Globalization and Regionalization of China's Economy

Implications for the Pacific Rim and Korea

Globalization and Regionalization of China's Economy

Implications for the Pacific Rim and Korea

Edited by
Denis F. Simon & Hong Pyo Lee

The Sejong Institute
Seoul, Korea

Globalization and Regionalization of China's Economy:
Implications for the Pacific Rim and Korea

Edited by Denis F. Simon and Hong Pyo Lee

Published by the Sejong Institute
CPO Box 8102, Seoul, Korea 100-681

The Sejong Institute is an independent, non-profit organization devoted to research on international affairs, national security, and Korean unification.

Printed in the Republic of Korea by the Kwangil Printing Co., Seoul, Korea.

ISBN 89-7429-322-6 93340

Contents

PART Ⅲ
Key Initiatives in China's Modernization

PART Ⅳ
Regionalism within China

PART Ⅴ
The Challenge of China in the Pacific Rim

Introduction

Denis F. Simon
(The Fletcher School of Law & Diplomacy, Tufts University)
and
Hong Pyo Lee
(The Sejong Institute)

Major Changes have taken place in China's economy since the onset of the four modernizations program in the late 1970s. These changes have included the introduction of significant economic reforms, fundamental changes in the structure and operation of the Science and Technology system, and inauguration of an "open door" policy designed to facilitate foreign investment and technology transfer to China. While there have been several false starts to each of these programs, and each has experienced a number of difficulties in terms of political opposition and financial shortfalls, the fact is that substantial progress has been made in moving China a way from reliance on the Maoist socialist model that dominated China's thinking about economics and technology since 1949.

Today, China is making its impact felt in a number of key areas in the global economy and the Pacific Rim regional economy. China's trade with the outside world, for example, has grown tremendously over the last ten years. In 1980, China was the 26th largest exporter in the world economy; by 1993, it had become the 11th largest exporter. Once a country that followed the principles of "self reliance," China is currently one of the most active nations in terms of trade activity in product markets ranging from commodities such as wool and petroleum to manufactured goods such as color TVs, clothing, shoes, and toys. The composition of China's trade has gone from being focused on primary goods (50.2% of China's trade in 1980 was accounted for by primary goods) to being heavily oriented towards manufactured products (in 1993, manufactured products made up 81.8% of China's exports). Chinese leaders have made known their intention to gain membership in the World Trade Organization for their country as part of an effort to offset trade disputes that China currently faces with the US and the EC. The OECD nations see Chinese membership as part of a process of harmonization, with the expectation that the rules and regulations governing China's trade regime will become both more transparent and more free market oriented.

In the field of foreign investment and technology transfer, many large multinational firms have responded to China's outward looking policies. Major companies such as NEC, Fujitsu, Xerox, IBM, Motorola, Siemens, Philips, Daewoo and Samsung have set up operations in China – some oriented towards the domestic market and some oriented towards exporting into other parts of Asia or the world. China has become the playing field for the playing out of global competition in industries ranging from telecommunications to auto mobiles. Peter Drucker, the noted management guru, once suggested that to be a global corporation, a firm had to have roots in three markets: the USA, western Europe and Japan. Today, without exaggeration, that statement requires modification; to be a true global player, firms must have a stragic presence in China. It is no accident, for example, that dynamic corporate leaders such as Bob Allen of AT&T, Jack Welch of General Electric, and Lee Kun-hee of Samsung, have noted the tremendous importance of China as one of the world's three "mega-markets" for the 21st century. The market of 1.2 billion that for so long had been thought to be simply a myth has now become a reality.

In 1991, two years after the turmoil of the Tiananmen incident, foreign investment into China seemed to take off, perhaps in response to the growing opportunities and perhaps in response to the growing belief that the violence in Tiananmen Square of June 4th 1989 was simply an aberration. A similar picture emerges regarding the import of foreign technology. China has spared little effort in encouraging foreign firms to transfer critical technologies, especially in key fields such as semiconductors, computers and peripherals, etc. The importation of foreign technology is designed to act as a catalyst to stimulate domestic technological upgrading, especially, in relation to the promotion of high technolgy industries. It also is designed to strengthen China's indigenous capacity to better meet its own technological needs over time.

In the midst of China's economic push both forward and outward, the Chinese economy has built stronger linkages with many of the key Pacific Rim economies, including South Korea and Taiwan. As the papers by Zhou Yuan and Lee Lai-to indicate, China's intra-regional trade has been growing quite fast as its neighbors in both Northeast and Southeast Asia seek to take advantage of the market of one billion plus. The role of ASEAN in China's foreign trade and foreign investment, in particular, appears to be growing quite rapidly. Foreign investment has grown as well as Korea in the north and Taiwan, Hong Kong, and Singapore in the south seek to harness China's increasingly skilled, low wage work force. China's leadership seems to have taken a greater interest in regional political and military affairs as well, perhaps in response to its perception of the present security environment and perhaps in response to its self-felt need to play a more central role in structuring the post Cold War regional order in the Pacific Rim – especially with the presence of the US and the former USSR having diminished significantly.

Yet, as the paper by Jin-young Suh indicates, the full consequences of China's larger regional posture portends a mixed picture. In contrast to the picture painted by Suh of a China best with succession and social problems, it is clear that China's willingness to assert itself as a more active participant in regional affairs has made some of the countries in the region quite apprehensive. A stronger, more self-confident China, suggest some observers, could become acerbic insofar as outstanding regional issues are concerned. Even putting aside the military dimensions of a more provocative Chinese foreign policy, the potential for there to emerge a more aggressive China in the economic and technology realm also worries some of the economies in the Pacific Rim. For example, what will China's role in APEC be? Will China play a constructive role in creating a new regional architecture for trade, investment, tourism, telecommunications, etc. or will China serve as a disruptive force? These are important regional issues that remain to be addressed as China's modernization proceeds ahead.

At the same time that China has revealed a stronger interest and willingness to participate in regional affairs, it also has begun to assert itself more actively in global economic and technology affairs. The paper by Denis Fred Simon indicates that China is steadily, albeit gradually, being tied into the evolving global economic system. While Hong Kong and Macao may be the largest source of foreign investment, for example, Philips of Holland is the largest foreign investor in China. Similarly, American firms continue to surpass Japanese firms in terms of the total value of foreign investment in the PRC – though as the paper by Roy Grow suggests, the Japanese account for more projects overall. He also suggests that Japanese influence within the Chinese economy should not be under-estimated. While Simon acknowledges the importance of the links with Japan, however, he strongly argues that the Chinese economy is being "globalized" in the sense that local industry is becoming increasingly enmeshed in the global sourcing networks of large MNCs, many of whom are anxious to utilize raw materials, labor, and distribution points in the PRC. While William Fischer argues that Chinese manufacturing and R&D capabilities are still 5-10 years behind that of Japan and the US, and China remains a reactive player rather than a driving force in the game of global competition, it still cannot be denied that Chinese economic influence is growing in importance.

In assessing the future position of the Chinese economy in overseas markets, two additional issues seem to stand out. The first is the disposition of China's so-called "third line" industries. These industries constitute the core of the PRC's military industrial complex. As the paper by Ding Jingping shows, many of the factories and research institutes in the defense sector have been converted to civilian production – some more successfully than others. The good news in this regard is that China's defense sector has always been advantaged insofar as personnel, financial and technological assets are concerned. If China can harness some of these defense assets and refocus them onto profitable civilian production and R&D tasks, the Chinese economy could receive a great big boost. It is not surprising, for example, to see companies such as NORINCO or San Qiu vying to establish business contacts with the world's leading automobile producers or manufacturers of wireless telecommunications devices.

Along with the conversion of military facilities to civilian production purposes, another key issue is the status of China's programs for promoting high technology industries. As the paper by Richard Suttmeier indicates, China is using a combination of plan and market to push ahead with the launching of a number of high technology sectors. As with the military conversion effort, some of these programs have been more successful than others. Some also have experienced more efficient coordination and management from the center than others. Budget limitations, personnel shortages, and equipment problems all plagues the effort to establish a solid foundation for high technology in China. While the abolition of COCOM and the relaxation of export controls by the US government has indeed given China greater access to advanced technology and equipment, the assimilation and digestion processes remain very uneven. Nonetheless, as Suttmeier implies, the Chinese should not be counted out as substantial progress in various fields has been made in a relatively brief period of time.

One of the more interesting aspects of China's expanded global and regional links is the fact that these linkages are growing at the same time that the internal dynamics and structure of the PRC economy are changing. More specifically, the forces of regionalism within China are becoming stronger, driven by both Beijing's lack of funding to support the modernization needs of every province and municipality in China and the growing driven for autonomy by localities via-a-vis the central government. In many ways, Chinese economic policymakers are looking to define and "bound" their economic tasks into smaller, geographically delimited, regional entities to make the task of resource allocation that much more manageable. Today, it is not uncommon to hear leaders in Beijing speak about China in terms of so-called "natural" economic regions. These would include 1) Southwestern China, including Sichuan and Yunnan; 2) Northeast China, including Liaoning and Heilongjiang; 3) East/central China, including Shanghai, Wuxi, and Hangzhou; and 4) South China, including Guangdong, Fujian, Hainan, and the so-called four "special economic zones" set up in the early 1980s.

Several factors give this trend towards regionalism a great deal of importance in terms of China's overall development pattern. Internally, this emphasis on a regional approach raises a number of critical questions about the relationship among the various regions in terms of specialization, allocation of resources by the central government, and domestic market development. The drive towards the development of a fully integrated domestic market could be undermined by excessive emphasis on economically and politically bounded regions. For example, what will happen to the efforts to create a national automobile industry or a national consumer electronics industry? Will regional blockades – which now constitute a serious problem – become even more difficult to handle if regional boundaries become formalized? Relatedly, what will be the relationship between the regions and Beijing? This is an especially sensitive question in terms of tax revenues and other fees collected by the center to cover the operating costs of the central government and to provide some discretionary funding to assist China's poorer areas. Moreover, as the paper by Keun Lee demonstrates, a weakened central government, financially or politically, will be in no position to address the issue of the future viability of the country's state-owned enterprises – one of the most critical bottlenecks to future reform and economic competitiveness.

From an external perspective, the questions are just as challenging and significant. If regional development does acquire momentum, how will this affect the way China interacts with the outside world? Will it be "regions" that are the units of action or will Beijing still have to give approval for various large projects and investment? Is it reasonable to expect a series of "natural" economic regions to incorporate a number of preferred foreign country partners? In some respects, this has already happened in Southern China with respect to the role of Hong Kong and Taiwan in the development of the Pearl River delta. As the paper by Hong Pyo Lee suggests, the creation of "Greater China" does promise to have a tremendous impact on the pace and path of development in the South – with Hong Kong and Taiwan helping to link this region of China into the world economy in a very effective and efficient fashion. Will it happen with the Japanese in Northeast China in places such as Shenyang and Dalian, with the Koreans in Shandong, and with the United States and Europe in Shanghai, Jiangsu, etc.? If this were to happen, would it mean the re-creation of "spheres of influence" as existed in the early years of the 20th century? While none of the authors seem to believe that this will happen in an explicit sense, the paper by Grow seems anxious to sensitize us to the fact, at a minimum, that many of the economic trades and forces that were in place in the early 20th century seem to once again have reared their head in the context of the Sino-Japanese relationship.

Obviously, there are a number of push and pull forces leading to more or less economic integration in China. The drive towards a more regionally-oriented development strategy in China need not mean economic disintegration; it is entirely possible that a well-orchestrated and coordinated effort on the part of Beijing could facilitate the overall modernization of the country by minimizing the complexity that accompanies any effort to deal with China as a whole. Yet, given the competition for scarce resources among organizations in China, combined with the historical desire for greater independence of action, the results could prove to be problematic – leading to an exacerbation of existing problems regarding policy coordination, reduction of duplication of equipment and technology imports, etc. The paper by Hieyeon Keum, for example, details the opportunities for commercial intercourse that are available to foreign firms in Southwest China – a region not widely known in the West. However, it remains to be seen whether foreign companies will seek out these opportunities in the face of that region's much less developed infrastructure and less cosmopolitan character.

Some experts have even gone so far as to argue that the post-Deng era in China will give rise to extensive tensions between the central government and the local provinces – fueled and exacerbated by the growing influence of foreign corporations, international organizations, etc. The paper by David Zweig tries to address some of the questions by putting forth a number of alternative scenarios that could lie ahead for China. One of these scenarios, Zweig suggests, could lead to the collapse of the Chinese economy and the eventual break-up of China. While such scenarios are indeed provocative and worthy of investigation over time, particularly as they might lead us to understand a new internal balance of power within China, the fact remains that China does not seem on the verge of either being dismembered by foreign commercial or political force. Nor do there appear to be radical secessionist forces with growing influence and power appearing on the scene. In fact, for the first time in its history, China will have a nationally integrated communications system, with each province, municipality and town being able to communicate with each other in ways never previously possible. The so-called "three goldens" project, which is China's version of the super-information highway, promises to expand national level credit card and banking, data, customs, and tax networks to facilitate commercial transactions across the country as well as strengthen the government's ability to understand just what is actually occurring in the economy on a nation-wide basis. Add to this the building a thousands of miles of roads, the expanded electrification of railways, and the modernization of the country's power grid and it all seems as if we are on the verge of one of the largest experiments in re-engineering in human history.

This volume examines the assorted dimensions and multiple consequences of globalization and regionalization for China's economic development, while at the same time exploring the overall interrelationship – real and potential – between domestic regional development schemes and China's integration into the Pacific Rim and global economic systems. The papers will assess the degree to which economic fragmentation has or will become a problem for China's economy in the years ahead. Moreover, they will also evaluate the viability of the current regionally – oriented economic strategy – one that has focused on the Eastern coast in the hope that the benefits of rapid growth growth would quickly "trickle-down" into the interior. As the paper by Ik Soo Kim highlights, this strategy has raised a series of critical questions insofar as growing regional disparities have become a source of new concern at the highest political levels in China. Finally, the papers examine the consequences of regionalization and globalization in terms of the role China has and will play in key industries such as textiles, electronics, petroleum, etc. This aspect of the volume holds special importance for countries such as US and Korea. For the US, as the paper by Donald Klein points out, growing economic interdependence with China, offers some substantial benefits; unfortunately, suggests Klein, there also are lots of minefields that could stand in the way of the improved relationship over the long-term. For Korea, if Korean firms, for example, can forge strong relations with key Chinese enterprises, this could help to provide greater access to the domestic market as well as provide access to key production resources for exports into the world economy. As Zhou Yuan stresses in his paper, this helps to explain China's growing interest in Northeast Asia and vice versa. On the other hand, the rapid development of certain Chinese industries could have a negative impact on the competitive position of Korean firms. While it is too soon to tell which of these scenarios will emerge, the fact is that it is essential for policymakers in Korea as well as the other Pacific Rim economies to understand China's economic capabilities, policy intentions, and technological strengths and weaknesses.

PART I

Globalization and Regionalization of China's Economy

1

The Impact of Globalization and Regionalization on China's Place in the World Economy

Denis Fred Simon
(The Fletcher School of Law & Diplomacy, Tufts University)

Introduction

Since the onset of its modernization drive and the open door policy in the early 1980s, China has emerged as an increasingly important player in global markets.[1] One merely has to examine the list of firms among the *Fortune Global 500* that have entered the PRC economy through foreign direct investment, licensing, and trade relationships to recognize that China is no longer a marginal player in international economic and technology affairs. More than 200 of the top 500 firms listed by Fortune in 1994 have started operations in China.[2] Between 1991-1995 (China's 8th Five

[1]Nicholas Lardy, *China and the World Economy* (Washington, D.C.: Institute of International Economics, 1994).

[2]Foreign Investment Structure Much Improved in China," *Xinhua* (April 14,

Year Plan), the Chinese economy averaged an annual growth rate of 11.7% – making it the fastest growing economy in the world. With its steadily rising demand for industrial and consumer products, China already has become a significant market – alleviating considerable doubt about whether the "market of 1.2 billion people" was real or simply a myth. In addition, China has become an important export production base for firms seeking to take advantage of either low cost labor or steadily improving skill base. And, in some selected fields, Chinese enterprises or R&D units even have become important partners to foreign firms seeking to leverage China's engineering and design capabilities for product and process innovation.

It was once thought that to be a true global player, a *Fortune Global 500* firm had to have a presence in each of three major markets: the US, Western Europe, and Japan. Today, it can be said without much reservation that to be a true global competitor, a corporation also must have a significant presence in China. In many ways, China already has become a battleground for the playing out of US-Japan-European competition. Firms that can capture significant revenues from even modest market shares in the PRC market can enhance their competitive potential. It is no wonder, therefore, that corporate leaders ranging from Lee Kunhee, CEO of Samsung to AT&T CEO Robert Allen have recognized that China is one of the mega-markets of the future.

China's growth has not only been felt in global terms, but also in regional affairs as well. In the context of East Asia, it has long been assumed that Japan would continue to be the catalyst for driving growth and development in the Pacific Rim. In fact, the so-called "flying geese model" that has long been used to analyze the patterns of industrialization in the Asia-Pacific region is largely Japan-centered. Even more recent analyses, which have suggested that the regional dynamics of economic and technology affairs in East Asia have moved beyond the flying geese model, have maintained an appreciable role for the Japanese economy. The rise of China, however, may now have called into question many of the prevailing assumptions about the sources of future growth in Asia. As one World Bank study has suggested, China may surpass Japan as the long-term engine of growth in the Pacific Rim. This transition from a Japan-centered to a China-centered regional economy, which has been exacerbated by the significant role played by overseas Chinese capital and know-how, holds tremendous implications for the ways in East Asia will interact with the rest of the world economic system in the 21st century.

The goal of this paper is to examine the nature of the interface between the global and East Asian regional economies, on the one hand, and the rapidly growing economy of the People's Republic of China, on the other hand. In particular, the paper examines the impact of globalization and regionalization on the development trajectory of the Chinese economy. It analyzes how the imperatives of globalization and regionalization are shaping: a) the patterns of foreign trade and foreign investment in China; and b) the thrust and direction of reform. The paper concludes by highlighting the ways in which the uneven and unpredictable pace of reform as well as the under-developed state of the PRC economic infrastructure have left some critical parts of the Chinese economy unable to respond to many of the evolving economic and commercial opportunities that have emerged over the last few years.

The Global and Regional Setting

Over the course of the last ten years, remarkable changes have taken place in the structure and organization of the world economy.[3] These changes have been engendered, in part, by a major transformation in the existing global trade regime, which has made demonstrable progress towards greater liberalization and harmonization of trade practices. In 1994, global trade topped US$8.5 trillion, an increase of 13.6% over 1993, when world trade was at a low ebb. The transition from the GATT regime to the

---

1995).

[3]Kenichi Ohmae, *The Borderless World* (New York: Harper Business, 1990).

World Trade Organization (WTO) promises to bring even faster growth in the movement of goods and services across national borders. Another important source of change has been the collapse of the former Soviet bloc and the so-called "socialist model." In contrast to the situation that prevailed for most of the postwar period, we can now seriously speak about one global market. And, while there are still appreciable differences in the level of economic integration among and between various nations and regions, the fact is that there is no longer a free world international economic order contending with the socialist economic order for global primacy.

In addition to these two significant sources of change in world economic affairs, two other critical factors must be considered. First, there has been a dramatic increase in the role and influence of the world's largest multinational corporations in international affairs.[4] Although the issue of the "global reach" of MNCs was analyzed and debated in the 1960s and 1970s, today the focus on the MNC has shifted away from the critical discourse that dominated the discussions twenty five years ago and is now centered on the ways in which national economic systems can better articulate their economic policies and priorities with the needs and requirements of foreign investors. The self-reliance models of development that were popular during the earlier period noted above were proven largely unable to provide a viable mechanism to stimulate rapid and sustained economic or technological development. Instead, based on a number of recent analyses, greater emphasis is being given to export-led development involving close and even intimate relations with the world s leading corporations.

The growing power and prestige of multinational corporations in world affairs also has fostered the steady, although at times uneven, globalization of markets and industries.[5] This process of globalization, which is best viewed as a micro-economic phenom-

---

[4]John Stopford and Susan Strange, *Rival States, Rival Firms: Competition for World Market Shares* (Cambridge: Cambridge University Press, 1991).

[5]George Yip, *Total Global Strategy* (Englewood Cliffs: Prentice Hall, 1992).

enon, has altered the nature and thrust of international competition; new patterns of collaboration, for example, are emerging in the midst of traditional forms of competition.[6] The nature and character of demand in many markets is becoming increasingly homogenized. MNCs now see the world as one big playing field in which they must seek out the most optimal locations for production, R&D, marketing and distribution. Globalization also has provoked numerous discussions about its true meaning for the nation-state, with some scholars already claiming the arrival of a "borderless world" and others still fixated on the competitive advantages to be derived from the critical assets within the nation-state.[7]

Yet, even if we acknowledge that the spread and impact of the globalization process has been uneven and heterogeneous, the reality is that its efficacy cannot be ignored insofar as the prevailing patterns of competition in industries ranging from food processing to telecommunications are changing.

One of the central aspects of globalization has been the shift from variable to fixed-cost competition. With the global integration of capital and factor markets, firms now increasingly compete on the basis of technology and time. The growing emphasis on technology has meant that the role of so-called "low-cost labor" is becoming less important; the percentage of overall production costs accounted for by labor in manufacturing has been steadily decreasing. In today s economic environment, innovation potential and time to market have become more central to the competition equation.[8] Not only must companies constantly create new products and improve their process technologies, but they also must do so at a time when product life cycles are becoming appreciably shorter.[9] Finally, along with being more

---

[6]Daniel Drache and M S. Gertler, eds., *The New Era of Global Competition* (McGill-Queens, 1991).

[7]See Philip Grub and Dara Khambata, eds., The Multinational Enterprise in Transition, 4th edition (Princeton: Darwin Press, 1993).

[8]Bruce Guile, ed., *Technology and Global Industry* (Washington, D.C.: National Academy Press, 1987).

focused on technology, competition has become more customer focused. Terms such as "mass customization" capture an entirely new competition dynamic – "the shift to flexible specialization." To succeed in a world of globalizing markets and industries, it is necessary to be able to draw upon the presence of manufacturing and R&D assets anywhere in the world; firms that can easily harness these assets have a distinctive advantage vis-a-vis their competitors.

The second additional factor that has generated important changes in the global landscape has been the emergence of East Asia as a new center, perhaps *the* new center, of dynamism in the global political economy. The East Asian market is comprised of over 800 million people (taking into account only China s coastal provinces) with an output value of over US $4 trillion. Since the mid-1980s, the economies in East and Southeast Asia have been growing at a much faster rate than the US or Europe – averaging 6% compared with only 2% among the OECD economies. By 1994, the region accounted for 25% of world trade. Per capita incomes are increasing rapidly as is the demand for high-value-added products and services in both consumer and industrial markets. Companies from within the region now constitute a significant percentage of those firms on the Fortune Global 500 list. It is therefore no accident that foreign direct investment in East Asia has grown from US $20.5 billion in 1990 to US $57 billion.[10]

As the economies of the region have grown economically, they have become more technologically sophisticated.[11] The emerging technological trajectory of the Pacific Rim promises to place the East Asian economies at center stage in terms of global competition. More and more of the world's leading companies are looking to forge joint ventures and strategic alliances with local Asian firms. These Asian firms are increasingly viewed as capable of

[9]Ove Granstrand, et. al., eds., *Technology Management and International Business* (New York: Wiley and Sons, 1992).

[10]*South China Morning Post* (May 9, 1995), p. 10.

[11]Denis Fred Simon, ed., *The Emerging Technological Trajectory of the Pacific Rim* (Armonk: M. E. Sharpe, 1995).

altering the international competitive balance in fields ranging from software development to semiconductor design.[12] Economies in the region (as well as around the world) that possess the necessary human and production resources as well as local infrastructure will be attractive partners in terms of the emerging patterns of competition and collaboration; economies that lack these resources or impose constraints on free and unencumbered access will become marginalized in terms of the mainstream of world economic and technology affairs.[13]

Interestingly, as these economies have grown and prospered, they have expanded their commercially-based interactions with each another.[14] As a result, concurrent with the spread of globalization, there has been a concomitant trend towards regionalization in East Asia – albeit "open regionalization" as defined by APEC. This trend towards regionalization in the Asia-Pacific may not seem so remarkable in view of the regionalization initiatives that have occurred in Europe (the European Union) and North America (NAFTA). Unlike the situations in these other parts of the world economy, however, East Asian regionalization has been driven largely by private sector actions rather than government policies or activities. In addition to the overseas activities of Japanese companies, firms from the so-called "four dragons" – Taiwan, Hong Kong, South Korea and Singapore, for example, have rapidly expanded their presence through equity and contractual investments in emerging markets such as China, Vietnam, and Indonesia. This trend toward regionalization in Asia has been especially important insofar as the PRC economy has been concerned. One of the striking features of regionalization in East Asia has been the appearance of a series of subregional economic zones, such as the "growth triangle" involving

---

[12]Dieter Ernst and David O'Connor, *Technology and Global Competition* (Paris: OECD Development Center, 1989).

[13]Saneh Chamarik, ed., Technological Independence: The Asian Experience (Tokyo: UN University Press, 1994).

[14]Kenichi Ohmae, "The Rise of the Region State," *Foreign Affairs* (Spring 1993).

Indonesia, Malaysia, and Singapore. What has made the appearance of these sub-zones even more significant is the fact that many of these sub-zones have appeared along the borders of the Chinese economy. In south China, for example, a sub-regional zone often referred to as "Greater China" has emerged linking together the economies of Taiwan, Hong Kong, and Guangdong and Fujian provinces.[15] In China's northeast, another sub-regional zone involving Japan, South Korea and Liaoning and Jilin provinces also has come into existence. These subregional groupings, while largely informal and non-institutionalized, have developed an economic momentum of their own. In some instances, their impact has been so pronounced that they have raised questions about the possible fragmentation of the Chinese economy into a series of regional economic units. These centripetal pulls have had even greater potency in view of the extensive decentralization of authority that has occurred in the relationship between the central government in Beijing and the local governments in China's various provinces and municipalities.

China's Economic and Technological Thrust

Anyone looking at the Chinese economy has to be impressed by the extent to which the PRC leadership has been able to pickup the scattered pieces of the reform program in the aftermath of the Tiananmen Incident in 1989 and move the economy back onto a steady development trajectory. While it is true that a sizeable degree of economic initiative has been passed on to the provinces and municipalities because of financial as well as political considerations, the central government has been able to intervene effectively to bring about the necessary credit controls, etc. to moderate the degree to which economic activities seemed to be "out of control." The so-called credit squeeze that was enacted in the aftermath of the Tiananmen violence and economic turbulence

---

[15]See the Special Issue on "Greater China," *The China Quarterly* (December 1993).

reflected the continued efficacy of the central authorities in the midst of the reforms that had occurred in enterprise management, the price system, the trade system, the banking system, etc. The economy has kept growing at very respectable rates, while a modicum of stability has been engineered into the system.[16]

This is not to suggest that the Chinese economy is without its problems. The situation inside of a large number of state-owned enterprises, especially in the northeast region of the country, remains rather bleak in terms of economic efficiency and profitability.[17] Some suggest that about 50% of the enterprises within the state sector are operating in the red; this has imposed a tremendous financial burden on the central government, which must make up any deficits to prevent massive layoffs and possible worker unrest.[18] The future disposition of many of these enterprises is a serious political issue in China because the current leadership remains hesitant to move as quickly as has happened in Eastern Europe and Russia regarding privatization.

Another serious problem confronting the leadership has to do with the emerging patterns of growth and inequality in China, derived in large part, from the fact that the leadership in Beijing has decided to rely on a trickle-down approach to economic development. The decision to focus on the so-called "fourteen coastal cities" as growth hubs runs absolutely counter to the Maoist policies of the 1950s and 1960s that were designed to prevent an urban-rural gap from being created or exacerbated. Of the US$96.56 billion foreign investment in China since 1979, only about 11% or US$10.42 billion has gone into central and western China (18 provinces and autonomous regions).[19] In a survey conducted at the Central Party School of the Chinese Communist

---

[16]World Bank, *Reform and the Role of the Plan in the 1990s* (Washington, D.C.: World Bank, 1993).

[17]Harry Broadman, *Meeting the Challenge of Chinese Enterprise Reforms* [World Bank Discussion Paper #283] (Washington, D.C.: World Bank, 1995).

[18]"State Enterprises To Be Rescued in 18 Cities," *Japan Economic Newswire* (Kyodo, August 27, 1995).

[19]*South China Morning Post,* (June 15, 1995), p. 10.

Party among department and bureau-level cadres, 84% of those surveyed pointed to excessive disparities in regional economic development as a significant problem. Among those who identified this problem as a major issue, three possible consequences were highlighted: unfair social distribution, social instability, and regional fragmentation.[20] The leadership was so worried about this issue that in mid-1995 it revised the prevailing foreign investment legislation to attract more foreign investment into the interior provinces. Moreover, by the end of the summer 1995, a lively debate raged among the leadership about whether the special incentive packages granted to the "special economic zones" (SEZs) should be removed to make the domestic playing field more level.[21]

The table below indicates China's own assessment of the concentration of economic, income, and technical resources in the country. Inland provinces are conspicuous by their relative absence.

The issue of the SEZs as well as the other economic development zones in the PRC promises to continue to occupy the attention of the leadership in the coming years. Initially, the zones were created to insulate the Chinese economy and society from direct exposure to foreign business activities. The zones also were areas where reform-oriented economic policies could be tried out without fear of contaminating the whole of Chinese society.[22] Similarly, the zones were created to highlight to Hong Kong and Taiwan as well as to the rest of the world that China could be comfortable with market-type economic entities on its doorstep. Today, with the reforms having advanced far beyond initial expectations and the symbolic aspects of the Hong Kong issue no

---

[20]"Party School Survey: Shocking Economic Gap Could Undermine Stability," *BBC Summary of World Broadcasts—Far East* (FE/2237/S1, February 25, 1995).

[21]"China Debates Special Tax Breaks Given to Coastal Zones," *Los Angeles Times* (September 24, 1995), p. 16.

[22]Susan Shirk, *How China Opened Its Doors* (Washington, D.C.: Brookings Institution Press, 1994).

Table 1. Evaluation of China's Development Level

Ranking	Economic Base	Income Distribution	Health and S&T
1	Shanghai	Beijing	Beijing
2	Guangdong	Shanghai	Shanghai
3	Hainan	Zhejiang	Tianjin
4	Beijing	Tianjin	Jiangsu
5	Tianjin	Guangdong	Jilin
6	Fujian	Fujian	Liaoning
7	Zhejiang	Jiangsu	Fujian
8	Jiangsu	Liaoning	Shandong
9	Liaoning	Shandong	Guangdong
10	Shandong	Hebei	Shaanxi

Source: Beijing Review (July 24-30, 1995), p. 19

longer as prominent a part of the Chinese decision calculus, the "unique" value of the zones may have simply been overcome by events. Add to this the fact that the zones increasingly have been associated with the problems of income and growth disparity in China, it is not surprising that new pressures have emerged regarding their future utility to the PRC leadership.

The problems of regional inequality highlight another issue related to role and status of regions in China, and that is the problem of regional parochialism and protectionism. As in traditional times, the problems associated with local interpretation of central government directives remain significant.[23] Guangdong, for example, which has been growing at a faster rate (18%) than the overall Chinese economy, has been reluctant to heed Beijing's admonitions about slowing down the rate of growth or reducing credit availability. During the Eighth Five Year Plan (1991-95), Guangdong received US$41 billion dollars in actual investment; as a result of this investment, Guangdong has been able to revamp a good deal of its economic base and become a major source of China's manufactured exports. Given its proximity to

[23]Kenneth Lieberthal and D.M. Lampton, eds., *Bureaucracy, Politics and Decision-Making in Post-Mao China* (Berkeley: UC Press, 1992).

Hong Kong and the fact that it is the home of three of the four special economic zones (Shenzhen, Zhuhai, and Shantou), Guangdong has perceived it more beneficial to respond to the economic forces within its immediate locale than to the dictates of Beijing. Multiplied across a larger number of provinces, this behavior pattern has the potential effect of muting or blunting Beijing's policies and distorting the impact of the central government's efforts to manage the economy.[24]

Localism also has had an impact on the flow of goods and services across the country. Given the growing degree to which local funds are being used to spur local development, there has been a tendency among local officials to impose explicit and implicit forms of "protectionism" to keep not simply foreign products out of the local market – which is actually a central government issue – but rather to keep out products manufactured in other parts of the country. This has led many foreign firms to view the Chinese market more as a series of geographically contiguous regional markets than as an integrated national market. And, it also helps to explain why there has been a proliferation of economic zones around the country, with each province and city looking to attract their own foreign investors and to "localize" the operations of these companies – whether they be small or large.

Much of the discourse that has been associated with the newly announced Ninth Five Year Plan (1996-2000) has been focused on addressing a large number of these problems.[25] The document issued by the leadership in October 1995 lays out the core features of the new plan; it reflects a great deal of sensitivity to the issues of inequality and regionalism and regional disparity as well as the problems associated with the viability of the state-owned enterprises. While not particularly provocative in its insights or its stated prescriptions, the document does highlight the fact that China does not intend to move ahead with either

---

[24]Howard Davies, ed., *China Business: Context and Issues* (Hong Kong: Longman, 1995).

[25]"CPC Proposal for Formulation 9th 5-Year Plan, Long-term Target," *Xinhua* (October 4, 1995).

economic reform or modernization in a socio-political vacuum.[26] The fact that the document also reflects an renewed commitment to retain the planning structures that have heretofore survived the onset of the quasi-market economy reinforces the evidence that the central government intends to maintain as much control over the current economic transition so that economic anarchy or social instability do not become serious problems.[27] Moreover, the central government via the State Planning Commission obviously intends to ensure that the development of the countries four pillar industries, including automobiles, electronics, petrochemicals and machinery, takes place in a coherent manner – without the same sort of chaos that was associated with the wasteful importation of 122 color television lines in the early 1980s.

Globalization of the Chinese Economy

As its modernization program has generated appreciable levels of growth and improvements in the quality and variety of Chinese products, the PRC has been transformed from being a relatively minor player in the global economy. Between 1980 and 1995, China's foreign trade grew substantially, making it the 11th largest trading nation in the world. In 1994, China's total trade with the world reached US$236.7 billion, up 21% from the previous year. Agricultural and related primary products now account for less than 15% of overall trade, while manufactured products on both the import and export sides have exploded. With trade becoming increasingly important as a source of Chinese economic growth, efforts have been underway to reform the existing foreign trade system. These efforts have been stepped up by China's stated desire to become a member of the newly established World Trade Organization. While the negotiations leading up to formal

[26]"Post-Deng Charter Dodges Issues," *South China Morning Post* (October 5, 1995), p. 11.

[27]"Ninth Five Year Plan to be Decided in August Beidaihe Meeting," *BBC Summary of World Broadcasts—Far East* (FE/2375/G1, August 7, 1995).

Table 2. China's World Trade (US $B)

	1992	1993	1994
PRC Exports	84.9	91.8	121.0
PRC Imports	80.6	104.0	115.7
Total	165.5	195.7	236.7
Balance	4.4	-12.2	5.3

Source: MOFTEC (Beijing, 1995)

membership pre-dated the creation of the WTO by more than two years, they have produced some appreciable improvements in the foreign trade structure, including greater transparency regarding the laws and regulations governing foreign trade activities.

The composition of China's imports and exports reflects the changing nature of the Chinese economy. Driven by a combination of two factors – the concerted effort to upgrade the overall technology base of Chinese industry and the need to overcome existing shortcomings in capacity, China has started to focus its imports on large quantities of machinery and related equipment. And, while China seems to have been able to overcome some of the trade deficits it was running during the earlier phases of the modernization drive, there are signs that the current surplus situation eventually will give way again in response to rising energy demands as well as the growing need for equipment and machinery.

As suggested, the growth in Chinese exports also reflects the general changes in the Chinese economy. One of the most important areas where improvements have occurred has been in the textiles industry, where many Chinese enterprises have imported a considerable amount of automated machinery from Western Europe to be able to move into higher quality, higher-value added garment and textiles production. Similar types of upgrading have occurred in the electronics industry, allowing China to move quickly beyond the embryonic state of the electronics industry that existed in the early 1980s. Today, as a result of foreign investment and the import of foreign production lines,

Table 3. China Top Imports, 1994 (US $B)

Category	Product(s)	Total Imports	% Change
84	Machinery	25.1	8.8
85	Elec Equipment	16.5	29.8
72	Iron & Steel	8.3	-31.2
39	Plastics	6.2	24.4
87	Vehicles	4.8	-11.8
27	Mineral Fuels	4.0	-30.6
88	Aircraft	3.5	53.2
54	Manmade Fibers	2.9	20.6
55	Manmade Staples	2.6	38.8
52	Cotton	2.5	104.3

Source: MOFTEC (Beijing, 1995)

Table 4. China's Exports, 1994 (US $B)

Category	Product(s)	Total Imports	% Change
62	Non-knit Apparel	15.0	30.1
85	Elec Equipment	14.1	45.5
61	Knit Apparel	6.3	25.6
64	Footwear	6.0	14.4
84	Machinery	5.6	33.8
95	Toys/Games	4.7	27.2
42	Leather	4.1	43.2
27	Mineral Fuels	4.1	-1.2
52	Cotton	3.2	16.2
39	Plastics	2.7	45.7

Source: MOFTEC (Beijing, 1995)

China has exhibited its potential of becoming another one of Asia's major manufacturers and exporters of consumer electronics products.

While the growth in China's foreign trade has been an important underlying cause of its increased integration in the global economy, the reality is that the PRC's main trading partners are still based in the Asia-Pacific region. Japan and Hong Kong remain China's top two trading partners. In 1994, if we include trade with Hong Kong, trade within East Asia accounted for over 50% of China's total trade; even if Hong Kong is excluded from the calculation, East Asia still was China's largest trading region. Japanese trading firms are especially active in China; unlike many Western firms, they are willing to move into China's interior and to develop commercial ties with companies in China's border regions as well as inland areas.[28] China's overall trade with the US is still slightly smaller than its trade with Japan, though it is clear that the American market has become the largest destination for Chinese exports in the world – reaching US$21.5 billion according to China's Customs Bureau in 1994. Moreover, whether measured in terms of exports or imports individually or grouped together, China's trade with the US is growing faster than Chinese trade with any other market.

Table 5. China's Trade by Trading Partner, 1994

Market	Exports (US $Billion)	Imports (US $Billion)
Global	121.0	115.7
Japan	21.6	26.3
Hong Kong	32.4	26.3
USA	21.5	14.0
Europe Union	14.6	16.9
–Germany	4.8	7.1
–Italy	1.6	3.1
–UK	2.4	6.3
–France	1.4	1.9
Taiwan	2.2	14.1
ASEAN	6.4	6.8
–Singapore	2.6	2.5
South Korea	4.4	7.3
Russia	1.6	3.5

Source: PRC Customs Bureau (Beijing, 1995)

[28] *Japan Chemical Week* (April 6, 1995), p. 8.

The bilateral trade relationship between China and the US has been an area of heightened controversy over the last several years. According to US statistics, in 1985, the trade balance between the two economies was roughly equal, but by 1994, the US claimed it was running a US $30 billion deficit with China. While China's overall export growth has been in the range of 13% year, it has been growing about 30% with respect to exports to the US economy. Ironically, China does not accept the claims made by the US regarding the deficit because it insists that products exported out of Hong Kong or shipped to Hong Kong should be counted as part of Hong Kong's trade – even if the exports had their origin in the PRC or the imports by HK will make their way into China![29] Yet, even allowing for some margin of error on both sides, it cannot be denied that the role of the US in China's foreign trade is rapidly expanding – thus further helping to integrate China more broadly into the world economy.

Along with trade, another important aspect of China's increased interaction and integration within the global economy has been the role and impact of foreign direct investment.[30] In contrast to the early 1980s when the Chinese were scurrying around for every investment dollar, today China has become a buyers market insofar as foreign investment is concerned. For every important project, there is a long line of suitors waiting to make concession after concession just to sink some roots into the Chinese economic landscape. While the overall level of foreign investment initially started to pick up in the mid-to-late 1980s, the big leap forward occurred in 1991, when overall FDI jumped from US $4.36 billion in 1990 to US $11.0 billion. The growth has been nothing less than extraordinary as China has now become one of the top two or three sites for foreign investment in the world. Total contracted foreign investment in 1994 was US $81.4 billion, a substantial reduction from the record of US $111.4 billion in 1993. More important, however, actually committed for-

---

[29]"The Trade Debate," *China Economic Review* (Hong Kong, April 1995), p. 13.

[30]Margaret Pearson, *Joint Ventures in the People's Republic of China* (Princeton: Princeton University Press, 1991).

eign direct investment reached US $33.8 billion, compared with only US$27 billion in 1993.[31] The slowing of foreign investment in contractual terms, however, was not a sign that somehow China has become less attractive as an investment site, though it is indeed facing competition for investment dollars from countries such as India and Vietnam. Rather, the immediate cause of the drop was a decline in investment in China's real estate sector as well as a dearth of local investment capital – counterpart investment funds – as a result of the credit controls imposed by Beijing.[32] Even with the slowdown in contracted foreign investment in 1994, China still stood as the second largest recipient of foreign investment after the USA.

Foreign companies have started to have a substantial impact on the shape and direction of China's modernization effort.[33] By early 1995, there were over 237,000 foreign investment projects approved in China – valued at US $104 billion; approximately 100,000 of these have actually gone into operation.[34] This amount is still relatively small, especially when looked at in comparison with Chinese private bank savings, which reached over two trillion yuan in early 1995.[35] Nonetheless, foreign investment is becoming increasingly important insofar as the changing nature of the economy is concerned. In 1994, the industrial turnover of foreign-invested enterprise reached 400 billion yuan or 12.8% of the national turnover. Even more significant, in that same year, foreign-invested companies accounted for US $87.56 billion in foreign trade – about 37% of the national total. This represented a significant increase over the previous year when total trade was US $67 billion; in contrast to 1993, however, the source of the increase was on the export side – with exports reaching almost US $35 billion (37.6% increase). In addition, the average size of

---

[31]South China Morning Post (June 7, 1995), p. 4.

[32]"Foreign Investment in China on the Rise," *Xinhua* (July 28, 1995).

[33]Geoffrey Murray, *Doing Business in China: The Last Great Market* (New York: St. martin's Press, 1994).

[34]"Foreign Investment Enterprises Rewarded," *Xinhua* (June 27, 1995).

[35]*South China Morning Post* (January 25, 1995), p. 12.

each investment project has been expanding, reaching US $1.9 million in 1994. Foreign invested companies in China employ over 14 million workers.

The largest source of foreign investment continues to be Hong Kong and Macao, which in 1994 supplied US $20.2 billion of actual foreign direct investment. The nature of these Hong Kong and Macao investments has been a source of critical debate among economists and investment analysts as it is not always clear as to the origins of the capital. In some instances, the monies may actually be Taiwan capital; in other instances, there is evidence to indicate that the monies are actually from within China itself – recycled through Hong Kong dummy companies so that the domestic entity engaged in the investment can secure official preferential treatment and tax incentives only available to foreign investors. Still, there is little doubt that overseas Chinese investment into the PRC continues to be an important source of capital, especially in the southern portion of the country.

The next largest sources of foreign investment have been Taiwan (US $3.39 billion) and the US ($US 2.49 billion). Interestingly, while the top three sources of foreign investment into the PRC all recorded significant declines in their total investment levels – ranging from 46% for Taiwan to 12% for the US, Japan (US $2.08 billion), Singapore (US $1.18 billion) and South Korea (US $720 million) experienced sizeable increases in the range of 35-40%.[36]

The steadily expanded role of foreign firms in the Chinese economy has made some government and Party officials nervous as they have started to perceive linkages between some of China's economic ills and the prevailing patterns of foreign investment. This has encouraged the government to tighten up some of its existing policies, especially with respect to those smaller investors from HK, Southeast Asia, and Taiwan. In 1994, for example, the government set limits to the number and type of small projects that could be approved.[37] In addition, the Chinese

[36] "Top Ten Investors Hong Kong and Macao Lead Mainland's Top Ten Investors," *Xinhua* (April 6, 1995).

Table 6. Foreign Direct Investment in China, 1994

Source of FDI	Actual FDI (US$Million)	Contracted FDI(US$Million)
Hong Kong/Macao	20,174	48,692
Taiwan	3,391	5,395
USA	2,491	6,010
Japan	2,075	4,440
Singapore	1,180	3,778
South Korea	723	1,806
United Kingdom	689	2,748
Germany	259	1,233
Italy	206	NA
Canada	216	890
TOTAL	33,767	82,680

Source: MOFTEC (Beijing, 1995).

government has made explicit for the first time those sectors where the country is encouraging, restricting, or prohibiting foreign investment.[38] This is designed to entice foreign firms to give greater consideration to possible investment in infrastructure-related and higher value-added projects. The PRC government also hopes to alleviate some of the controversy associated with the desire of foreign firms to invest in such sectors as telecommunications services, energy, and railways – the latter two which have been opened up to foreign investors while the former has not.[39]

At the same time, as the PRC business environment has improved and many of the world's largest multinational firms have started operations inside of China as foreign investors, they

[37]"Foreign Investment Structure Much Improved in China," *Xinhua* (April 14, 1995).

[38]"China Issues Policy Guidelines on Foreign Investment," *Xinhua* (June 27, 1995).

[39]New Guidelines Mark End of "Short-term" Quantitative Strategy," *BBC Summary of World Broadcasts—Far East* (FE/2342/S1, June 29, 1995).

have come to be followed by their suppliers and subcontractors – all of whom feel it is necessary to be in close proximity to their major customers. As a result, China has begun to experience the arrival of a host of small and medium firms from around the world along with the expansion and upgrading of business activities by companies with established operations inside of the PRC economy. This has been viewed in a positive light by Chinese officials who believe that this "second tier" of firms will lead to an increase in local content through expanded technology transfer and management training. It also has helped to stimulate a shift by foreign firms into more technologically sophisticated operations as the availability of higher quality parts and components has improved.

In contrast to the early 1980s when foreign firms entering the Chinese economy could only dream about potential profits and earnings, the current situation has improved considerably. According to a report prepared by Andersen Consulting based in Hong Kong, 47% of the seventy multinational companies that were surveyed reported having become profitable within two years after start-up; a total of 64% said that they were making money – though margins in China were lower than many other emerging markets.[40] What makes foreign firms even more optimistic is that consumerism in China with respect to foreign branded items is now beginning to gain momentum. With China's eventual entry into the WTO and the greater degree of economic liberalization that will be obligated by that membership – plus the growth in per capita incomes, there is little doubt in anyone's mind that current levels of demand and profits will increase in the years ahead.

In essence, foreign investment in China has been a significant factor in helping to facilitate the country s integration into the mainstream of global business affairs. The planes flying to Beijing or Shanghai seem to be always full with eager business executives vying with each other to get the best deal, the five-star

---

[40] "Business Basics Put an End to Myths," *South China Morning Post* (September 22, 1995), p. 14.

hotels seem to have fewer and fewer vacancies as foreign firms seek out attractive Chinese partners and develop the necessary "*guanxi*" to get their deals approved by either the local or national authorities. In the process of bringing their capital, equipment and technology, and managerial know-how to China, foreign firms have begun the process of orchestrating the formation of a new industrial architecture in the Chinese economy. In 1994, China s state-owned enterprises grew at a rate of only 6.5%, while the industrial output generated by foreign-invested and private firms and township and village enterprises grew almost 42.2% and 29.4% respectively.[41] Foreign firms have a degree of mobility inside of the Chinese economy that allows them the opportunity to create their own supplier networks and source components from other foreign-invested firms or from Chinese producers located throughout the PRC economic system. Of course, foreign companies are subject to the pressures of local government to source locally and vulnerable to the inadequacies of the Chinese transportation and communications infrastructure. Nonetheless, a process has already been started that promises to place much of the old economy in a subordinate or declining role to the new economic system that is being forged.

The problem with the economic transformation taking place in China is that the process is simply much too slow for firms responding to or being driven by the higher imperatives of global business.[42] For firms merely directed towards the Chinese domestic market, the situation is less problematic, though not without difficulties. For firms hoping to manufacture in China for external markets, the situation is much more troublesome. One of the major problems is simply the weight of the existing government bureaucracy, which while more streamlined than in earlier years and more economically inclined than its Communist Party-driven predecessors, is still a far cry from acting as the economic

---

[41]"Market Conditions," *Investing Licensing and Trading* (Economist Intelligence Unit, February 1, 1995).

[42]Susan Shirk, *The Political Logic of Economic Reform in China* (Berkeley: UC Press, 1993).

facilitator found in many other countries. The weight of the bureaucracy makes itself especially felt in the process of negotiation and project implementation.[43] Many provincial and local government authorities may have tried to reduce the formal steps for approval of foreign-invested projects via the establishment of the so-called "one-chop shop" in places such as Shanghai and Tianjin, but this has not necessarily reduced the number of individuals who must be won-over in the process of securing overall project ratification.[44]

Added to this problem is the continued leeway that exists at both the national and local level for ad hoc government intervention. The immaturity of the Chinese legal and regulatory systems does not help the situation; while the sanctity of contracts and the efficacy of the law may preclude such indiscriminate interventions by government officials in most Western countries, this is not the case in China. The building of appropriate political alliances and relationships must still be a high priority for foreign firms operating in China as these companies cannot count on the law or the courts to protect their interests in the face of such problems as technology piracy. In addition, the situation has been further worsened by the growing prevalence of corruption among local government officials. If the problems were simply ones of "business facilitation," the situation might not be so bad. The reality, however, is that the problem of corruption has become quite severe – so much so that the present Chinese leadership under Communist Party Secretary Jiang Zemin has made a crackdown on corruption one of its paramount initiatives. Aside from his ability to possibly use the anti-corruption drive as a means to weed out potential political enemies in the succession to the post-Deng Xiaoping era, Jiang apparently recalls that along with an inability to control inflation, the other reason for the collapse of the Kuomingtang regime in 1949 was the rampant cor-

---

[43]Kenneth Lieberthal and Michael Oksenberg, *Policy Making in China: Leaders, Structures and Processes* (Princeton: Princeton University Press, 1988).

[44]Preston Torbert, "New Foreign Investment Regulations Clarify China's Priorities," *East Asian Executive Reports* (July 15, 1995), p. 7.

ruption that existed throughout the government bureaucracy. More than just a few foreign companies have come face-to-face with this problem in China. Moreover, with each foreign company looking for an edge in the intensely competitive Chinese market, the problem of corruption has only been further deepened.

Both the problems with the bureaucracy and corruption have added an element of uncertainty to the Chinese business environment that has raised questions in the minds of some major companies about their ability to rely on China as a partner in their efforts to build global or regional production, sourcing, R&D and distribution networks. In this era of globalization, because of the premium placed on time and customer responsiveness, firms have attached a high priority to three key elements: flexibility, agility, and mobility. They must be able to move people, products, raw materials and information easily across markets and borders.[45] The types of constraints imposed by the realities and uncertainties of the Chinese market serve as an important constraint on the rapid expansion of higher value-added business activities in the PRC.[46] Foreign companies operating in the PRC still have a difficult time extricating themselves from the vagaries and ambiguities associated with the overall Chinese political economy. And, if they cannot get the guarantees that require, they simply will got to other investment locations where the situation is much less difficult and the requirements for success much less demanding.[47]

China's ability to play a more essential role in the game of

---

[45]Gijsbert van Liemt, *Industry on the Move* (Geneva: International Labor Office, 1992).

[46]For a discussion of some of the problems experienced by Boeing, see "No Pain, No Gain," *Far Eastern Economic Review* (August 31, 1995), p. 45.

[47]This helps to explain why the Chinese government announcement that it will grant 'national treatment' status to foreign enterprises was so welcome. Under the Chinese plan, foreign companies will be given the right to set up their own networks to sell imported products and buy raw materials and components at the same prices that local Chinese enterprises pay. See "Equal Treatment for Foreign Firms Hailed," *South China Morning Post*(October 5, 1995), p. 11.

global competition also is constrained by the simple fact that its cost structures are becoming non-competitive in some areas. The salaries of workers in foreign funded enterprises in China rose by 24.2% in 1994, up 22% from 1993. According to a survey conducted by the Wyatt Company in Hong Kong, Chinese wages are being driven up from a combination of inflation, high employee turnover, and foreign exchange-related factors.[48] In cities such as Shanghai and Tianjin, operating costs also have soared, making it increasingly expensive to operate in China's more dynamic coastal locations. Here again, China's inability to maintain price stability could prove detrimental in terms of its capacity to attract future investment, especially if foreign companies do have other investment options in Asia or other parts of the world.

Even more critical is the current and future availability of capable domestic firms to enter into joint ventures and other collaborative partnerships with foreign companies. The problems inside of the state sector already have been referred to above. One important key to China's ability to attract foreign firms in the future will be the degree to which the program of technical transformation of enterprises can be carried out. Xu Penghang, Vice-Minister of the State Economic and Trade Commission, which now has responsibility for the program on technical transformation of enterprises, indicated in a May 1995 national meeting on industrial technology that the upgrading of domestic enterprises using indigenous technologies is a high priority task. Even in China's textiles industry, where tremendous progress has been made in moving beyond the antiquated equipment and obsolete production facilities that were prevalent just a few years ago, major difficulties still exist. In a speech to a National Textile Work Conference in August 1994, Vice-Premier Li Lanqing cited the following issues as important constraints to future progress and financial viability: a) ow-quality equipment; b) an irrational technical structure; c) a product mix non-responsive to international market demand; d) heavy debt burdens in some enterprises while there is a capital shortage in the industry as a whole; e) ris-

[48]*South China Morning Post* (February 4, 1995), p. 1.

ing costs; and f) worsening economic efficiency.[49]

The program on technical transformation of enterprises is designed to upgrade the production facilities, manufacturing processes, management systems, and physical plant layout within Chinese factories.[50] It is structured to provide limited monies for acquisition of new domestic or foreign produced equipment and machinery to replace obsolete and worn out items. In contrast to the acquisition of turn-key plants from abroad, the program is focused on the "software" side of the production process rather than simply looking to new hardware purchases as the solution to China's pressing production issues. Towards this end, during the initial three years of the Eighth Five Year Plan (1991-95), China invested a total of 467.9 billion yuan in technical transformation – exceeding the total investment during the entire Seventh Five Year Plan (1986-1990).[51] The program has started to yield very positive results, especially as it has moved away from being simply a "grants" program supported by the government to a commercially-driven program where most of the capital is now drawn from bank loans and the enterprise's own funds.[52] The case of Hubei province illustrates just how much the program has helped boost output and quality. In four years of technical renovation in state-owned enterprises in Hubei, over 26 billion yuan was invested – almost twice as much as was provided during the previous five years; over 3,000 projects were completed. Approximately 516 projects had foreign investment introduced, while the rest depended on the direct introduction of new

---

[49]"Li Lanqing on Serious Difficulties of the Textiles Industry," *BBC Summary of World Broadcasts—Far East* (FE/2091/G9, September 3, 1994).

[50]"Technical Renovation Benefits Enterprises," *Xinhua* (December 1, 1994).

[51]"Further Commitment to Support for Technical Transformation," *BBC Summary of World Broadcasts—Far East* (FE/W0336/W6, June 8, 1994).

[52]For example, in the case of two major technical transformation projects consummated in 1993, only 1.1% of the capital was drawn from the state budget, while 35.5% was from domestic loans, 3.8% was from foreign funds, 53.2% was from the enterprises' own earnings, and 6.4% was from other investment sources. See "Further Commitment to Support for Technical Transformation," *BBC Summary of World Broadcasts—Far East* (Fe/W0336/W6, June 8, 1994).

hardware and software. As a result of this investment, industrial output in the province increased by 16.57 billion, with the output of steel increasing by 14% and the output of cement increasing by 41% between 1990-1994.[53]

Within the electronics industry as a whole similar progress also has been made as a result of technical transformation investments. Between 1980-1995, China invested more than US $5.36 billion in technical renovation to boost the output and improve the quality of such products as color televisions, semiconductors, computers, VCRs, and related electronic components. As a result, the performance of the industry has been quite commendable; it has grown at an average annual rate of 25%, reaching an annual output of US $21.87 billion in 1994 – up from US $1.19 billion in 1980.[54] While the Chinese electronics industry is still a long way off from becoming a true global competitor, there is little doubt that over the next five years, China's electronics industry will begin to make its impact felt beyond simply producing low-end products for overseas markets.

The revitalization of the technological base within Chinese enterprises is being complemented by the on-going effort to substantially upgrade the overall technical foundation of Chinese industry.[55] Chinese leaders have expressed their strong determination to make a breakthrough in high technology industries by the end of the century, which perhaps is an overly ambitious goal, but nonetheless an important one. The essential elements of the program to raise the technological level of Chinese industry through R&D and innovation were presented in a Central Committee and State Council document on "accelerating scientific and technological progress" in May 1995.[56] The document was

---

[53]State-owned Sector Technical Renovation Brings Benefits to Hubei State Businesses," *Xinhua* (June 4, 1995).

[54]"State Plans $71 Billion Re-Charge for Electronics Industry," *China Daily-Business Week* (April 30, 1995).

[55]Richard Conroy, *Technological Change in China* (Paris: OECD, 1992).

[56]"Decision on Accelerating Scientific Progress," *BBC Summary of World Broadcasts—Far East* (FE/2322/S2, June 6, 1995).

issued in the aftermath of the National Conference on Science and Technology held in Beijing earlier in that same month. While the conference document may have been short on details regarding specific initiatives, it left little doubt as to the intent regarding the promotion of China s high technology industrial capabilities.[57] To accomplish this goal, China has established 52 state-level high technology development zones, has reinvigorated technological promotion programs such as the Torch Plan and the 863 Plan, and has created a host of technological incubators around the country to energize high technology development.[58]

In essence, it is increasingly clear that the PRC government recognizes that the simple infusion of foreign capital, while a necessary requirement for moving the economy ahead in a rapid and sustained fashion, is simply not sufficient by itself to further enhance the composition of China s industrial output. The goal is to ensure that there is a shift from "extensive" to "intensive" development whereby more and more indigenous resources can be called upon to meet the demands of Chinese modernization. While these issues are being sorted out, however, the PRC leadership wants to ensure that foreign investment keeps flowing into the country. This helps to explain, in large part, the decision by CCP General Party Secretary Jiang Zemin to issue his third book on China's modernization – this one focused on the "utilization of foreign capital."[59] In Jiang's preface, he highlights the continued significance of the open door policy, articulating six key reasons why foreign capital is so critical to China's economic development; a) it is conducive to making up for shortages of domestic

[57]"Jiang Zemin and Li Peng address Conference on Science as Primary Productive Force," *BBC Summary of World Broadcasts—Far East* (FE/2317/G1, May 31, 1995).

[58]"Goals Set for High Technology Industry Development," *Xinhua* (December 9, 1994).

[59]The other two books deal with the definition of the socialist economy and the role of science and technology respectively. See "Text of Jiang Zemin's New Reader on Use of Foreign Capital," *BBC Summary of World Broadcasts—Far East* (FE/2312/G1, May 25, 1995).

investment; b) it is conducive to bringing in technology for industrial upgrading; c) it is conductive to transmitting modern managerial know-how; d) it is conducive to employment creation and generating revenue for the state; e) it is conducive to promoting foreign trade; and f) it is conducive to the establishment of the socialist market system.[60]

To reinforce the stated commitment of the PRC government to provide an attractive business environment for foreign firms, the State Economic and Trade Commission reiterated in May 1995 a series of seven preferential policies for foreign investors that will continue to be in force.[61] These policies include the following items: a) foreign firms are permitted to use currency, machinery and equipment and industrial property rights as capital investment. If so used, these relevant items can be exempted from customary import duties and tariffs; b) there are no restrictions on the proportion of shares held by overseas investors in joint ventures; c) there is no time limit on investment projects for foreign firms; d) foreign-invested firms can purchase directly raw materials and sell their products directly in the international market; e) foreign-invested firms can employ the workers they need directly, including technical experts and managers from abroad; f) tax incentives will continue to be provided to foreign-invested firms; and g) extra tax incentives and preferences will be granted to foreign firms investing in key projects identified by the PRC government as high priority.

Regionalization and the Chinese Modernization Drive

The rapid and sustained integration of the Chinese economy with that of East Asia s other market economies has made China increasingly interdependent with important segments of the

---

[60]"Text of Jiang Zemin's New Reader on Use of Foreign Capital," *BBC Summary of World Broadcasts—Far East* (FE/2312/G1, May 25, 1995).

[61]"China: Seven Preferential Policies for Foreign Investment," *BBC Monitoring Service—Far East,* (May 24, 1995).

regional economy – a significant development in view of China's almost continuous adherence to a policy of self-reliance since the onset of the Sino-Soviet dispute in the late 1950s. As suggested earlier, China's role in the East Asian region is helping to redefine the character of the regional political economy. Rather than merely becoming a participant in regional economic and technological affairs, China has the potential to become the principal driving force behind regional growth during the early phase of the 21st century.

The most important regional relationship for China is the Sino-Japanese bilateral relationship. The multifaceted ties between the two countries involve numerous agreements covering foreign assistance, foreign investment, trade, and scientific cooperation. Japan is China's largest creditor, extending US$15.8 billion since 1979, including aid and yen- denominated low-interest loans.[62] In 1994, trade between the two countries totaled US $47.9 billion, up 22.8% from 1993.[63] Unfortunately, since the countries established diplomatic relations in 1972, China has had a 20-year trade deficit totaling US $50 billion. This deficit remains an important concern of the Chinese government. Despite the yen appreciation during the last 24 months, Japanese exports to China keep on increasing due, primarily, to the cost-cutting practices of Japanese firms.[64] This also is a reflection of the complementarities that exist in economic structure between the two economies as well as the fact that Japanese trading companies have developed a broad base of activities in the PRC.

Along with the bilateral trade relationship, increases in Japanese foreign investment in China also have become an important source of growing economic interdependence. By the end of 1994, Japanese firms had initiated 10,332 foreign-invest-

---

[62]"Chinese Premier Lashes Tokyo Over Aid Cut," *Agence France Presse* (September 19, 1995).

[63]"China: Japan to Become Bigger Partner," *China Daily—Business Week* (August 13, 1995).

[64]"Yen Appreciation Won't Harm Sino-Japanese Trade," *Xinhua* (April 13, 1995).

ment projects in China with a value of US $14.2 billion.[65] Japanese-invested firms operating in China now account for 30% of PRC exports to Japan; these same enterprises also are an important source of demand for Japanese machinery and equipment imports. In 1994, for example, the Chinese economy substantially increased its imports of machinery, electronics products, precision instrumentation, and chemical products. While the appreciation of the yen did result in some decline in imports from Japan, in many instances, Japanese firms operating in China have been left with no alternative but to rely on Japanese imports to meet quality requirements or production schedules.

One of the most interesting aspects of Japanese foreign investment in China has been the growing flow of investment capital into Dalian, a coastal city in Liaoning province. Dalian has established an "economic and technology development zone" (ETDZ) that has two sub-sections, one for Japanese companies and the other for Taiwan firms. The substantial presence of Japanese firms in this northeastern industrial city is conspicuous given the tumultuous relationship that has existed between the two countries as a result of the Japanese invasion and takeover of "Manchuria" in the 1930s. Still, recognizing the potential benefits of its close proximity to Japan, Dalian municipal officials have worked hard to attract Japanese foreign investment. Thus, it is not surprising to find that Japanese foreign investment has become the principal source of growth in Dalian.

Among the major Japanese companies that have set up operations in Dalian are Toshiba (electronic home appliances and components), Canon (toner cartridges), and Mabuchi Motors (micromotors). The operations of Toshiba are quite interesting because they are part of a series of manufacturing networks being set up by Japanese companies throughout the Asia-Pacific region. Toshiba has brought with it several of its supplier firms from Japan, and has linked its Dalian based operations with the operations of its suppliers in Hangzhou and its own related operations

---

[65]"China: Exports to Japan Rise, Despite Tiffs," *China Daily-Business Week* (August 27, 1995).

in Thailand. This type of network manufacturing structure is being replicated by a number of other Japanese firms in China; they have become an important mechanism for drawing China into the larger regional division of labor that heretofore, for the most part, did not include the Chinese economy. These firms not only sell products within the Chinese market, but also use China as part of their regional production base for exporting products back to Japan and other markets around the world.

Of course, Japanese foreign investment in China has spread beyond the Dalian region to include Shanghai as well as southern China. One of the most interesting examples of Japanese manufacturing activities in southern China involves NEC, which uses its offices in Hong Kong to oversee the production of computers, printers, and hard disk drives. NEC Hong Kong, which is often called "a company without a factory" has developed a series of localized production networks linking to together a number of dedicated factories in southern China with a team of twenty-six production engineers that manage and coordinate manufacturing, assembly, and sourcing activities.[66] There is no Japanese equity investment in any of the Chinese-based factories. Yet, through NEC's use of information technology, it is able to transmit production design and specifications data and statistics from the local production sites in China to Hong Kong and from Tokyo and even the US (NEC has computer factories located in Massachusetts in the US) to the local factories in southern China.

While the overall total value of Japanese investment in China is still modest, the reality is that the total number of projects has started to grow as "China fever" has steadily grown in Japan. In addition, projects such as that orchestrated by NEC indicate the full extent of Japanese involvement in China is not simply reflected in many of the standardized statistical measures. As the

---

[66]Denis Fred Simon and Yongwook Jun, "Technological Change, Foreign Investment and the New Strategic Thrust of Japanese Firms in the Asia Pacific," in Edward Chen and Peter Drysdale, eds., *Corporate Links and Foreign Direct Investment in Asia and the pacific* (Sydney: Harper Collins, 1995), pp. 203-226.

Japanese have looked at their own needs in terms of domestic economic re-structuring, more and more Japanese investment in all likelihood will move into China. Whether it be telecommunications – involving NEC and Fujitsu – or automobiles – involving Toyota – Japanese firms are actively involved in competing for the most important projects in the PRC. Of course, the Japanese are not always welcome as the first choice of the Chinese due to historical factors. Nonetheless, China cannot ignore the value of developing a close, intimate working relationship with Japan.

For this to happen, however, one of the paramount issues that must be resolved is the Chinese dissatisfaction with Japanese firms in terms of technology transfer. In 1994, China introduced 93 technology transfer projects from Japan with a value of US $769 million; this represented a 56% decline from the situation in 1993. Japanese companies have been constantly admonished by Chinese officials for offering "show how" rather than know how. This may be an extreme perspective in view of Japan s high standards of quality and reliability regarding manufacturing. As was the case with their earlier investments in economies such as Taiwan and Korea, Japanese firms believe in an incremental approach to technology transfer. Their hesitancy in the past as well as today stems from concerns about the quality of local management in China; there is not much confidence that the current cadre of enterprise managers can easily handle the challenges of technology acquisition and assimilation. China, on the other hand, believes that Japanese reluctance to transfer technology is a reflection of its concerns about the so-called "boomerang effect." While the appreciation of the yen has fostered a more forthcoming attitude on the part of many Japanese companies, the reality is that conditions in Japan have necessitated the expanded offshore movement of a great deal of industrial activities too. Add to this the fact that more and more of the products manufactured in China by Japanese firms will be exported back to Japan, it is safe to say that these circumstances may serve to enhance the willingness of Japanese firms to bring more advanced technology and know-how to the PRC. This is exactly what has happened with respect to other Japanese investment activities in Southeast

Asia, especially in Singapore and Malaysia.

China's relationship with South Korea represents another import element in the PRC's growing linkages with the East Asian regional economy. Sino-Korean trade reached US $11.72 in 1994, a 42.5% increase over the previous year. Estimates are that total trade will reach over US $15 billion in 1995. South Korea has become China's sixth largest trading partner overall and China has become Korea s third largest trading partner, next to Japan and the US (not including Hong Kong).[67] Korean trading companies have been especially active in expanding their activities in the PRC economy. As of mid-1995, Korea's general trading corporations had established 56 offices in China, up from only 6 in 1990. While this level of activities is small when compared to the Japanese or American presence, it has grown rapidly – reflecting the more intimate relationship between the two countries. It also is part of South Korea's growing involvement in what is often referred to as "Greater China" – Taiwan, Hong Kong, and the PRC. In 1994, Korean exports to Greater China amounted of US $16.95 billion; growth in bilateral trade during the first half of 1995 indicates that the level of exports as well as total trade easily will surpass this level as well as the level of Korean exports to the United States – once Korea's principal export market.[68]

In a similar fashion, Korean foreign investment in China also has grown. Total Korean foreign investment in China reached US $1.96 billion by February 1995 with a total of 2,248 cases.[69] This growth is complemented by the rapidly expanded presence of PRC companies that have set up branch offices in Korea. As of the end of 1994, Chinese companies had set up a total of 85 branches in Korea, the fourth largest following the 518 they set up in Japan, 501 in the USA, and 223 in Hong Kong.

The steadily expanding trade and investment flows between

---

[67]"ROK Trade Relations Enter New Stage," *Xinhua* (May 8, 1995).

[68]"Exports to the China Region Outpace Those to the US," *Korea Economic Daily* (July 27, 1995).

[69]GTCs Show Remarkable Expansion of Branch Offices in China," *COMLINE Daily News* (Korea, May 9, 1995).

China and South Korea underscores the fact that the two economies are developing a more intimate overall relationship. As a June 1994 article in *Business Korea* suggested, "Korea has become a foil for China to lessen its dependence on Japan for technology transfer..."[70] At the government-to-government level, cooperation in the field of industrial technology has steadily grown to include everything from high-definition television to aerospace. The initiative in the aerospace field is potentially an important one because the goal of the cooperation is to produce mid-size commuter aircraft for use in the Asian region. Under a memorandum signed in March 1994, South Korea will assemble the engines for the new aircraft, while China will manufacture the airframe. The two countries hope to create an alliance with an established Western aerospace firm that will bring to the relationship its design technology and know-how. China has manufactured parts and components for both Boeing and McDonnell Douglas in the US as well as Airbus in Europe. The PRC and South Korea hope that they can use the project to establish themselves as credible players in the aerospace industry. While there are many questions about whether an actual aircraft will ever be produced, the fact that the two countries are even considering such a complex venture as part of a collaborative relationship reveals just how far the bilateral relationship has evolved.[71]

Another indicator of the state of the Sino-Korean relationship in the commercial realm is the degree to which Korea's major chaebols (conglomerates) now are willing to make an extensive commitment to China. The case of Samsung, Korea's leading chaebol, highlights the importance attached to the China market by South Korean firms. In April 1995, Samsung announced plans to invest US $4.0 billion in China over the next several years. Initially, about US $1.6 billion will be invested in electronics, $300 million in textiles, $200 million in chemicals, and $400 million in distribution and other related fields.[72] It will set up five industrial

[70]"China Prefers South Korean Technology and Investment," *Business Korea* (June 1994), p. 42.

[71]"Flight of Fancy," *Far Eastern Economic Review* (August 3, 1995), pp. 50-51.

Table 7. Korea's Foreign Investment in China

Year	# of Approved Cases	Investment Value (US$M)
1989	12	10.0
1990	38	55.0
1991	112	85.0
1992	269	222.0
1993	629	622.0
1994	809	1051.0

Source: Korea Economic Weekly (March 27, 1995), p. 2.

bases in the PRC: Tianjin, Jilin province, Sichuan province, Suzhou, and Guangdong. One of the more provocative of Samsung's investments is its decision to build a US$100 million semiconductor plant in Suzhou.[73] The Suzhou site was chosen because development of the Suzhou Industrial Zone is part of the joint venture between Samsung and the Keppel Group of Singapore.[74]

The Chinese relationship with ASEAN also has become an integral part of the evolving Asian economic structure. China's trade with the ASEAN economies reached US$13.2 billion in 1994, an increase of 23.5% over the previous year.[75] In fact, trade with the ASEAN region grew at a higher rate than China's overall trade growth, which was 20.9% in 1994. ASEAN has become China's sixth largest trading partner. Singapore, which is China's largest trading partner within the group (followed by Malaysia), also has become an active investor in China. Similarly, Thailand, led by the CP Group, also has become an active foreign investor

---

[72]"Samsung Announces Plans for Investment in PRC," *FBIS-EAS-95-070* (April 12, 1995), p. 46.

[73]"Samsung Sets Up Semiconductor Plant in China," *Korea Herald* (July 8, 1995), p. 8.

[74]"Samsung Group to Launch China Electronics Complex," *Korea Economic Weekly* (October 3, 1994), p. 11.

[75]"Business with ASEAN Hits $13.2B," *China Daily-Business Week* (February 19, 1995).

in the PRC. In many respects, the rapid growth of trade and investment between ASEAN and China is linked to the economic and financial power of the overseas Chinese business communities residing in these countries. It also is linked to the fact that as China's economic influence grows, government officials in the ASEAN countries recognize that they cannot afford to ignore Chinese commercial power as well as the opportunities created by the PRC modernization drive.

The last aspect of China's regional relationships to be discussed in this section involves the PRC's links to Taiwan. The paper by Lee Hong-pyo in this volume addresses this topic in greater length. Suffice to say at this point, however, that the growing trade and investment ties between the two economies via Hong Kong has often been viewed optimistically as the first step towards peaceful political integration. Taiwan-PRC trade reached US $16.5 billion in 1994, an increase of over 20% from 1993. Estimates are that Taiwan companies have invested in the vicinity of US $15 billion into China, moving many of their labor-intensive operations that have become non-competitive on the island over to the China mainland. Taiwan has become the second largest source of investment capital into China. This transfer, combined with the transfer of similar types of labor-intensive manufacturing operations by Korean and Japanese companies, helps to explain a large part of the sizeable increase in the trade deficit between the US and China. In essence, these economies have transferred the trade surpluses they had been running with the US in manufactured products to the China mainland as part of their own economic restructuring.

Taiwan, using Hong Kong as its main point of entry into the China market, continues to run a huge trade surplus with the PRC – of the US $16.5 billion in trade in 1994, US $14.1 billion was composed of Taiwan exports to China. Taiwan mainly exports machinery and production-related items to the PRC, while the PRC primarily exports low-end electrical products and clothing. In the short-term, being able to have access to the rapidly growing China market is clearly advantageous to Taiwan companies, especially as they try to cope with rising wages and production costs on the island. Nonetheless, it also is clear that Taiwan government officials believe that the island's future prosperity lies less in the economic orbit of China and more within the context of its emerging technology-based relationships with the US, Japan, and Europe. Taiwan s ability to maintain and promote the future growth of information-intensive industries on the island will directly determine the degree to which the PRC market will have leverage over Taiwan in commercial terms. The crisis over Taiwan's sovereignty in the aftermath of the collapse of its diplomatic relationships with most of the major countries of the world has been abated by the continued interest of the world s leading companies to invest on the island. Thus, while there is a definite pull being exerted by the China mainland to expand Taiwan s dependence on the mainland market, there also is a push coming from the side of the government on Taiwan to ensure that the island s economy remains a player in such global industries as microelectronics, computers, and telecommunications. This may not be the direction that China has anticipated insofar as Taiwan's economic position is concerned. Nonetheless, it does suggest some definite limits to the degree of integration between the two economies.

Prospects and Conclusion

As China sets out to implement the various elements contained in its Ninth Five Year Plan, it will have to increasingly come to terms with two major forces: globalization and regionalization. Chinese leaders cannot simply shut the door and insulate the economic and technology system from the changes being wrought by the dynamic world economy during the last half of the 1990s. As China seeks to extend and expand its role and position in the global economy, it must adapt itself to the fact that the world system is in the midst of a fundamental transformation insofar as the patterns and terms of international competition are concerned. It is no longer a question of domestic versus foreign markets as globalization ensures that most markets are best viewed as being borderless. China's ability to adapt itself to the new rules and requirements for success will, in large part, affect the extent to which it is able to move into an important position in the mainstream of the world economy.

Regional forces clearly have had and will continue to have an important shaping affect on China's economy – in terms of both trade and investment. There is little doubt that China s relationships in the East Asian region are becoming more central to its economic well-being and future prosperity. In many ways, Asia provides a type of comfort zone for China in economic terms. Yes, there is some trepidation among the various economies in the region as to the bigness of the Chinese economy and the dramatic impact a major Chinese export push could have on certain countries. Still, the reality here too is that these economies cannot afford not to have a positive-sum relationship with the world's most rapidly expanding economy. The pivotal question for these Asian economies is whether or not China, like Japan in the 1970s and 1980s, can serve as a catalyst for long-term growth within and across the entire region. While the Asian economies do not want to be dominated by China, they certainly do not want to bypass an opportunity to give a boost to their own economies via closer commercial engagement with the PRC.

In looking to the future, there is little doubt that the growing foreign presence in China will shape the course and character of the Chinese modernization drive. It is becoming increasingly difficult for China to extricate itself from the plethora of economic and technology relationships it has established with the world's leading corporations. Perhaps the best example of this is the automobile industry, which highlights just how necessary foreign investment is to facilitate China's transition from a bicycle to an automobile society. Without judging the costs or virtues of this transition, it is safe to say that the current participation of companies such as Volkswagen, Peugeot, and Chrysler, and the pending participation of Ford, General Motors, and Toyota in terms of car and truck production, has helped to push the industry to the next level in economic and technological terms. The idea that "the Chinese will grab the technology and kick the foreigners out" is becoming less and less likely – though it is never totally impossible given the fact that political imperatives still frequently distort the way China s makes its economic decisions.

Over time, the foreign business community, whether it be defined in regional or global terms, will remain anxious about the degree to which China is prepared to abide by the standard rules of international business and commerce as its economic and technological power grows. From one perspective, there are clear limits to China's growth, particularly in qualitative terms, if the PRC is not able to re-construct and re-engineer much of its industrial enterprises and the overall structure in which they sit. Viewed from another perspective, however, the more China's influence does grow, the more likely it may be for the PRC leadership – even the post-Deng Xiaoping leadership – to still define its interests in traditional national terms. This will pose significant problems for China as global economic intercourse is conducted more and more within the domain of a borderless world unencumbered by traditional forms of xenophobia or even strident nationalism. Thus, as we look into the future, it will be interesting to see if China becomes a vestige of Jurassic Park – a dinosaur seeking to play by a set of rules and attitudes no longer relevant in the 21st century – or whether through the program of reform still underway, it can make the necessary adjustments. Globalization and regionalization promise to remain ever present, and thus whatever type of leadership comes to power after the death of Deng Xiaoping, it must learn to cope with the pressures and opportunities created by the interactions between these two powerful external forces.

2

China's Role in the Pacific Rim Economic Order

Jin-young Suh
(Korea University)

Introduction

There have been increasing concerns about China's role as one of the most critical factors shaping the Pacific Rim economic order. Yet there are two contrasting views on the role of China in the post-Cold War world. Some argue that China will be the next hegemon during the 21st century due to its rapid economic growth along with its huge population and mighty military power. On the other hand, others are cautious and even pessimistic about the role of China. They argue that because China is still an economically backward country, and China confronts various internal problems such as regional imbalance, political instability, and rampant corruption, she will face serious chaos or political disintegration.[1]

[1]On the contrasting views on the future of China, see Melvin C. Gurtov,

In spite of the contrasting views on the role of China in the post-Cold War era, most China experts agree that China's role will substantially rise. China has the world's largest population, the third largest territory, and the fastest growth rate in the last decade. In fact, China has already become a military superpower with nuclear weapons and three million troops, but also has emerged as an economic power. Because the death of Deng Xiaoping, as the champion of economic reform and liberalization, is imminent, concerns about the future of China after Deng have been intensified recently.

The main aim of this paper is to assess the rise of China, and to discuss the changing role of China during the post-Cold War era. The main argument of this paper is that the rise of China is an opportunity as well as challenge to neighboring countries, including Korea. It is an opportunity in the sense that China's economic dynamism is a driving force for East Asian economic development, providing a huge new market and a cheap labor force. Yet it is a challenge because China begins to compete with other countries in the world market, and Chinese military build-up may cause tensions and an arms race in this region. The following issues are examined by this paper. First, I discuss how the economic, as well as military, status of China has risen. Second, the perceptions by major powers and Korea of the rise of China are examined. After that, I explore China's perceptions of the post-Cold War order and the role of China. Finally, I assess China's role in the Pacific Rim economic order.

The Rise of the Pacific Rim Economic Order

The Pacific Rim has experienced profound structural change in the last few years. During the Cold War era, the Pacific Rim was a place in which the U.S. and the Soviet Union faced each other, and the U.S. troops resided to defend the region from the com-

"The Future of China's Rise," *Asian Perspective*, 18:1 (Spring-Summer, 1994), pp. 109-128.

munist threats. The end of the Cold War has changed the nature of the Pacific Rim economic order. Previous rules and norms dictating the Pacific Rim have changed and the power balance has been restructured.

Above all, the Pacific Rim has emerged as the world's most dynamic economic region. Pacific Rim countries have recorded a higher growth rate than any other region in the world. In addition, under the trend of globalization, direct investments and financial capital have been concentrated in the Pacific Rim countries which are dynamic as well as relatively open. As a result, the Pacific Rim, which used to be on the periphery of world history, has emerged as a center of the new world order. Naisbitt and Aburdene argue that the center of world trade is moving from the Atlantic to the Pacific.[2] Northeast Asia, in particular, has emerged as the most dynamic region in the world.

The second feature of the Pacific Rim economic order is the relative decline of the U.S. hegemony and influence. During the Cold War era, U.S. dominance was accepted by other countries mainly due to the necessity of a defense umbrella by the U.S. Yet the end of the Cold War era diminished the military threats and confrontation in this region, though there remain potential tensions in this region. In addition, the United States itself has tried to reduce defense burdens in this region due to its huge fiscal deficits and domestic economic problems. In spite of domestic constraints, the U.S. tries to maintain its influence in the Pacific Rim. The Clinton administration emphasizes the importance of the Pacific Rim to U.S. interests. While the U.S. reduced defense burdens, the U.S. tries to increase its economic linkages to this region.

Another feature of the Pacific Rim economic order is the rise of Japan. During the Cold War era, Japan emerged as an economic superpower under the United State's defense umbrella and as part of the U.S. market. Japanese industries, which grew under the U.S. support, have dominated the U.S. market and put many

[2]John Naisbitt and Patricia Aburdene, *Megatrend 2000* (New York: William Morrow and Company, 1990).

U.S. industries in a difficult position. Since the mid-1980s, Japan has tried hard to transform East Asia into a Yen-bloc economic zone, by increasing direct foreign investments and moving domestic production facilities to developing countries of the region. In fact, the amount of Japanese direct investments and foreign aid to Asian regions has surpassed that of the United States since the mid-1980s. It is clear that Japan has become an economic hegemon in the Pacific Rim.[3]

The final feature of the Pacific Rim economic order is that a strong regional economic bloc is not formed, unlike other regions, such as Europe and North America. In this region, countries differ significantly in terms of the size and level of economic develpemnt. There are, of course, various efforts toward regional economic cooperation in this region. The most important effort for regional economic cooperation is APEC (Asia-Pacific Economic Council) which began in 1989. APEC has recently grown as a key organization for reginal cooperation. The increasing economic importance of APEC reflects the economic dynamism and growing status of this region in the world economy. Yet APEC does not have exclusive cohesiveness, unlike EU and NAFTA. Member countries are geographically dispersed, and their differences are larger than their similarities, and the interests of member states are different. Thus, there is little possibility of becoming a cohesive eocnomic cooperative organization.

The Rise of China in the Pacific Rim Economic Order

Even though U.S.-Japan rivalry is the most crucial determinant of Pacific Rim economic order, another important factor determining the Pacific Rim order in the long term is the role of China. China has already become a military superpower, and has also rapidly upgraded its economic status due to its successful eco-

[3]On the increasing influence of Japan in Asia, see Richard Cronin, *Japan, the United States, and Prospects for the Asia-Pacific Century* (Singapore: Institute of Southeast Asian Studies, 1992).

nomic reform. Since 1978 China has pursued its integration into the capitalist world economy under the leadership of Deng Xiaoping, while maintaining the socialist power structure and ideology. The Chinese economy has recorded an average annual growth rate of 9% since 1978. Recent economic performance is more impressive, recording 12.8% in 1992, 13.4% in 1993, and 11.8% in 1994.[4]

Due to the rapid economic growth, the size of the Chinese economy also has been enlarged. In terms of the size of its GNP, China is the third in the world, behind the U.S. and Japan. Trade volume increased from US$ 20.6 billion and the degree of trade dependence from 10% to 45% from 1978 to 1994.[5] Within the Pacific Rim economic order, China has become a manufacturer of cheap products due to low wages and the huge reserve army of the labor force. In addition, the immense size of its domestic market makes China a huge importer of capital goods and consumer goods from neighboring countries.[6] In fact, China now plays a role as an economic driving force of Asian economic dynamism. This role can be identified in the rapid rise of the "Greater China Economic Community."[7] Greater China expands economic activities and increases its importance in the world economy, by combining the capital and technology of Hong Kong and Taiwan with the labor force of mainland China. According to a World Bank report, it is expected that the GNP of Greater China will

---

[4]On the economic performance of China in the last decade, see K.C. Yeh, "Macroeconomic Issues in China in the 1990s," *The China Quarterly*, No. 131 (September 1992), pp. 501-544; *Zhong Guo Tong Ji Nian Gan* [*Statistical Yearbook of China*] (PRC State Statistical Bureau, various issues).

[5]About trade volume and the degree of trade dependence, Nicholas R. Lardy, *China in the World Economy* (Institute for International Economics, Washington D.C., 1994), pp. 29-47.

[6]On a purchasing power basis, the Chinese economy in 1990 accounted for over 6% of world output, ranking third behind only the U.S. and Japan. See Lardy, *Ibid*.

[7]About the concept of "Greater China," see Harry Harding, "The Concept of 'Greater China': Themes, Variations and Reservations," *The China Quarterly*, No. 136 (December, 1993), pp. 660-686.

reach US$ 9.8 trillion in 2002, surpassing US$ 9.7 trillion of the U.S. in the same year. The same report estimates that trade volume of Greater China will reach US$ 639 billion in 2002, compared to US$ 521 billion of Japan in the same year.[8]

Based on growing economic power, China has also tried to increase its military status. China has rapidly increased its defense budget and pursued military modernization. ⟨Table 1⟩ indicates that the official defense budget increased three times from 1988 to 1995. China's actual annual military expenditures are estimated to vary from US$ 10 billion to US$ 50 billion.[9] China's military build-up has raised concerns from neighboring countries and may cause an armament race in this region. In fact, Japan mentions China's military build-up as an excuse for her own military expansion. China is currently engaged in disputes over land and sea borders with various countries. The Chinese military build-up is a major destabilizing factor in East Asia, along with North Korean nuclear program. As China continues to build military muscle, it is difficult to eliminate the tensions of the Cold War era in this region.

In spite of the rise of Chinese economic and military status in the post-Cold War world order, China has confronted various

Table 1. Growth in the Chinese Defense Budget (1988-1995)

(unit: hundred million Chinese renminbi)

	'88	'89	'90	'91	'92	'93	'94	'95
Defense Budget	217.9	251.4	290.3	330.3	377.8	425.8	550.6	630.9
Increase Rate (%)	(3.9)	(15.3)	(15.5)	(13.8)	(14.4)	(12.7)	(29.3)	(21.2)

Sources: The Research Institute for National Unification, *The Intensification of Reform and Liberalization in China and Northeast Asia Order* (Korean), Research Report 93-04, p.29; Korean International Economic Policy Institute, Regional Economies (April 1995), p. 9.

[8]World Bank, *Economic Trends in Developing Countries* (Washington, D.C., 1993).

[9]About the Chinese military build-up and neighboring countries' response, see "New Menance or Misunderstood Giant?" *Far Eastern Economic Review* (April 13, 1995).

internal problems. First, Western influences, occurring in the process of integration into the capitalist system, have undermined the legitimacy of the Communist Party. China, during the Deng era, has adopted a dual approach, which pursues the radical economic reform, while maintaining the dominance of the Communist Party and socialist ideology. This dual approach has been successful in controlling the political ramifications, of economic reform, and has been able to maintain political stability, unlike other socialist countries where economic reform virtually destroyed the Communist Party-dominated political system. Nontheless, there have been increasing challenges to the socialist ideology and legitimacy of the political system. Since China responded repressively to political challenges, as seen in Tiananmen Incident, rule by the Communist Party is expected to be maintained for the forseeable future. However, as loyalty to Communist Party and acceptance of its legitimacy have substantially diminished, it remains to be seen whether China can maintain socialist ideology and Communist Party domination.

As for the economy, the Chinese government has increased fiscal deficits. Nonproductive expenditures have increased due to the rise of military spending and government subsidies to state enterprises, and the decrease of revenues. A high inflation rate which reached 24% in 1993, the relative decay of the rural sector and migration to the urban sector, and unequal income distribution have resulted as adverse effects of economic growth.

Furthermore, economic reform has increased other social conflicts. Egalitarianism and communitarianism, traditional virtues of the socialist system, have been destroyed, while social cleavages have been intensified and spread. In addition, there have been huge regional imbalances in the speed and degree of economic reform. Moreover, the power of the central government over local governments has declined, and conflict between the central government and local governments has become conspicous. Because of the above problems, some scholars even mention the possibility that China will disintegrate into separate regions.[10] Furthermore, corruption, crime, and moral degradation are rampant throughout government institutions and social sectors. Finally, China is facing a strong possibility of a succession crisis.

Various domestic problems imply that the rise of China as a military and economic superpower is not so smooth and easy. These problems will be the source of political instability and social conflicts in China after Deng.[11] China's new role in the post-Cold War world order largely depends on the solution of the domestic problems.

The Perceptions of China's Neighbors: Regarding the Post-Cold War Order and the Rise of China

To assess the role of China in the Asia-Pacific Rim order, we have to analyse how the major neighboring countries perceive China. Unquestionably, the neighbors that are strongly interested in the China's role, since their policies have been closely related to the Chinese foreign policy, are the United States, Japan, Southeast Asian countries (including Vietnam, the Philippines, and Malaysia) and Korea. This section deals with those countries perceptions and policies towards China.

The United States

In the post-Cold War world order, whether we may call it a multipolar system or a unipolar one, the United States is only one nation with a global reach – economically, politically and militarily. Yet it is also clear that the US has neither the capacity nor the will to play a global hegemonic role. Like all other major nations, its priorities are increasingly domestic in nature, aimed at resolving a number of economic, social and political problems that are the result of decades of rapid economic transformation.[12]

---

[10]About the regionalism as a result of reform and liberalization, see Suisheng Zhao, "From Coercion to Negotiation: The Changing Central-Local Economic Relationship in China," *Issues and Studies*, 28:10 (October 1992).

[11]Harry Harding, "China at the Crossroads: Conservatism, Reform or Decay?" *Adelphi Paper* 275 (1993), pp. 36-48.

Warren Christopher, the U.S. Secretary of State, mentioned that the Clinton administration has placed Asia at the core of its long-term foreign policy strategy, and Asia's future will depend greatly on the future of China. Christopher, in an article, while emphasizing the continuity of America's core interests by quoting Harry S. Truman's words, "Circumstances change, but underneath, the great issues remain the same – prosperity, welfare, human rights, effective democracy, and above all, peace," showed that obviously the U.S. began to have more specific interests in promoting economic security and relations with China.[13] This stance reflected the circumstances, the post-Cold War world.

After the diplomatic normalization between the U.S. and China in 1979, both countries had had congruent interests; the U.S. needed the China "card" against the Soviets, and China needed American capital, technology, and market for its invigorating open-door policy. On the basis of mutual interests, both countries could keep rather friendly relations in the 1980s. But this rapprochement faced a severe crisis provoked by the Tiananmen incident, during which the Chinese government brutally suppressed demands for democratization from within the Chinese civil society. This incident made the human rights factor resume its strong position in the U.S. foreign policy.[14]

Since the Tiananmen incident, such issues as China's political repression, its nuclear technology and weapons sales to Iran and other volatile regions of the world, along with some illegal trade practices and a mounting trade surplus with the U.S. have added to the tensions in a relationship already strained by the unnecessary and tragic violence of June 1989 and subsequent repression.[15]

---

[12]Robert A. Scalapino, "Chinese Foreign Policy in the Post-Mao Era," Ilpyong J. Kim and Hong Pyo Lee, eds., *Korea and China in a New World* (Seoul: The Sejong Institute, 1994), p. 9.

[13]Warren Christopher, "America's Leadership, America's Opportunity," *Foreign Policy*, No. 98 (Spring 1995), pp. 6-27.

[14]On the U.S. policy response to that incident, see Robert G. Sutter, "American Policy toward Beijing, 1989-1990: The Role of President Bush and the White House Staff," *Journal of Northeast Asian Studies*, 9:4 (Winter 1990).

Simultaneously, in order to understand the U.S. perception of China, one should consider the rise of isolationism in America.[16] In the post-Cold War era, the top priority of American policy lies in domestic affairs rather than in international affairs. The Clinton administration was launched with much concerns and hopes of solving domestic problems in 1993. During the 1992 election campaign, Clinton attacked the Bush administration which made efforts lest Tiananmen crackdown should not affect the U.S.-China relations.

In fall 1994, however, the Clinton administration, separating human rights from MFN(Most Favored Nations) treatment, recommended the unconditional renewal of China's current tariff status. President Clinton proposed only the mildest of sanctions: continuing the few measures imposed after the Tiananmen crisis that remained in effect and banning the import of munitions from China. This dramatic turn-around may be interpreted in some ways.[17]

First, the U.S. perceives that China can play a major role in building and consolidating stability in the Asia-Pacific region. If Chinese economic development continues the way it is presently going, China will be a world power equipped with enormous military build-up, a power that is able to compete with the U.S.[18] This scenario seems to make the U.S. have more pressing than

---

[15]Barber B. Conable, Jr. and David M. Lampton, "China: The Coming Power," *Foreign Affairs* (Winter 1992/93), p. 133.

[16]Bill Clinton says, "There is a struggle now going on between those of us who want to carry on the tradition of American leadership and those who would advocate a new form of American isolationism." Current isolationism is a tenet of the Republican Party, but it is increasingly popular among the American people. *Far Eastern Economic Review* (April 13, 1995), pp. 14-15.

[17]Harry Harding pointed out that Clinton administration's Asia predicament before 1994 was the result of deficiencies in the policy process and misunderstandings of the region's situation. Harding, "Asia Policy to the Brink," *Foreign Policy*, No. 96 (Fall 1994).

[18]Of course, a superpower economy does not necessarily mean a military superpower. The perception of China as a 'threat' owes much to the fear that economic success could be translated into an offensive military capability. But

pacific attitude towards China.

In fact, military analysts, who dismiss Beijing's official 1995 defense-budget figure of 63.1 billion renminbi (US$ 7.5 billion) as ridiculously low, are in the dark over how such purchases are financed. Independent estimates of China's actual annual military expenditures vary from US$ 10 billion to US$ 50 billion. What official figures do reveal is a 200 percent increase from 1988, when China listed its defense budget as the equivalent of US$ 2.5 billion.[19] The U.S., however, seems to share with Japan and India the view that China does not pose an immediate threat. Accordingly, China is unlikely to become a foe of the U.S. in an arms race, such as the Soviets did in the Cold War era.

Second, in the post-Cold War era, American foreign policy is likely to be determined by economic interests, as was when American businessmen pushed the government to separate human rights from trade issues. Indeed, economic factor has much increased in the past few years. China's drive for a market economy and industrialization can provide more opportunities to cure American economic stagnation and provide overseas outlets for American investment.

Third, and finally, the new world order provoked American political leaders to focus their main concerns on the domestic affairs. This trend makes it more likely in the future that the U.S. will not be involved directly in the Asia-Pacific region, but will make efforts to organize a multilateral security council, like APEC in the economic field. Currently, the American attitude towards China is ambivalent.

Japan

Japan is China's major partner in economic modernization as the largest supplier of loans and grants, first in trade after Hong Kong, and an important source of technology and investment

---

there are no strict historical parallels and those that exist are ambiguous. Vincent Cable and Peter Ferdinand, "China as an Economic Giant: Threat or Opportunity?" *International Affairs*, 70:2 (April 1994), p. 258.

[19] *Far Eastern Economic Review* (April 13, 1995), p. 25.

(See Table 2). China ranked second only to the United States as the provider of Japan's imports and held ninth place for exports. As recession worsened in Japan, markets and development projects in China became increasingly important, thanks to the astonishing continued growth of that economy.[20]

As the PRC has come of age economically and diplomatically, there has been a corresponding growth in national pride and a desire for respect and acknowledgment of Beijing's status as a great regional power capable of independently protecting its interests. This ambition provides powerful incentive behind the drive for expanded military budgets and defense modernization. A great deal of homage is currently being paid to the role of economics as the future source of international power, and the PRC is surely committed to becoming a world economic power.[21] In this age of capitalist market economy, China needs, and will con-

Table 2. Share in Total PRC Exports/Imports

	1981-85		1986-90		1991-92	
	export	import	export	import	export	import
Asia	67.7	46.0	69.0	51.2	73.0	60.0
Hong Kong	25.5	9.1	38.9	20.8	44.4	26.3
Japan	21.5	29.7	21.5	20.4	14.0	16.4
North America	9.1	20.7	8.9	14.8	10.2	14.2
U.S.A.	8.2	15.5	8.0	12.1	9.4	11.7
Europe	15.9	22.1	17.5	25.8	13.2	19.9
EU	9.9	13.6	9.3	16.0	9.2	12.6
USSR	1.8	1.9	3.5	3.5	-	-
E.Europe	3.2	4.2	3.5	3.7	0.4	0.9
Africa	3.7	1.4	2.6	0.6	1.5	0.6
Latin America	2.5	4.8	1.2	3.5	1.2	2.4
Australia S.	1.1	4.0	0.9	2.8	0.9	2.6

Source: Robert F. Ash, "Mainland China's Emerging Role in the World Economy: Implications and Future Prospects," *Issues & Studies*, vol. 31, no. 1 (January 1995), p. 8.

[20]Allen S. Whiting, "The Future of Sino-Japanese Relations," p. 84.

tinue to need, economic exchange with Japan for the foreseeable future, which implies that China and Japan basically have a shared interest, and have a necessary condition for maintaining their cooperative relations.

However, although Japan has identified herself with the economic power, but not with either political or military power even in the region, China, along with most Asian countries that suffered Japanese imperialism, is wary of Japan's technological edge and its military potential. Japan also thinks of the rise of a heavily nuclear armed China, that could proclaim herself a regional hegemon, as a catalyst for insecurity. In order to offset this possibility, Japan tries to get the U.S. involved in Asia, calling for a continued presence of U.S. troops in Japan. Accordingly, unless Japan would like to become a military superpower, Japan's perception and Japan-China relations will depend upon the U.S.-PRC relations for the time being.

Southeast Asian Countries

With China's open-door policy expanded, there have emerged two contrasting views on the continuing validity of the Chinese market. A more openly pessimistic view would be that government efforts to dampen an overheated economy and reform the financial system, combined with increased nervousness in the face of widespread economic and social unrest, have made mainland China less attractive to overseas investors. Many foreign investors have complained about the difficulties of the commercial environment in which they have to operate. The introduction of new tax rules at the beginning of 1994, which reduced preferential treatment for FFEs(foreign-funded enterprises), has deterred new foreign investment, as may the cancellation of duty-free imports of foreign cars by such enterprises. Rising labor costs in coastal region, as well as higher property rentals in some

[21]Ralph A. Cossa, "The PRC's National Security Objectives in the Post-Cold War Era and the Role of the PLA," *Issues and Studies*, 30:9 (September 1994), p. 25.

major cities, are likely to have had a similar deterrent effect.[22]

The fact that foreign investment has increased can support a more optimistic interpretation.[23] Also, Chinese authorities have sought to discourage nonproductive and low value-added investment and to direct foreign capital toward areas that lend more direct support to industrial policy goals. By contrast, the manufacturing sector has been much less seriously affected, and foreign funds have been increasingly reallocated toward weak links in the domestic economy, such as agriculture and infrastructure. Such changes are reflected in shifts in the geographical origins of foreign investment. Increased investment in more capital- and technology-intensive projects by American, Japanese, Taiwanese, and Korean firms indicates that mainland China's investment environment is changing. A crucial factor to change such an environment has come from the Southeast Asian countries.

Vietnam has for several years competed with mainland China for foreign – especially Asian – capital and recent rises in labor costs in coastal regions of the mainland economy have improved its competitive edge. Hyundai, one of the biggiest companies in Korea, recently made a contract to invest the total sum US$ 2.2 billion in Vietnam, which would be larger than any investment from a Western country.[24] There is evidence, too, that other countries in Southeast Asia (for example, Indonesia and the Philippines) are actively seeking to improve their investment environments in order to attract more overseas capital. In this respect, the Southeast Asian countries began to regard China as an economic rival.

Basically, however, the small countries of East Asia have long thought of China as a latent power to intervene and seriously influence that larger region, as well as the individual countries. Table 3 shows the imbalance of military power in the region very

---

[22]Robert F. Ash, "Mainland China's Emerging Role in the World Economy: Implications and Future Prospects," *Issues and Studies*, 31:1 (January 1995), p. 16.

[23]The first three-quarters of 1994 showed expansion by 49 percent. *Financial Times* (November 7, 1994).

[24]*Chosun Ilbo* [*Chosun Daily Newspaper*] (July 20, 1995).

well. Especially Vietnam, equipped with the largest military facilities in Southeast Asia and having experienced border conflicts with China, has a great interest in preventing an expansion of Chinese influence, which may make its security situation unstable. Though Beijing's relations with Hanoi have improved since the mid-1980s, the latter's worry about the former is most unlikely to disappear in the near future. The normalization of relations between Hanoi and Washington and Hanoi's approaching the member states of the Association of Southeast Asian Nations(ASEAN) can be understood as Hanoi's efforts to offset the PRC's expansionism. It actually means that Vietnam may one day become a new ASEAN or U.S. "card" to be played against the PRC.[25]

Since late 1987 China has paid attention to the Spratly issue. Before then, the Spratly dispute was a minor issue in China's regional policy. Beijing was more concerned about the strategic significance of the South China Sea in the superpowers' rivalry and their policies toward China than about the sovereignty dispute, which did not show signs of becoming a potential regional flashpoint. But China's view of the Spratly dispute began to change qualitatively in late 1987.[26] East-West detente and the concomitant loss of China's influential role in superpower strategic

Table 3. Comparison of Armament in Three Southeast Asian Countries

	CHINA	VIETNAM	PHILIPPINES
Tanks	9,200	2,000	126
Submarines	51	-	-
Destroyers and Figates	55	7	1
Patrol and Coastal Craft	870	55	44
Combat Aircraft	5,845	190	43
Armed Forces	2,930,000	572,000	106,500

Source: *IISS* (London), *FEER* (April 13, 1995), p. 26.

[25]Ralph A. Cossa, *op. cit.*, p. 8.

[26]For more detailed analysis of China's Spratly policy, see Chen Jie, "China's Spratly Policy," *Asian Survey*, 34:10 (October 1994).

relations substantially shifted the attention of Chinese strategists to the nation's own peripheral region and to factors that could lead to limited wars there. By 1989-90 it was widely agreed in China that the Spratly dispute was likely to become a new hot spot in post-Cambodian Southeast Asia and a source of more friction between China and ASEAN.

In response to Beijing's active commitment to the Spratlys, the ASEAN countries have started to internationalize this dispute. A growing trend is underway to establish dialogues on regional security issues at the annual ASEAN Ministerial Meeting and Post-Ministerial Meeting, as well as at other international forums. Internationalization would only enhance the positions of the smaller regional claimant countries in relation to China and strengthen international sympathy for them. In the meantime, the ASEAN countries have tried to involve the U.S. and Japan in South China Sea security by establishing new security links with the U.S.

Korea

The post-Cold War order provided the South Korea rapprochement with China. In the worldwide mood of detente, the PRC's open-door policy, oriented towards the market system, and the ROK government's Nordpolitik provided the immediate conditions that led to the diplomatic normalization in 1992. The volume of trade between both has increased almost four times from US $3 billion in 1988 to US $12 billion in 1993 (see above Table 2). What is more interesting is that, despite the Tiananmen tragedy, the scale of exchange between the two countries was widened and deepened. While there exists a stubborn fear of the advent of a strong China among the Korean people, China is perceived not only as having strategic importance, but also as economic partner, without which the Korean economy would have exhausted its foreign markets. Indeed, what is a more significant factor contributing to friendly relations between the two countries is that they share similar policy goals and have viewpoints in common concerning the Korean issues.

In fact, to improve relations with China has been a major goal of the Korean government's Nordpolitik from 1988 on. Nordpolitik, since it had an ultimate goal of changing fundamentally the structure of South-North Korean relationship, intended to change China's Korea policy from unilateral support for North Korea.

However, the two countries have at this moment slightly different views of Pyongyang's insistence on nuclear armament. Whereas Seoul takes it seriously and thus worries about its impact on the balance of power on the Korean peninsula, Beijing views it as motivated primarily by Pyongyang's diplomatic goal of establishing relations with the United States and Japan. The different assessments of North Korean intentions may well constrain the joint measures between Seoul and Beijing against the problem.[27] But the tentative conclusion of the North Korean nuclear issue through the Geneve Agreement seems unsatisfactory to both countries for different reasons. The ROK government complains that it was almost left out of the overall negotiation process between the U.S. and the DPRK, and their compromise was not helpful to the South-North Korean dialogue. Doubting the genuine intention of the U.S. approach towards the DPRK, China does not conceal her view that the U.S. government is trying to make full use of North Korea against China.[28]

China seems to maintain a two Korea policy and to continue to support the Kim Jong Il regime, not only for survival of her Socialist "brother," but also to prevent possible migration, which must hurt the stablity of Chinese society, from North Korea when the DPRK system collapses.[29] Accordingly, as long as the ROK government keeps its alleged non-absorbing unification policy

---

[27]Dong Sung Kim, "China's Policy toward North Korea and Cooperation between South Korea and China," *The Korean Journal of International Studies*, 25:1 (1994), p. 44.

[28]*SiSa Journal* (August 4, 1995), pp. 46-47.

[29]This observation can be applied to China. If Chinese economy fails and subsequent political turmoil occurs, mass migration of Chinese is not only a nightmare but reality. A Japanese puts the tragic scenario: "If China becomes

and acceptance of Kim Jong Il's offical status, South Korea and China will maintain more than necessary conditions for rapprochement. Furthermore, there are few, if any, incongruencies or conflicts in economic matters that would do harm to their relations. However, the recent aggravated relations between the U.S. and China will become a major factor influencing on the ROK's China policy.

China's Perceptions on the Post-Cold War Order

In this section I will discuss China's own perception regarding the role of China in the emerging new international order. China's role is closely related to the self-image of China's present capability and future potentials. Traditionally China tends to have conflicting self-images. On the one hand, China portrays itself as a part of the poor, developing Third World. On the other hand, it views itself as a great nation, possessed of a rich cultural heritage, massive size, and huge military power.[30] Recently a positive self-image becomes stronger in China. Impressive economic performance has enhanced China's confidence and capability of playing a major role in the world order. This positive self-image has been reflected in China's recent foreign policies. China's recent foreign policies have three major goals.

The first goal of foreign policy is to promote economic growth and modernization. Ever since the reform program and open-door policy was adopted at the Third Plenum of the CCP in December 1978, China began to emphasize economic development as a key goal of foreign policy. In the post-Cold War era,

---

embroiled in turmoil, Hong Kong will be deluged by 500,000 Chinese, 10 million Chinese will go to Thailand and 100 million will go to Indonesia." Takashi Sugimoto, *Mass Migration Pressures in China*, Policy Paper 80E (Tokyo: International Institute for Global Peace, 1992); quoted in Cable and Ferdinand, *op. cit.*, p.259. In this respect, the most serious security threats posed by China or North Korea would originate not in their economic success but in the consequences of economic failure.

[30]Scalapino, *op. cit.*, p. 15.

China gives even higher priority to economic growth than before. In reality, economic interests replace ideology as the most important goal of foreign policy.[31]

The second goal of China's foreign policy is military build-up to keep sovereignty and independence.[32] Even though this goal has been pursued consistently since the inauguration of the PRC, economic power made possible recent military modernization in China. This military build-up has also been accelerated by the territorial disputes with neighboring countries such as Vietnam and the Phillippines.[33] Furthermore, on the basis of the principle of "independence and non-interference," China does not permit interference in unification with Taiwan by other countries, especially the U.S. which as yet maintains strong bonds with Taiwan.

The final goal of China's foreign policy is to enhance its national status by the improvement and diversification of foreign relations. After the end of the Cold War era, China has tried to improve diplomatic relations with countries, with which it had previously adversarial relations. The best examples are normalization with South Korea in 1992 and rapprochement with Russia. China also has made efforts to improve its relationship with European countries and Middle-East countries like Saudi Arabia. The internationl isolation due to Tiananmen massacre and the related embargo by the Western countries, and the collapse of East European socialist countries also forced China to pursue diplomatic diversification.

When China adopts her foreign policy toward individual countries, these three goals are mixed differently in each country. In the relations with some countries like South Korea, economic

---

[31]*Ibid.*, p. 4.

[32]Samuel S. Kim, "Mainland China in a Changing Asia-Pacific Regional Order," *Issues and Studies*, 30:10 (October 1994), p. 9.

[33]Since independence, Chinese leaders have proclaimed that China's foreign policies are guided by the Five Principles of Peaceful Coexitence, which include acceptance of political differences, non-interference in the international affairs of another country, and recognition of the equality and independence of all states.

interests tend to be a major goal. Toward other countries, like Vietnam, territorial claims are the most important goal of foreign relations. Hereafter I will discuss China's perceptions and relations with, major countries, including the United States, Japan, Korea and Southeast Asia.

None is more important than the relationship with the United States. China currently has a multitude of problems with the United States. The major pending issues between the two countries are human rights, China's weapon sales, and trade imbalance.

The first issue is human rights abuses in China. The U.S. government and American public have protested that human rights are abused extensively in China. Thus, the U.S. government has demanded an improvement of human rights as a neccesary condition to develop relationship between the two countries. Regarding the human rights issue, however, the PRC's leaders have taken a position that the human rights issue is basically an domestic problem. Therefore, they insist that in discussing human rights, the principles of sovereignty and noninterference in the internal affairs of a nation must be observed. According to their opinion, the standards of human rights are closely related to the socio-cultural conditions of each country and, thus, standards for human rights vary with a nation's political and economic circumstances.

This discrepancy in views on the human rights between U.S. and China has not changed yet. When U.S. Secretary of State Christopher visited Beijing in early 1994 and criticized the PRC for human rights abuses, Chinese leaders replied that it was not fair to impose the standard of an advanced country on human rights on China.[34]

Another pending issue between the U.S. and China is the China's weapons sales abroad. China is the fifth largest exporting country in the world weapon market. From 1987 to 1991, China exported US$ 7.8 billion worth of arms, following the U.S., the

---

[34]John F. Copper, "Peking's Post-Tiananmen Foreign Policy: The Human Rights Factor," *Issues and Studies*, 30:10 (October 1994), pp. 49-73.

USSR, Great Britain, and France. The U.S. has criticized that China's weapons sales to hostile countries arguing that the sales may threaten peace and stability of post-Cold War order and renew arms expansion. On the other hand Chinese leaders, however, regard weapons export as a commodity export or as a measure of foreign policy. Chinese leaders downplay the political and economic impact of China's weapons sales, pointing out that China made only 5% of the world weapons sales and exported only US$ 0.3 billion to the developing countries in 1991.

The final crucial pending issue is the trade imbalance between China and the U.S. In 1994, China recorded about US$ 30 billion trade surplus with the U.S, and that surplus is expected to grow more. In order to reduce the huge trade deficit with China, the U.S. government has demanded the opening of the Chinese market. Yet China has been very reluctant to open her market. Thus, the U.S government has threatened to cancel various trade measures (most notably, MFN treatment), that have contributed to the rapid rise of China's exports to the U.S. market. In addition, the U.S. government opposes China's entrance to the WTO(World Trade Organization) until China opens her market to a satisfactory level. China regards entrance into the WTO as a critical step for continued economic growth. To enter the WTO, China needs to gain two thirds consent of the member nations, but in reality it cannot be achieved without support of the United States. Recently Sino-American relations have been deteriorated due to Taiwanese Prime Minister Li Denghui's visit to the U.S. The Chinese ambassador to the U.S. was summoned home after Li's visit to America. The relationship between China and America is in the worst condition since normalization of diplomatic relationship in 1979.

Dealing with these pending issues between the two countries that I have discussed so far, Chinese leaders have a basic perception that the U.S. pursues a containment policy toward China. Chinese leaders perceive that a U.S. containment policy is shown in the diplomatic normalization with Vietnam, the rapprochement with North Korea, and the recent policy toward Taiwan. Against this U.S. policy, China is trying to formulate a counter-containment policy. For example, China makes efforts to improve diplomatic relations with European countries. China is also trying to improve the relations with Russia, CIS, and Middle East countries including Iran and Iraq.[35] In addition, Chinese leaders can wield the Taiwan card at any time. This is proved by the recent military trainings in the Straits of Taiwan.

In short, China perceives that the U.S. is the most important country for China's foreign economic relations. At the same time, China has the perception that the U.S. is the most threatening country to China's sovereignty.[36]

China's foreign policy toward Russia has also changed significantly in the post-Cold War era. The two countries maintained an adverse relationship during the Cold War era. In the post-Cold War era, however, the two countries began to show friendly postures toward each other. This change began with the clearing of previous obstacles between two countries: Soviet troops at Sino-Soviet and Sino-Mongol front, Soviet support of the Vietnamese invasion of Cambodia, the Soviet invasion to Afganistan. Gorbachev's visit to Beijing in May of 1989 brought about the rehabilitation of relations between the two countries. Even after the collapse of the Soviet Union, this friendly relationship has been maintained between China and CIS.[37] Yet the Sino-Russian relationship is fragile at present. It is because ideological links are

[35]Prior to Jiang Zemin's visit to Germany, Hungry, and Finland starting from July 5th of this year, Li Peng visited Russia, Ukraine, and Belorus. These diplomatic movements imply that China's counter-containment policy to the U.S. has been initiated. Especially, during Jiang's visit to Germany, he appointed Benz as the partner of China's motor company. It brought Crrysler great disappointment, because it has tried continuously to extend its business to China. China's effort to sell the atomic technology to Iran is intended to construct a diplomatic foundation in the Middle East. *Chosun Ilbo* (July 18, 1995).

[36]In a joint public poll conducted in Japan and China, 59.4% of Chinese picked the U.S. in response to the question of which is the most important country to the Chinese economy, and only 19.9% picked Japan. At the same time 71.6% of Chinese regard the U.S. as a most threatening country to China in terms of national security. *Hangyore Sinmun* [*Hangyore Daily*] (June 2, 1995).

[37]Yasuo Onishi, ed., *Reisen-go no hokuto ajia—aratana sogo kankei no mosaku*

completely broken, and Russia and China are destined to be economic competitors for the World's scarce capital resources. Furthermore, Chinese leaders worry about the continuing deployment of Russian military forces in the Far East.[38]

Let us now turn to China's relations with Japan, Korea, and Southeast Asian countries. Chinese leaders have an ambivalent attitude toward Japan. In fact, China has two contradictary sets of images and perceptions of Japan. One set includes negative perceptions of Japan as a ruthless historical enemy and predator. The other set includes positive perceptions of Japanese as a developmental model for China's modernization. In other words while China wants to expand her economic relations with Japan, China remains suspicious of Japan's motives, especially concerning the re-militarization of Japan.[39]

Beijing has made strong efforts to improve relations with Japan, primarily for economic reasons. Its trade with Japan has expanded significantly in recent years. It also hopes for greater Japanese investment and technology transfer. In other words China worries that Japan's economic power will be tranformed into military power. Thus, Chinese leaders now pay attention to Japanese participation in peace keeping activities abroad. A joint public poll in Japan and China reveals that 31.3% of Chinese respondants regard Japan as a competitor; on the other hand, 19.8% of Japanese respondants did. Regarding Japan's membership in the standing committee of the Security Council of the UN, 26.1% of Chinese were affirmative but 45.9% were negative.[40] In short, while China and Japan are expected to expand their economic partnership on the one hand, they will compete for militay power, as well as political influence in the new Pacific Rim order, on the other hand.

China's policy toward Korea has also changed in the post-Cold

---

[*Northeast Asia after the Cold War: Groping for New International Relations*] (Tokyo: The Institute of Developing Economies, 1993), pp. 14-15.

[38]Scalapino, *op. cit.*, pp. 22-23.

[39]Samuel. S. Kim, *op. cit.*, p. 14.; Scalapino, *ibid.*, pp. 20-21.

[40]*Hangyore Sinmun* (June 2, 1995).

War era, adjusting to the changing domestic, regional, and global situations. According to Samuel S. Kim, China's policy toward Korea has evolved through several phases, shifting from the familiar one-Korea policy to one-Korea *de jure*\two-Korea de facto policy, and then again to a two-Korea *de facto* and *de jure* policy.[41] China's Korea policy has been guided by two different goals, economic growth and international legitimation. In pursuing these goals, China has adopted a dual-track approach of maintaining its traditional ties with North Korea, even when China's economic ties with South Korea increased.

China's diplomatic normalization with South Korea in 1992 reflects the change of Chinese strategic thinking. From diplomatic normalization with South Korea, China has tried to gain several benefits. These are to strengthen Chinese cooperation with Seoul, to isolate Taiwan, and to control increasing Japanese influence in this region. South Korea was regarded as a potential ally against Japanese hegemony.[42]

To its Southeast Asian neighbours, China is currently following a more pragmatic approach than in the past. In general, economic considerations replace ideology in the China's Southeast Asian policies. This trend is shown in the fact that China's assistance to guerrilla movements in this region has ceased. China worries about Japan's growing economic stake in Southeast Asia, which has been regarded for centuries as traditionally a Chinese sphere of influence. India, with which China has been engaged in periodic border disputes since the late 1950s, is considered another rival in this region.

China is involved in teritorial disputes with Southeast Asian countries such as Vietnam and the Philippines. China has shown willingness to use military force to resolve the territorial disputes. To defend China's territorial interest, the PRC tranformed its naval strategy to an offshore strategy instead of its previous coastal defense strategy. As a consequence, China has recently tried to strengthen its naval power, which has been considered to

---

[41]Samuel S. Kim, *op. cit.*, p. 16.

[42]*Ibid.*, pp. 16-18.

be a weak point in China's military capabilities.

As mentioned above, there are three major goals in China's foreign policy – economic, military, and diplomatic goals. In China's foreign policy, these goals are intertwined with each other, and the relative importance of these goals differs by countries or by issues. But a significant trend is that China's foreign policy is increasingly guided by China's economic interests, rather than ideology. Chinese leaders also appear to have growing self-confidence and willingness to strengthen China's role in the Pacific Rim economic order. Because this growing self-confidence and the rise of China's role can be a favorable opportunity or serious challenge and threat, the rest of the world, especially neighbouring countries, is paying special attention to China with high expectation as well as grave concern.

China's Role in the Pacific Rim Economic Order

In this section I will discuss and predict China's role in the newly formed Pacific Rim economic order. After fifteen years of incessant trial and error and several changes, China's economic reform has reached a critical point. China has made tremendous economic growth since 1979. The reform policy was accelerated by Deng's 1992 'South China Talk,' China recorded more impressive growth performance. China revealed annual growth rates of 12.8% in 1992, 13.4% in 1993, and 11.8% in 1994 respectively.

Due to its rapid economic growth, China has become third in the world behind the US and Japan in terms of the size of GNP. In particular, China's trade with Hong Kong and Taiwan reached US$ 49 billion which ranked first in the Asia-Pacific region. With its huge labour force, immense domestic market, and rapidly growing trade cooperation with Hong Kong and Taiwan (what we call the "Greater China Economic Community") China has great potential to be an economic giant in the coming decade.

In military terms, China has recently paid much attention to the military sector and has increased its defense budget, contrary to world trends. At the Fourteenth National Congress held in

1992, General Secretary of CCP Jiang Zemin emphasized the urgency of military modernization. He argued that the military should enhance combat strength all around, to defend the country's territorial sovereignty and to safeguard the unification and security of the motherland.[43]

Another important factor contributing to China's military modernization has been the restoration of Sino-Russian arms connections since 1991. Russia has played a major role in the modernization of the PRC's military industry. Over 1,000 Russian military scientists and technicians have worked in China on defense-industrial exchanges since 1991.[44] China also bought US $ 1.8 billion worth of arms from Russia reportedly making it Russia's most important arms customer. This kind of military build-up not only threatens neighboring countries but other countries around the world.

In the post-Cold War era, China faces a new opportunity to improve its diplomatic status. With the demolishing of the USSR, China became one of the last and certainly the most powerful socialist country in the world. China increased its diplomatic relations from 132 states in 1989 to 158 by the end of 1993. During this time, China has made substantial progress in its ties with Russia and South Korea. The Sino-Soviet Summit in May 1989, and Boris Yeltsin's visit to Beijing in December 1992, lessened tension on the Sino-Russia border so that it is no longer a flashpoint.

China normalized diplomatic relations with South Korea in 1992. Sino-Korea trade has seen a dramatic increase from a mere US $ 40,000 in 1978 to US $ 9 billion in 1993. China also has some leverage over North Korea. Beijing has been willing and able to play a decisive role in controlling Pyongyang's nuclear program. After the Security Council of the UN adopted a resolution by a vote of 13 to 0, with only China and Pakistan abstaining, on May 11, 1993, China's leverage over North Korea became stronger

[43]Jiang Zemin, *CCP's Fourteenth National Congress Political Report* (September 1992).

[44]Tai Ming Cheung's article in *Far Eastern Economic Review* (July 8, 1993), p. 24.

than before. In general, China seems to be more vulnerable to U.S. pressure than other countries, but its occasional resistance to American pressures have maintained the tension between the two countries.

Despite some remarkable economic, military, and diplomatic achievements abroad, China today confronts a variety of domestic problems. The role of China abroad is related to how it can handle these problems. First, China is losing its ideological authority, the legitimacy of the Communist political system is declining. Post-Mao China has tried to build a society with the ideology of so called "market Leninism." China seems to have been successful at grasping the people's support with the idea of "market Leninism." But in the long run, especially if economic growth stagnates and other social problems, like corruption,[45] become serious, there is a strong possibility that China's government will lose political legitimacy.

Second, China is faced with serious regional imbalances. There have been huge regional differences in the speed and performance of economic reform. Since Mao stressed the even development of regions in his famous article, "On Great Ten Relations," regionally-balanced development has been a key goal of Chinese economic policy. In contrast, Deng Xiaoping chose an uneven development strategy. He believed that for successful economic transformation certain strategic areas should be chosen.

Third, China's central government has lost control over local governments and ethnic minorities. In order to boost economic growth, the central government has transfered much of its power to local governments since 1978. This power shift has reduced the central government's control over local governments and ethnic minorities. Losing traditional levers of control, the central government increasingly depends on coercive forces. The Tiananmen

---

[45]Harry Harding advanced a three-eyed view of corruption as symptomatic of political decay in post-Mao China : 1) the abuse of public power for private gain; 2) the decline in the capability of the state; and 3) the decline in the legitimacy of the political system such that the state can no longer evoke popular compliance. Harding, "China at the Crossroads," p. 44.

massacre in 1989 is a good example.

Finally and the most importantly, China is faced with a leadership succession crisis. There has been much concern about the future of post-Deng China. I have suggested four scenarios for the post-Deng era. The first scenario is the continuation of the present political system. It can be labeled as a "neo-authoritarian regime," which pursues economic liberation and an open policy for economic development on the one hand, with political conservatism on the other. In this scenario, Jiang Zemin could be considered the core leader of such an authoritarian regime.

The second plausible scenario is the re-emergence of conservatives backed by the military. In this scenario, Deng's death would leave China in a power vacuum, with different factions struggling for power. In this confused situation, conservatives with military support might seize power, reducing the speed and scope of the reform at home, while maintaining the existing socialist system with an emphasis on Chinese nationalism in foreign relations.

The third scenario is the seizure of power by radical political reformists. In this scenario, with demands for radical reform from the bottom, radical reformists will throw away one-party communist rule and pursue radical political reform. This would see China follow the road of USSR and East European countries.

The final scenario is of political chaos in China. As the struggle between power elites of the central government becomes heated, the central government would lose control over local government, and conflict among local governments would increase.

Each scenario is plausible, but each ignores the time variable. I think that the plausibility of each scenario differs in its time frame. In the short run, China is more likely to develop a neo-authoritarian regime under Jiang's leadership. There are a number of reasons for this. First, there is currently no strong alternative leader except Jiang and second, the power elites fear chaos. Nevertheless, I predict that a power struggle between elites after Deng's death will probably end as a "typhoon in a tea cup." In other words, a post-Deng power struggle is not likely to advance beyond the "redistribution of power" within elites.

To summarize, there are two sets of contradictory factors which facilitate or constrain China's role in the post-Cold War international order. The facilitating factors – dynamic economic growth, military build-up, and increased international status – will contribute to enhancing China's role in the Pacific Rim economic order in the coming decade. Constraining factors – legitimacy crisis, regional imbalance, declining power of central government, and the succession problem – will be obstacles to China's increasing role in the Pacific Rim economic order. Therefore, China's role in the Pacific Rim economic order will depend on how China tackles two sets of contraditory factors. In order to enhance China's status in the Pacific Rim economic order, China needs to utilize facilitating factors on the one hand, and should overcome domestic constraints on the other hand. The ways and means of handling this task differ with the types of regime that emerges after Deng's death. The success or failure in accomplishing this task will determine the fate of China after Deng. At the same time, the Pacific Rim economic order of the next century will be substantially shaped by the role of China.

PART Ⅱ

China and the Asian RegionalEconomy

3

Sino-Japanese Economic and Technology Relations

Roy F. Grow
(Carleton College)

> Among the other countries confronting our own, there is none that surpasses us in proximity to China, in close access to all of its ports, and in convenience of navigation. It must be said that our country occupies the best position with respect to the China trade. Ito Hirobumi (1898)

> There is little question as to where our real future lies; it is not so much as in North America or in Europe. Japan's real economic future lies on the Asia mainland – especially in China. Murayama Tomichi (1994)

Taguchi Noboru looked around as he walked out of the north train station in Dalian.[1] The city was booming and the area's famous port appeared to be the center for an enormous flow of exports. In the mid-1990's, Dalian looked like it was one of China's main links to the world of regional and international economic activity. Taguchi had first came to Dalian in the 1930's as a

[1]I have changed some of the names used in this paper at the request of the interviewees.

young employee. He had worked as an engineer in a company controlled by the Mitsubishi conglomerate and he had helped install a complex switching network for a branch of the South Manchuria Railroad Company.[2] Taguchi had been proud of his work, both for the level of the new technologies he had helped install and for the role that the rail line played in economic development across Asia. "We helped open all of the northeast China with that line," he said during his later visit. "The trade that came out of our work was good for both China and my company."

Now, more than fifty years after his first assignment in China, Taguchi was back in Dalian as a "returned elder" for Mitsubishi. At first, his attention was riveted on all of the continuities; he could still pick out the downtown landmarks, and many of the streets – although renamed – were familiar thoroughfares. Even the Japanese presence in the city appeared to have strong and continuous threads and Taguchi was surprised at the very public presence of so many Japanese firms. "It seems even more heavy than when I was here in the '30's," he said at one point. "If I didn t know the history of the years in between so well, I could almost imagine that I had never left."

After a few days, however, he could see more clearly the changes a half century had brought. Some were obvious, such as the modern infrastructure and the new buildings and factories. Others were more subtle and Taguchi, as he began to check in with other Japanese companies and listened to the stories of the young business people who now worked in Dalian, could sense how deep many of the changes had been. "Some things are really different now," he said. "The presence of our Japanese companies seems as strong as it ever was, maybe even stronger. But the things our companies are doing, the ways we are doing them, and our relationships with our Chinese counterparts – a good deal of this seems changed. We are important, but we are important in very different ways than when I was first here."

---

[2]There is a wonderful description of Mitsubishi's early involvement in China. See Mitsubishi Electric, *Kengyo Kaiko* (Reflections on Business) (Tokyo, 1951).

Taguchi was right. Japanese business activity was (and remains) the most important factor shaping the regionalization and internationalization of the Chinese economy. But important parts of this relationship have changed during the past one hundred years. Japan's involvement in China is commonly divided by the war years from 1937-1945. The years before the war – especially from 1900 to 1937 – show an extraordinary expansion of Japanese economic influence in China and also show Japan taking on the most important role in shaping the flow of capital and goods into China. The years following the war show this role becoming more subtle and flexible, as Japanese firms become the conduit for the inward and outward flows of technology, managerial expertise, and organizational strategy. Taken together, these two periods outline a remarkable record of one nation's involvement in the transformation of another. This chapter will examine both the changes and continuities in Japan's economic relationships with China.

Early Japanese Involvement in China, 1890-1937

Japan has not always played the most prominent foreign role in China, of course. For most of the 1800's, the important foreign actors in China were from Europe and North America. Great Britain was both a leader and a role model for much of China's nascent industrial sector and, especially in the period immediately following Opium Wars period (1840-57), British entrepreneurs became the most active agents in China.

Many analysts have commented on the juxtaposition of Britain's military presence and the expansion of the influence of English businessmen. But the role of Britain's military and naval power – although important to China's politics – was in fact limited when it came to the economic sphere: by and large, the expansion of British economic activity was the province of private entrepreneurs.[3] Family names such as Jardine and Perkins

[3]See the argument in Peter Duus, Ramon Myers and Mark Peattie, *The*

were more important to both British and American economic activity than were the names of military and naval commanders.

The strong European economic presence began to give way to a rising tide Japanese activity by the late 1880's. Japanese business people were beginning to move across Asia and these entrepreneurs looked at China as a source of inexpensive inputs for their developing industry and as sites of new markets manufactured products.[4]

At first, most of Japanese business activity in China was located in the Yangtse river basin and was concentrated in only a few sectors – most notably cloth spinning mills and railroad building. But Japan's military actions of the 1890's and early 1900's against China and Russia had the effect of focusing Japanese public attention northward and gave the Japanese military its first important footholds in China proper. The concessions that were granted after these military actions spurred Japanese commercial activity and gave both military and industrialists an important entree to cities such as Mukden and Port Arthur.[5] Japan's commercial activity grew rapidly throughout north and northeast China and by the turn of the century the center of gravity for Japanese economic activity had moved north, with China's three northeast provinces becoming the primary focal point.

The new Japanese rail lines became especially important agents of change. Earlier, many Japanese military and government offi-

---

Japanese Informal Empire in China, 1985-1937 (Princeton: Princeton University Press, 1989), pp.-6 (chapter introduction). For a more detailed discussion, see Ian Nash, "An Overview of Relations Between China and Japan, 1895-1945," in *The China Quarterly*, No. 24 (December 1990), pp. 601-623.

[4]Mizoguchi Toshiyuki, "The Changing Pattern of Sino-Japanese Trade, 1884-1937," in Peter Duus, Ramon Myers and Mark Peattie, *The Japanese Formal Empire in China, 1895-1937*, pp. 11. *The China Quarterly*, No. 124 (December 1990), pp. 601-623. See also the argument in Francis V. Moulder, *Japan, China, and the Modern World Economy* (Cambridge: Cambridge University Press, 1977), Introduction.

[5]See Phyllis Genther's description of the war's impact on the redirection of Japanese industry, *A History of Japan's Government-Business Relationship: The Passenger Car Industry* (Ann Arbor: Michigan Papers in Japanese Studies, No. 20, 1990), pp. 18-21.

cials had looked warily at the construction of branches of the Trans-Siberian Railroad across China's northeast and the concessions gave Japanese businesses the right to compete with the Russian branch lines and to develop commercial centers in the same areas. The South Manchuria Railroad Company became one of the early agents for shaping Japanese economic activity across north China during the first part of this century and linked Japanese interests in a number of Chinese cities. The firm's activities became an important counterweight – both politically and economically – to Russian influence.[6]

The decades that followed mark a tremendous expansion of

Chart 1. Japan and Britain in China, 1899-1931

	1899	1914	1931
Direct trade with China (millions of HK taels)			
Great Britain	53.9	113.3	170.9
Japan	53.1	184.9	543.7
Population in China			
Great Britain	5,562	8,966	13,015
Japan	2,440	80,219	255,686
Number of firms in China			
Great Britain	401	590	1,027
Japan	195	1,269	4,633
Shipping Capacity in China (tons)			
Great Britain	23.3	61.2	52.2
Japan	2.8	23.4	45.6
Investments in China (millions US dollars)			
Great Britain	260.3	607.5	1,189.2
Japan	1.0	219.6	1,136.9

Source: C.F. Remer, *Foreign Investment in China,* as cited in *The Japanese Informal Empire in China, 1895-1937,* p. 3.

[6]See the argument by Ramon Myers, "Japanese Imperialism in Manchuria: The South Manchuria Railway Company, 1906-1933," in Peter Duus, Ramon Myers and Mark Peattie, *The Japanese Informal Empire in China, 1895-1937,* pp. 101-132.

Japanese economic involvement in China. While World War I was an important break point for European economic activity in Asia – with British, French, and American efforts focused mainly on central Europe – Japanese involvement in China had overtaken even that of Britain well before the war broke out; in almost every category of activity – from direct trade to the number of firms in China – Japanese economic activity had surged past Great Britain by the first decade of this century.

This robust Japanese involvement in China coincided with a rapid structural change that was sweeping across the Japanese economy itself and many analysts argue that the extraordinary expansion of the Japanese economy during this period was one of the primary motive forces shaping Japan's increasingly deep involvement in almost every kind of industrial activity in north China.[7] These analysts have also pointed out the increasingly symbiotic relationship between Japanese domestic industrial development, the growing thirst for raw materials, and the need for protected markets to absorb the output of the yet inefficient industrial sector.[8] The energy that emerged from this structural change pushed Japanese economic interests deeper into China and set the stage for the incorporation of the entire region into Japan's "formal empire."[9]

By the early 1930's, therefore, a number of distinct and important categories of Japanese involvement in China had emerged, and many of the trends begun during this period would have

---

[7]Herbert P. Bix, "Japanese Imperialism and the Manchurian Economy, 1900-1931," in *The China Quarterly*, No. 51 (July-September 1972), pp. 425. Rob Stern describes the origins of Japanese "low-cost production" techniques during this period and its links to Japan's increasingly robust international economic activity. See his "Structural origins of Japan's foreign direct investment," in Jonathan Morris, *Japan and the Global Economy* (London: Routledge, 1991), pp. 46-47.

[8]Mizoguchi Toshiyuki, "The Changing Pattern of Sino-Japanese Trade, 1884-1937," in Peter Duus, Ramon Myers and Mark Peattie, *The Japanese Informal Empire in China, 1895-1937*, p. 24.

[9]Ramon Myers and Mark R. Peattie, *The Japanese Colonial Empire, 1895-1945* (Princeton: Princeton University Press, 1984), pp. 30-38 (Introduction).

important consequences for the ways this relationship renewed itself in the post-1945 period:

• Trade

By the 1920's, trade with Japan was accounting for 20-30% of both exports and imports from China (a pattern that would resume after the war and continue into the 1990's).[10] The commodity composition of Sino-Japanese trade changed dramatically between 1900 and 1930. At the turn of the century, China was the primary Japanese market for goods that come from its nascent industrial sector. Because many Japanese firms could not compete directly with their western counterparts – in factor costs, quality, technical standards – regions of China become captive markets in which Japanese goods can be sold with little competition.[11]

In the late 1930's, however, Chinese industrialists had mastered most of the earlier Japanese process and product technologies and the Japanese business advantage began to disappear and China's primary exports to Japan were more complex industrial products – such as machinery and motor vehicles. In 1937 – the date commonly used to mark the beginnings of Japan's "formal empire" in China – the balance of trade had swung in China's favor: Japan had become a net importer of Chinese goods.

• Foreign Direct Investment

As the Kuantung army strengthened its hold on Manchuria in the 1930's (and at the same time began to play a more prominent role in Tokyo politics) the patterns of direct Japanese investment in China changed as well. By the mid-1930's, Japan's major

---

[10]Mizoguchi Toshiyuki, "The Changing Pattern of Sino-Japanese Trade, 1884-1937," in Peter Duus, Ramon Myers and Mark Peattie, *The Japanese Informal Empire in China, 1895-1937*, p. 30.

[11]See the commodity composition tables in Mizoguchi Toshiyuki, "The Changing Pattern of Sino-Japanese Trade, 1884-1937," in Peter Duus, Ramon Myers and Mark Peattie, *The Japanese Informal Empire in China, 1895-1937*, pp. 17-21.

exports to China were finance capital and state of the-art industrial technologies that ranged from machinery to management techniques. Many analysts have noted the almost counter-intuitive consequences of this investment:

> although northeast had China become, in effect, a colony, Japan became a net exporter of both capital and industrial equipment to the region it controlled – reversing the process found in European colonial empires.[12]

There were several sources for this Japanese investment. The most important were a series of government agencies whose officials saw in China a safe location for new industrial development, a source of raw materials for both this new industry and the older industry in the Japanese home islands and, most importantly, a locus of strategic advantage against an increasingly powerful Soviet military machine. As well, there were a series of newcomer entrepreneurs – the so-called new Zaibatsu – who saw in China opportunities not open to them in the home islands.

For China, the most important consequence of this pattern of Japanese FDI was the development of a series of regional industrial centers. The most prominent – the Showa complex at Anshan, the coal centers at Fuxun, and the port facilities at Dalian – became China's most important industrial centers and shaped Chinese economic activity for the next half century.[13]

---

[12]Nakajane Katsuji, "Manchukuo and Economic Development," in Peter Duus, Ramon Myers and Mark Peattie, *The Japanese Informal Empire in china, 1895-1937*, pp. 152, 157.

[13]There is considerable debate bout the real impact of this Japanese investment and the ways that it shaped indigenous Chinese economic activity. In agriculture, for example, analysts disagree about how important this Japanese investment was in skewing land holding patterns and wage rates, and altering a process of change that was already in motion. But there is little question that the massive movement of Japanese capital and technologies into north and northeast China set in motion a process of industrial development, the logic of which is still felt in the 1990's. See Herbert P. Bix, "Japanese Imperialism and the Manchurian Economy, 1900-1931," *The China Quarterly* (July-September 1972), pp. 425-443; and the critical comments about this article by Ramon Myers in *The China Quarterly* (July-September 1973), pp. 547-556.

• Organizational and Managerial Styles

There is no question that Japanese organizational strategies and management patterns differed from both those of their western counterparts in China and from those already well-developed in indigenous Chinese factories.[14] The decision-making patterns of managers, the tendency to avoid the use of compradors, and the new industry/government relationships were all part of this Japanese pattern in the 1920's and 1930's.[15] As well, there were important Japanese experiments with Soviet models of planned input/output relationships, especially in those industries under the administrative guidance of the Kuantung Army and the War Munitions Board.[16]

Some Long-Term Trends

The deep Japanese push into China generated four important trends. First, as Japanese involvement in China increased, the dependence of the Japanese economy on things Chinese also began to increase. Several studies have noted the increasing Japanese appetite (and need) for markets and raw materials and, as Duus notes, "China was a convenient source of both" – even more so than Korea and Taiwan.[17]

Second, Japan's economic activity in China increasingly

---

[14]See, for example, the description in Peter Duus, "Zaikabo: Japanese Cotton Mills in China, 1895-1937," in Peter Duus, Ramon Myers and Mark Peattie, *The Japanese Informal Empire in China, 1895-1937*, pp. 90 & 97-98.

[15]Mark Fruin makes the point about a reverse-learning process during this period, as Japanese firms also adopted Chinese strategies. See his *The Japanese Enterprise System: Competitive Strategies and Cooperative Structure* (Oxford: Clarendon Press, 1994), pp. 34.

[16]Ironically, it was fear of the Soviet military that led many Kuantung Army officers and the War Munitions Board officials to experiment with Soviet models as one of the best ways of organizing resources in the region. These models – as they were applied to the great Japanese Showa iron and steel complex and in some of the mining regions – laid the groundwork for the later Soviet aid efforts in 1948, the bulk of which went to the old Japanese industrial and infrastructure projects.

[17]Peter Duus, Ramon Myers and Mark Peattie, *The Japanese Informal Empire in China, 1985-1937*, p. 4.

became the lynch pin for a rigorous and growing intra-Asian trade as China's economic transactions with Japan easily outpaced those between Japan and both Korea and Taiwan.[18] At the same time, a broad of division of labor developed in Japanese international trade and foreign direct investment, with China becoming the focal point for the greatest part of Japan's high-tech industrial investment.[19]

Third, Japan became a major conduit for the movement of China's export goods abroad – both to Japan and into other markets in Asia.[20] As the Korea/Taiwan/China division of labor became more pronounced, Japanese merchants became one of the primary mechanisms channeling the flow of Chinese goods throughout the region, as well as shaping the flow of international capital into China.[21]

Fourth, the increasing dominance of Japanese commercial activity in China had the function of reshaping the nature of foreign business activity in China itself. By the end of the first decade of the 20th century, most Japanese commercial activity had as its core a strong partnership with a series of government agencies – a relationship which was much stronger for those operations located in China than for those in the Japanese home islands.[22] Although the South Manchuria Railroad company

---

[18]Mizoguchi Toshiyuki, "The Changing Pattern of Sino-Japanese Trade, 1884-1937," in Peter Duus, Ramon Myers and Mark Peattie, *The Japanese Informal Empire in China, 1895-1937*, pp. 12-16.

[19]Duus makes the important distinction between Japan's informal and formal empires in China and argues that as the informal gave way to the formal, the very basis of Japan's economic activity was undermined. See Peter Duus, Ramon Myers and Mark Peattie, *The Japanese Informal Empire in China, 1895-1937*, p. xxiv.

[20]Note the argument made by Bruce Cumings, "The origins and development of the Northeast Asian political economy: industrial sectors, product cycles, and political consequences," in *International Organization*, 38:1 (Winter 1984), pp. 1-40.

[21]This is the argument made by Kenichiro Hirano in The Japanese in Machuria, 1906-1931 (Ph.D. dissertation, Harvard University, 1984).

[22]Nakajane Katsuji, "Manchukuo and Economic Development," in Peter

became the prime example of this sort of government/industry relationship, it came to characterize almost all of the Japanese commercial activity in China's coastal and northeast regions.[23]

Japan's Post-War Role

The war years were devastating for both China and Japan. In China, the years of revolution and occupation had brought economic life to a standstill and, along with such cataclysmic events as the Great Famine of 1942-43, scarred a generation of Chinese. For Japan the destruction of its military capability and the trauma of the war's end were equally devastating. In 1945 both economies were in a shambles and cross-national transactions were almost non-existent.[24]

Yet fifty years later the Sino-Japanese economic relationship is again Asia's most dynamic. Most interestingly, many of the economic trends that were so important in the 1920's and 1930's have continued into the present – almost as if the disruption caused by the war had not occurred. To be sure, many of the underlying forces that shape these trends are very different: Patterns of trade and investment have changed, flows of technology have been altered, and organizational strategies used in Chinese enterprises have evolved. But the underlying dynamic remains much the same in the 1990's as it was in the 1930's: At most levels of economic interaction, Japan remains China's most important economic link with the outside world.[25]

Duus, Ramon Myers and Mark Peattie, *The Japanese Informal Empire in China, 1895-1937*, pp. 137-141.

[23]W. Mark Fruin, *The Japanese Enterprise System: Competitive Strategies and Cooperative Structures* (Oxford: Clarendon Press, 1994), pp. 126-127.

[24]For a note on the impact of the war's end on the Japanese auto industry in China, see Phyllis Genther, *A History of Japan's Government-Business Relationship: The Passenger Car Industry* (Ann Arbor: Michigan Papers in Japanese Studies, No. 20, 1990), p. 43.

[25]This is the argument of Christopher Howe, "China, Japan, and Economic Interdependence in the Asia Pacific Region," in *The China Quarterly*, No. 124

This section will outline the important continuities that shape China's move into regional and international economic activity. Then, the important factors underlying this continuing relationship will be outlined and Japan's role as an agent of China's movement into these larger economic arenas evaluated.

Building on the Japanese Heritage: The Soviet Interlude

By late 1945, most of Japan's industrial centers in China were occupied by Soviet troops and Japanese nationals in China had been forcibly expatriated to the Japanese home islands – even those born in China.[26] Chinese communist forces followed Soviet military units into most of the Japanese-occupied areas and began the process that would result in the larger sweeps south the following year.

With most of the region's factories and rail lines out of service, there was a sense on the part of many Chinese communist leaders that economic rehabilitation required outside help. Two of China's revolutionary leaders – Gao Gang and Liu Shaoqi – traveled to the Soviet Union in 1948 and negotiated the first Soviet aid agreements. By 1949-50, there were formal Soviet commitments to rehabilitate 141 different economic sites in China. Most of this Soviet aid went into the repair of the economic infrastructure created by Japanese industrialists and the military in the prewar years, and most of these projects (over 85%) were located in north and northeast China.

More significant than the location of the aid was the form and content of the Soviet projects. Already we have noted the fascination of Japanese leaders in the Kuantung Army in Manchuria and the War Munitions Board in Tokyo with Soviet central planning strategies. From the Showa Iron and Steel Works to the South

(December 1990), pp. 662-693.

[26]The battle between Japanese and Soviet troops that flooded into the area continued after the Japanese surrender to the United States; the Soviet army sent most of the captured Japanese military personnel into Siberian prisons and occupied many of the Japanese industrial centers, claiming the machinery as reparations.

Manchurian Railway, Japanese authorities in Manchuria had carried out important experiments with various forms of planned allocation, structured input/output relationships, and Soviet accounting methods.

The Soviet aid that began in 1949-50 had the effect of resurrecting many of these old industrial organization patterns, accounting practices, and management techniques in the old Japanese centers. In terms of management practice, for example, a number of Soviet models with roots in the 1930's came with the aid; one-man management, the "responsibility system," and the coal industry's "Kovalev method" had been used both in the Soviet Union and in Japanese industry in China during the 1930's. To the degree that the Soviet rehabilitation projects became important to the larger Chinese economy in the 1950's, Soviet aid had the effect of continuing many of the important Japanese-sponsored organizational policies and economic trends that flourished in China during the 1930's. More important consequences came in the area of trade. Most of the Soviet aid was tied to a series of repayment agreements – the first coming due in 1955-56 – which required the shipment of specific goods from China. The great portion of these goods were in two categories: raw materials (both agricultural and mineral) and output from the Japanese-built industrial centers in China's northeast. The commodity compositions lists show Sino-Soviet trade in the 1950's resembling almost exactly the lists of Sino-Japanese trade in the 1930's. During the 1950's, the Soviet Union replaced Japan, by and large, as the recipient of China's raw materials and manufactured goods.

The strains that emerged from this Sino-Soviet relationship highlight some of the tensions that continue to shape China's interaction with the larger Asian regional economy. The most important strain centered on a growing awareness by Chinese managers of issues having to do with technological compatibility. Although many of the *management* strategies used in Chinese industry from the mid-1930's to the 1950's had their origins in Soviet practice, much of the hardware itself – the machinery, assembly lines, and building arrangement – was decidedly

Japanese. That part of Soviet aid that came in the form of machinery and equipment (about 65%) thus had to be grafted onto a well-developed Japanese base and in most cases the graft proved difficult, if not impossible. Thus, in sites such as Anshan Iron and Steel, Soviet help soon put the steel factories in the complex back into production and was largely responsible for the early gains in Chinese steel output. But Chinese technicians soon reported that the Soviet equipment simply did not mesh well with the older Japanese machinery, and many of these managers were becoming disenchanted with Soviet equipment and the Soviet experts that came with this equipment.

Perhaps more important was the deep antipathy in China that was stirred by the Soviet aid and it was not long before there was serious grumbling from many Chinese officials – especially the revolutionary cadres who had moved in to the factories – about Soviet aid "resurrecting Japanese imperialism." This grumbling spread to the heart of Chinese politics when Northeast leader Gao Gang – who championed more egalitarian and autarkic policies – confronted Liu Shaoqi over the question of Soviet aid and in 1954 labeled him a "counter-revolutionary" for his support of these industrial bases. The ripple effect of these charges continued through the 1950's, resulting in Gao's purge (and suicide) in 1955 and the 1959-60 polemics with the Soviet Union.

The Re-emergence of Japan: The Important Trends

The first contacts with Japanese business groups occurred almost immediately after the proclamation of the People's Republic of China in 1949 and developed in the context of the growing Chinese disenchantment with Soviet process and product technologies. The Korean War had put some of these post-war contacts on the backburner, but by 1955-56 Japan was again China's leading trading partner.[27] Sino-Japanese trade increased

---

[27]Still, the China trade continued to hover at its traditional 3-4% of Japan's GNP. Christopher Howe, "China, Japan, and Economic Interdependence in the Asia Pacific Region," in *The China Quarterly*, No. 124 (December 1990), p. 680.

steadily throughout the 1950's. By 1959, in the wake of the Great Leap Forward and the cessation of Soviet aid, many Chinese ministries began to issue "unofficial" official invitations to their Japanese counterparts. Similarly, Japanese business groups began to find their voice (almost completely silenced since the American occupation) and in Tokyo began to press for a more active role in inter-Asian trade.[28]

The late 1970's saw a series of agreements between China and Japan. The most important was the declaration of February, 1978, that formalized the commercial transactions that been going on in an informal way for almost a decade.[29] This declaration was followed by some four dozen supplementary agreements that opened economic channels in almost every trade category.[30] Perhaps the most prominent of these agreements was the protocol that brought Japanese companies into the construction of the ill-fated Baoshan complex near Shanghai – an on-again-off-again project that almost destroyed official Sino-Japanese trade relationships.[31]

The real logic of the Sino-Japanese economic relationship became clear as these agreements took affect and analysts note a series of trends that underscore the changing nature of this relationship. The most trends are summarized below.

- Direct and Indirect Trade

Chart 2 outlines the dramatic increase in Sino-Japanese trade beginning in the late 1950's. The figures also show that for both

---

[28]For an overview, see Akira Iriye, "Chinese-Japanese Relations, 1945-1990" in *The China Quarterly*, No. 124 (December 1990), pp. 623-638; and Wendy Dobson, *Japan in East Asia: Trading and Investment Strategies* (Singapore: Institute of Southeast Asian Studies, 1993), pp. 9-12.

[29]Allen S. Whiting, *China Eyes Japan* (Berkeley: University of California Press, 1989), pp. 95-99.

[30]Bill Clifford, "Japan's Lending Program in China," in *The China Business Review* (May-June 1993), pp. 30-35.

[31]See "Steel Industry: The Baoshan Complex," in Chae-jin Lee, *China and Japan: New Economic Diplomacy* (Stanford: Stanford University Press, 1984), pp. 30-75.

Chart 2. China's direct trade with Japan
(as % of China's total trade)

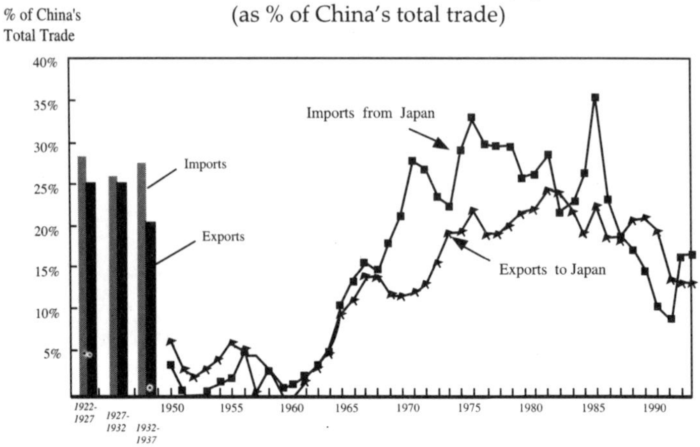

Source: *Handbook of Economic Statistics*, 1977, p. 61; *Trade Statistics Yearbook*, various issues.

Chart 3. China's direct trade with Japan
(total value of trade)

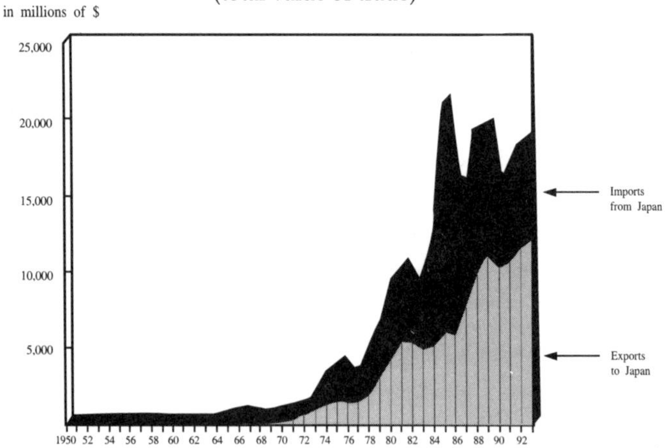

Source: *Handbook of Economic Statistics*, 1977, p.61; *Trade Statistics Yearbook*, various issues.

Chart 4. Commodity composition of Sino-Japanese trade

China's Imports from Japan

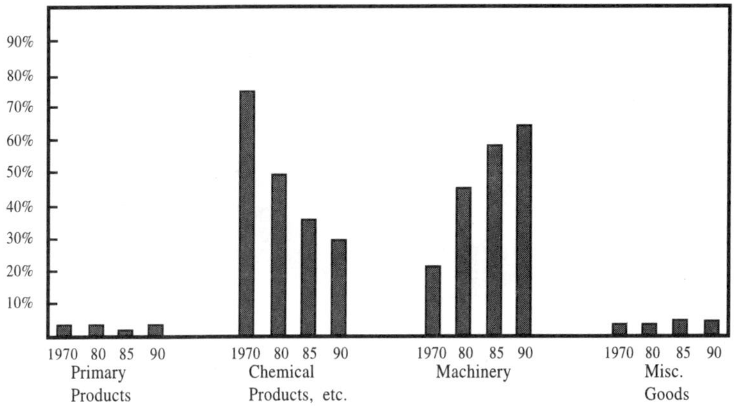

China's Exports to Japan

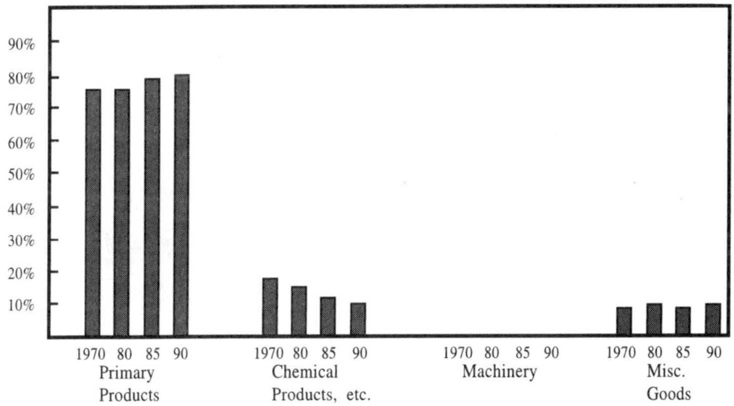

Source: *EIU Country Report, China/North Korea,* various issues and Howe, *The China Quarterly,* No. 124 (December 1990), p. 629.

exports and imports the peaks – reached in the 1970's and the 1980's – are at about the same levels of those in the 1920's and 1930's.[32]

At first, most of this growing trade channeled Chinese raw

Chart 5. Direct and indirect trade

China's Exports to Japan

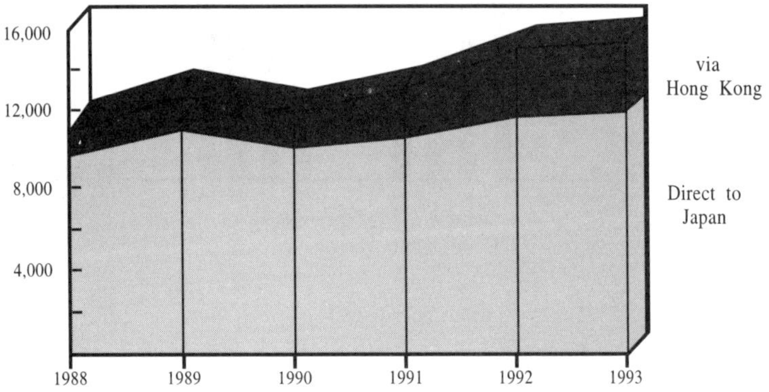

China's Imports form Japan

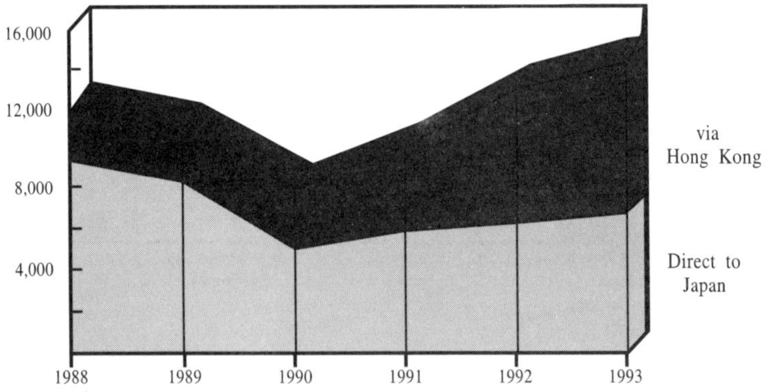

Source: *CTR* (October 1992 & May 1993).

[32]Shigeru Ishikawa, "Sino-Japanese Economic Cooperation," in *The China Quarterly*, No. 109 (March 1987), pp. 2-6.

materials – and especially energy products – to Japan.[33] However, commodity composition lists show that most of this trade in raw materials was temporary, driven more by the oil embargoes and the "Nixon shock" than by fundamental and deep-seated economic needs.[34]

The volume of Sino-Japanese trade is only a surface indicator for more important and deep-seated changes that were taking effect. One of the most important changes has to do with the changing geographic locus of much of this trade, especially in the indirect trade that was flowing through Hong Kong. *Chart 5* shows just how fast Hong Kong's role changed: by the early 1990's, indirect Sino-Japanese trade via Hong Kong almost equaled that of direct trade between the two countries.[35]

A closer look at some of the details of this indirect trade further highlights the changing nature of Japan's economic relationships with China, as southern China began to play a very different role from northern China in Japanese trade.[36] As well, Hong Kong became the most important Japanese entry point for its own consumer goods into China.[37] By the 1980's, therefore, most of Japan's consumer exports to China flowed through Hong Kong, while the great portion of Chinese industrial products flowed directly to Japan via ports such as Shanghai and Dalian. Hong Kong took on an even more important role for Japanese imports to China and by 1993 over 50% of all Japanese imports were flowing through Hong Kong.[38]

---

[33]Qingxin Ken Wang, "Recent Japanese Economic Diplomacy in China: Political Alignment in a Changing World Order" in *Asian Survey*, 33:6 (June 1993), p. 628.

[34]Chae-jin Lee, *Japan Faces China: Political and Economic Relations in the Postwar Era* (Baltimore: Johns Hopkins University Press, 1976), pp. 140-150.

[35]Christopher Howe, "China, Japan, and Economic Interdependence in the Asia Pacific Region," in *The China Quarterly*, No.124 (December 1990), p. 682.

[36]For an overview of Japanese intra-industry specialization, see Bela Belassa and Marcus Noland, *Japan in the World Economy* (Washington D.C.: Institute for World Economics, 1988), pp. 62-69.

[37]David Kilburn, "Japan's retailers travel to China," *Advertising Age*, 64 (March 15, 1993), pp. 115-116.

• Direct Investment

Much the same pattern appears when Japanese FDI in China is examined. *Charts 6 and 7* show Japanese investment – as a percentage of total investment – increasing in the Greater Shanghai area and in Guangzhou, while decreasing in other regions, especially in China's northeast.[39] These charts also demonstrate the shifting rationale for investment.[40] By the mid-1980's, the greater part of Japanese investments in Shanghai and Guangzhou was channeled into projects that furthered Japanese commercial and merchandising activity in China, while investment in China's northeast was used primarily to facilitate sourcing and sub-contracting.[41]

Japan's auto industry provides an especially interesting case in point. The industry's tendency to use sub-contractors is well known and is one of the primary ways the Japanese industry differs from its European and North American counterparts. The FDI figures point to the speed with which this sub-contracting work began to move away from the main Japanese islands.[42] *Chart 8* shows just how this sub-contracting in China has

---

[38]Note the case study in John Quansheng Zhao, "The Making of Public Policy in Japan: Protection in Raw Silk Importing," *Asian Survey*, 28:9 (September 1988), pp. 926-944.

[39]Note the figures in Wendy Dobson, *Japan in East Asia: Trading and Investment Strategies* (Singapore: Institute of Southeast Asian Studies, 1993), pp. 38-39.

[40]Tessa Morris-Suzuki, "Reshaping the international division of labor: Japanese manufacturing investment in Southeast Asia," in Janathan Morris, ed., *Japan and the Global Economy: Issues and Trends in the 1990's* (New York: Routledge, Chapman and Hall, 1991), pp. 135-153.

[41]Yoichi Yokoi, "Plant and Technology Contracts and the Changing Pattern of Economic Interdependence Between China and Japan," *The China Quarterly*, No. 124 (December 1990), pp. 700-01; Todd Thurwachter, "Japan in China: The Guangdong Example" in *The China Business Review* (January-February 1990), pp. 7-17.

[42]Peter Dicken, "The changing geography of Japanese foreign direct investment in manufacturing industry: a global perspective," in Jonathan Morriss, ed., *Japan and the Global Economy: Issues and Trends in the 1990's* (New York: Routledge, Chapman and Hall, 1991), pp. 14-44.

increased into the 1990's: China (along with Southeast Asia, Australia, and the United States) had become one of the primary locations for this sub-contracting work.[43]

Chart 6. Japan's FDI in China
(by region and by purpose)

(a) By region

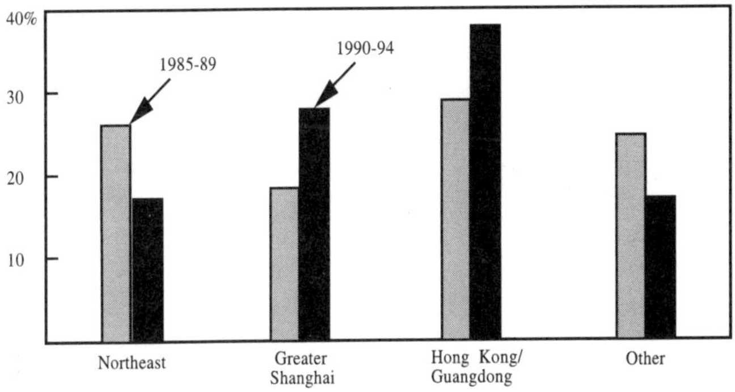

(b) By purpose, within each region (raw materials excluded)

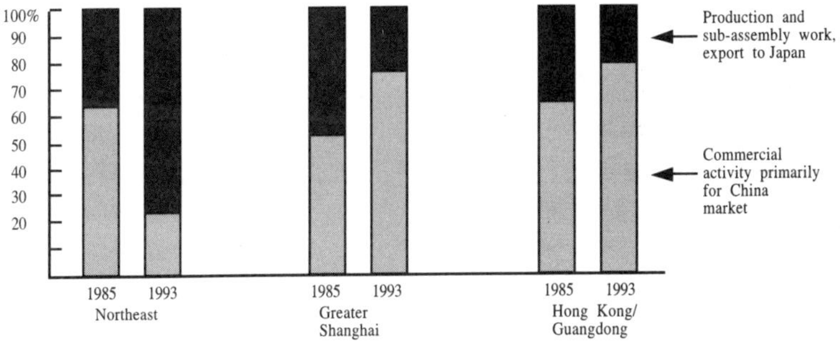

Source: Roy F. Grow, data gathered in China from various Japanese interviews

---

[43]Richard Johnson, "Japan Seeks Passport to China's Auto Mart," *Automotive News* (November 15, 1993) p. 3; Gwen Zonghetti, "Japan in Shock," *Word's Auto World*, 29 (January 1993), pp. 33-34.

Chart 7. Japanese FDI
(rationale for investment)

(a) Project type

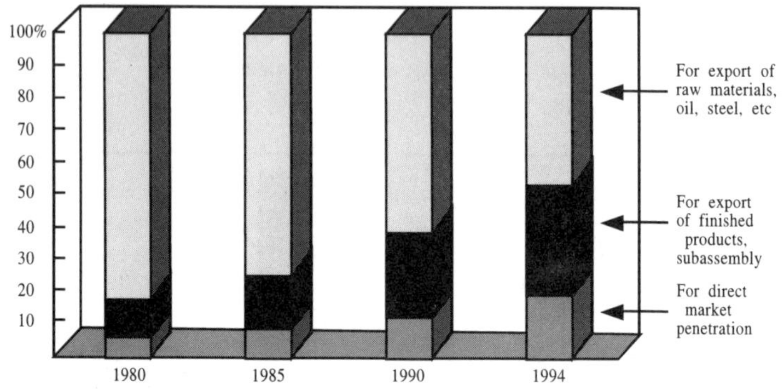

(b) Managers' attitudes

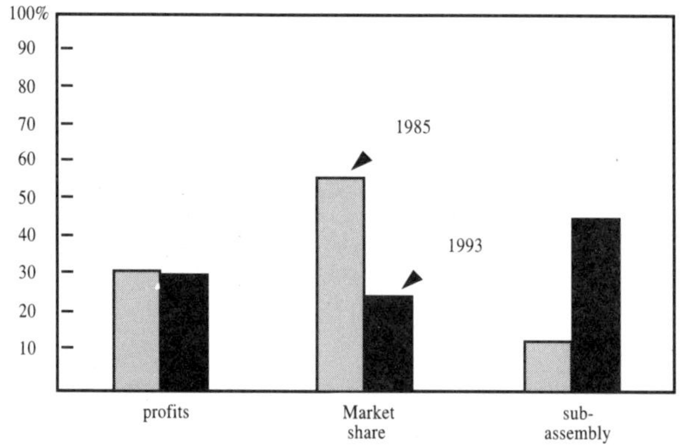

Source: Roy F. Grow, data gathered in China from various Japanese interviews

Analysts have noted a series of factors that shape the way this investment pattern structures the Sino-Japanese economic relationship. The first factor has to do with location. Unlike the American automobile industry, Japan's sub-contractors tend to group themselves more in close geographic proximity. In the United States, for example, both Ford and General Motors work with sun-contractors across the United States and, by and large, it

Chart 8. Outsourcing in the Japanese auto industry
(Externally produced component as a percentage of total manufacturing cost)

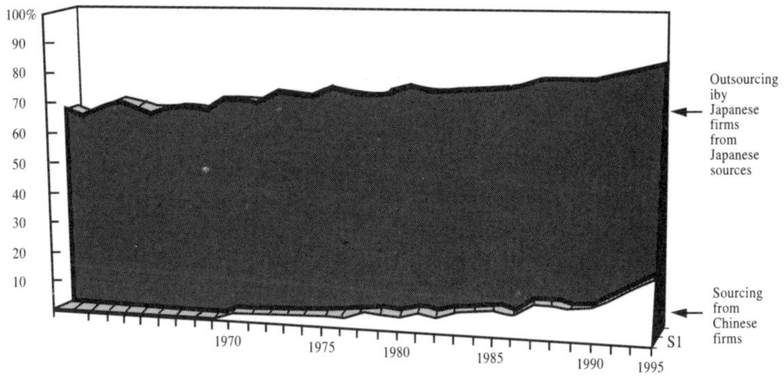

Source: Chinese figures from State Planning Commission and Roy F. Grow; Japanese figures from Toshihiro Nishiguchi, *Strategic Industrial Sourcing: The Japanese Advantage*, p. 97.

is price (as opposed to location or length of working relationship) that is the guiding criterion for the American firms. Japanese production in the United States, on the other hand, tends to rely on sub-contractors clustered together geographically – regardless of product.[44] 200 miles is considered a long distance in most Japanese sub-contracting relationships.

The same location pattern is characteristic of Japanese industry in China. Most Japanese sub-contracting work (indeed, most investment) is grouped in three main areas: the northeastern provinces, Shanghai, and Guangdong.[45] This contrasts with

---

[44]Richard Florida and Martin Kenney, "Japanese Foreign Direct Investment in the United States: the case of the automotive transplants," in Jonathan Morriss, ed., *Japan and the Global Economy: Issues and Trends in the 1990's* (New York: Routledge, Chapman and Hall, 1991), pp. 91-114. For comparable trends in Australia, see David W. Edgington, Japanese Business Down Under: Patterns of Japanese Investment in Australia (New York: Routledge, 1990), pp. 99, 109, 221.

[45]Richard Johnson, "Japan seeks passport to China's auto mart," *Automotive News* (November 15, 1993), p. 3.

Chart 9. Location of important Japanese assembly/subassembly operations

Source: Charts derived from David Edington, *Japanese Business Down Under: Patterns of Japanese Investment in Australia*, pp. 99, 219, 221; Richard Florida and Martin Kenney, "Japanese Foreign Direct Investment in the United States" in Jonathan Morris, *Japan and the Global Economy*, pp. 91-114.

American investment patterns in China which are more widely dispersed and in joint venture locations which appear in greater numbers in areas such as those around Chengdu and Xian.

• Production Complexity

During the 1980's, there was an increasingly rapid tendency for Japanese production activity in China to move along a continuum from "simple production" to "complete assembly." *Chart 10*

Chart 10. Transition to subcontractor work

(a) Transition by Japanese firms in Japan, 1962-72

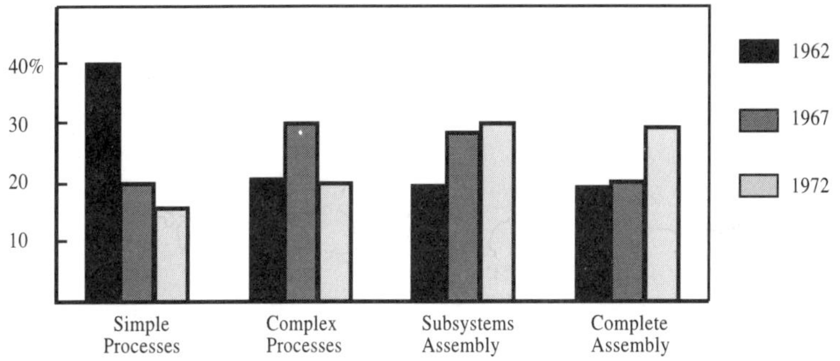

(b) Transition by Japanese firms in China, 1983-93

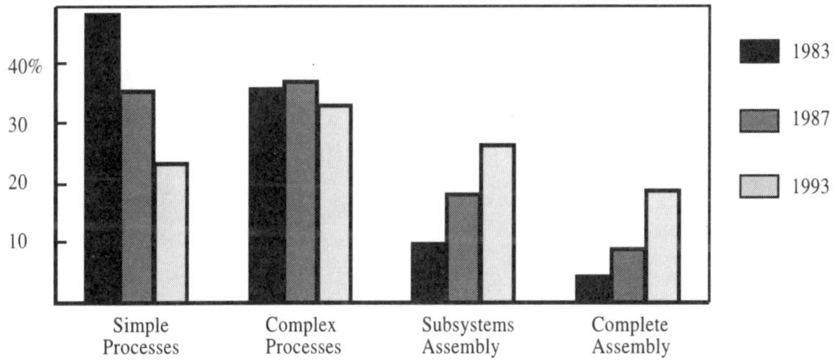

Simple process:	single discrete process, such as grinding or polishing
Complex process:	multiple processes, such as grinding and polishing combines
Subsystems assembly:	assembly of subsystems or systems components consisting of multiple processes
Complete assembly:	assembly of complete products that can be sold in final product market

Source: Japanese figures from Toshihiro Nishiguchi, *Strategic Industrial Sourcing: The Japanese Advantage*, p. 112; Chinese figuresfrom Roy F. Grow, sample of 14 Japanese firms (categories modified to fit Nishiguchi's framework).

shows this transition in the Japanese sub-contacting industry during the crucial 1962-72 period in the Japanese home islands.[46] Looking at a similar (although later) period in Japanese work in China, we note a similar movement along the continuum. While the movement is not as rapid nor complete as in the earlier case in the Japanese home islands, there is still no question as to the direction of the movement, and it shows the general tendencies at work in Japanese production activity in China.

• Organizational Structure

Accompanying the movement of Japanese capital and growing complexity of production activity in China was the diffusion of organizational style. Two trends have shaped the assembly process in Japan's international manufacturing activity across the world. The first trend has to do with the ways that Japanese firms and their sub-contractors work toward decisions, design new parts, and figure out cost.[47] The tendency has been toward participatory and inclusive kinds of behavior, with all of the parties involved in an active way that is far different than industry from other countries.[48] The second trend has to do with organizational structure, as these participatory themes become formalized in a first-tier second-tier strategy. As *Chart 11* indicates, the first tier generally handles most of the interaction with sub-sub-contractors, speeding the process, keeping organizational pyramids relatively flat, and minimizing span-of-control issues.[49]

Many of these same tendencies have found their way into

---

[46]Michael J. Smitka, Competitive Ties: Subcontracting in the Japanese Automobile Industry (New York: Columbia University Press, 1991), Chapter 3; Toshihiro Nishiguchi, *Strategic Industrial Sourcing: The Japanese Advantage* (New York: Oxford University Press, 1994), p. 112.

[47]Mark Fruin, *The Japanese Enterprise System: Competitive Strategies and Cooperative Structures* (Oxford: Clarendon Press, 1994), pp. 294-5.

[48]Michael J. Smitka, *Competitive Ties: Subcontracting in the Japanese Automobile Industry* (New York: Columbia University Press, 1991), pp. 1-22.

[49]Toshihiro Nishiguchi, *Strategic Industrial Sourcing: The Japanese Advantage* (New York: Oxford University Press, 1994), pp. 122-3.

Japanese industrial organization in China. Most Japanese companies begin their production and sourcing activities in China by using relatively static and simple one-on-one relationships with a Chinese supplier – usually through a simple joint venture rela-

Chart 11. Fuji Electric subcontracting in Japan and China

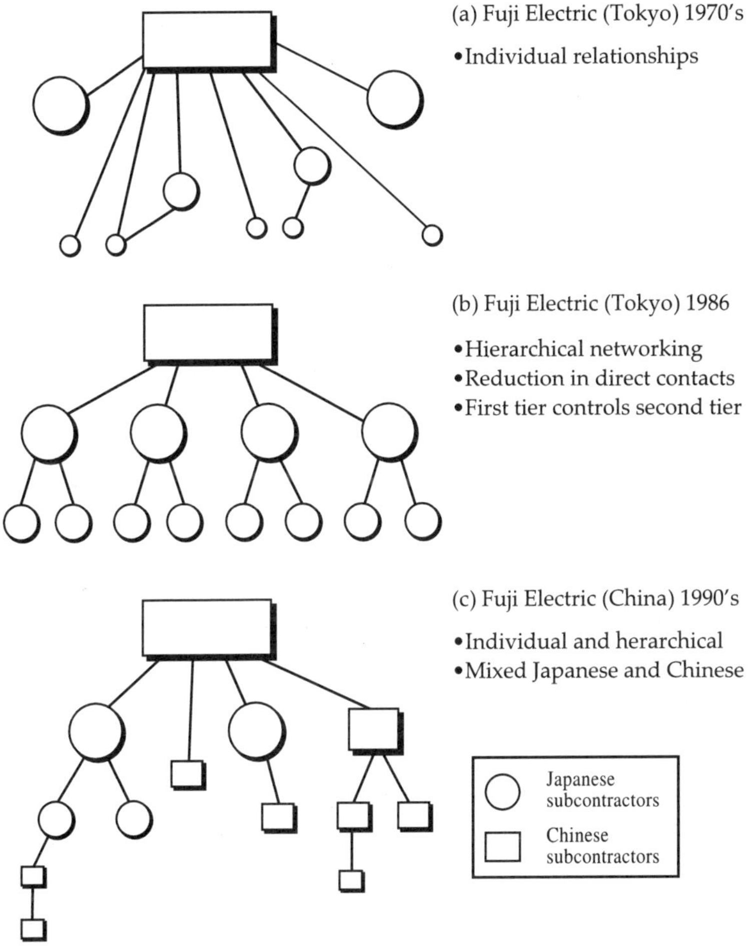

Source: Chinese chart by Roy F. Grow, interviews in Japan and China; Japanese charts adapted from Toshihiro Nishiguchi, *Strategic Industrial Sourcing: The Japanese Advantage*, p. 123.

tionship. In this model, the China joint venture stays in direct contact with a central administrative point and reports to Japan in much the way that Japanese first-tier sub-contractors report to headquarters units. Increasingly, however, the entire Japanese first-tier second-tier relationship is finding its way into Japanese production work in China. More and more, complex webs of sub-contracting units (and even complete sub-assembly relationships) are developing in the wake of Japanese investment and, as *Chart 11* shows, are reshaping the ways that Japanese firms do business in China.

• Technology Transfers

No issue has been more volatile to China's managers and ministry officials than that of technology transfer. Over and over, the complaint most heard from these managers and officials is that "Japanese technology transfer is simply not as good as that of American firms."

The actual situation is more subtle and nuanced, however. As most studies show, there is no question that American firms are more likely to bring with them to China advanced machinery with all of its "bells and whistles." Japanese firms, on the other hand, are more likely to focus on the kinds of technology transfer that has to do with organization and instruction.[50] Japanese managers tend to be more "hands on" in their management role than are their American counterparts, tend to place a higher value on direct training of Chinese workers, and focus more on implementing "Japanese styles" of organization – the "software" of technology transfer. As a result, Japanese technology transfers to China tend to emphasize the less visible "software" side of technology transfer. And, more importantly, Japanese technology transfer more often result in successful China projects.[51]

[50]Denis Simon provides the most insightful and detailed evaluation of these transfers. See Denis Simon, *The Emerging Technological Trajectory of the Pacific Rim* (New York: M.E. Sharpe, 1995), Introduction.

[51]Roy F. Grow, "Comparing Japanese and American Technology Transfer in China," in *Technology Transfer in International Business* (New York: Oxford University Press, 1991), pp. 193-222.

• Distribution Networks.

Distribution remains an area which is, for many Japanese firms, the most innovative area part of their economic activity in China. At the same time, it is also a "black hole" that into which their product often disappears. In Japan, distribution networks are quite often complex and multi-layered – some of the most inefficient in the industrial world. The movement of simple product to family store sometimes requires as many as seven or eight separate transactions.[52]

But in their non-Japan activity, many Japanese firms have been among the most innovative in building new channels and distribution networks.[53] Toyota's marketing and distribution efforts in the United States beginning in the late 1950's are one of the most visible examples.

Japanese firms have been equally innovative in their distribution efforts in the China market. In this market, there is now an almost 100 year history of working with (and through) Japanese trading companies, and the experience has diffused into a number of different Japanese companies.

• Management

Perhaps the most subtle and troublesome aspect of Japanese firms' role in China has to do with actual management (as opposed to the training of Chinese workers.) Here we note a tendency seen in other Japanese operations around the world:

> the inability of Japanese managers to distance themselves from direct management, and to operate adequately in a crosscultural environment.[54] In

---

[52]Masayoshi Maruyama, "The Structure and Performance of the Japanese Distribution System," in Michael R. Czinkota and Masaaki Kotabe, *The Japanese Distribution System: Obstacles and Opportunities, Structures and Practices* (Chicago: Probus Publishing Company, 1993), pp. 23-30.

[53]Takeshi Suzuki, "Trade Connections and Trade Patterns in the Japanese Distribution System," in Michael R. Czinkota and Masaaki Kotabe, *The Japanese Distribution System: Obstacles and Opportunities, Structures and Practices* (Chicago: Probus Publishing Company, 1993), p. 219.

[54]Hiroshi Komai, *Japanese Management Overseas* (Tokyo: Asian Productivity

China, the most common failing of Japanese firms has to do with the relationships between Japanese managers and Chinese employees; there is frequently an inability of these Japanese managers in China (as in other parts of the world) to manage as effectively away from their home base in Japan.[55]

Conclusion

For a century, Japan has been the most important outside agent facilitating China's entry into the world market. Even though China has built relationships with new trading partners and developed new sources of technology from across the world, the Sino-Japanese relationship remains China's most important link to regional and global economies.

Three decades ago, Ray Vernon described relationships like those between Japan and China in terms of product cycle theory. In Vernon's view, product innovation in one part of the world was followed frequently by a chain of events that included the maturation of product and process technologies. Then, as the enterprises using technologies reached out to new markets, production itself tended to move into these markets (since certain factor costs might be lower) and the innovation which had developed in the originating economy moved across borders.[56]

A number of studies have examined Japan's early role in China

---

Organization, 1989) Chapter 6; John C. Beck and Martha N. Beck, *The Change of a Lifetime: Employment Patterns Among Japna's Managerial Elite* (Honolulu: University of Hawaii Press, 1994), Chapter 7; Peter Lorange and Johan Roos, *Strategic Alliance: Formation, Implementation and Evolution* (Cambridge: Blackwell, 1992), pp. 177-8.

[55]Roy F. Grow, "Comparing Japanese and American Technology Transfer in China," in *Technology Transfer in International Business* (New York: Oxford University Press, 1991), pp. 193-222.

[56]Ray Vernon, *Sovereignty at Bay* (New York: Basic Books, 1971); and Louis T. Wells, "Economic Man and Engineering Man," in Robert Stobaugh and Louis T. Wells, eds., *Technology Crossing Borders: The Choice, Transfer, and Management of International Technology Flows* (Boston: Harvard Business School Press, 1984), pp. 47-68.

in terms of Vernon's theses. These studies examined especially the movement of Japanese enterprise activity into north and northeast China and evaluated the consequences of this activity in terms of long-term structural change. By and large, they concluded that the impact of the Japanese economy on China was real and profound, and that this impact changed the course of China's economic development in both the pre-war and the post-war periods.[57]

The evidence outlined in this chapter, however, supports the view that the diffusion of Japanese innovation across China – and the accompanying movement of Chinese enterprises into regional and global economies – is based on a more complex set of factors than envisioned by Vernon. The interplay of the factors examined here falls more in line with the view of analysts such as Grosmman and Helpman. They argue that the interaction between two economies such as China's and Japan's not so uniform and uni-directional as Vernon suggested and that a sort of "ebb and flow" model more adequately describes the impact of developed economies on the developing.[58]

This "ebb and flow" model more fully captures the essence of Japan's current importance to China. There is no questions as to the overall significance of the role that Japan plays; as in the past century, Japan today is, arguably, the primary conduit for capital, process technology, and organizational models to China.[59] Yet this Japanese role has increasingly become more complex and multifaceted. Patterns of trade, direct investment, and technology

---

[57]See especially Bruce Cumings, "The origins and development of the Northeast Asian political economy: industrial sectors, product cycles, and political consequences," in *International Organization*, 38:1 (Winter 1984), pp. 1-40.

[58]Gene M. Grossman and Elhanan Helpman, *Innovation and Growth in the Global Economy* (Cambridge: The MIT Press, 1991), p. 311.

[59]See the summary arguments in William E. James, Sieja Naya, and Gerald M. Meier, *Asian Development: Economic Success and Policy Lessons* (Madison: University of Wisconsin Press, 1989), Chapter 7; and Nicholas R. Lardy, *Foreign Trade and Economic Reform in China*, 1978-1990 (New York: Cambridge University Press, 1992), pp. 141-147.

transfer have changed dramatically during the past century and, especially since the war, have moved in several different directions at the same time. For example, sourcing and sub-contracting activity has become concentrated in several specific locations – such as China's northeast – while merchandising-related activities have been grouped more on the coastal south, especially in areas in and around Guangdong.

Japan's influence on other sectors of the Chinese economy has similarly become more variable, multi-faceted, and subtle. As the level of Japanese production in China has changed – moving (in many cases) from simple sub-contracting and assembly work to full-scale production of finished goods – there has been a parallel movement in other kinds of production-related tasks. As this paper outlined, Japanese firms in China have moved toward more complex organizational structures, more formal and stratified input relationships, and more complex forms of technology transfer.

At the same time (and as Grossman and Helpman argue is the case across the "developing" world), the move of Japanese firms into China has not been a record of unmitigated success. Quite often Japanese enterprises and their managers have been stymied in their China activities, just as in other parts of the world. For example, adapting management strategies that work well in the Japanese home islands (and even North America) to different realities in China has been a persistent problem that has troubled Japanese enterprise in China for a century. Even more serious has been the inability of many Japanese firms to find access to China's evolving distribution systems and to use models that are successful in other parts of the world.

Yet the impact of the Japanese economy on China has been powerful and important, far outweighing these shortcomings. Already we see the demonstration effect of many of the Japanese successes on Chinese enterprises, as state enterprises, collectives, and township-level organizations in those areas where the Japanese presence is most concentrated evolve and change in ways different from their Chinese compatriots in other parts of China.[60] As well, there has been a dramatic ripple effect in the development of new rules in many of the economic zones, and Japanese macro-economic theories and keiretsu strategies have been studied by Chinese managers and agency officials for insights about decision-making strategies and resource allocation models.[61]

Thus, the Japanese impact on China has moved well beyond the simple and almost uni-directional model described by product cycle theorists. Perhaps Jonathan Morris captures Japan's role in China more completely when he speaks of a process he calls "global localization" and distinguishes this process from a "more simple process of globalization."[62] He argues that in a first-stage globalization activity, Japanese firms established fairly basic manufacturing operations in China. These operations were controlled closely by their Japanese parent headquarters and, at best, the new enterprises engaged in assembly line operations, most often with only a limited amount of Chinese domestic content.

"Global *localization,*" argues Morris, is a fundamentally different and more complex process. It represents a further stage of involvement as Japanese investment "deepens" and Japanese firms attempt to become "insiders" in the Chinese economy by transforming every aspect of their key in-house component production. Morris argues that this process includes transferring key parts of the decision-making cycle as well as some of the parent firm's key R&D activities. As with Vernon, Morris argues that such movements are market driven – perhaps an almost inexorable process for firms search for expanding sales and returns on investment. But his analysis of the interplay of the additional factors that shape this movement of economic interaction and technology transfer comes closer to the model put forward by

---

[60]Keun Lee, *Chinese Firms and the State in Transition: Property Rights and Agency Problems in the Reform Era* (New York: M.E. Sharpe, 1991), pp. 150-1.

[61]George T. Crane, *The Political Economy of China's Special Economic Zones* (New York: M.E. Sharpe, 1990), pp. 164-5.

[62]Jonathan Morris, *Japan and the Global Economy* (London: Routledge, 1991), pp. 2-3.

Grossman and Helpman.[63]

The overview in this article supports the view of Morris, Grossman, and Helpman – especially as they point to the real variability of Japan's impact on China. In many cases, Japanese activity in China follows a pattern of "deepening" and there is little doubt that a number of Japanese firms – such as Mitsubishi and Ajinomoto – are moving along a continuum described by Morris. Yet we have also seen that many Japanese firms are unwilling or unable to follow this lead. The hold of organizational and management patterns developed in the Japanese home islands is still too strong for many of these firms (and their managers) and the activities of these Japanese firms in China quite often run into self-imposed roadblocks that hinder their full movement into the kind of global localization described by Morris.

Tuguchi Noburu, who returned to Dalian after over a half century absence, again seems to best catch best the flavor of the mixed Japanese record. "We Japanese," he said after his stay in Dalian, "sometimes seem unable to grasp the real meaning of working in China. We are there, but many of our companies don t always seem to participate in China's new ways; we sometimes insist on doing things in Dalian like we do them in Osaka. But life doesn t always work that way, and our insistence that we can do it a 'Japanese way' is getting in the way of our full participation in Chinese business activity. We have our successes; but we seem to have even more failures."

Taguchi is right; the record of Japanese enterprises in China is one of success and failure, and Japan's overall role in the regionalization and globalization of the Chinese economy is mixed as well. But there is little question that this role – for all of its successes and failure – will continue to be one of the most important in shaping China's full emergence into the global system.

---

[63]See also Ryoshin Minami, *Industrialization and Technological Progress of China: Comparison with Japanese Experiences* (New York: Macmillan, 1994).

4

Greater China: A Reality or An Illusion?

Hong Pyo Lee
(The Sejong Institute)

Introduction

One of the most explicit manifestations of international relations in the period following the end of World War II has been the trend toward globalism. The term "globalism" is generally used to describe increasing interdependence among the economies through various means: international trade, foreign investment, technology transfers, and official development aid, to name a few. The trend toward globalism was further accelerated in the 1980s when the bipolar world system, caused by the Cold War, came to a close. In the process, countries vigorously pursued economic cooperation that transcended differences in ideology and systems, thus opening an era of peaceful coexistence and detente.

As a recent phenomenon, however, globalism has increasingly given way to regionalism as evident in the emergence of economic bloc.[1] Regionalism is defined broadly as preferential trade agreements among a subset of nations located in the same region. These agreements usually depend on government initiatives, largely with both political and economic objectives, and involve discrimination in trade policy against non-members. The term "regionalism" is also used to mean regional economic integration, not as a result of inter-government arrangement such as the free trade area, but as a result of private economic forces. With the burgeoning of a new international order in which economic competition is replacing military and political confrontation, the trend toward regional integration to ensure economic prosperity has been rapidly spreading around the world as manifested by the formation of the European Union(EU) in 1991 and the North American Free Trade Agreement(NAFTA) in 1992. In response to this development, there have been various discussions going on in East Asia, a region that is generally considered as the nucleus of world economic growth for the remainder of the 20th century given the economic dynamism it has sustained over the past decades. The goal is to search for a mechanism or approach to form a region-wide economic cooperative arrangement similar to the European Community (EC) and NAFTA. Although there are favorable factors existing subjectively and objectively in the region, formation of an economic community like the EC will unlikely occur overnight. Thus the emergence of cooperating subgroupings is often portrayed as one possible scenario for the future of the Asia-Pacific region.[2]

It is within this context that the emergence of what analysts call "Greater China" has recently drawn increasing attention. This concept is a complex and multifaceted phenomenon involving the interaction among the world's various Chinese economies.

---

[1]For a succinct analysis of this trend and a conceptual discussion on globalism and regionalism, see Jagdish Bhagwati, "Regionalism versus Multilateralism," *The world Economy*, 15:5 (September 1992); see also, Jeffrey J. Schott, "Trading Blocs and the World Trading System," *The World Economy*, 4:1 (March 1991).

[2]See, for example, Duck-Choong Kim, "Open Regionalism in the Asian Pacific Region: A World of Trading Blocs?," *AEA Papers and Proceedings* (May 1992).

According to Harding, this phenomenon can be best explained by examining the interaction among the three most prominent Chinese economies – i.e., Taiwan, Hong Kong and mainland China (especially, "Southern China defined as inclusive of Guangdong and Fujian) at three levels: economic linkages, cultural ties and political reunification.[3] In essence, however, the concept of "Greater China" refers to the rapidly expanding commercial relations among the three Chinese economies, overcoming the political boundaries that once divided and isolated them. If taken together, these three entities' combined economic prowess presently accounts for the world's third largest GNP, largest foreign exchange reserves and third largest foreign trade turnover. In light of the rapid growth of the Chinese economy over the past fifteen years and high degrees of economic complementarity among the countries involved, it is often portrayed that "Greater China" has huge potential to become one of the world's most vibrant economies.[4]

Although "Greater China" implies an informal economic connectedness, it is often used in tandem with other concepts – trade bloc, economic integration – that suggest a comparison with other regional associations and connote a greater degree of institutionalization given the current state of de facto economic integration. Many reports forecast that if current growth trends continue, China's economic might will exceed or at least reach the level of the United States by the year 2010.[5] Given this, when this forecast is added to the other parts of the Greater China economy through the formation of an organized economic community, the economic and political implications of the extension of current trends into the twenty-first century become awe-inspiring. Some of the questions which arise in this context are: What force has been behind the emergence of Greater China? In what man-

---

[3]Harry Harding, "The Concept of 'Greater China': Themes, Variations and Reservations," *The China Quarterly*, No. 136 (December 1993), pp. 660-661.

[4]See, for example, "Greater China: A New Economic Colossus," *The Washington Quarterly*, 16:4 (August 1993).

[5]See, for example, *The Economist*, "A Survey of China" (November 28, 1992).

ner does it affect the relationships among the three countries involved and their own societies as well? Is "Greater China" likely to evolve into a formal economic community such as a regional bloc and by extension, an economic superpower? What will be the effects of the transborder economic interaction among the "three Chinas" on the rest of the region?

To answer these questions, this paper will first examine the contours of "Greater China." The purpose is to gain an insight on the current state of inter-relationships among the three economies. Drawing on theoretical literature, this paper will examine the possibility that Greater China will turn into an organized economic community. In so doing, a brief account will be made as to the impact that the emergence of Greater China has rendered on the three countries to date. Prospects for the future and the implications of current trends toward the integration of the principal Chinese economies for the rest of East Asia will also be discussed to conclude the paper.

The Contours of "Greater China": Trends Toward Increasing Interdependence

By all accounts and trends so far, the economic links among China, Hong Kong and Taiwan have been growing at a stunning pace.[6] Trade among the principal Chinese economies was greatly attenuated, if not entirely suspended, by the political and ideological barriers constructed in the early 1950s. Trade was first revived between Hong Kong and mainland China following the adoption of the open door policy by Deng Xiaoping in the late 1970s. Soon Hong Kong resumed its historic role as entrepot for Southern China and then gained a prominent place as entrepot for the country as whole.[7] Hong Kong's trade with mainland

---

[6]For overall trends toward the expansion of trade and investment among the three economies, see Robert F. Ash and Y.Y. Yueh, "Economic Integration within Greater China: Trade and Investment Flows Between China, Hong Kong and Taiwan," *The China Quarterly*, No. 136 (December 1993), pp. 711-745.

China grew from $5.7 billion in 1980 to more than $80 billion in 1992, making Beijing Hong Kong's number-one trading partner.[8] Taiwan joined this trading relationship soon thereafter. Given Taiwan's more remote location and its ban on direct shipping and air links with the PRC, Taiwan's level of trade with the mainland has remained significantly lower than Hong Kong's. Even so, the increase – from $320 million in 1980 to $21 billion in 1994 – has been even sharper, averaging some 40 percent per year.[9] By 1994, Taiwan has become the mainland's fourth largest trade partner, the fourth largest export market, and the seventh largest import market. As relations between Taiwan and China have improved since the mid 1980s, Taiwan has shown more interest in Hong Kong as an entrepot. Previously, Taiwan's commercial relationship with Hong Kong were limited, primarily due to Hong Kong's future reversion to Chinese sovereignty. Now, Taiwan is Hong Kong's fourth largest trading partner with its total trade amounting to US $22.8 in 1994 and Hong Kong has become Taiwan's second largest export market next to the United States, although 40 percent of the goods are re-exported to China.

Investment has also been rising rapidly during the period of 1979 and 1994 as the PRC established its "special economic zones," adopting various incentives for foreign capital and creating a more flexible legal framework for foreign investment. From the inception, Hong Kong has been the chief beneficiary of these

---

[7]For the most recent (post-1978) expansion of Hong Kong's trade with China, see Yun-wing Sung, *The China-Hong Kong Connection :The Key to China's Open Door Policy* (Cambridge: Cambridge University Press, 1991).

[8]Statistical figures cited in this paragraph and the following paragraph are drawn from quarterly issues of *EIU Country Report :Taiwan, China & Mongolia* (The Economist Intelligence Unit Limited, 1993-1995). It should be noted that there is slight difference on relevant figures among several different issues. So the goal is not to present precise figures here. Rather, this paper intends to show the pattern and the trends pertaining to trade among the three economies by presenting relevant figures.

[9]The true figure for total Taiwan-PRC trade is undoubtedly higher, as some if conducted through areas other than Hong Kong (e.g., Singapore), and direct trade is still restricted and therefore hidden.

developments initiated by the pragmatic leadership in the mainland, and it has so far invested approximately $60 billion in China and $1.2 billion on Taiwan. Taiwanese investors waited until the late 1980s, when the Taiwan government finally authorized investment in the mainland. Nonetheless, their stake in the PRC has approached a total sum of $8.4 billion (amount implemented) by 1994. It is also estimated that China has invested a cumulative total of $20 billion in Hong Kong, although none yet in Taiwan.

As a result of this development, the Chinese-based economy in Asia is rapidly emerging as a new epicenter for industry, commerce and finance despite the continued Japanese dominance of the region. By absolute standards and in holistic terms, the area covering the three Chinese economies contains substantial technology and manufacturing capacity, outstanding entrepreneurial, marketing, and service acumen, a tremendous pool of financial capital and huge endowments of land, resources and labor. In this regard, the rapid expansion of economic interaction among the three economies is truly notable. However, the emergence of Greater China is of great interest not only because of quantitative growth of trade and investment, but also due to the striking changes caused by the emergence of Greater China both in the participants and the nature of their relationships.

For each of the three Chinese economies, intra-trade has become an important part of its global economic relations. Moreover, the nature of economic cooperation has tended to become more intensified over time. For example, at first, investments by Taiwan and Hong Kong in the PRC were relatively small-scale projects, involving rapid amortization and simple technology.[10] Examples include real estate development in major coastal cities and the transfer of labor-intensive manufacturing, processing, and assembling operations from Hong Kong and Taiwan into the mainland. In a recent move, however, there has

---

[10]Yunwing Sung, "The Economic Integration of Hong Kong and Taiwan with the mainland of China," in R. Garnaut and Lin Guogang, eds., *Economic Reform and Internationalization* (London: Allen and Unwin, 1991), p. 149.

been a tendency toward larger-scale projects, involving more advanced technology and penetrating broader sectors of the mainland Chinese economy. Suffice to say that buoyed up with some positive results of their initial ventures in the mainland, Hong Kong and Taiwanese investors have recently tended to get involved in heavy industrial projects and infrastructure-building.

There has also been a reverse flow of mainland Chinese capital back into Hong Kong. By the end of 1988, the mainland had become a major foreign investor in Hong Kong, with stakes in banking, real estate, trade and communications worth over US $10 billion. It has been recently estimated that mainland Chinese investment in Hong Kong amounted to $20 billion in 1992 alone – equivalent to the sum of all previous years combined. The influx of capital is pouring into Hong Kong for a variety of reasons: to increase mainland China's economic stake in Hong Kong, to use Hong Kong as a jumping- off place for its excursions into international capital market, to acquire the level of "foreign capital" for reinvestment back into China, to qualify Chinese entrepreneurs for regular permission to leave the country, and to earn high financial returns outside the supervision of the Chinese state.[11]

Equally important to this trend is the gradual growth of economic interaction between China and the other two economies beyond the confines of Southern China. Although China's foreign trade and investment remain disproportionately concentrated in Guangdong, there are growing signs that foreign entrepreneurs are actively exploring opportunities elsewhere, partly in response to the rise of the cost of doing business in Guangdong and the Chinese government's deliberate policy to divert foreign investment to other regions of the country which still remain relatively underdeveloped.[12] Recent statistics indicate that investment by Hong Kong and Taiwan businessmen is moving north into

---

[11]Gerald Segal, *The Fate of Hong Kong* (New York: St. Martin's Press, 1994), pp. 85-86; Harding, *op. cit.*, pp. 664-665

[12]For further discussion on this trend, see Margaret M. Pearson, "Foreign Investment and Trade," in William A. Joseph, ed., *China Briefing: 1994* (Boulder, CO: Westview Press, 1994), pp. 60-61 and pp. 67-70.

Greater Shanghai, and Bohai Gulf and west Guangxi and Sichuan.

The most powerful explanation for the expansion of economic interaction among the three principal economies is the economic complementarities that presently exist among Hong Kong, Taiwan and the mainland. The three areas each have their respective strengths and weaknesses with regard to production endowments. Mainland China, for instance, possesses rich resources and a huge labor force and market but is handicapped by a shortage of capital, a lack of modern production technology, and backward management practice. Conversely, economic development in Taiwan and Hong Kong has recently been hampered by limitations of land and resources, labor shortages and rising wages, and the pressure of international protectionism. This situation, coupled with geographic proximity, has undoubtedly served as a powerful inducement for these three economies to increase economic intercourse among themselves as close economic cooperation would benefit all three areas simultaneously.

From a non-economic perspective, the emergence of Greater China is often explained as a decisive result of a common culture embracing the three economies in question. It is often asserted that a common heritage, cultural background, language and customs, family ties and ancestral roots all make it somewhat easier for Chinese to do business with one another than to engage in commercial relations with foreigners. Besides, many prosperous Chinese entrepreneurs outside mainland China may be more willing to absorb some losses with the People's Republic due to the belief that they are contributing to the economic development and modernization of their homeland. As Harding sums up, this sentiment – the desire to help the modernization of the motherland, or to participate in the development of one's native place, even at a lower financial return – has been a powerful motivation for many older Chinese entrepreneurs, thus facilitating the realization of economic complementarities.[13]

The interplay of economic complementarity and cultural com-

---

[13]Harding, *op. cit.*, p. 665.

monality makes the Greater China economy one of the best examples of "natural economic territories": economic systems and social networks that can form naturally and spontaneously across political boundaries as long as governments do not interfere.[14] It is true that one of the most important factors accountable for the emergence of Greater China has simply been governmental decision to lower the barriers to commercial activity. For example, following the adoption of the open-door policy in 1978, mainland China has decentralized its foreign trade apparatus, removed various barriers which in the past had discouraged foreign trade and investment.[15] Also to be noted is the Taiwan government's decision in the late 1980s to remove some of the barriers to commercial relations with its rival on the mainland.[16]

To a large degree, the growing commercial interactions among Hong Kong, Taiwan and the mainland do represent the resurrection of the normal economic ties that had been interrupted by 30 years of central planning in the PRC and by 35 years of enmity across the Taiwan Straits. Hong Kong is resuming its original role as the intermediary regarding commercial intercourse between China and the West, whereas Taiwan is developing the natural position as the growth center for Fujian and much of the Chinese coast. However, it would be misleading to portray the govern-

---

[14]Robert Scalapino, "China in the Late Leninist Era," *The China Quarterly*, No.136 (December 1993), p. 958; For a brief discussion of the term "natural Economic Territories," see Robert Scalapino, "The Politics of Development and Regional Cooperation in Northeast Asia," in Won Bae Kim, et al., ed., *Regional Economic Cooperation in Northeast Asia* (Honolulu: East-West Center, Proceedings of the Vladivostok Conference, August 25-27, 1992); see also his *The Last Leninsts: The Uncertain Future of Asia's Communist States* (Washington, D.C.: Center for Strategic and International Studies, 1992), p. 20.

[15]For some of these measures taken in the early years following the adoption of the open door policy, see Samuel P.S. Ho and Ralph W. Huenemann, *China's Quest for Open Door Policy: The Quest for Foreign Technology and Capital* (Vancouver: University of British Columbia Press, 1984), pp. 33-56.

[16]See George W. Tsai, "An Analysis of Current Relations between Taiwan and Mainland China: A Political Perspective," *Issues and Studies*, 27:9 (September 1991), pp. 18-41.

ments involved as simply "getting out of the way" in order to allow natural economic forces to proceed. All three of the governments centrally involved in the emergence of the Greater Chinese economy have been adopting more positive measures to promote their economic interaction. Beijing deliberately placed its first special economic zones opposite Hong Kong and Taiwan in part to promote commercial ties with these other Chinese economies.[17] From time to time it has also adopted special trade and investment incentives targeted at entrepreneurs from Hong Kong and Taiwan.

These three governments have distinctively different motivations for expanding trade and investment, although all their calculations revolve around the relationship between economic integration and political unification. The consolidation of the economic complementarities between these Chinese economies reveals that more than economic forces are at work. The governments of the principal Chinese economies are not simply removing past obstructions and adopting a neutral posture towards economic relationships. Instead, each government has deeply involved in promoting and guiding the commercial ties with the other two economies as a means to further its perceived interests. For the leaders of mainland China, the strengthening of economic integration with Hong Kong and Taiwan is a prominent strategy to accelerate the process toward political reunification of China.[18] Some in Taiwan share this motivation but would add that economic interaction is simultaneously a way of encouraging the social and political change on the mainland that would eventually make reunification feasible.[19] Hong Kong views it as a way of

---

[17]Ho and Huenemann, *op. cit.*, pp. 33-56.

[18]For China's strategy pertaining to Hong Kong, see Segal, *op. cit.*, especially Chapter 5 "China: Taking Charge," pp. 77-95; for an overview of Beijing's Taiwan strategy, see An-chia Wu, "Peking's Taiwan Policy in the Post-Cold War Era," *Issues and Studies*, 30:7 (July 1994).

[19]Parris H. Chang, "Beijing's Relations with Taiwan," in Parris H. Chang and Martin L. Lasater, eds., *If China Crosses the Taiwan Strait: The International Response* (Lanham and New York: New York University Press of America, 1993), pp. 13-15; see also Chien-min Chao, "David and Goliah: A Comparison

softening its return to Chinese sovereignty in 1997 by allowing Beijing to have a large and direct stake in preserving the territory's political viability and economic prosperity throughout the transition. And for Taipei, economic integration can be used as a kind of leverage over the mainland, discouraging Beijing from using force against the island. Moreover, some Taiwanese view economic integration as a more acceptable form of national unity than formal political reunification, and thus as a substitute for it.[20]

Accordingly, the governments in question have been trying to shape the evolution of the Greater Chinese economy in ways most favorable to their own interests. Beijing is encouraging the formation of additional "economic circles" along the Chinese coast and the country's inland borders,[21] so as to break Guangdong's virtual monopoly over foreign trade and incoming foreign investment. The goal is to expand the region where the open door policy and reform measures can be extensively implemented, thus alleviating the situation of uneven development of the country. Conversely, Hong Kong is expanding its shipping and airport facilities so that it can remain the entrepot not only for southern China, but also for the upper Yangze basin and perhaps for the entire Chinese economy. Taipei is actively promoting the expansion of its investment into Southeast Asia and Hong Kong so as to reduce its dependence on the mainland and to secure diplomatic leverage over Beijing. Although all three governments share the vision of a Greater Chinese economy, their respective vision of a "Greater China" differ significantly from one to the other.

Despite the conflicting motivations and interests of the nature

---

of Reunification Policies Between mainland China and Taiwan," *Issues and Studies*, 30:7 (July 1994), especially pp. 31-35.

[20]Chang, *op. cit.*, pp. 13-15.

[21]The other two economic subregions or circles are Pan Yellow Sea Economic Circle linking the east coast of China to South Korea, and Pan East Sea (Japan Sea) Economic Circles linking Northeast of China to Japna, Russia and both North and South Koreas.

of the Greater China economy, rapid economic growth was precisely what followed after the three governments began introducing some policy measures designed to promote cooperation with the other two partners. From the adoption of the open door policy, Guangdong has been the center of economic dynamism of which annual growth rate surpasses the average growth of the entire country.[22] Hong Kong capital now accounts for an overwhelming share of external economic activity in Guangdong, amounting to approximately 80 percent in trade and 70 percent in investment respectively.[23] As many as an estimated 3 million workers are employed in factories owned by Hong Kong investors, as opposed to only 670,000 employed in the manufacturing sector in Hong Kong itself. Thus one can conclude that Hong Kong has been instrumental in getting Guangdong on its present pattern of development.[24] But at the same time, one can claim that Hong Kong has taken advantage of the opening of China to restructure its economy by relocating en masses its labor-intensive and sunset industries to the Pearl River Delta and beyond.[25]

In the same way, Taiwan investors have relocated their industrial plants to China in response to rising wages and rent at home.[26] They have tended to concentrate in Guangdong and

---

[22]Yukari Sawada, "Guangdong's Reforms and Their Impact on Society," *JETRO China Newsletter*, No. 97 (March-April 1993).

[23]Unless specifically cited, the figures in this paragraph and the following one are drawn from Yeung Yue-man, "Growth Triangles in Pacific Asia: A Comparative Perspective," in *Tumen River Area Development Project: The Political Economy of Cooperation in Northeast Asia* (Seoul: The Sejong Institute, Proceedings of the international conference, August 4-5, 1994), pp. 65-66.

[24]David K.Y. Chu and Yue-man Yeung, eds., *Guangdong: Survey of a Province Undergoing Rapid Change* (Hong Kong: Chinese University Press, 1994); Pearson, *op. cit.*, pp. 67-69.

[25]Since 1988, Hong Kong has shed 446,000 manufacturing jobs. In 1988, close to half of Hong Kong workers were in manufacturing; now less than a fifth are. During the period of 1988-94, 670,000 service jobs were added in Hong Kong. Gary Silberman, "The Price of Success," *Far Eastern Economic Review* (July 6, 1995), pp. 54-55.

Fujian, particularly in Shenzhen, Xiamen, Guangzhou and Fuzhou. The major industrial investment has been in footwear, electrical engineering, plastics and apparel, some already on decline in Taiwan and losing their competitive edge in the international market. Initially, investment was made through intermediaries in Hong Kong and Japan, when the official policy forbade direct contact with Chinese counterparts. By 1994, nearly 30,000 firms were operating in China with pledged investment of approximately US $30 billion.[27]

Although Hong Kong and Taiwan have derived substantial gains in the subregional cooperation, the most profound impact has been the physical and economic transformation experienced in Guangdong and Fujian. Both provinces have grown at rates and within such a short period that their miracle growth has surpassed the experience of the Asian dragons in a certain sense. Besides, recent developments within the South China region point to the greater integration of the three economies. For example, as already stated, investment is far from unidirectional, from Hong Kong and Taiwan to China. Chinese direct investment in Hong Kong has been substantial and continues to grow. In 1992, investment amounted to US $20 billion, which is approximately the total Hong Kong investment in China. Massive Chinese direct investment not only partakes in the booming economy in Hong Kong, but provides as well, opportunities for on-the-job training for Chinese personnel in the skills and rigors of a free market economy at its unfettered best. The growing integration between southern China and Hong Kong is also manifested in the de facto monetary union, with the Hong Kong dollar freely circulated in Guangdong and Fujian. It has been estimated that up to 30 percent of Hong Kong dollars are in circulation in China.[28]

Overall, as the result of the emergence of Greater China, the three economies are becoming interdependent more than at any

---

[26]Liu Jinqing, "Trends in Cross-Straits Relations," *JETRO China Newsletter*, No. 116 (May-June 1995), p. 15.

[27]*South China Morning Post* (September 4, 1995), p. 1.

[28]Yeung, *op. cit.*, p. 67.

time since the Chinese Revolution in 1949.[29] China presently conducts about half of its global trade with Hong Kong and Taiwan, up from only 17 percent in 1981. China receives about 70 percent of its in-bound direct investment from the other two Chinese economies and directs the bulk of its out-bound foreign investment into Hong Kong. Hong Kong relies on both mainland China and Taiwan for about 45 percent of its domestic exports and for about two-thirds of its re-exports. These ratios are all substantial increases over those of 1981. Mainland China has also become Hong Kong's most important source of new in-bound foreign investment. Taiwan presently conducts approximately 11 percent of its global trade with mainland China and Hong Kong, and direct 27 percent of its officially reported out-bound foreign investment there. Each of these ratios is between two and three times higher than it was in the early 1980s.

As exemplified by their sustained economic dynamism over the past 15 years, this development of economic interdependence has undoubtedly enabled participant countries to derive substantial benefits. The pattern of interdependence, however, has been uneven. Mainland China is now heavily dependent on the rest of Greater China as a source of investment and a partner for trade; although Hong Kong is significantly integrated with mainland China and Taiwan, it is less fully dependent; and Taiwan is least integrated into Greater China of the three economies. In each case, however, the degree of dependence has tended to increase substantially over the last decade.

Noting this trend toward increasing integration, many scholars claim that all three parties would further benefit if they could create a more organized "Greater China Economic Community" as it would promote economic cooperation and exchanges among

---

[29]For the figures cited in this paragraph, see Pamela Baldinger, "The Birth of Greater China," *The China Business Review* (May-June 1992), pp. 13-17; Sally Stewart, Michale Tow Cheung, and David W.K.Yeung, "The Latest Asian Newly Industrialized Economy Emerges: The South China Economic Community," *Columbia Journal of World Business*, 27 (Summer 1992), pp. 31-37; Lee A. Brudig, "The Fifth Dragon," *The China Business Review*, 20:4 (July-Aug. 1993), p. 18-25.

Chinese populated areas and thereby increase their prosperity. The question which will be addressed in the following section is whether or not Greater China will evolve into an organized economic community similar to that of a regional bloc. Is it desirable? Is it feasible in a practical sense?

"Greater China": Evolving into a Formal Economic Community?

In practice, an organized economic community exists in one of the five forms (in ascending order of economic integration): preferential trade arrangement, free trade area, customs union, common market and economic union.[30] Among the most frequently proposed forms for the case of Greater China are "free trade area" which would link the three Chinese economies through the elimination of tariff barriers to goods passing among them, and "common market," which would involve the establishment of a common set of tariffs for all goods entering the region from abroad.[31] Drawing a parallel with the European Economic Community, some analysts recommended the organization of a Chinese Economic Community, which would entail not only free trade within the area and common tariffs with non-members, but also the unrestricted mobility of factors of production (especially capital and labor), the co-ordination of monetary and fiscal policies, and the creation of common social welfare mechanisms.

Aside from the argument that a formal economic community, if realized, would further integrate the three economies and contribute to their economic growth as a whole, it is often claimed that it would be desirable for the three principal Chinese

---

[30]For a brief discussion on sequential regional trade bloc movements, see Joseph L. Brand, "The New World Order: Regional Trading Blocs," *Vital Speeches of the Day*, 58:5 (December 15, 1991), pp. 155-60; For further discussion on these forms of economic integration, see Bela Balassa, *The Theory of Economic Integration* (London: Allen and Unwin, 1962).

[31]Harding, *op. cit.*, p. 668.

economies to stick together for defensive reasons. As a common feature, the PRC, Taiwan and Hong Kong have pursued export-oriented management with varying degrees of emphasis to achieve rapid economic growth. One common characteristic of economic blocs, whatever the form, is that blocs espouse trade liberalization internally but achieve trade protection externally. Of particular note in this context is that the consumer markets of North America and Europe have ingested the overwhelming majority of exports by these countries in holistic sense. For this reason, growing protectionism in the world system stemming from the formalization of economic blocs in Europe and North America now portends to stifle the future growth potential of these countries. It is thus urgent for these countries "circle the wagons"[32] in the region, i.e., to promote economic integration among themselves.

Economic integration is generally defined as "movement towards one price throughout the global economy, for a piece of merchandise, a service or a factor of production.[33] Theoretical literature on economic integration in general suggests that when possible, it is desirable for countries to pursue economic integration for a variety of reasons.[34] Economic integration benefits participating nations of a formal economic grouping mainly in two ways. Firstly, it improves the fundamental economic situation of the countries involved. Given that economic integration creates a division of labor among the participating nations, it enlarges domestic markets, permits the exploitation of economies-of-scale, and brings into play the effect of specialization. The enlarged scale of production enables businesses to invest more in research

---

[32]The term "circle the wagons" is taken from Karl J. Fields, "Circling the Wagons: The Trend Toward Economic Regionalism and Its Consequences for Asia," *Issues and Studies*, 28:13 (December 1992).

[33]See, for example, H.W. Arndt, "Anatomy of Regionalism," *Journal of Asian Economics*, 4:2 (1993), p. 273.

[34]See, for example, Eduardo Linzano, "Integration of Less Developed Areas and of Areas on Different Levels of Development," in Fritz Machlup, ed., *Economic Integration: Worldwide, Regional, Sectoral* (New York: Macmillan, 1976).

and development, thus raising productivity, improving the industrial structure and accelerating economic growth. Secondly, increased integration among the economies involved creates a much stronger economic force for them to deal with other regional economic groupings or individual countries. Cooperation would prevent the integrated economies from competing against each other while a united economic policy would strengthen their bargaining power toward the outside world.

In addition to these two effects, economic integration also breaks down boundaries among the member countries and strengthens competition among different industries. This may improve economic efficiency or prompt businesses to increase their investments in order to strengthen their competitiveness. What is more, the elimination of tariff barriers among members and their adoption of higher tariffs against the outside world combine to attract investments from non-member countries in exchange for tariff-free benefits. In short, economic integration would give smaller economies the large market needed to create the "critical mass" of production and sales needed to be competitive.[35]

One crucial point is that forming an economic community is a purposive activity. Political leaders work to weave their national economies together for any variety of reasons. If the EC serves as a guide, for these sorts of endeavors to succeed, there must be a foundation of interdependence and reciprocal economic ties of some importance to all involved countries. It is because that economic integration is a process to formalize the pattern of interdependence, reflecting world market forces as well as national policies. In this regard, interdependence is considered a necessary, though not, sufficient condition for successful integration. There are two points that support this conclusion. First, interdependence is a reflection of economic practice and therefore, reveals how traders and investors understand risk and efficiency. Second, interdependence creates domestic political constituencies for integration and bolsters national "political will". Opposing

---

[35]P. F. Drucker, *The Realities* (New York: Harper and Row, 1989), p. 131.

political forces may be unleashed by interdependence, but without it, the voices in favor of integration would weaken.

As a corollary, the primary motivation for economic integration through a formal economic grouping consists in the rapidly expanding trade and investment among the three economies, which reflect the comparative advantage of each nation. In addition, there are indeed several powerful forces conducive to integration: a natural economic complementarity, the common cultural and ethnic background among the three Chinese economies, the strong family ties linking various segments, and the age-old sense that a powerful China should be a unified China. Despite these various sinews for integration, however, a close look at the situation surrounding each country and the relationships among the three reveals that the formation of a formal economic community is not likely to occur in the near future.

One crucial obstacle pertains to the desirability of countries involved. Experience in Europe and elsewhere indicate that for a regional economic body to work usually requires a political commitment to dilute national sovereignty in favor of broader regional policies. Of course, one key variable affecting one country's political will must be related to potentiality of an economic grouping in question to increase the welfare of the member countries. Hence, the single most important factor is whether or not an organized economic grouping under consideration will substantially accommodate the countries' interests in comprehensive terms, i.e., beyond the dimension of national economic welfare. Do benefits to be rendered by the formation of a formal economic community exceed the costs involved?

The rapidly expanding trade and investment among the three Chinas have greatly helped them sustain economic dynamism in recent years. But at the same time, the economic interdependence of the three Chinese economies has significantly contributed to their internal transformation. For the PRC, investment from Taiwan and Hong Kong and Hong Kong's central role as an entrepot for foreign trade have been critical in creating the high rates of growth in both its exports and GNP. In addition, trade and investment relations with Taiwan and Hong Kong are promoting the evolution of the PRC from a state-owned and state-planned economy to a market economy with more diverse forms of ownership. In short, the dynamism of the mainland Chinese economy is inextricably linked with the emergence of Greater China as a whole.

However, these same interactions are steadily changing the status quo on the mainland in some undesirable ways as well. Perhaps the most evident change is that growing commercial ties with Hong Kong and Taiwan is producing disparities between the provinces, and between urban and rural areas. The growing prosperity enjoyed by many localities (especially in South China) is undermining the traditional political relationships between Beijing and provinces,[36] just as the rise of a new class of private entrepreneurs is eroding the old relationships between the government and the people. Popular culture from Hong Kong – with its emphasis on materialism rather than sacrifice, and on individualism rather than collectivism – is creating new values and attitudes on the mainland, especially among younger people.[37] And the influx of democratic values and institutions accompanied by growing commercial ties with Taiwan and Hong Kong may well have an impact on political culture in the PRC as well. So far, there have been no signs of either the geographic disintegration of the mainland or a level of popular mass protest that the regime cannot control. Nonetheless, the emergence of a Greater Chinese economy is increasing the pressures on Beijing for meaningful

---

[36]There has recently been a flood of articles on this issue in the domain of Chinese studies, see Maria Hsia Chang, "China's Future: Regionalism, Federation or Disintegration," *Studies in Comparative Communism*, 15:3 (September 1992), pp. 211-227; see also Geral Segal, "The Middle Kingdom: China's Changing Shape," *Foreign Affairs*, 73:3 (May-June 1994), pp. 43-58; For a recent account of this issue, see Lincoln Kaye, "The Grip Slips," *Far Eastern Economic Review* (May 11, 1995), pp. 18-21; see also his "Southern Cooking: Coast's Hot Economies Find Center Distasteful," *Far Eastern Economic Review* (May 25, 1995), pp. 22-24.

[37]For example, see Thomas B. Gold, "Go with Your Feeling: Hong Kong and Taiwan Popular Culture in Greater China," *The China Quarterly*, No. 136 (December 1993), pp. 920-923.

political reforms such as further liberalization and decentralization. With the passage of Deng Xiaoping from the political scene in the near future, China is now in ever-urgent need for maintaining domestic stability. In this regard, the PRC cannot afford to stand for mounting pressures for democratization, a situation dubbed "peaceful evolution" by the Beijing authorities.[38]

For Hong Kong and Taiwan, the most pressing challenges are more economic in nature. Both economies have witnessed the rapid relocation of their labor-intensive assembly manufacturing operations to the mainland. Furthermore, there are signs that other economic activities, including financial administration and research and development are being transferred as well. As a result, there have been rising fears that economic integration with the mainland would lead to a "hollowing out" of local industry.[39] According to Harding, paradoxically parallel concerns have been expressed in the PRC: that the complete removal of barriers to trade and investment relations with Hong Kong and Taiwan would confront mainland manufactures with unbeatable competition, and thus would exacerbate the problems of bankruptcy and unemployment in the state sector in the PRC.[40] Furthermore, Hong Kong will have to prepare for a time when Taiwan will trade directly with the mainland and when other Chinese coastal cities assume the role of entrepot for their own hinterlands, thus undermining Hong Kong's present position as the economic capital of Greater China.

The emergence of the Greater Chinese economy is also posing a political challenge for Hong Kong. On the one hand, the growth of interdependence between Hong Kong and the mainland is helping cushion Hong Kong's return to Chinese sovereignty in

---

[38]For further discussion on this situation, see Yang Kai-huang, "Mainland Chinese Society and the Campaign Against 'Peaceful Evolution'," *Issues and Studies*, 28:6 (June 1992), pp. 26-32.

[39]According to one report, about 36 percent of Hong Kong's industry has moved across the border to the Pearl River delta, Pamela Baldinger, "The Birth of Greater China," *The China Business Review* (May-June 1992), p. 14.

[40]Harding, *op. cit.*, p. 670.

1997 by limiting Beijing's ability to exercise arbitrary political authority over the territory. On the other hand, however, the rapidly increasing level of Chinese investment in Hong Kong, as well as the steady immigration of Chinese workers into the territory, is increasing China's ability to exercise control from the bottom up as well as from the top down. Moreover, there is growing apprehension about the spread of corruption from mainland China into Hong Kong, which, if unchecked, will erode the effectiveness of political institutions and may increase the cost of commercial transactions as well.[41]

Explicit in the above argument is that the growing economic interdependence has contributed to their internal transformation both in positive and negative ways. Although growing interdependence has contributed to economic dynamism of each nation, it has also brought about some consequences which are in play against their national interests. Accordingly, there presently appears to exist no unanimity among Chinese about the desirability of developing "Greater China" into a highly institutionalized economic community. Instead, different groups of Chinese approach the idea of economic integration with distinctively different motivations and interests. In mainland China, there is interest in extensive interaction among the PRC, Taiwan and Hong Kong, but largely as a way of securing political reunification.[42] Beijing sees economic exchanges as a way of establishing its influence over Taiwan; the quicker Taiwan becomes economically dependent on the mainland the sooner Beijing will be able to force unification under the "one country, two systems" formula. On Taiwan, there is also interest in promoting economic ties with the mainland, but these newly-formed relationship is wide-

---

[41]Kari Huus, "The Reckoning Bejins," *Far Eastern Economic Review* (March 2, 1995), p. 16

[42]For a detailed explanation of Beijing's and Taiwan's motivation for trade and investment, see Dennis Van Vranken Hickey, "Will Inter-China Trade Change Taiwan or the Mainland," *Orbis*, 35:4 (Fall 1991), pp. 522-525; see also T. Clifton Morgan, "Economic Ties, Influence, and Taiwan-Mainland China Relations," *Issues and Studies*, 29:3 (March 1993), pp. 1-3.

ly regarded as an alternative to political reunification, rather than as a means to achieving it.

Taipei, while fully aware of the pitfalls involved in seeking economic benefits from the mainland, intends to use its present economic and trade advantages to win from Beijing a promise not to launch a military attack on Taiwan and recognition of Taipei as a distinct political entity. Taiwan also hopes to publicize its development experience on the mainland and hasten the process of democratization in order to reunify China on the basis of freedom, democracy, and an equitable distribution of wealth. In Hong Kong, the greatest interest in the development of economic ties with South China, largely as a method for cushioning the transfer of political sovereignty to Beijing in 1997. By increasing the economic stakes for Beijing, Hong Kong wants to prevent Beijing from suppressing the economic vitality of Hong Kong by changing the latter's current economic and political system. All in all, no convergence of interests among the three Chinese countries has occurred albeit a rapid increase in economic cooperation among them. Furthermore, it appears that in each country, the process of full economic integration is viewed with some apprehension. The concerns are that their respective economies will gain the least benefit and suffer the greatest dislocation, and experience undesirable consequences which have political ramifications.

The question of desirability aside, there also appears to be great difficulties on forming a highly organized economic community in terms of feasibility. A formal economic community, whatever the form, must be an inclusive entity, encompassing a wide array of economic issues, from the reduction and/or removal of tariffs and to cultural exchange and joint development and preservation of natural resources. As for one essential feature, it must include a set of binding measures and devices to resolve various issues pertaining to "responsibility sharing" which in turn would determine the division of potential gains, which is a major economic and political problem of almost any association.[43]

To be specific, one main constituent of an organized economic community is the readjustment or establishment of a division of labor. In groupings of developed countries, this is accomplished by the elimination of marginal industries in the existing production structure through trade creation guided by price mechanism. Groupings involving LDCs, however, tend to do this prior negotiations in accordance with the principle of comparative advantage. These negotiations are decisive to the success of integration, since ascertaining the scope and direction of profitable specialization affects not only the distribution of the benefits and costs of integration among members, but also the level and speed of industrialization.

In practical terms, economic integration has a quite different function for the countries involved.[44] As the division of labor is achieved through negotiation rather than the price mechanism, a conflict of interests among members is inevitable. Although certain remedial measures – such as fiscal compensation, investment location guidance, and agreed specializations – may be adopted, the success of the economic integration still hinges on the attitude of the participating countries during the negotiations. In theory, if the member countries have similar economic systems, social structures, and consumption patterns, and a similar level of economic development, the process of negotiation will be less complicated, as it would pose no serious problem pertaining to the "division of gains."

According to this theoretical argument, the differences in economic structure among the participants would hamper the formation of any regional economic community. Given the difference in economic system, no common price index or standards for evaluating projects exists among the three countries, and naturally they differ in their understanding of comparative advantage. It would thus be difficult for them to reach a consensus on

---

[43]J.J. Schott, *Free Trade Areas and US Trade Policy* (Washington, D.C.: Institute for International Economics, 1989), p. 71. Cited from his "Trading Blocs and the World Trading System," *The World Economy*, 14:1 (March 1991), p. 2.

[44]For further account of this point, see Peter Robson, *The Economies of International Integration*, 3rd ed. (London: Allen and Unwin, 1987), pp. 202-205.

division of labor. For instance, it would be more appropriate in view of the principle of comparative advantage and its resource base, for Taiwan to develop capital-intensive or technology-intensive industries, and, by the same reasoning, for mainland China to develop labor-intensive industries. But a division of labor that would benefit the region as a whole would not necessarily correspond with the expectations of each individual area. Although mainland China is economically backward and has a labor surplus, Beijing may still want to develop capital-and technology-intensive industries in order to accelerate its economic growth. It would therefore be reluctant to follow a regional economic policy that would demand that it develop labor-intensive industries like textiles or clothing which are on the decline in Taiwan and Hong Kong but still command an international market. Taiwan and Hong Kong businesses would also be reluctant to give up these still profitable industries. It is problems like these that would stand in the way of a division of labor among the three principal economies in question.

A far more serious obstacle than the ones outlined above is related to political relationship among the three countries. The establishment of an organized economic community would necessitate prolonged negotiations among the parties concerned, but in view of the political differences and enmity between Taiwan and mainland China and lingering political tension between the PRC and Hong Kong over the latter's status after 1997, it is difficult to envisage the three sides agreeing on such negotiations. At least, on the surface, Hong Kong's retrocession to China in 1997 will bring two legs of the triad together, but the third will probably remain apart. Political tension between Taiwan and China has undoubtedly eased considerably in recent years; nonetheless, it still exists. Beijing, suspecting that the Taipei government is actually seeking independence, refuses to renounce the option of using force against Taiwan as a means to realize the unification of China.[45] Taipei, for its part, maintains

[45]For Beijing's position on this issue, see Li Liaquan, "Taiwan Independence, 'Independent Taiwan' and Reunification," *Beijing Review*, No. 32 (August 10,

that Beijing's "four fundamental principles"[46] and the "one country, two systems" formula are aimed at downgrading Taipei to a local government under Chinese Communist leadership, thus constantly refusing to Beijing's overture for unification talks.[47] In this connection, Taipei has been careful to limit the ratio of its economic dependence on China to the current level[48] and by extension, to discourage further integration of its economy into mainland China by ostensibly maintaining a "three Nos": no contact, no communications and no compromise. Accordingly, before these political differences are fundamentally worked out, there can be no confidence between the two sides and normal economic and trade exchanges cannot develop.

All these points considered, it is too early to herald the arrival of Greater China involving Taiwan, mainland China, and Hong Kong even in the form of a free trade area, let alone a full-fledged economic community. Hong Kong's status as a free port makes it impossible to envisage its inclusion in a Chinese free trade area, unless the rest of Greater China were also willing to eliminate tariffs on imported goods. In the absence of official relationship, direct transportation links and a trade or investment agreement between the PRC and Taiwan, it is hard to find a mechanism to accelerate the process toward a higher level of economic integration in a practical sense. The gaps between the standards of living, economic institutions and legal systems on the

---

1992), pp. 22-25.

[46]The PRC's "four fundamental principles" are 1) the socialist road, 2) the dictatorship of the proletariat, 3) the primacy of the communist party, and 4) Marxism-Leninism-Mao Zedong thought.

[47]An-Chia Wu, "Taipei-Peking Relations: The Sovereignty Issue," *Issues and Studies*, 29:5 (May 1993), pp. 29-32.

[48]Analysts suggest that the Taiwan government now informally imposes the ceiling of 10 percent of total trade on the belief that anything above this figure would result in excessive dependence on the mainland market and give Beijing undue leverage in its dealings with the island. See Baldinger, *op. cit.*, p. 15; For a conceptual base of this policy, see Ramon H. Myers and Londa Chao, "Cross-Strait Economic Relations and Their Implications for Taiwan," *Issues and Studies*, 30:12 (December 1994), pp. 108-112.

Chinese mainland and those in Taiwan and Hong Kong, internal transformation undergoing in all three economies as a result of growing economic interaction among them also indicate that extensive economic integration would be highly problematic for these countries both in economic and political terms. Based on these points, together with the intermediary role of Hong Kong as a free port connecting the two economies, one can conclude that the three nations should at best undertake a partial form of economic cooperation or group themselves into a loosely constructed economic bloc pending the resolution of fundamental problems that make government-to-government negotiations among the three virtually impossible.[49]

Conclusion: Prospects for the Future and Implications for the Region

To sum up, Greater China has emerged as a favorable conjunction of political and economic circumstances prevailing in the three territories as well as in the world. On the surge of globalism following the end of WWII, Taiwan and Hong Kong have achieved phenomenal economic growth over the past decades forming two integral parts of the Asian Newly Industrialized Economies (NIEs). The PRC began to follow in the footsteps of these two countries in the late 1970s, thus having significantly contributed to the rise of economic might in the region. China's inauguration of its open door policy coincided with the needs of Taiwan and Hong Kong to change their economic structures. Wages had been rapidly rising in these two countries, forcing a shift from labor-intensive manufacturing to capital-intensive and skill-intensive activities. There are few parallels to the contribution that market-driven economic integration is making to eco-

[49]Weidenbaum predicts that Greater China will resemble the Hanseatic League more than the European Community, in that it is more likely to be a cooperative grouping of like-minded trading entities than a tightly integrated economic bloc. Wiedenbaum, *op. cit.*, pp. 71-83.

nomic growth in the coastal regions of South China.[50] The stimulus of deregulation and opening up and advantage of geographical proximity have been powerfully reinforced by cultural affinity between the businessmen of the "three Chinas," thus leading Greater China to one of the most dynamic sub-regions in East Asia. As a result of this development, the growing economic interdependence has become one definite aspect of both their tripartite relationship and bilateral ties. Sticking to the export-oriented development strategy, the three countries now in common have growing needs to effectively deal with increasing protectionism in the world economic system. In light of the exclusiveness of the regional economic blocs, the rise of regionalism would make it imperative for these countries to establish some kind of economic community.

However, the foregone analysis indicates that the emergence of Greater China remains an indeterminate process and the final dimensions are yet unclear. This is not to say that it is impossible, however. Experiences in Europe and elsewhere indicate that it is a time-consuming process to form an organized economic grouping with various obstacles being removed along the way. Judging from the current situation revolving around the issue, the future process toward full integration of Hong Kong, China and Taiwan hinges upon the development in the relationship between Taiwan and the PRC. In short, full economic integration of these three economies cannot be achieved until some sort of political accommodation is reached between the two countries across the Taiwan Strait. Taiwan and the PRC still maintain various barriers such as the ban on direct transportation of goods and people and on capital transfers which together prevent them from cashing in on the potential benefits of free trade and capital movement.[51] Given the political stand-still across the Taiwan Strait, a breakthrough in bilateral economic cooperation cannot be expected in the near

---

[50]Yeung Yue-man, *op. cit.*, pp. 60-66.

[51]For the political reasons why Taiwan still upholds this ban, see Chien-min Chao, "Obstacles in Taiwan-Mainland Relations: The Issue of Direct Transportation," *Issues and Studies*, 29:2 (February 1993), pp. 24-27.

future. Accordingly, progress toward full integration among three economies, if there will be any, will only be made incrementally.

One crucial point to be made pertaining to the emergence of Greater China is that the growing economic interrelationships among the "three Chinas" are not necessarily part of organized efforts by governments only. Rather, these economic ties have been initiated and expanded by individual enterprises of Taiwan and Hong Kong seeking to serve their own interests. To a certain degree, it has been so in the case of the PRC.[52] Given this, the momentum of the forces at work and the complementarity of the economies involved and geographic proximity all suggest that the process will continue in the future. To put it differently, in light of the on-going global trend toward regionalism, the existence of powerful integrative forces among the three economies will continue to serve as a "push factor" for higher degrees of integration as long as the private sector remains the main pillar of Taiwan's and Hong Kong's economy despite the lingering political difference between the two sides across the Taiwan Strait.

Although the evolution of Greater China into a formal economic community presently appears to be merely an illusion, current trends towards increasing economic cooperation among the three economies would be alarming to the rest of the region. In light of high growth rate and high degrees of complementarity, the combined economic strengths of the "three Chinas" would be truly immense. Yet mainland China is presently a low-technology economy and that it is absorbing technology from Hong Kong and Taiwan. It is true that, partly as a result, China's global exports have grown rapidly at an average rate of nearly 14 percent between 1980 and 1994. This implies that China is becoming a serious competitor for other developing countries, especially

---

[52]A significant portion of Beijing's overseas business ventures are controlled by enterprises owned by the PRC government. A prominent example is the China International Trust and Investment Corporation (CITIC). Although it is still owned by the government, it gets involved in business activities as an independent enterprise in many ways. See Tai Ming Cheung, "Middle of the Kingdom," *Far Eastern Economic Review* (January 21, 1993), pp. 48-52.

for some of the NIEs in the region, as they tend to face stiffer competition over the export markets especially in their traditional strongholds such as the United States and Europe. Also implicit in the current trends toward increasing integration among the three Chinese economies is that China siphons off jobs from Hong Kong and Taiwan, and capital from Taiwan, Hong Kong and elsewhere. All these points lead to the conclusion that China will be a formidable competitor for countries like South Korea over foreign capital in the future.

The dynamism of the Chinese economy has also tended to give rise to a sense of insecurity among Beijing's neighboring countries.[53] Based on its ever-growing economic might, China has increased its military expenditures at a stunning pace in recent years.[54] The extent to which such military modernization will occur in the upcoming years and the purposes to which it might be put, are not yet clear, thus serving as a main source of increasing tension in the region.[55] It is in this context that there has arisen concern that the combination of economic and military resources available to Greater China will pose a significant threat to the commercial vitality and the strategic stability of the rest of the world. If the three countries were to be reunified under a powerful central government, such an aggregation of resources would be possible, making China more powerful in the international community than the present. However, it is all but clear that a single central government which would be able to gain firm control of the economic and military resources of the main-

---

[53]See Denny Roy, "Hegemon on the Horizon: China's Threat to East Asian Security," *International Security*, 19:1 (Summer 1994), pp. 149-160.

[54]For a brief account of this trend, see June Teufel Dreyer, "The People's Army: Serving Whose Interests?" *The Current History* (September 1994), pp. 267-268.

[55]On this point, see Samuel S. Kim, "China as a Regional Power," *Current History* (September 1992); see also Andrew Mack and Desmond Bell, "The Military Build-up in the Asian-Pacific Region," *The Pacific Review*, 5:3 (1992), pp. 200-203; and Michael T. Clare, "Great Arms Race," *Foreign Affairs*, 72:2 (Summer 1993); for a recent account, see Nayan Chandra, "Fear of the Dragon," *Far Eastern Economic Review* (April 13, 1995), pp. 24-28.

land, Taiwan and Hong Kong is not likely to come into existence in the near future. Without such a centralized political will, Greater China will not evolve into a strategic superpower of the magnitude that could be attained. Additionally, it seems improbable that the various Chinese economies will form a closed bloc, buying primarily from themselves while seeking to sell to others. China's coastal area and other regions of the country have been open to foreign investment and trade from the inception of the open door policy, serving as the center for economic intercourse with its neighboring countries. In this regard, one can claim that the economic networks springing up along China's coast are increasingly linking the Chinese economies not just among each other but to other economies as well. Given the economic structure of the three economies in which trade with the outside world plays a significant role, such a trend is likely to continue in the future.

Accordingly, the rise of Greater China presents opportunities rather than threats to the outside of the area.[56] Although trade among the three principal economies has increased dramatically, they still heavily rely on the developed countries both for exports and imports. Additionally, all three of the major economies seek the so-called, "high technology" and "big capital" that still come primarily from outside the Greater China area. In this regard, the rise of Greater China has potential benefits for such countries as South Korea and Japan. Indeed, these two countries have participated in the growth of Chinese economy in significant ways as evident in their increasing trade with and investment into the PRC over the past decade.

With the emergence of Greater China, China has rapidly emerged as one of major exporting nations in the region, becoming a potential competitor for some of the NIEs in the region. As China exports increase, however, it will also gain the ability both to import and to invest abroad. Sales to China are already an

---

[56]For a similar perspective, see Vincent Cable and Peter Ferdinand, "China as an Economic Giant: Threat or Opportunity," *International Affairs*, 70:2 (1994), pp. 243-261.

increasing factor in the global exports of South Korea, Taiwan and Japan to a certain extent. Similarly, investment from mainland China is an increasing factor in the prosperity of Hong Kong, and capital from Hong Kong and Taiwan is flowing into the rest of Southeast Asia. In a period when the growth of the advanced economies is slowing and when international capital is in short supply, China may begin to play a role as one of the engines of growth for the rest of the regional economy.

5

China and ASEAN in the 1990s: Cooperation or Competition

Lee Lai To
(The National University of Singapore)

Haunted by its residual links with fraternal communist parties and the so-called overseas Chinese problem, Sino-ASEAN relations did not really improve markedly in the 70s even with the establishment of diplomatic relations between China and Malaysia in 1974 and between China and Thailand and the Philippines in 1975. After China's adoption of its economic reforms and opening to the outside world under the guidance of the four modernizations mapped out by Deng Xiaoping starting from the late 1970s, there were hopes that closer cooperation, especially that in economic terms, could be expected in Sino-ASEAN relations. However, China's initial focus of its "open door" policy was more on the industrialized countries and not really on developing areas like Southeast Asia. With the demise of the cold war and its ramifications for global and regional developments,[1] China, just like others, began to reorient, among other things, its policy towards the ASEAN region. More importantly, the Tiananmen incident of 1989 and the subsequent setback in China's relations with the industrialized world had in many ways forced Beijing to pay closer attention to neighbouring states, including the ASEAN states. The more "rational" reactions of these states to China's June 4th Incident[2] and the booming economies of the ASEAN region would probably lure China to pay more attention to the area under its independent policy of befriending neighbouring states. In view of the rise of protectionism and its strained relations with the West over human rights, democracy, proliferation of arms and other issues, China must have decided that more has to be done to gain the support of the developing world, particularly nearby states. Its persistent emphasis on the need to have a prolonged period of stability at home and peace in the Asia Pacific for development after the 1989 Tiananmen incident would suggest that the ASEAN region could be of some importance to China. ASEAN's remarkable economic performance and its active diplomacy would also provide not only economic opportunities but also ways and means to plug into the regional dialogue processes promoted by ASEAN in the 1990s. Although its major focus is domestic development, Beijing also realizes the importance of playing a part in regional and global activities in an increasingly inter-dependent world. It is the purpose of this chapter to examine China's moves, especially those of a political nature, in building a closer rapport with the ASEAN region as a whole in the 1990s and their implications for the Asia Pacific region.

---

[1]For an analysis of major power politics in the post-cold war era, see, for example, Lee Lai To, "Beyond Containment: The Future Utility of the US Military Presence in the Asia Pacific – A View from Southeast Asia" in Robert Monteperto, ed., *Cooperative Engagement and Economic Security in the Asia Pacific Region* (Washington, D.C.: National Defense University Press, 1993), pp. 119-136.

[2]See Lee Lai To, "Domestic Changes in China Since The 4 June Incident And Their Implications For Southeast Asia," in *Contemporary Southeast Asia*, 13:1 (June 1991), pp. 17-43.

The Diplomatic Breakthrough

One of the most urgent tasks in China's policy towards the ASEAN was no doubt the normalization of relations with all the members of the area. After the establishment of official ties with Malaysia, Thailand and the Philippines in the 70s, the logical target of diplomatic efforts for China would be Indonesia, the biggest state of ASEAN. However, marred by bitter exchanges after the attempted coup of the Indonesian Communist Party (PKI) in 1965 and alleged links with the ethnic Chinese minority in Indonesia , Beijing had not been successful in resuming suspended ties with Jakarta since 1967. Even with the changed international and regional environment like the Sino-American detente and establishment of official ties between China and some members of ASEAN, China did not seem to be able to remove its stigma as a threat to the security of Indonesia. However, China's diplomatic efforts like the Southeast Asian visits by President Li Xiannian and Foreign Minister Wu Xueqian in 1985 and Premier Li Peng in 1988 and the recognition of the changed international and regional environment in Indonesia, particularly the views from its Foreign Ministry and Chamber of Commerce and Industry (KADIN) seemed to have born some fruits by the second half of the 1980s. Although it was reported that Foreign Minister Wu might have missed an opportunity to have a meeting with President Soeharto due to scheduling difficulties while the former was in Indonesia for the 30th anniversary of the Bandung conference of Asian and African countries in April 1985, direct trade between Indonesia and China was restored later on after the visit.[3] In spite of the differences related to the procedure on commodity inspection in Sino-Indonesian trade and consequently temporary setbacks in direct trade, further progress seemed to have been made after a meeting between President Soeharto and Foreign Minister Qian Qichen while they were in Tokyo attending Emperor Hirohito's funeral in February

[3]*South China Morning Post* (April 27, 1985), *Hongkong Standard* (April 25, 1985) and *Dagong Bao* (January 3, 1986).

1989. It was learned that President Soeharto was satisfied with the Chinese assurance that Beijing would not interfere with the domestic affairs of Indonesia and it was agreed that both sides would take steps to normalize Sino-Indonesian relations.[4] After a number of technical meetings, Jakarta and Beijing finally resumed official ties on 8 August 1990. Indonesia's decision to normalize relations with China reflects obviously its confidence in coping with possible repercussions of the move on its domestic scenes, especially those related to security and the opposition against the normalization at home. More importantly, the decision must be motivated by the economic incentive. With economic problems like the drop in oil earnings and increase in debts, Jakarta might think of banking on China's four modernizations, a move spearheaded by its own businessmen even before the normalization. In addition, to play a leading role in regional affairs, like the Cambodian conflict and later on the South China Sea disputes, it was becoming more evident that it would be unrealistic for Jakarta not to have any dealings with a major actor like China. At a time when the West was extremely critical of Beijing's 1989 crackdown in Tiananmen Square, Jakarta's move also signaled to others that while it might not agree with the Chinese move, it was useful to resume a dialogue with Beijing and that it had no intention of interfering the domestic affairs of others. Quite obviously, an isolated and unstable China would not only affect Beijing but also other regions, especially nearby areas like Southeast Asia.

With the resumption of Sino-Indonesian relations in 1990, China do doubt scored a major breakthrough in Sino-ASEAN relations. From China's perspective, the move helped not only in economic terms but also more importantly in diplomatic and political terms. Notably, at a time when it still had to face the chorus of criticisms against Beijing from the West after the 1989 Tiananmen incident, the breakthrough was particularly valuable. It not only diluted its "odd man out syndrome" in world and regional affairs after 1989, but also paved the way for the eleva-

---

[4]*China Times* (February 24, 1989).

tion of its position in Asian and particularly Southeast Asian affairs. Specifically, the normalization would help expedite China's desire to have formal ties with the remaining ASEAN states, namely, Singapore and Brunei. This was particularly true in the case of Singapore which had over the years increased its economic linkages with China, notably after its recession in 1985-86. These included increased air links and visits between the two countries, setting up of trade offices, frequent trade missions from China to Singapore and vice versa, consultations at the top by the political leaders, notably in visits to China by Prime Minister Lee Kuan Yew and by the appointment of former first Deputy Prime Minister Goh Keng Swee as an economic adviser in China. As it turned out, China and Singapore established diplomatic ties in October 1990, just about two months after the resumption of official ties between China and Indonesia. Apparently, China did not consider Singapore's "practical" relations with Taiwan, including its military ties with Taiwan under the "Star Light Project," an impediment in establishing diplomatic relations with Singapore. In fact, with regard to the military ties, Li Peng indicated that he understood the situation and that "this is a fact and we should not mind too much" when he was in Singapore in August 1990.[5]

Having established or resumed official ties with five of the ASEAN states, it was just a matter of time before China could link up with Brunei when the latter was ready. As it turned out, Brunei and China set up diplomatic ties on 30 September, 1991.[6] By that, China had managed to have official ties with all the ASEAN states, a major diplomatic success for Beijing after the 1989 Tiananmen incident. At a time when western sanctions, albeit softening by the early 1990s, still remained, it augured well for Beijing in adhering steadfastly to its determination to steer its own course in battling with the West over human rights, democracy, protectionism and other issues.

---

[5]*United Daily* (August 13, 1990).

[6]*Dagong Bao* (October 1, 1991).

The Political and Security Front

China's wooing of ASEAN in the 1990s perhaps was best demonstrated by the increased political and diplomatic offensive in polishing its image and befriending the region. In fact, the 1990s started with two well publicized visits by Premier Li Peng to the area. The first visit took place at the time of the resumption of Sino-Indonesian relations in August 1990 when Li went to Indonesia, Singapore and Thailand. The move, together with American consultation with China on the Middle East conflict, notable the invasion of Kuwait by Iraq, signaled Beijing's comeback to the world scene soon after the June 4th incident. Li's visit dealt with bilateral political and economic relations with three of the ASEAN states. Moreover, it provided opportunities for Chinese and ASEAN leaders to examine the Cambodian conflict and the changing situation in the Middle East. As the territorial conflicts in the South China Sea began to emerge as a potential bone of contention between China and some of the ASEAN states, Li proposed that the sovereignty issue be shelved and that the parties involved should work together to explore the resources in the area.[7] Li's visit to the three ASEAN states was unusual in many ways as it had been China's practice to invite political leaders to visit Beijing. One is only reminded of the homages paid by Prime Minister Kakuei Tanaka, President Nixon and President Mikhail Gorbachev in normalizing relations with Beijing. The departure from China's traditional way in normalizing relations with other countries signaled a new way of conducting its diplomacy, at least towards the so-called third world like Southeast Asia. The new diplomatic offensive after the June 4th incident was reconfirmed by Li's other trip to Sri Lanka and Southeast Asia, including two of the ASEAN states, namely, Malaysia and the Philippines, later on in December 1990. As far as ASEAN was concerned, that was the second trip to ASEAN for Li in the same year. The increased meetings between China and ASEAN in 1990 was also augmented by numerous visits to China

[7] *Far Eastern Economic Review* (August 30, 1990), p. 11.

by top ASEAN leaders, notably the first state visit by President Soeharto to China in November 1990 after the suspension of diplomatic ties between Indonesia and China in 1967. In view of the changing international and regional changes in the post-cold war era, especially the reduced presence of Moscow and Washington in the Asia Pacific, Beijing might find it timely to reap the benefits arising from the normalization of relations with ASEAN, or for that matter, Southeast Asia, and upgrade its political and diplomatic activities in the area. This was probably facilitated by the decrease, if not termination of, Beijing's support to the local communists, notably by the declaration of the end of armed struggle against Malaysia by the Malayan Communist Party. Moreover, as elaborated later on, in view of Taiwan's economic diplomacy in ASEAN, Beijing might also feel it necessary to work on the ASEAN states and impress on them the importance of upkeeping the one-China policy.

On the whole, China's relations with ASEAN got off to a fresh start by the end of 1990. Beijing was not only able to establish diplomatic ties with all ASEAN states except Brunei, but also to promote closer consultation and interactions with the ASEAN region by exchange visits of top leaders. This prompted a review in the *People' Daily* to consider 1990 as the year that China had already developed full-blown relations with the ASEAN states.[8] While ASEAN leaders continue to stream to China, the momentum of conducting ASEAN visits by Chinese leaders also seems to pick up in the 1990s. China's ASEAN visits included two trips of President Yang Shangkun to the ASEAN region, one to Indonesia and Thailand in June 1991 and another to Singapore and Malaysia in January 1992, visits of Qiao She, Chairman of the Standing Committee of the National People's Congress, to Indonesia, Malaysia, Singapore, Thailand and the Philippines from July to August 1993, visits of Foreign Minister and Vice Premier Qian Qichen to ASEAN since 1991 as a guest of the annual ASEAN Ministerial Meeting (AMM) and the representative of China to the annual ASEAN Regional Forum (ARF) from

[8]*People's Daily* (PD) (December 19, 1990).

1994 onwards as a consultative partner, visits of Liu Huaqing, Vice Chairman of the Central Military Commission of the Chinese Communist Party, to Thailand and Indonesia with a stopover in Singapore in January 1994, and last but not least, visits of President Jiang Zemin to Singapore, Malaysia, Indonesia and Vietnam in November 1994. In the light of the numerous China visits made by top ASEAN leaders, it was obvious that the place of ASEAN in China's diplomacy had moved upwards considerably. In fact, 1993 was dubbed as the "ASEAN Year" in China's diplomacy because of the numerous mutual visits by top leaders from both sides.[9]

While the exchange visits may promote mutual understanding, consultation and cooperation in a wide range of subjects, especially in the economic arena as demonstrated later on, China also seemed to be very keen on building a more concrete and lasting political relationship with the ASEAN region. With a region that it used to having political liabilities like links with local communists and the so-called overseas China and where there was still residual suspicions of China's motives in moving closer to ASEAN, Beijing probably would like to utilize its unprecedented cordial relations with the ASEAN to build up more good will and reap more concrete diplomatic and political gains. As noted earlier, Beijing's strained relations with the West after the Tiananmen incident had made it more urgent for it to woo the ASEAN region. This was especially true with regard to issues like human rights and the importance of political stability in development and other issues, Beijing had found it more rewarding in working closely with the ASEAN states as the latter seem to find western standards and values disagreeable. To boost its image in the ASEAN region, China had made it known that it supported the Malaysian proposal of establishing the East Asian Economic Caucus (EAEC) and the Zone of Peace, Freedom and Neutrality (ZOPFAN) and Southeast Asian Nuclear Free Zone (SEANFZ) as endorsed by ASEAN.[10] It has also made known on numerous

[9]*Wenhui Bao* (July 25, 1993).

[10]See, for example, *PD 4* (October 1990) and *Wenhui Bao* (January 12, 1992).

occasions that it would like to work with ASEAN in restoring peace in Cambodia.[11] As the territorial disputes in the South China Sea could be a stumbling block in warming up relations with some of the ASEAN states, China decided to shelve the sovereignty issue and take part in discussions on joint development in the area in spite of its initial reluctance to talk about the issues with others. That was demonstrated by its participation in the Indonesian initiative of having "informal" workshops on "Managing Potential Conflicts in the South China Sea" since 1991.[12] While China does not want to internationalize the issues and that it has its doubts about multilateralism in resolving problems, it has, nevertheless, been taking part in the workshop that could provide dialogues and a better understanding of the issues involved.

At the official ASEAN level, China had indicated that it would like to be a dialogue partner of the sub-regional organization, just like some other major Asia Pacific states.[13] However, for the ASEAN states, it seems that they had reservations in roping in China as a full dialogue partner immediately because of their lingering fear of China, especially its military modernization and consolidation of claims in the South China Sea, and of their residual suspicions, at least on the part of some observers in the ASEAN states. As always, China's size, proximity, ethnic outreach and its renewed dynamism could instill fears in some of the small states of the ASEAN region.[14] However, in view of the vast potential for furthering Sino-ASEAN economic cooperation and

---

[11]See, for example, *PD* (August 17, 1990).

[12]The annual workshop started in 1990. The first one was only for the ASEAN participants. China and others have been taking part since 1991. For an analysis of the workshops, see Lee Lai To, "Defusing Rising Tension in the Spratlys – An Analysis of the workshops on Managing Potential Conflicts in the South China Sea in Indonesia" in *American Asian Review* (forthcoming).

[13]*PD* (April 28, 1991) and (July 23, 1991).

[14]See Lee Lai To, "ASEAN-PRC Political and Security Cooperation – Problems, Proposals and Prospects," in *Asian Survey* (November 1993), pp. 1095-1104.

need to engage China in security dialogues in the post-cold war era, ASEAN had decided to take a step-by-step approach in promoting dialogues with China. For a start, ASEAN has been inviting Beijing to attend the AMM as a guest since 1991. And starting from 1994, Beijing has also become a consultative partner of the newly formed ARF. To Beijing, these occasions in ASEAN may be useful for it to dispel the "China Threat" or its desire to fill the so-called "vacuum" left behind by the reduced presence of Washington and Moscow. It would try to reiterate the common ground taken by China and ASEAN with regard to issues like human rights and highlight the importance of maintaining peace and stability for China and the whole Asia Pacific region. As such, China, as made known notably by its Vice Premier and Foreign Minister Qian Qichen, would like to promote not only economic, cultural, scientific and technical cooperation with ASEAN, but also "a multi-level and multi-channel dialogue mechanism on security."[15] This will be pursued at the ASEAN level and with the individual states of the sub-region. By the mid-1990s, if not earlier, it seems that China had already carved a niche for itself in ASEAN foreign affairs. No doubt it has yet to become a full dialogue partner, otherwise, its place in security dialogues was well in place as demonstrated vividly by its participation in the ARF. Sino-ASEAN economic interactions, as analyzed later on, were also on the increase. In addition, numerous exchange visits between top political and defense officials of both sides not only discuss economic cooperation and nation-building experiences but also possibilities of defense cooperation.[16] In fact, in the case of Malaysia, which has been harbouring misgivings against Beijing because of the latter's links with the local communists and "overseas Chinese," changed dramatically its perception of the PRC, at least by its Prime Minister Mahathir and Deputy Prime Minister Anwar Ibrahim. As stated by Deputy Prime Minister Anwar, China "is a special friendly country" and

---

[15]*Beijing Review* (August 3-9, 1992), p. 4.

[16]See, for example, the discussions on Sino-Malaysian defence cooperation as reported in *Lianhe Zaobao* (September 15, 1994).

outstanding issues must be resolved without delay.[17] More importantly, Prime Minister Mahathir stated clearly that there would be greater Sino-Malaysian cooperation as the economies of the two countries expanded. He further noted that because of ideological differences, Sino-Malaysian relations had not been as good as it should have been for a long time. As things had changed greatly, Prime Minister Mahathir considered Sino-Malaysian relationship to be as normal as it could be and that the past was very much forgotten and in many ways irrelevant.[18] With reference to the dispute in the Spratlys, he emphasized that "Malaysia does not regard China as a potential enemy, therefore these talks about having security arrangements as if it seemed China was going to be the enemy, to us are quite irrelevant."[19] From all indications, pragmatism and the search for mutual benefit, especially that of an economic nature, seems to have prevailed in Sino-Malaysian, or for that matter, in most, if not all, of the dealings between China and the ASEAN states in the 1990s.

It remains to be noted that while emphasizing the cooperative aspects between China and ASEAN, the PRC is at the same time concerned with possible forces which could undermine the cordial relations. Firstly, it would probably be wary of the impact of the inclusion of Vietnam as a member of ASEAN on Sino-ASEAN affairs. Vietnam, together with Laos, acceded to the Treaty of Amity and Cooperation of Southeast Asia in 1992, thus becoming an observer of the sub-regional organization. More importantly, the AMM in July 1994 held in Bangkok decided to invite Vietnam to be a member of ASEAN when the latter was ready. And before the end of 1994, it was already known that Vietnam had applied to be a member of ASEAN. As such, Vietnam would be a member of ASEAN in due course. Although there are signs showing that Sino-Vietnamese relations are normalizing, it is obvious that it will take a long time before the two sides could resolve their differences, notably their boundary disputes on land, the Gulf of

---

[17] *Straits Times* (*ST*) (August 29, 1994).

[18] *ST* (May 1, 1993).

[19] *Sunday Times* (Singapore) (August 22, 1993).

Tonkin and the South China Sea. It remains to be seen to what extent Vietnam's membership in ASEAN will affect Sino-ASEAN relations. Secondly, and as far as the South China Sea conflicts are concerned, Beijing is probably aware of the fact that there may be forces in ASEAN which would like to internationalize the issues. In fact, the adoption of the South China Sea Declaration by the AMM in Manila in 1992 was looked upon with suspicion by China, at least to a certain extent, as it showed vividly to China that ASEAN might want to regionalize, if not internationalize, the issues and increase its say in the handling of the conflicts. Suggestions by ASEAN leaders, like the convening of a conference on the South China Sea conflicts under the auspices of the UN mooted by President Ramos or Foreign Secretary Raul Manglapus' idea to call for an international conference on the Spratlys, certainly reinforce Beijing's impression that the issues could be internationalized.[20] As China has always favored bilateral discussions, and at the most, discussions among the claimants or South China Sea states, it is naturally concerned with all these moves from ASEAN. In fact, it has made known its wish that the Spratlys and Paracels should not be discussed at the workshops on "Managing Potential Conflicts in the South China Sea" hosted by Indonesia and it has suggested that the Spratly issues should not be included in the agenda of the ARF.[21] However, to some in ASEAN, the South China Sea could be used as a buffer zone between China and Southeast Asia in view of their residual worries about China's long term intention.[22] Moreover, China is also aware of the fact that the ASEAN claimant states, at least in the cases of the Philippines and Malaysia, are trying to consolidate their claims not only for security reasons but also for economic gains. Thirdly, in spite of the differences in value judgments with the West, Beijing could not help but notice the western inclination of at least some of the ASEAN states in economic and political

---

[20]*ST* (July 15, July 20, 1992).

[21]*ST* (August 26, 1993) and *Lianhe Zaobao* (April 5, 1994).

[22]See, for example, the statement by General Hashim on the need for ASEAN to be wary of China's military expansion as reported in *ST* (March 29, 1992).

and security terms.[23] From China's perspective, it is possible that the West and some of the ASEAN states might find it mutually beneficial to restrain China's ambitions in Southeast Asia and the Asia Pacific.[24] In fact, to China, some observers in ASEAN might have accepted the western "theories" about the "China threat" and "China filling the vacuum" in the Asia Pacific. In view of their colonial heritage and close links with the West, ASEAN could be influenced into taking steps against Chinese interests as suggested by some in the PRC.[25]

As a result, China, just like ASEAN, would agree that it would be useful to have more dialogues on political and security matters, not only on a bilateral basis but also in multilateral forums like the ARF to promote mutual understanding of the issue involved. As the ARF meetings include participants from a vast number of states in the Asia Pacific, it was suggested that a separate round of meetings just between China and ASEAN on political and security issues should be launched. And for a start, senior officials of China and ASEAN will meet to discuss political and security issues in April 1995 in Beijing.[26]

It remains to be emphasized that in terms of China's priorities in the security arena, Beijing would probably be much more concerned with separatist tendencies in the so-called autonomous regions like Tibet and especially in Taiwan and not so much in areas like the South China Sea or Senkaku (Daiyutao) islands. In the case of its policy towards Taiwan, Beijing has found it most difficult to convince Taipei of the wisdom of following the "one country, two systems" for the reunification of China. Instead, Beijing is witnessing a de facto "one country, two governments" and calls for independence in Taiwan.[27] What is relevant to Sino-

---

[23]See, for example, the analysis by Lu Wenjun, "Luelun Dongmeng De Fazhan Qushi Ji Dui Wo Guo De Yingxiang" (A General Treatise on Trends in ASEAN Development and Their Impact on China), in *All-Round Studies of Southeast Asia*, No. 4 (1993), p. 13.

[24]*Ibid.*

[25]*Ibid.*

[26]*Lianhe Zaobao* (July 25, 1994).

ASEAN relations is that the ASEAN states are seen to be pursuing a de facto one China on Taiwan policy. Numerous high officials of ASEAN and Taiwan have visited each other to promote, inter alia, economic cooperation. Taipei's "elastic diplomacy," "money diplomacy" or "holiday diplomacy" seems to have been able to create a place for itself in Southeast Asia and it is possible that the KMT government could upgrade its relations with some of the ASEAN states from that of economic in nature to a higher level. This no doubt will be of much concern to Beijing as witnessed by its protests to the ASEAN states in instances like Manila's move to pass the Philippines-Taiwan Beneficial Act and the invitation of Taiwan leaders to visit the region by some of the ASEAN states in what Taipei calls "holiday diplomacy."[28] Beijing will definitely exercise constant vigilance on possible ASEAN acts to move closer to Taipei. Any ASEAN gesture that is seen to be conferring official standing to Taipei will be protested by the PRC.

The Economic Incentive

With China's diplomatic successes in ASEAN in the early 1990s as analyzed above, it is not surprising that closer Sino-ASEAN economic ties are forthcoming. The numerous visits conducted by leaders of both sides to visit one another have certainly provided the environment to help strike more business deals. From the trade statistics released by Beijing, it could be detected that the volume of trade has certainly increased in the 1990s. With only slightly over US $ 4 billion of Sino-ASEAN trade in 1990, the figure is increased to US $ 7.96 billion in 1991, US $ 8.46 billion in 1992, US $ 10.68 billion in 1993 and US $ 5.52 billion for the first six months of 1994.[29] It has been noted that by 1992, Sino-ASEAN

[27]For details, see Lee Lai To, *The Reunification of China – PRC-Taiwan Relations In Flux* (New York: Praeger Publishers, 1991), pp.1-104.

[28]See *Ibid.*, p. 76.

[29]*PD* (November 1, 1992 & July 21, 1993) and *Business Weekly* of *China Daily*

trade had already increased 15 times over the volume in 1975.[30] By 1993, Sino-ASEAN trade accounted for 5.4 per cent of China's foreign trade, making ASEAN China's fifth largest trade partner after Japan, Hong Kong, the US and the European Community.[31] As both China and ASEAN have had sustained rapid growth and are expected to grow continuously in the remaining of the 1990s, Chinese officials are optimistic that Sino-ASEAN will be doubled that of 1993 at the turn of the century. As projected by a senior official of the Ministry of Foreign Trade and Economic Cooperation, "by the year 2000, Sino-ASEAN trade volume will reach around $20 billion (US)."[32] That means the trade volume should increase by 10 to 20 per cent per year from 1994 to 2000.

The optimistic forecast is produced not only by the expected economic growth on both sides and the unprecedented warm relations between China and ASEAN, but also the fact that the potential or room for further increase is great as ASEAN had only accounted for 5 to 6 percent of China's foreign trade and China had only accounted for 2 to 3 per cent of ASEAN foreign trade in the past.[33] China no doubt is aware that there could be competition between China and ASEAN in selected areas. Notably, some natural resources, labour-intensive and agricultural products and manufactured goods may compete for overseas markets. However, it is argued that China has a big market and a complex technical and production structure, thus allowing it to develop complementary or mutually beneficial economic interactions with states at various levels of development.[34] Moreover, it has been argued that if the competition is healthy, it could promote the necessary structural adjustment, diversification and value-

---

(October 9-15, 1994).

[30]*PD* (July 21, 1993).

[31]*Business Weekly* (October 9-15, 1994).

[32]*Ibid.*

[33]*PD* (November 1, 1992).

[34]See, for example, the remarks made by Pu Shan of the Chinese Academy of Social Sciences on Sino-ASEAN economic cooperation as reported in *Wenhui Bao* (December 7, 1990).

addition for the products concerned.[35] China's general assessment of Sino-ASEAN trade is that there should be ample room for expansion and that such interactions may be more complementary in nature.[36] While this could be an expression of goodwill and best wishes, at least to a certain extent, and that the business interactions may be used by China for political purposes in promoting relations with the ASEAN region, it seems that in most instances, pragmatism, hard-headed calculations and complementarity are the primary basis for the increase and sustaining of the projected increase of Sino-ASEAN trade in the 1990s, just like China's economic dealings with Taiwan.[37] To facilitate Sino-ASEAN trade, both sides signed an agreement to set up a joint committee on economic and trade cooperation in 1994.[38] The move, coupled with bilateral agreements between China and some of the ASEAN states on investment protection and avoidance of double taxation, will probably help push Sino-ASEAN economic cooperation to a higher level.

With the economic reforms and the policy of opening to the outside world fully entrenched in China in the 1990s, Beijing will continue to source for overseas capitals to prop up its modernization process. In the case of ASEAN, it has met with some successes as evidenced by the increasing investments from the region in the PRC. By the end of 1991, the ASEAN states had already committed US $1.41 billion in 1042 projects approved by the Chinese government.[39] Of the six ASEAN states, Singapore leads not only in trading with China, but also in investing in the country. By mid-1994, Singapore became China's fifth biggest overseas investor after Hong Kong, Taiwan, the US and Japan.[40] With its drive to regionalize its economy and to create a second wing in

---

[35]*Ibid.*

[36]See, for example, *PD* (September 1, 1993), (July 21, 1993), *Dagong Bao* (July 19, 1993) and *Wenhui Bao* (July 25, 1993).

[37]See Lee Lai To, *The Reunification of China……*, p. 125.

[38]*Sunday Times* (July 24, 1994) and *ST* (September 15, 1993).

[39]*PD* (November 1, 1992).

[40]*Business Weekly* (October 9-15, 1994).

its development, Singapore had invested in 3,834 projects in China with promised investment of US$ 6.817 billion by mid-1994.[41] Of these, the agreement between Beijing and Singapore to jointly develop the multi-billion dollar project at the Suzhou Industrial Park in Jiangsu Providence is most notable. The project is not only to raise capital but to transfer the "software" in development, especially advanced management experiences – the Singapore way, to Suzhou in particular and to China in general.

China is not just the receiving end of the capital transfer. It is also investing moderately in the ASEAN region. From 1979 to 1992, 296 Chinese enterprises have invested US $ 290 million in the ASEAN.[42] Beijing is also collaborating with some of the mainland Southeast Asian states including Thailand, an ASEAN member, in the development of the Mekong River.[43] In addition, quite a number of Chinese companies have already set up operations in ASEAN, notably Singapore, as a base to penetrate global markets. These include Chinese companies in finance, insurance, manufacturing, construction, trading and labour recruitment.[44] In view of its surplus labour, China has been successful in clinching labour contracts with the ASEAN region. And in 1993, it was revealed that Beijing managed to clinch 609 labor contracts with ASEAN states and completed US $250 million of business turnover.[45]

China's economic interactions with ASEAN are not just on trade and investment. It is also interested in promoting scientific and technological cooperation mainly to further each other's competitiveness in the international business world. As noted by the Chinese, China has a strong base on scientific and technological research. However, there is still a lot of room for improving in applying the research results into the production process and

---

[41] *Ibid.*

[42] *PD* (July 21, 1993).

[43] *ST* (September 17, 1994).

[44] *ST* (November 30, 1993).

[45] *Business Weekly* (October 9-15, 1994).

marketing the products abroad. As some of the ASEAN states do have some experiences in the commercialization of science and technology and application of the findings to the production process, there could be cooperation between China and ASEAN.[46] In view of the reluctance of some of the industrialized nations and their multinational corporations in transferring technology to other states, it would be wise for China and ASEAN to work together in this area. As a result, China has signed agreements on joint scientific and technological cooperation with some of the ASEAN states. It has also signed an agreement with ASEAN to set up a joint committee on scientific and technological cooperation in 1994.[47]

With all these economic interactions, plus the cultural exchanges and tourist visits between the two sides, it is obvious that Sino-ASEAN relations in the 1990s are no doubt on a much better footing than before. The relatively new found rapport between China and ASEAN signals that the two indigenous parts of Asia are now finding it mutually beneficial to have closer links. While they still bank heavily on having economic links with the industrialized world, notably the US, Japan and the European Union, they also realize that closer Sino-ASEAN links would certainly cushion the impact of protectionism and strengthen the bargaining power of Asian states in the Asia Pacific economy.

It remains to be noted that the "China fever" has caused concerns in some quarters in ASEAN. Questions could be asked if it is wise to divert capital to China, especially when it is done at the expense of domestic development. In view of the large number of ethnic Chinese in ASEAN doing business with China and the seemingly enthusiasm of Beijing in cultivating the support of these ethnic Chinese for its four modernizations, it could lead to criticisms from other racial groups against the Chinese minority in their respective country. The talk of forming some kind of Greater Chinese Economic Circle that would include Taiwan, the

---

[46]*Wenhui Bao* (December 7, 1990).

[47]*Sunday Times* (July 24, 1994).

PRC, Hong Kong, Macao and even Singapore and other "overseas" Chinese to promote economic cooperation would cause misgivings and disquiet among the non-Chinese in the ASEAN region, particularly those who want to branch into the China market.[48] As a result, it was timely for Senior Minister Lee Kuan Yew to highlight that ethnic Chinese who came from certain "sensitive" ASEAN countries should exercise care that their investments in their own countries did not diminish as a result of their China investments in a gathering of Chinese entrepreneurs in Hong Kong in 1993. Malaysian Deputy Finance Minister Loke Yuen Yow also emphasized that it was Malaysia's view that while it was good to invest in China and explore the huge market there, the businessmen should also not neglect the investments needed at home. He noted that "overzealousness on the part of Malaysian businessmen of Chinese origin could have adverse repercussions racially in their own country."[49] Likewise, the same could be applied to Indonesia where the dominance of ethnic Chinese in the economy has always been a political and economic issue.[50]

Major Implications

Closer Sino-ASEAN relations in the 1990s should not obscure the reality that while ASEAN may find the market and investment opportunities in China attractive, others in the Asia Pacific may also be lured to the PRC for the same reasons. If the industrialized countries, like the US, Japan and members of the European Union compare trade and investment packages in ASEAN with those of China and find China much more attractive, the implication is that the ASEAN states, especially countries like Indonesia,

---

[48]See Lee Lai To, "ASEAN-PRC Political and Security Cooperation……," p. 1097.

[49]*ST* (December 2, 1993).

[50]See, for example, the remarks made by Research and Technology Minister B. J. Habibie as reported in *Sunday Times* (December 12, 1993).

may lose out. Even in the case of highly-rated Singapore, as noted by its political leaders, China is a big "vacuum cleaner" that could suck up a lot of foreign investments. Prime Minister Goh Chok Tong, upon learning that a very big European electronics giant had decided to invest more than $ 1 billion in China instead of making any new investments in Singapore, remarked that the move sent a chill down his spine.[51] He feared that more multinational manufacturing companies might be calculating in the same way as that electronics giant.[52] Even in the cases of other newly industrialized economies, like Taiwan, Hong Kong and South Korea which have been investing and trading with ASEAN, they may find the attractions in China too tempting to miss and switch more attention to the PRC. This is especially true in the cases of Hong Kong and Taiwan where geographical proximity, linguistic and cultural affinity, and Beijing's accommodative policy towards its compatriots would make China more attractive than the ASEAN region. As for South Korea, no doubt it is a dialogue partner of ASEAN, however, it knows that its place in ASEAN is not as high as the other major powers and that ASEAN may not be as useful or helpful when compared with China in political and economic terms in view of its major concern with North Korea, or for that matter, the development in the Korean peninsula and Northeast Asia.

Nevertheless, as a growth region and an increasingly active actor in regional political and security affairs in the 1990s, ASEAN will continue to enjoy a certain level of importance in the eye of China. The closer and increasing interactions between China and ASEAN as noted above will in many ways have significant implications for major power politics in Southeast Asia. At a time of reduced presence of Washington and Moscow in Southeast Asia, China's advances in the region, coupled with its rapid economic growth and ability to project power abroad, sig-

---

[51]*ST* (November 9, 1994).

[52]*Ibid*. It was later on clarified that the German firm would still continue to invest in Singapore. However, the worry is probably unchanged although lessened to a certain extent. See *ST* (November 15, 1994).

nal that China will play a critical role in the balance of power. Thus ASEAN's policy of engaging the PRC is a timely and useful strategy in seizing opportunities to further political and economic cooperation between China and Southeast Asia. Sino-ASEAN relations in the 1990s highlight the cooperation between two developing and neighbouring areas in Asia for mutual benefit. Chances are, the voices of China and ASEAN would carry more weight in the post-cold war era. As far as China is concerned, it would consider its success in promoting cooperation with ASEAN as an elevation of its place in the so-called third world and south-south cooperation.

It remains to be emphasized that China's move towards ASEAN could have serious implications for Taiwan. As noted earlier, China cannot help but notice the close links, especially those of an economic nature, between Taipei and the ASEAN states. Trade between Taiwan and ASEAN in the 1990s amounts to US $ 9.68 billion in 1990, US $ 11.28 billion in 1991, US $ 12.92 billion in 1992 and US $ 14.13 billion in 1993.[53] The figures show that Taiwan-ASEAN trade has been on the increase in the early 1990s and are more than Sino-ASEAN trade for the same period. In addition, Taiwan has been investing in the ASEAN region. Its approved investment figures in the ASEAN region for the 1990s are US $ 3.93 billion in 1990, US $ 2.99 billion in 1991, US $ 1.46 billion in 1992 and US $ 0.7 billion in 1993.[54] Although Taiwan's investment in ASEAN is on the decline in the early 1990s, it is still one of the important investors in the ASEAN region, at least in the cases of some of the states and the amount is significantly more than that from the PRC. More importantly, with the "go south" policy mooted by President Lee Teng-hui in the 1990s and armed with promises of economic assistance through its

---

[53]The figures exclude trade between Taiwan and Brunei. Figures of Indonesia, Philippines, Singapore and Thailand are from *Taiwan Statistical Data Book 1994*, Council for Economic Planning and Development, Taipei (June 1994), pp. 197-199. Figures of Malaysia are from *Issues and Studies* (April 1993), p. 105, *China Post* (September 1, 1994) and *China Times* (December 30, 1993).

[54]The figures exclude Brunei. See *Sinorama*, 19:10 (October, 1994), p. 102.

Overseas Economic Cooperation and Development Fund, the dispatch of technical missions and other devices, it is not surprising that Taipei has, to a certain extent, managed to conduct successfully its holiday diplomacy with at least some of the ASEAN states.[55] Thus one of the motivations of China in interacting with ASEAN in the 1990s could be to lessen the economic clout of Taipei in the area and dampen Taipei's hope of raising its political and diplomatic profile in Southeast Asia. As always, it will insist that ASEAN should upkeep the one-China policy. Any move that is seen to be giving official standing to Taipei would be blocked by Beijing, making it more difficult for Taipei to operate in the ASEAN region.

Concluding Observations

As a fast growing state having the greatest potential to be a dominant Asian power in the 21st century, China will be able to exert considerable influence on its neighbours, including the ASEAN region. While China's economic and political clout will probably not be able to overshadow the other major powers, notably the US, in the Asia Pacific for the remaining of the 1990s, it is clear that its weight in regional and sub-regional affairs will be increased. And as such, the ASEAN states will find it beneficial to broaden their links with China and avoid banking on the industrialized nations alone. However, the lack of transparency of Chinese policies, especially that in the security arena, may give rise to different interpretations on how a new and revitalized China would behave. As a result, both sides see the wisdom in having more Sino-ASEAN dialogues and interactions. The hope is that with more discussions and dealings between China and ASEAN, each side will not only understand each other's positions and problems, but will also see the usefulness in continuing

---

[55]For an analysis of the help given by Taipei to ASEAN, see, for example, Chan Jie, "The 'Taiwan Problems' in Peking's ASEAN Policy," in *Issues and Studies* (April 1993), pp. 102-112.

the cooperative relationship for a long time to come. The integrating of China into the community of nations in the Asia Pacific, or for that matter, the world, would hopefully serve as a useful process in enticing a strengthened Beijing to playing a constructive role in regional and world affairs.

PART Ⅲ

Key Initiatives in China's Modernization

6

State Sector Reform in China: The Last Frontier of the Reform

Keun Lee
(Seoul National University)

Introduction

As the economy entered the boom again in 1992 after a three year's contraction, the Chinese communist party plenary session held in October 1992 adopted the slogan of "socialist market economy" replacing the former planned commodity economy. When the Chinese used as their model the planned commodity economy in the mid-1980s, the term "commodity economy" was used in stead of market economy for ideoligical reasons; at that time, the Chinese leadership still did not like the term market. The "planned commodity economy" was to combine plans and markets, and state enterprises were supposed to be under plans while non-state enterprises were under markets. Namely, different enterprises were treated differerntly. Now the idea of "socialist market economy" means equal treatment for all kinds of enterprises, regardless of their ownership. Both state and non-state enterprises are now supposed to compete on an equal basis in markets.

Then, what is socialism? Now, socialism means the continuing dominance of large and medium-sized state enterprises in important sectors of the economy. In other words, they do not intend to launch major scale privatization. This is the critical points which impinge upon the future of the Chinese economy. In the past 15 years of reform, Chinese authorities tried really many measures to revitalize their state enterprises. However, as is well known, all they failed, and about two-thirds (mostly large and medium sized ones) of the all state enterprises in China are now making losses. Those loss-making state enterprises are responsible for the budget deficits, excessive and unprofitable fixed investment drive, and relative stagnation of heavy industry contrasted while non- state enterprises dominated booming light industry. Actually, they are the real bottleneck of the sound take-off of the Chinese economy or transition from a refrom miracle to an East Asian miracle. This paper aims at addressing again the issue of state sector reform which emerged as the last battle ground of the reform. However, this frontier is ever important since it is not a simple and small isolated combat but can determine the direction of the whole war.

State enterprise reform has been at the core of a decade of economic reform in China since 1978. In its effort to cope with continuing economic inefficiency, the Chinese enterprise system has evolved from the profit retention and profit contract systems (1979 to the early 1980s) to the tax-for-profit system (1983 to 1985), the contracted management system since 1986, the experiment of the shareholding system since the late 1980s, and finally to the "corporatization" since the 1993.[1] However, the general judgement is that there is no significant success and that performance of state enterprises is worsening, particularly in financial

[1]Keun Lee, "Economic Reform and Privatization in China: Case Studies of Enterprises (in Korean)" Working Paper (Department of Economics, Seoul National University, 1994); Keun Lee, "Property Rights and Agency Problems in China's Enterprise Reform," *Cambridge Journal of Economics*, No. 17 (1993).

performance.[2]

This paper will review the whole evolution of the state sector reform to clarify the issue and analyze the continuing problems facing the state enterprises. Section 3 is devoted to such review, while section 4 address a more recent situation, and focuses on the issues of "corporatization" and "legal person socialism." Before these, the paper begins in the next section by first setting the background for the coming analysis and discussing the role of the state sector in the overall Chinese economic reform.

State Sector as a hindrance to Growth

Out of about 10,000 state-owned industrial enterprises, large and medium sized one accounts for less than one tenth of the total and less than 3 percent of the total industrial enterprises in China.[3] However, large-and-medium sized state industrial enterpries produce roughly half of the total industrial gross outputs and, more importantly, account for about 70 percent of the total fiscal revenues for the central government. Furthermore, if we accept that some industries are more important than other industries for a developing country like China, importance of state enterprises is greater than is represented by their shares in outputs. They are in charge of the so-called back-bone industries of energy, transportation, electricity, large-scale machinery, iron and steel, chemical, and so forth.

The Chinese dillemma is that performance of the state sector is more and more worsening in spite of a series of reform measures during the last 15 years. In 1992, about one third of the state

---

[2]Wing T. Woo, Wen Hai, Yibiao Jin and Gang Fan, "How Successful Has Chinese Enterprise Reform Been?: Pitfalls in Opposite Biases and Focus," Journal of Comparative Economics, 18:3 (1994); Lee, "Economic Reform and Privatization in China……."

[3]Beijing Weekly Press, ed.0, *Zhongguo guoyouqiye zhouxiang shichang* (China's State-owned enterprises running for markets), (Beijing: Shingxing chubanshi, 1993).

enterprises were making losses according to official statistics although it was believed that actual proportion of the loss-making enterprises was as high as two thirds due to many hidden losses. According to a recent report in the *Chinese Economic Daily* cited in Sin,[4] now about a half of all the state enterprises are now in deficits even by official standard. In other words, it seems to be certain that the trend of deteriorating performance is not stopped.

Of course, there exist a relatively large volume of literature finding improving performance of the state sector in China. Chen, et al. found total factor productivity growth of 5.5 percent in the 1979-85 period, which is much higher than the pre-reform period of 1957-78 of 0.9 percent.[5] Dollar got basically similar results by enterprise data.[6] As a more recent performance for the 1984-87 period, Jefferson, et al. found an annual TFP growth of 2.4 percent at the city/county level by estimating a gross-output production function.[7]

However, these empirical findings were challenged by a recent research results by Woo, et al. that there were zero TFP growth in state-owned enterprises.[8] Woo, et al. argued that the previous results confirming a positive TFP growth might be due to the underdeflation of gross output and overdeflation of intermediate inputs.[9] More importantly, they emphasized that criteria for performance assessment should include not only physical TFP but

---

[4]Taiyong Shin, "China trying hard to reduce the losses by state enterprises," *Silmul Kyungje* (in Korean), (October 26, 1994).

[5]Kuan Chen, et al., "Productivity Change in Chinese Industry, 1953-1985," *Journal of Comparative Economics*, 12:4 (1988), pp. 570-591.

[6]David Dollar, "Economic Reform and Allocative Efficiency in China's State-owned Industry," *Economic Development and Cultural Change*, 39:1 (1990), pp. 89-105.

[7]Gary Jefferson, et al., "Growth, Efficiency, and Convergence in China's State and Collective Industry," *Economic Development and Cultural Change*, 40:2 (1992), pp. 239-266.

[8]Woo, et al., *op. cit.*

[9]*Ibid.*

also financial performance (profitability), intertemporal efficiency, and implications for macroeconomic stability.

Woo et al. argued that an increase in technical efficiency does not necessarily mean that government revenue would increase commensurately.[10] They found that the proportion of net output of state-owned enterprises dispensed, directly and indirectly, to workers and managers has increased over time. This development has created a fiscal crisis for the government that threatens infrastructure investment and macroeconomic stability.

With my own empirical analysis of the state enterprise performance,[11] I agree with Woo et al.s view that there has been relatively few improvement of performance of the state sector, and the financial performance is specially important owing to implications for macroeconomic performance.

To the extent that the state sector's inferior performance resulted in lowering the average growth rate and that its financial behavior resulted in undesirable diversion of investment funds away from infrastructure construction, we can say that China's state sector played the role of a "hindrance" to growth.

A more detailed picture of the role of the state vs. non- state sectors during the last 15 years can be seen by the following analysis dividing the 15 years into the four sub- periods. The anlaysis begin with a brief description of China's reform strategy. China's reform strategy was to decentralize state property rights in mainly two dimensions. The first decentralization involved the transfer of state property rights to economic entities with a view to changing the behavior of existing entities or to create new entities. The second decentralization was to create a macroeconomic environment where new economic entities were to operate. The main processes of decentralization and the underlying economic rationale were as follows.

First, to change the behavior of existing state enterprises,

---

[10] *Ibid.*

[11] Keun Lee, "The Chinese Model of the Socialist Enterprise; An Assessment of its Organization and Performance," *Journal of Comparative Economics*, No. 14 (1990), pp. 384-400.

supervisory state organs transferred to the enterprises a part of their control rights in the area of production plans and marketing, while they maintained monitoring rights and income rights (taxation). To strengthen incentives, enterprises were granted a fraction of income rights in the form of profit retention, with workers obtaining a fraction of retained profits as bonuses. In rural areas, new economic entities were created with the demolition of the commune system. Independent household farming was revived on the basis of a separation of the state's income rights and peasants' control rights over production matters. Decentralization of property rights also involved privatization, which allowed emergence of private and collective enterprises, as well as selling and leasing of small state enterprises. The rather conservative rationale for allowing growth of the private sector has been that certain economic activities can be better performed by private actors, rather than by the state.

The second form of decentralization, to create a macroeconomic environment, involved the transformation of the resource allocation mechanism from one based on central planning to one that had a market orientation. Introduction of markets implied the possibility of competition for, and free transfer of, property rights. Market competition involved replacement of a disciplinary mechanism based on vertical control by another mechanism based on autonomous horizontal competition. It was expected that this change would result in higher economic efficiency in resource allocation.

In aggregate terms, China's reform strategies were successful in that the economy achieved an average 9.0 percent real GNP growth per annum and 7.5 percent real per capita GNP growth per annum over the last 14 years from 1978 to 1992 (see Table 1). The last 14 years can be divided into four sub- periods. We can investigate economic changes in each of the four sub-periods with a view to reveal the success secrets.

The first period is from the initiation of the reform in late 1978 to late 1984 when the Chinese declared the extension of the reform to include urban areas. Initiation of economic reform had an important impact on the performance of the Chinese economy.

Table 1. 15 Years of Reform in China

A. VALUES AND SHARES	1978	1984	1985	1988	1991	1992
1) Basics						
GNP, bil.RMB	358.8	696.2	855.7	1406.82	2023.63	2403.62
Fix.Prod.Inv. 100mil.RMB	58.3	82.9	115.6	201.2	217.6	418.2
Fix.Prod.Inv. '78 pr	58.3	49.7	61.4	80.1	73.8	125.4
GNP Index	100	166.9	188.2	251.2	295	333.4
GNP ('78 price)	358.8	598.8	675.3	901.3	1058.5	1196.2
growth rates		14.8%	12.8%	11.3%	8.2%	13.0%
GNP deflator	100.0	116.3	126.7	156.1	191.2	200.9
Population, mil.person	962.59	1038.7	1050.44	1110.26	1158.23	1171.71
Per capita GNP, Yuan	372.7	576.5	642.8	811.8	913.9	1020.9
Grain Product. 10000 tn	30477	40731	37911	39408	43529	44266
2) Gross Output by Sectors and Ownerships (current 100 million RMB)						
Agriculture	1397.0	3214.1	3619.5	5865.3	8157.0	9084.71
Industry, Total	4237.0	7617.3	9716.5	18224.6	28248.0	37065.71
Large & Med. size			4110.0	7422.5	12366.1	15917.44
State	3289.2	5262.7	6302.1	10351.3	14954.6	17824.15
Collective	947.8	2263.1	3117.2	6587.5	10084.8	14101.19
Rural collective firm	385.3		1423.3	3550.3	5935.4	8957.07
urban cooperatives				39.3	69.0	101.88
rural cooperatives			151.8	400.1	500.3	767.94
Urban collective firm			1542.2	2597.8	3580.1	4274.3
Individual business			179.8	790.5	1609.1	2806.8
rural			146.4	722.0	1479.8	2611.42
urban			33.4	68.5	129.3	195.38
Other Ownership			117.4	495.4	1599.6	2633.58

B. Average Annual Growth Rates	78-92	78-84	84-88	88-91	91-92
1) Basics					
GNP	14.6%	11.7%	19.2%	12.9%	18.8%
Fixed Productive Invest	15.1%	6.0%	24.8%	2.6%	92.2%
Fix.Prod.Inv.('78 price)	9.5%	3.4%	16.0%	-4.1%	82.9%
GNP Index	9.0%	8.9%	10.8%	5.5%	13.0%
GNP ('78 price)	9.0%	8.9%	10.8%	5.5%	13.0%
growth rates					
GNP deflator	5.1%	2.5%	7.6%	7.0%	5.1%
Population	1.4%	1.3%	1.7%	1.4%	1.2%
Per capita GNP	7.5%	7.5%	8.9%	4.0%	11.7%
Grain Production	2.7%	5.0%	-0.8%	3.4%	1.7%

2) Gross Ouput	78-92	78-85	85-88	88-91	91-92
Agriculture	14.3%	17.2%	17.5%	11.6%	11.4%
Industry, Total	16.8%	14.8%	23.3%	15.7%	31.2%
Large & Med. size	ERR	ERR	21.8%	18.5%	28.7%
State	12.8%	11.4%	18.0%	13.0%	19.2%
Collective	21.3%	21.9%	28.3%	15.3%	39.8%
Rural collective firm.	25.2%	24.3%	35.6%	18.7%	50.9%
urban cooperatives	ERR	ERR	ERR	20.7%	47.6%
rural cooperatives	ERR	ERR	38.1%	7.7%	53.5%
Urban collective firm	ERR	ERR	19.0%	11.3%	19.4%
Individual business	ERR	ERR	63.8%	26.7%	74.4%
rural	ERR	ERR	70.2%	27.0%	76.5%
urban	ERR	ERR	27.1%	23.6%	51.5%
Other Ownership	ERR	ERR	61.6%	47.8%	64.6%

Source: Calculations based on figures from *Zhongguo tongjinianjian* (Statistical Yearbook of China), 1993 and various years.

A closer look at the Chinese reform path reveals the important fact that the success of the reform was mainly due to the creation of new economic entities. Efforts to change the behavior of old economic entities such as urban state enterprises were generally unsuccessful. From 1978 to 1984, the main source of growth arose from the initial shock arising from the decentralizing reforms, and, in particular, the successes in agriculture that occurred with the transformation to individual peasant farming. Agricultural net output recorded a real growth of 7.4 percent per annum between 1978 and 1984, compared to the pre-reform period average of 1.8 percent (see Table 2 in Lee 1994a).[12] However, industrial net output maintained a growth rate that was almost the same as that of the pre-reform period, indicating no improvement in the performance of the state industrial sector.

The initial success with the agricultural reform brought in more than 800 million peasant families as strong support group for the reform. With confidence, the Chinese leadership declared the extension of reform to urban areas in late 1984, which was the

[12]Of course, there was a rapid increase in prices of agricultural products. However, there was also significant growth in physical terms, as seen by the average 5 percent growth of grain outputs.

beginning of the second sub-period ending in late 1988 with the macroeconomic cooling down of the overheated economy. During the second subperiod, the engine of growth switched to new economic entities in the non-state sector, especially private and rural collective enterprises.

After a peak harvest in 1984, grain harvest consistently declined in physical terms (see Table 1).[13] In contrast, during this period, the average annual growth rate of industrial net output jumped from 14.8 percent in the first period to 23.3 percent in current terms (Table 1). This increase was not due to the vitalization of the state sector but due to the remarkable growth and increasing importance of the non-state industrial sector. During this period, gross industrial production of state units increased less than 20 percent per annum in current terms, while gross industrial production of collective units, and individual businesses grew almost 30 percent and more than 60 percent, respectively (Table 1). Industrial output values of other ownership including foreign ventures grew at an average of 61.6 percent per annum.

The third sub-period was macroeconomic contraction and adjustment period, which run from late 1988 to 1991. Since the late 1980s, the economic situation worsened with serious inflation, material shortages, corruption, and emerging income inequality. All of these factors contributed to the Tiananmen crisis in 1989 and gave impetus to the partial recentralization drive. However, in 1991 a slow recovery began, and from 1992 up to the present is another boom for the Chinese economy. Table 1 shows that during the third sub-period real GNP grew at an annual average of 5.5 percent, while over the 1991 and 1992 period, it grew at 13 percent. The growth rates of industrial output by non-state economic entities dropped down siginificantly during the

[13]Although one reason for this would be the possible exhaustion of the shock effects of the reform, a more important reason is that individual farming weakens investment in irrigation and fertility maintenance which requires collectivist cooperation. State-initiated investment has also decreased since 1984. The 1984 record level of grain harvest was recovered only in 1989 as a result of massive investment since 1988.

third sub-period of recession. However, throughout the second, third, and fourth sub-periods, the relative order of growth rates was, in decreasing order, individual and other ownership firms, collectively-owned firms, and last state-owned firms.

In sum, any success that arose from the reform was mainly due to the creation of new economic entities domestically and inviting foreign entities from abroad. China succeeded in creating new dynamic economic entities in rural areas by a "revolutionary" demolition of the People's Commune to create individual family farming. The demolition of the Commune and distribution of communal assets to individual families in China provided the material basis for the emergence of non-state industrial enterprises in rural towns and suburban areas. In contrast, efforts to change the behavior of old economic entities such as urban state and large collective enterprises were relatively unsuccessful. In other words, China's state sector has now emerged as a hindrance to more rapid growth as it served to reduce the average growth rates. As a matter of fact, the inferior performance of the state sector is continuing in 1994; during the first half of 1994, the average growth rate of China's gross industrial output was 15.8 percent, whereas that by state industrial enterprises was only 4.4 percent.

Evolution of the State Sector Reform in China

In state ownership charactering the pre-reform state sector in China, property rights is centralized by the state apparatus, with the state bearing risks associated with these rights. Enterprises function as parts of the state apparatus. Thus, the entire decision process (initiation, ratification, implementation, and monitoring of decision-making) is allocated within the state apparatus. Neither the state bureaucracy nor enterprise managers and workers bear the value consequences of their decision-making, while the central leadership bears only the political riskassociated with economic performance. Economic risk is borne by the whole society. In other words, if the system does not perform well in terms of output, the whole society suffer in terms of less consumption.

Under the traditional state ownership, each state enterprise, as simply a part of the entire economic organ of the state, was not expected to be responsible for its own profit or loss. Profits were submitted to the state, and losses are covered by the state. The principal duty of enterprises was to accomplish plan targets. Profitability used to be only one of the many performance indicators and fulfillment of output targets was emphasized as the primary goal. While the objective function of the socialist state enterprise can also be operationalized into the framework of constrained maximization, the profit constraint, if any, tended to be weak or soft. If sufficient state credits and subsidies are assured as the result of the "soft budget constraint," the manager of the state enterprise had less concern for its profitability. In other words, state assets would not be used in a financially efficient manner.[14] In the socialist state enterprise, enterprise profits remitted to the state take the nature of combination of dividends and income taxes since the state is the owner of the enterprise assets. In contrast with capitalist corporations where dividends are alienable residual claims of shareholders, remitted profits are not completely alienable to socialist enterprises; profits of socialist state enterprise are first remitted to the state and then re-invested at the state's discretion.

As the behavioral assumption for human agents of opportunism has become increasingly valid in socialism, proper allocation of decision and control processes among enterprise members and adequate incentive provisions have emerged as important tasks in socialist enterprises, just as in capitalist firms. First of all, the owner in socialism, i.e. the state, is not a person but an abstract entity, and lower level bureaucrats are supposed to work

---

[14]Kornai argues that the budget constraint of socialist enterprises is "soft" due to substantial state intervention in the form of "soft taxation, soft subsidies, and soft credits." In this concept, allocative and productive inefficiencies persist because state enterprises can always count on state budgetary and financial resources to subsidize unprofitable operations. See Janos Kornai, "The Soft Budget Constraint," *Kylos*, 39:3 (1986), p. 30.

on behalf of the state. However, state bureaucrats are supervisory agents who also need to be properly motivated and monitored. Otherwise, there is always the possibility that the interests of the owner-state would be neglected by agents seeking irregular private benefits. Furthermore, the combination of state ownership and central planning results in a highly hierarchical structure of economic management, ranging from the top state bureaucrats down to lower level bureaucracy and party organs, managers, and finally workers. With this setup, the possibility of collusion among agents emerges. As Tirole argues, collusion is typical of most multi-tier hierarchical structures.[15] The more tiers a structure has, the more serious the problem of collusive activity. In state enterprises, the negative side-effects of collusion include the loosening of the monitoring mechanism and, in some cases, outright corruption.[16] The material basis for this loosening is the possibility of, or the temptation for, expropriation of the state assets.

In China, reform of the traditional model of the socialist state enterprise began with greater enterprise autonomy, which necessarily implied a change in the contract structure regarding enterprise management. In particular, enterprises were to assume responsibility for their own financial conditions. In the so-called "profit retention system," state enterprises were allowed to retain some portion of realized profits. The retained profits could be used for investment, collective welfare, and bonus funds. The idea, as opposed to the central reallocation, was that decentral-

---

[15]Jean Tirole, "Hierarchies and Bureaucracies: On the role of Collusion in Organization," *Journal of Law, Economics and Organization*, No. 2 (1986), pp. 181-214

[16]Here we use the term collusion only in a negative sense. For the positive aspect of collusion, we reserve the term, cooperation. As Aoki (1987) argues, the Japanese firm would be the case of cooperation among the owner, the management, and the workers. Masahiko Aoki, "The Japanese Firms in Transition," in Yamamura K. and Y. Yasuda, ed., *The Political Economy of Japan* (Stanford: Stanford University Press, 1987). Also for comparison of firms in China, Korea, and Japan, see Keun Lee, *Chinese Firms and the State in Transition: Property Rights and Agency Problems in the Reform Era* (New York & London: M.E. Sharpe, 1991). Especially Chapter 8.

ized investment and bonus payments would be more effective in stimulating enterprise and worker incentives. The enterprise funds accumulated from retained profits are also to play the role of risk or mortgage funds. In the event that realized profits were short of quota profits to be remitted to the state, the gap is filled with the enterprise funds.[17]

In terms of the decision process, lower level state bureaucrats are now supposed to be responsible for decision control, while the enterprise leadership, including the manager and the enterprise party committee, would be in charge of decision management.

The problems with this model of Chinese enterprise were mainly twofold: the incompleteness or ambiguity of the contract and the ex post weak enforceability of the contract. With the reform, property rights relations between the state and enterprise, in terms of both income and control rights, remained somewhat ambiguous, especially with regard to the retained profits. State control over the relative distribution of the retained profits into investment, collective welfare, and bonus funds was also arbitrary or ambiguous. The state function was to see to it that sufficient amounts of investment were guaranteed, while excessive bonus payments were checked. However, state enforcement was soft, and bonus payments and housing construction out of collective welfare funds grew beyond control. Given loose monitoring devices and a weak power base, the managers tended to collude with workers in paying bonuses and using collective welfare funds for worker housing construction in an extraordinarily generous and still egalitarian manner.[18]

In the past implementation of the profit retention or contract system, the most serious difficulties were encountered in setting the profit remission quota at an appropriate level and with an objective base. This difficulty has resulted in soft ex post enforce-

---

[17]Lee, "The Chinese Model of ……."

[18]Empirical analysis of the collusion is done in Keun Lee and Shelly Mark, "Socialist Egalitarianism and the Agency Problem in China's Economic Reform," *Seoul Journal of Economics*, 2:4 (1989), pp. 383-401.

ment of profit remission quotas, as well as substantial ex ante bargaining between the state authorities regarding the determination of the profit quotas. The later improved version of the profit contract system, the so-called contracted management system (chengbaozhi), sought to formalize the relationship between the state and the enterprise by introducing legal enforcement of contracts by the People's Court and public notarization.[19] However, the collusive behavior between local state organs and the enterprises in the determination and enforcement of the profit remission quota appears to have persisted throughout the reform decade.[20]

The main consequences of the various versions of profit remission systems were limited improvement of enterprise performance and the persistence of state fiscal deficits, although some improvement of the enterprise performance with the CMI model was verified.[21] In China, the mixed achievement with previous forms of enterprises generated debate on the strategies of enterprise reform. Two contrasting perspectives on continuing enterprise reform had emerged since the mid 1980's.[22] The first group sought to further improve the CMS, while the second and newer group focused on property right relations in the enterprise. This latter group argued that the source of the problem was that ambiguous property rights relations between the state and the enterprise turned into ambiguous distributional and control relations. This group also argued that the CMS did not promote efficient resource allocation. The reasons were that under the CMS, there was no automatic mechanism that inefficient enterprises were closed and merged, and new more efficient enterprises were created, and that enterprise investment behavior was constrained

[19]Lee, "The Chinese Model of ······."

[20]For more details on what collusive behavior remained and for the reasons, see Lee, *Chinese Firms and the State in Transition* ······.

[21]Lee, "The Chinese Model of ······."

[22]Conference (on the China's economic reform), "Quanguo jingi tizhi gaige lirun yantaohui zongshu (summary of the national conference on the theories of economic system reform)," *Zhongguo jingi tizhi gaige*, No. 12 (1988), pp.18-20.

by short-term profit considerations during the contract period, which was at most three or five years. Furthermore, under the CMS the state was still directly involved in bargaining and contracting with enterprises. Thus, it tended to preserve the state's habit of direct controls over enterprises. In this light, the CMS was not consistent with China's long term design of a new economic mechanism in which indirect controls substitute for direct control over enterprises.

The latter line of argument provided theoretical justification for the experiments with shareholding systems beginning the late 1980's. This motivation contrasts with the origin of the shareholding company in capitalism where it emerged mainly as a device to pool capitals. In the early days, most of the Chinese shareholding corporations were formerly collective enterprises, although the Chinese authorities had later enlarged the scope of their experiment to include state enterprises. What they aimed at with the shareholding system was the real separation of ownership and control. The experiment with shareholding system was an important innovation in that it, for the first time, dealt with property rights relations. It was politically sensitive because it meant that socialism was introducing one of the most typical capitalist institutions, the corporation, violating Marx's propostion that socialist distribution is according to labor, and not capital (property).

Introduction of the shareholding system in the late 1980s is to deal with arbitrariness in the distributional relations between the state and the enterprise and related incentive problems by addressing property rights issues. While the Chinese shareholding system represented a new move in China's continuous search for enhanced economic efficiency, however, the process has been constrained by various economic environmental and ideological conditions, and hence the status of the Chinese shareholding system was still marginal and in mixed form, keeping some elements of the traditional socialist state enterprises and attempting to incorporate some of the attributes of modern corporations.

In contrast to the state sector reform without much success, non-state sector grew rapidly since the mid-1980s and started to cause some problems in their interaction with state sector. Non-state enterprises took advantage of the general gap between the demand and the supply ability of state enterprises in a variety of items ranging from intermediate goods to consumer goods. The underdeveloped nature of China's distribution mechanism and infrastructure, including the transportation and communication systems, have also been taken advantage by non-state enterprises. Successful enterprises were more flexible and active in exploiting new markets, in seeking information about products, and in marketing beyond the boundary of their base localities.

As sales and purchasing activities expanded, rapid growth of the non-state economy increased interaction between the urban and rural economies and across different regions of the country. Subsequently, a competition problem between non-state and state enterprises arose, although China's non-state enterprises grew under both restrictive and supportive state policies.[23] Since the late 1980s, the problem has been most prevalent in competition for raw materials and energy, as the rapidly growing national economy required more and more intermediate inputs while more and more inputs were transactioned in markets rather than allocated by plans. Only those enterprises who could afford to pay higher market prices were able to obtain necessary inputs, and state enterprises found it increasingly difficult to obtain an adequate amount of inputs.

In the late 1980s, at a time of serious inflation, the general recognition was that financial decentralization and rapid growth of non-state sectors were the main causes of inflation.[24] This situation led to hot debate on the competition issue as well as on the issue of how to judge the nature of growth of the non-state sector. Especially since 1989, rural enterprises were increasingly criti-

---

[23]On the diverse attitudes toward non-state enterprises by state bureaucrats in China, see Chapter 7 of Lee, *Chinese Firms and the State* ······ and William Byrd, "Rural Industrialization and Ownership in China," *Comparative Economic Studies*, 32:1 (1990), pp. 73-107.

[24]The dual pricing system and price reform are also responsible for the shortage of intermediate inputs and inflation.

cized as being economically inefficient, causing pollution and nature destruction, engaging in tax evasion, and as being under unjustifiable protection by local state bureaucrats pursuing local interests.[25] The success of the rural enterprises was mainly attributed to strong private incentives, which, however, were not always consistent with the benefit of the whole economy. Such arguments provided an excuse for recentralization measures after the Tiananmen crisis in spring 1989.

The 1989 partial recentralization reenlarged the scope of centralized allocation of key materials and reemphasized the priority of large and medium-size state enterprises.[26] Many rural enterprises were closed or merged, and others were subject to strict taxation and controls. Non-state enterprises were urged to rely solely on locally available resources. Furthermore, the conservative leadership stopped the experiment of transforming state enterprises into shareholding companies. This situation signifies the dilemma facing the leadership between the rapid modernization and socialist emphasis on the state-owned industry. The recentralization and contractionary policies led the economy into an abrupt and serious downturn with the reemergence of the unemployment problem in 1989 and 1990.

Concerned about the social implications of economic stagnation, the central leadership had to again promote the positive role of non-state enterprises in creating jobs even before the end of 1989. Since then, the contractionary macroeconomic continued to be loosened, and finally Deng Xiaoping ordered the resumption of rapid growth in early 1992 when he visited Guangdong, the China's reform hub. In October 1992, the Chinese communist Party meeting adopted the so-called "Socialist Market Economy" as a new model for China, replacing the former slogan of the

---

[25]R. Delfs, "Jiangsu's Dynamic Rural Industry Comes Under Attack," *Far Eastern Economic Review* (September 14, 1989); A. Ignatius and A. Barnett, "China's Economic Wooes Post Risk of New Unrest," *The Asian Wall Street Journal* (August 7, 1989).

[26]On more detailed aspects of the recentralization, see Chapter 9 of Lee, *Chinese Firms and the State in Transition* …….

"Planned Commodity Economy." Since 1992, the Chinese economy entered a strong boom although it received another round of macroeconomic contractionary measures to cool down the overheating in mid 1993. Although the boom is continuing in 1994 with higher inflation rates than in 1993, performance, especially measured by profititability, of the Chinese state enterprises is showing no clear sign of improvement.

As about the two-third of the state enterprises turned out to be in de facto deficits, the Chinese authorities issued a new provisions, the so-called "transformation of the operation mechanism of the state enterprises" in July 1992. Basically, this provision was to further enlarge the autonomy of the state enterprises in the areas of production, input procurement, marketing, foreign trade, personnel managment, etc. Since then up to now, there is no clear sign that that measure stopped the trend of worsening performance of the state enterprises. It is within this background that the Chinese authorities has been recently trying the "corporatization" as a solution to the state sector problem. Transformation of the state enterprises into shareholding companies are now being tried as one form among many forms of corporatization.

Sources of the Problem and Seeking a Solution in Corporatization and "Legal Person Socialism"

The nature of the problem facing China's state enterprises can be seen in many dimensions. As is well known, worsening profitability is wide-spread throughout the China's state sector. One of the direct reason for this is considered as the shortage of operating capital. According to a survey done on 443 firms in Liaoning province, July 1993, more than 90 percent of them answered that the lack of funds are the first cause for the production abnormality.[27] These firms argued that especially during the

---

[27]Yaochun Sun, et al., "Shenhua guyougiye gaige jidaijiejuede nantiyuduici (Several Difficulties and Policies requiring Prompt Solution in deepening the reform of state enterprises)," *Jingji Yanjiu*, No. 30 (1994).

first half of financial disorder and inflation excessive financial diversion further aggravated the funds problem facing state units vis-a-vis non- state units where funds were flowing into.

Related to the funds shortage is the excessive financial burden of the state enterprises. The same survey in Liaoning reported that these firms have a cumulative total of 19.74 billion Yuan as debts, which is roughly two times as big as the total realized profits by these firms during the Seventh Five Year Plan period of 1986-90. The debts include losses in operating losses, to-be-paid welfare benefits including those to retired workers, and overdue-loans from banks. These firms estimate that "surplus" workers amounted roughly 23 percent of the whole workforce in them, and the number of retired workers is as large as 41.3 percent of the whole workforce. These retired or surplus workers simply mean the increasing financial burden of the enterprises since enterprises have to support them notwithstanding they do not produce at all or not as much as they are paid.

Since the ratio of profits to the operating funds is lower than the borrowing interest rates charged by the banks, enterprises cannot afford to have enough funds to pay back their loans. The survey reported that the amount used to repay interest and principal is as big as three times the amount of realized profits.[28]

Another direct cause for the worsening performance would be rising input costs problem, which can be regarded as more serious for the state enterprises than non-state enterprises. Owing to both price reform and inflation, prices of raw materials and many intermediate goods were liberalized from control and hence mostly increased substantially. This eliminated one of the last benefits state enteprises used to enjoy. In the past with the dual track system, state enterprise were able to get inputs at lower prices than market prices. Not only raw materials but also increasing transportation costs and wage rates are the aggravating factors for the state units. The Chinese estimate is that about 30 percent of the losses can be accounted for by these cost push factors.[29]

[28]*Ibid.*

If the above mentioned aspects are about the nature itself or more direct causes of the worsening performance of the state enterprises, more important would be structural or more fundamental causes for the performance deterioration.

First, rising and often unfair competiton between state and non-state enterprises should be pointed out in this regard. In the past, different-ownership-based firms have been treated differently in many aspects. Especially important is the tax treatment. Only in 1994 the comprehensive fiscal reform equalized the income tax rates for all kinds of enterprises across different ownership. State enterprises used to be subject to higher 55 percent income tax rates, whereas foreign-capital-invested firms (*sanzi qiye* in Chinese) and township-and-village enterprises(TVEs) were subject to lower tax rates in average, or benefitted from tax exemptions as long as their accouting profits are negative.

Another disadvantage of state units are their limited access to cashes. Most of their transactions are done in their bank accounts using bank checks, whereas transactions of non- state units rely heavily on cashes. Given the situation of wide-spread circular debts among enterprises, access to cashes has been a critical instrument for competition, which can give users a better deals in transactions.[30]

In sum, it can be said that the above-mentioned disadvantages and other disadvantages assciated with the regulation and practices of central planning contributed to the worsening performance of the state enterprises. However, a more fundamental issue is that of property rights between the state and enterprises and within an enterprises as has been well documented by section 3 above.

Despite numerous effort in this regard by the Chinese authoriteis, it can still be argued that property rights issues are not solved clearly in many state enterprises. Although enterprises were given the status of a legal person and the rights of ownership and management were declared to be separated by legal

---

[29]Shin, *op. cit.*

[30]Sun, et al., *op. cit.*

measurs, the legally independent status in name does not seem to have really freed enterprises from arbitrary interference by state authorities and bureaucrats who seek to protect thier vested interests.[31]

The property rights problem between the state and enterprises leads to the distribution problem between the state and enterprises. As well documented in section 3, the determination of the profit remission quota and value of state shares and their corresponding dividends has always been subject to arbitrary bargaining and practices. A vicious cycle has been working such that small profits lead to small profit tax and small retained profits, and hence to small investment or operating funds, and to small profits in the next year.

Internal managment practices have not improved much, either.[32] They are still not so much sensitive to economic efficiency in the management of physical and human resources. Although rising input prices were mentioned above, the real problem is that they are not used efficiently; socialist inefficiency in energe uses are quite well-known. Distribution of bonuses and promotion is still more or less based on egalitarian principle, and the same is true of hiring and inside placement. These features, combined with out-dated machinery and equipment, are the cause for the worsening performance of the enterprises.

A short term response by the Chinese authorities to the ever-aggravating situation in the state sector seems to be a "more selective subsidizing combined with a more tough discipline." They are going to allow more and more enterprises into bankruptcy based on a more rigorous assessment of their potentials or nature of problems. For those enterprises whose losses are judged as temporary, the authorities have decided to resume bank loans or subsidies despite the overall policy direction for macroeconomic contraction to low inflation rates.

An increasing incidence of bankruptcy has been confirmed, and there have emerged many new factors which would let

[31] *Ibid.*

[32] *Ibid.*

bankruptcy happend more.[33] One of the new factors include the 1994 tax reform, which has changed the incentive structure facing the local government in the direction to allowing more bankruptcy.[34] In the past, the local government had incentives to keep loss-making enterprises by giving subsidies or loans because the enterprises paid back the local government turnover taxes as long as they kept producing something. However, with the tax reform, most of the turnover taxes goes to the central government. Thus, the local governments would feel less inclined to expend their own money to loss making local state-owned enterprises.

A more important, longer term response by the Chinese authorites to the worsening performance of the state sector seems to be the "corporatization." By corporatization, they seems to mean establishing inside Chinese enterprises such institutions and organizational structure as seen in modern corporations in capitalist economies, including the board of directors, auditors, shareholder's meeting, president, and corporate constituion. The objective of corporatization is to establish firmly the legal person status of the enterprises and a more clear-cut separation of ownership and management by modernizing corporate government structure.[35]

In the past, such instituions were introduced in only those firms which transformed themselves from an state-owned enterprises to a shareholing corporations. The new "corporatization" means that state-enterprises are to be transformed into corporation and introduce such institutions as the board of directors, auditors, and so forth, regardless of whether they adopt the shareholing system or not. A total of 100 large-and-medium sized

---

[33]Wuyi Wang, "Guanyu woguo guoyouqiye pochanqing quangde yinsu fenxi (On the Causes of Bankruptcy in China's State-owned Enterprises)," *Jingji Yanjiu* (June 1994).

[34]*Ibid.*

[35]Shuangyin Dong, "Gongyouzhi qiye tuishing gongcizhede tantao (Probing into Public Ownership Practicing Corporate System)," *Jingjililunyu jingjiguanli*, No. 2 (1994).

state enterprises are selected for this experiment of corporation. Three forms of corporations are tried, including a corporation with 100 percent state shares (*duzi gongci*), a limited corporation (*youxian ziren gongci*) invested by 2-5 shareholders with limited responsibility, and a limited shareholding corporation (*gufen youxian gongci*) based on a large number of shareholders.

The third form, a limited shareholding corporation, is nothing other than the most typical capitalist corporate form. In other words, shareholding corporation, for which they used to show some reservation for an ideological reason, is now allowed more openly as one form of corporatization. It is certain that among the three forms a shareholding corporation will be the most important experiment because it can leads to real privatization as the aggregate share of private shareholders increases beyond the 50 percent or higher. The Chinese authorities know this possibilities, and, therefore, they have declared that they will keep the spirit of public ownership by encouraging not individual shareholders but public-oriented legal person shareholders.[36]

In their design, the so-called public-oriented or publicly-owned legal persons include the state asset management committee under the standing committee of the People's Congress, banks, People's Insurance Company of China (PICC), investment companies, the pension funds, the labor unions, other state enterprises, and other non-profit organizations.

By maintaining the shares held by these pubic institutions, they are going to keep socialization of share ownership and prevent its concentration on any individual's hands. Such model can be called "legal person socialism," which is neither socialist state monopoly nor capitalist private monopoly. The basic idea behind the legal person socialism seems to be the ideological concern that people's socialism allowing a large share for indiviudal shareholders for state enterprises can, sooner or later, end up with people's capitalism.

---

[36]Jinglian Wu, "Directions of Development and Prospects of Market Economy in China (in Korean)," paper presented at the seminar hosted by Korea-China Friendship Association (Seoul, 1993).

Along this line of argument for the legal person socialism lies closely such idea of "running by people (minying)" which is recently emphasized in opposition to both "running by bureaucrats (guanying)" and "privatization (siyouhua)."[37] They seems to hope shareholding corporation to promote running by people with maintaining the basically public nature of ownership. Therefore, they are to avoide the old style "running by bureaucrats" under the state ownership as well as capitalist "privatization" under the private ownership.

The idea of "legal person socialism" seems to be already being implemented. When I visited the Nanhai Polyester shareholding corporation in the Nanhai city of Guangdong province, I found that although the enterprise was transformed into a shareholding corporation, the authorities did not allow individual shareholders.[38] Individual workers in the company, therefore, put their money into the labor union, and the union became a shareholder for the company. The interviewed personnel told me that Chinese people knew well how to get around the state regulations. In this form, the labor union participates as one legal person shareholder in the enterprise decision making, however, dividends go to each investor individual. I was, of course, told that not such disguised legal person but real legal person sharehoders also exist.

Now, let me ask where the great potentials of the shareholding corporations would lie, in other words, what is the chance for success. My visits in 1993 to several state enterprises which are transformed into shareholding corporations have found that the most important contributions of this new system are the following two.[39] First, according to interviews, the shareholding corporatization helped to increase capital through the issuance of stocks. This seems natural because the shortage of funds has been one of the most serious difficulties facing Chinese state firms.[40]

---

[37]Yingqiu Liu, "Zhongguo jingji minyinghuade biyaoxinghe xianshixing fenxi (Analysis of the mecessity and feasibility of denationalization in China)," *Jingji Yanjiu*, No. 6 (1994).

[38]For details, see Lee, "Economic Reform and Privatization ……."

[39]*Ibid.*

This finding is actually re-confirmation of my earlier argument based on the case studies done in 1988 in Lee and Mark where capital expansion was identified as the important contribution as well as motivation for transformation into a shareholding corporation.[41]

Second, the transformation into shareholding corporations is also regarded to have worked positively in reducing arbitrary interference of state authorities, and this finding is also the same as the finding of case studies in 1988 in Lee and Mark.[42] In my opinion, the first benefit can come only through the transformation into a shareholding companies, however, the second benifits can come independently from such transformation. As a matter of fact, in the case of the Shanghai Second Textile Machinery Corporation, the cutting of interference seemed to have happened owing to special favors given by the Shanghai Municipality expanding enterprise autonomy.[43]

If we accept the expansion of capital as the most important contribution of shareholding corporations, then the offical idea of legal person socialism comes under some doubt regarding its chance for success. Since, in current Chinese society, those who are getting rich are neither the state nor public institutions, but individuals, the potential of shareholding corporations can realize only when they can attract more and more individual shareholers' money. However, more individual shareholders means "people's socialism" which can soon result in people's capitalism, but is distant from the vision of legal person socialism. If anything similar to legal person socialism continues, that will be a disguised legal person socialism as seen by the case of the Nanhai polyester company where individuals invest through the labor union.

Then, we can say that if the idea of the legal person socialism is going to succeed, performance of state enterprises has to improve

---

[40]Sun, et al., *op. cit.*

[41]Lee and Mark, *op. cit.*, pp. 157-173.

[42]*Ibid.*

[43]Lee, "Economic Reform and Privatization ⋯⋯."

"now" when the state is yet the dominant shareholders for most state enterprises. The current success will lead into further accumulation of investable funds at the public hands, and public share can expand. However, if it fails, which seems more likely, the share of the state or public organs will diminish in relative terms and the idea of legal person socialism will be difficult to realize.

Then, we have to ask what is the chance for success with the model of a shareholding corporation. In this regard, the first difficulty would be how to solve the arbitrary distribution problem between the state and the corporation persists, being translated into the problem of how much should be paid as dividends for the state share and how much is the value of the original state asset. As Lee and Mark observes,[44] the phenomenon of expropriation of state asset for irregular private continues, and the problem of who should represent the state share in the shareholder's meeting also continues.

As Lee and Mark[45] and Ma[46] argues, the problems arise not only from the intrinsic characteristics of the shareholding corporation system, but also from the external institutional environment. That is, various agency cost-reducing mechanisms such as capital markets, the managerial and ordinary labor markets, markets for corporate control, and the final threat of bankruptcy are not institutionalized nor fully functioning in China. Without such devices, the simple pursuit of separation of ownership and control would have limited potential for micro and macro efficiency. In sum, the experiment of shareholding corporations can be said to be yet constrained by various economic environmental and ideological conditions, and hence there lies a great uncertainty in the future of this experiment.

---

[44]Lee and Mark, *op. cit.*, pp. 157-173.

[45]*Ibid.*

[46]Jun Ma, "Gufenzhide guojijinglianju jidui zhongguode jiejianyiyi (International experiences with shareholding corporations and their implications for China)," *Jingji Yanjin*, No. 4 (1994).

Conclusion

The reform of the state enterprise system in China has evolved from the traditional state enterprise to the initial reform models with various profit retention systems, the contracted management system, and to the shareholding corporation system, and recently has adopted the corporatization as the catch-phrase. The analytical review in this paper has traced the evolution and identified continuing problems in the reform process. The whole enterprise reform process had centered around the issues of property rights regarding the relative distribution of profits among the state, enterprises, and workers, as well as the agency problem typified by the dual collusion.

Transformation of the old state enterprises into shareholding corporations is now tried as one form of corporatization. In order to avoid both old socialist state monopoly and capitalist private monopoly, the Chinese authorities intend to encourage public-oriented legal persons as shareholders for these shareholding corporations. Feasibility of such idea, which can be termed as "legal person socialism," depends critically on the current performance with shareholding corporation movement. However, to the extent that the potentials of the shareholding corporation experiment has to do with its ability to attract new financial resources by selling shares, it has certainly to invite more and more individual shareholders. That is because it is not public- oriented institutions but individuals who accumulate money and get rich in contemporary Chinese society.

Then, the Chinese dillemma is that more individual shareholders mean "peoples' socialism" which can soon degenerate into people's capitalism. Regardless of this dillemma, the transformed shareholding corporations should have themselves look attractive enough to sell stocks to individuals, if they are going to absorve private money anyway. That means, only aready-well-performing state enterprises will be transformed into shareholding corporations. For those many inefficient state enterprises, simple change of the name to a shareholding corporation would be neither permitted nor a solution for the problem.

7

China's Strategy for High Technology: Reform, R&D, and the Global Search for Asset Complementarity

Richard P. Suttmeier
(University of Oregon)

Introduction

The image of an increasingly powerful and prosperous China has captured the attention of business leaders, security planners, environmental activists, and ordinary citizens around the world. However, though much in demand, accurate assessments of the balance between China's impressive strengths and quite formidable problems continue to be elusive. Enough is known of the promise to make China a favored destination for foreign investment by firms from the OECD world and from the Asian region, and an object of foreign policy concern among its friends and neighbors.

Important variables in shaping China's future economic and military courses, and thus our understandings of its regional and global impacts, are those pertaining to how China acquires, develops and uses modern technologies. China is engaged in the global economy as never before, and has imported technologies worth over $US 40 billion since the open door policy was launched in 1978, with these technology transfers now yielding impressive economic returns.[1] In the past three years, many of the world's high technology leaders have been streaming to China to help launch a series of important and ambitious ventures. Meanwhile, China continues to develop plans for its own high technology research projects and industrial development. With particular attention to these domestic programs, this chapter explores the nature and prospects for China's strategy for high technology and its implications for China's regional and global roles.

Background Considerations

China's current high technology development is occurring under conditions of rapid domestic and international change. Domestic economic institutions are the object of major redesign, with reform policies in science and technology both following the wider economic reforms and serving, more independently, as a prod for continuing institutional change in the political economy more generally. The international context is also changing rapidly.

The end of the cold war has meant that mechanisms to restrict the international flow of high technology on security grounds, such as COCOM, have either been abolished or have been drastically liberalized. International concerns for global ecological sustainability are raising new questions about the uses of technologies, and the trajectories technological development should take. Technological capabilities are diffusing more widely to a variety of countries and a highly integrated global economy is becoming a reality. The Asian region has become a magnet for attracting

[1]Ryuji Sato, "China High-Tech Spree Pays Dividends," The Nikkei Weekly (November 7, 1994), p. 24.

technologies from around the world, and increasingly sophisticated indigenous research and development capabilities in the countries of the region are making Asia a source for new technologies and scientific understandings as well.[2] China's high technology, increasingly, is intertwined with both this Asian regional technosystem and the knowledge flows of the global economy.

China shares with other nations many of the challenges of finding the special conditions which seem to be required for high technology development, i.e., the often elusive combinations of research competence, capacity for technological innovation, and ability to realize new wealth from technical mastery. As recent comparative studies of the dynamics of technological progress make clear, such progress is usually the product of a series of interacting factors – a virtuous combination of technological opportunities, public policies, market conditions, human resources, and institutional and organizational resources.[3]

In the suggestive terms of David J. Teece, commercial success in technological innovation involves the ability to orchestrate an ensemble of "core" technological resources and "complementary assets" (competitive manufacturing capabilities, distribution channels, service provision and complementary technologies). These must then be harmonized with the relevant stages of product development and the characteristics of the extant "appropriability regime" (understood as a function of the legal protections for intellectual property and the ease with which a technology can be copied).[4] For China, the elements of the ensemble are being assembled from technical resources found in the international environment and from its own rich pool of human talents

---

[2]See, Denis Fred Simon, ed., The Emerging Technological Trajectory of the Pacific Rim (Armonk, NY. M.E. Sharpe, Inc., 1995).

[3]See, for example, Nathan Rosenberg, Ralph Landau, amd David Mowery, eds., *Thchnology and the Wealth of Nations* (Stanford, CA. Stanford University Press, 1992).

[4]David J. Teece, "Strategies for Capturing the Financial Benefits from Technological Innovation," in Rosenberg, et al., pp. 175-206.

and organizational assets. The orchestration involves the progressive solution of a series of challenging policy problems pertaining to the institutional arrangements for high technology in China.

The language of complementarity assets is appealing in trying to understand China's high technology development experience. China's early commitment to building scientific and technological capabilities after the Communist victory in 1949 indicated that the new Chinese leadership had more than a passing appreciation for the importance of developing "core technologies." But, as in other socialist economies, serious misunderstandings of the roles of "appropriability regimes" and "complementarity assets," meant that the considerable investments China made in R&D in support of core technologies over the years had, at best, marginal economic impact during the Maoist period.

Nevertheless, we can trace China's commitment to new, science-based technologies back to the 1950's, with its adoption of the 12 year plan (1956-67) for S&T development. This plan led to the introduction into China of capabilities in such fields as computers, semi-conductors, automation, radio electronics, nuclear and jet propulsion technologies.[5] These early efforts were successful in giving China a knowledge base for mastering a whole series of technical challenges in the then "new" technologies. Yet, the mid-1950's goal of developing a broad base of generic, science-based technological capacities, fell victim to the development of more specialized (and highly classified) competence in the military sphere, to the great detriment of the economy and of scientific research. Except for military applications, not much was gained from this expensively acquired knowledge base for many years; indeed, even in the military realm, the value of the knowledge base seemingly declined over the course of two decades as the radical politics of the Cultural Revolution decade (1966-76) disrupted established research projects and the training of new cohorts of scientists and engineers.

---

[5]State Science and Technology Commission, *Guide to China's Science and Technology Policy, 1986* (*White Paper on Science and Technology, No. 1. Hereafter, White Paper*),(Beijing, 1987), p. 16.

By the end of the Maoist years, then, China's national system of innovation had become distorted by the demands of poorly formulated national security missions, and had seen its capacity for innovating core technologies dissipated. Years of political interference in the R&D system, isolation from international centers of research and innovation, and an economic system which was indifferent - if not hostile - to the challenges of product and process innovations, had taken their toll.

China's current high technology aspirations must be seen against this background. The reform program which began in 1978 has been addressed to the righting of the wrongs of the Maoist past, both in terms of the R&D system and the system of complementarity assets needed to capture value from technological opportunities. Since 1978, as Chinese high technology objectives have become clearer, and understandings of innovation more sophisticated, the high tech strategy has - in stages - become more complex and differentiated.6

In many of its essentials, the strategy resembles those of other countries in Europe, Asia, and North America. To participate profitably in the global high technology economy, it calls for the development of domestic capabilities through high profile national programs and for mutually beneficial, complementary linkages with high tech players abroad. China's strategy is distinctive, however, because of the special legacy of scientific and technological development from the Maoist period, and the intimate linkage of current high tech efforts to a wider, economic and political reform project. China's underlying justification for its high technology efforts – why a poor country with abundant inexpensive industrial labor resources should pursue high technology – are tied to these features.

China entered the post-Mao era with an enormous technical

---

[6]An excellent alalysis of the evolution of S&T reform policy is found in Gu Shulin. "A Review of Reform Policy for the S&T System in China: From Paid Transactions for Technology to Organizational Restructuring," Paper presented to the UNU/INTECH Workshop on "Restructuring of Industrial R&D Institutions in China" (Maastricht, June 29-July 1, 1994).

establishment which, by 1990, had grown to over 5,000 research and development organizations, employing 617,000 personnel, of whom 407,800 were scientists and engineers.[7] Largely because of the industrial dispersion program of the 1960's and 1970's (known as the "Third Front Construction Project"), which moved strategic industries to China's interior for national defense reasons, China's R&D assets for high technology are also found at a number of centers around the country, and are not confined to the eastern coastal areas of the country, as is often assumed.[8] With such a relative abundance of human and material resources for high technology, China's leaders ask themselves why the country is not richer and stronger.[9] Since the beginning of the 1980's, the answer has been that the policies and institutions of the Maoist

---

[7]State Science and Technology Commission, *China Science & Technology Statistics: Data Book, 1992*.(Bejing: State Science and Technology Commission, 1993), p. 9.

[8]Sichuan, Yunnan, and Shaanxi provinces, for instance, all have large concentrations scientists and engineers and facilities, and are actively seeking to employ these in new high tech efforts. See, for instance, Ma Lie, "Shaanxi Gears Up High-Tech Production," *China Daily* (February 8, 1994),. p. 1. in Foreign Broadcast Information Service(FBIS) FBIS-CHI-94-027. (February 9, 1994), p. 62; He Zhiquiang. "Orient Towards the Twenty-First Century in the Development of Yunnan's High Technology Industries," *Yunnan Ribao* (February 11, 1993), p. 6. in Joint Publications Research Service(hereafter, JPRS)JPRS-CST-93-009 (May 13, 1993), pp. 4-5.

[9]Writing in 1981, one of China's senior science policy analysts bemoaned the fact that,

"China and Japan began their respective research on semiconductors at about the same time and China succeeded in the experimental production of a transistorized computer before Japan did, and China successfully developed a laser less than one year after the first laser came on the international scene. Today China has substantial production in its semiconductor industry, computer industry and laser industry and tens of thousands of production workers in these industries, but we have fallen behind international standards in these areas."

Luo Wei, "The Position and Role of the Academy of Sciences in the Chinese Research System," *Ziran Bianzhengfa Tongxun.*, 3:3 (June 10, 1981), in JPRS 81620, p. 20.

era have been inappropriate and were in need of reform. With reformed institutions, and the right policies, high technology – not low cost factory labor – can become China's ticket to wealth and power.[10]

---

[10]An important question for understanding the rationales for Chinese high technology has to do with comparative advantage and how it is perceived in China. While much of China's rapid economic growth over the past decade seemingly supports a view that China's comparative advantage in manufacturing lies in the availability of low cost labor, it is clear that some people in China are skeptical about the viability of a labor intensive development strategy. Writing in 1990, for instance, Li Xu'e, Vice-Minister of the State Science and Technology Commission(SSTC) argued that,

"⋯although in labor-intensive industries China has the advantage of cheap labor, we lack clear advantages in such other factors critical to product competitiveness as product quality, modern management, and after sales service ⋯the added value produced by these industries is small, and the competition among undeveloped countries is fierce," Li Xu'e, "Some Problems in the Development of China's High Technology Industry," *Zhongguo Keji Luntan (Forum on Science and Technology in China*), No. 6 (November 18, 1990) in JRPS-CST-90-008.

This same sentiment was expressed more recently in a report on a 1992 work conference on science and technology which stated that,

"China sees a grim future for its labor intensive processing industry in the present technology-intensive world. Developing its own high-tech industry is the way out," *China Daily* (March 11, 1992), p. 1 in FBIS-CHI-92-049(March 12, 1992), p. 35.

Cleary, for some Chinese leaders, the determination of comparative advantage is not a simple matter. Although China remains an underdeveloped country by many measures, in one respect- its large number of scientists and engineers - it is more like a developed country. Furthermore, China has also had considerable experience with high technology research and production as a result of its strategic weapons programs, and already has a high tech industry capable of producing goods and services annually worth more than 1100 billion yuan. When the rates of labor productivity found in hanicrafts, traditional industry and high tech industry are compared, China's high tech boosters conclude that

"If China is to reach a comfortably well-off standard of living with a fairly short period of time and catch up with the moderately developed countries, it must energetically developed high technology industries," He Zhiqiang, "Orient Towards⋯⋯"

High Technology Development in the Deng Xiaoping Era - Evolution and Key Programs

The first major effort to rectify the problems of the Maoist period came at the 1978 National Science and Technology Conference. The S&T development plan announced at that occasion was strongly oriented towards high technology. It identified 108 key projects in 8 priority areas: agriculture, energy, materials, microelectronics, lasers, space, high energy physics, and genetic engineering. Within a year of its announcement, however, this plan was being reconsidered. By the early 1980's its emphasis on basic research and high technology had been toned down considerably in the face of judgments that these were too far removed from China's immediate economic needs, and that shortages of both money and high quality manpower argued against a major push into high technology at that time.

Key Technologies R&D Program

Policy and planning attention for S&T, therefore, turned to the more pragmatic concerns of the 6th Five Year Plan (FYP) (1980-85) for the economy. High technology development was not entirly excluded, however; work on large-scale integrated circuits, computers, computer software, communications (including optical fibers, microwaves, satellites, digital exchanges, and networks), biotechnology, new materials, space technology and remote sensing, lasers, and isotopes and radiation technology was supported under the Plan.[11] Many of these areas of research received a boost when they were included in the "Key Technologies R&D Program"(keji gongguan jihua, lit., "Scientific and Technological Key Projects Program") of the 7th Plan when it was adopted in 1986.[12] Support of research relevant to high technology through the key Technologies R&D Program and the regular planning process continues into the current 8th plan, albeit

[11]White Paper, 1986, 189-215.

[12]White Paper, 1986, p.153.

with a growing emphasis on reform. Administration of the plan now has a multilevel structure – national, sectoral, regional- instead of being a single, nationally administered effort as in the 6th and 7th plan periods. Sources of financing have becoming more diverse, and elements of competition are being introduced into funding decisions.[13]

The "863" Program

Attitudes towards more focused commitment to high technology development began to change in the mid-1980's. More funds were becoming available for S&T, the technical manpower pool was expanding with new graduates and the return of technical personnel from advanced study abroad,[14] and the understanding and appreciation of the world high technology revolution among Chinese policy makers was deepening. A consensus began to emerge, therefore, that China could not afford *not* to get into high technology more ambitiously. In March of 1986, laser specialist Wang Dahang and three other senior scientists wrote to Deng Xiaoping urging the initiation of a new national high technology program. The Party Central Committee approved the idea in October, and the program began in early 1987 as the National High Technology Development Program, or "863" Program (as in 86/3 - March, 1986 – when the original proposal was drafted). As originally conceived, the Program aimed,

> "… to pool together the best technological resources in China over the next 15 years to keep up with internatioonal high technology development, bridge the gap between China and other countries in several most impor-

[13]Department of Planning, State Science and Technology Commission. *The Main Programmes of Science and Technology* (Beijing: State Science and Technology Commission, 1992), p. 8.

[14]The number of individuals working in S&T in state organizations increased by 38..6% between 1982 and 1987. In this same period, there were 1.863 million college and university graduates, and some 69,000 recipients of graduate education in China(in all fields), *Liaowang*, 15 (April 11, 1988) in JRPS-CAR-88-023, p. 17.

> tant areas, and wherever possible, strive for breakthroughs.The program also aims to provide technological backup for economic development and train large numbers of talents for the future."[15]

The Program identified seven priority fields (based on then current capabilities in China, and Chinese assessments of what will be the truly important areas in the year 2000). These included biotechnology, space technology, information technology, laser technology, automation, energy, and advanced materials.

The overall management of the Program is divided between the Basic Research and High Technology Department of the State Science and Technology Commission and the National Defense Science, Technology and Industry Commission. Its actual administration employs an innovative (for China at the time) competitive peer-review system. Each of the seven areas above has a senior expert advisory committee. Below these are 15 "expert task groups"(involving a total of 106 scientists and engineers) who designate projects warranting support, and who review the progress of grants on an annual basis. In project selection, the Program uses both a "bottom up" approach, with project ideas originating from potential investigators (inspired by US practice), and the "top down," more targeted approach favored by the Japanese.[16]

The 863 Program has been a source for additional R&D resources and more enlightened research administration since its inception. Chinese officials have reported that there were some 400 important achievements from the program during the 7th plan period, with 54 of these being world class. Successes to date have been reported in projects dealing with opto-electronics, lasers, rice germination, hepatitis b vaccine, and new materials. In addition, 15 new research centers in the fields of biology, information, automation, new materials and energy have been estab-

---

[15]*An Outline of the Hi-Tech Development Program in China* (Beijing: The Science and Technology Leading Group of the State Council, 1987).

[16]The "top down" priorities for the 1990s can be found in *The Main Programmes of Science and Technology* , pp. 11-14.

lished to support the program, including R&D centers working on computer integrated manufacturing systems (CIMS), intelligent computers, intelligent robots, optoelectronic processing, artificial crystals, and genetically engineered vaccines, medicines, and other bio-products.[17]

As originally conceived, the primary purpose of the 863 Program - through research and international technology monitoring - was to prepare China for the high technology challenges of the turn of the century. Nevertheless, some of the results of "863" are finding their way into applications, and research results during the remainder of the 1990's are expected to have commercial potential.

The "Torch" Program

Concerns for the commercialization of research, including, but not limited to the 863 Program, prompted the initiation of the "Torch" Program in August, 1988. Torch is administered by the Torch High Technology Industry Development Center (established in 1989) under the Industrial Science and Technology Department of the SSTC. Like other high tech initiatives, Torch is very much a product of the broader reform environment. Its approach to problems of moving research to production shows the influence of 10 years of exposure to foreign innovation systems, and its foci of attention are the new organizational forms (eg., start-up firms), and institutional possibilities (eg., high tech development zones) which emerged in the 1980s and early 1990s.

The Plan's main objectives include the following:[18]

1. *Policy Guidance.* Provide policy guidelines conducive to the growth of high technology industry and the transfer of knowledge from laboratory to

---

[17]*The Major Programmes,* p. 16; Yang Zhaobo and Yang Ning, "863 Plan Promotes High Technology Application," *XINHUA Domestic Service* (August 16, 1993) in FBIS-CHI-93-165 (August, 27, 1993), p. 26.

[18]See three important articles translated from *Zhongguo Keji Luntan* (*Forum on Science and Technology*), No. 16 (November 18, 1989), pp. 2-1 in JPRS-CST-90-008 (March 15, 1990), pp. 1-13.

enterprise. The main focus of this work is to cooorditate policy for, and oversee, existing(or planned) special economic zones for high technology enterprises(see below).

2. *Establishment of Technology Enterprise Service Centers.* Some 30 of these were to be established during the first few years of the Program. Borrowing from the Western concept of "technology incubators," the centers provide comprehensive services and information pertaining to finance, equipment procurement, marketing, taxes, foreign travel, etc. to those(especially scientists and engineers) seeking to establish new companies. The Donghu New Science and Technology Startup Services Center in Wuhan served as the prototype.

3. *Training.* During its first few years, the Program sought to provide management training for up to 20,000 individuals(typically, scientists and engineers with no prior commercial experience) in many aspects of operating high technology firms for both the domestic and international markets.

4 .*Finance.* The Torch Program was established with a limited budget, and thus approaches the financing of high tech start ups more as a broker than a banker. The Program uses its influence to facilitate loans and investments from banks and local governments with promises of payback periods of 3-4 years. The Industrial and Commercial Bank of China was especially active in supporting the Program initially, providing RMB 200 million and $US 10 million in 1988 and 1989.[19]

5. *Organize Specific Projects Valued by the State.* Some 272 such projects(out of 1,500 project proposals received) were supported during 1988 and 1989 in five major areas designated as priorities - new materials, microelectronics and information, energy (high efficiency and conservation technologies), biotechnology and electromechanical devices("mechatronics"). Approximately RMB 1.5 billion has been invested in support of these projects. This investment was expected to produce returns of RMB 5.6 billion annually and earn some $US 580 million in annual exports.[20] By the end of 1991, the number of nationally supported projects of this sort had grown to over 800, drawing investments of RMB 4.6 billion and $US 123 million.[21]

When it began, the Torch Program assumed an active level of international cooperation as part of its efforts to build a structure of complementary assets. The program was opened to foreigh

---

[19]XINHUA(April 19, 1990) in FBIS-CHI-90-077 (April 20, 1990), p. 34.

[20]*Ibid* .

[21]The Main Programmes, p. 24. These figures do not include locally projects conducted under the Torch policy umbrella. These unmber some 1,900 and involve RMB investments which approximate the national projects.

investment, and contacts have been made with foreign venture capital firms. Since the Chinese market for high tech was believed to be still relatively small, the international market was – and *is* very important for the Program. China, of course, also hoped to enter into joint ventures which would combine Chinese expertise and the "critical elements" – finance, special materials, management and marketing expertise – from abroad which are not available in abundance in China. Although progress towards the internationalization of Torch was slowed by the events of June, 1989, the perceived importance of international cooperation increased. At a national Torch conference held in May, 1990, the questions of internationalization received prominent attention. Emphasis was placed on the establishment of "brideg" and "showcase" firms in the US, Japan, Germany, Hong Kong and Macao, and on more foreign participation in the training of management personnel for high tech enterprises.[22] As foreign investment, joint venturing, and Chinese international commercial expansion[23] have accelerated in the 1990s, the original internationalization goals of Torch are both being exceeded and becoming more irrelevant. Nevertheless, during the past year, the SSTC, in cooperation with four foreign firms, took the initiative to establish a new "China Torch Hi-Tech Investment Fund" which is targeted on projects under the Torch Program.[24]

---

[22]XINHUA (May 9, 1990) in FBIS-CHI-90-092, p. 31.

[23]China's high tech firms are increasingly energetic in establishing beachheads abroad. In April 1993, for instance, the International Development Company, Ltd. because the first Chinese firm to establish a presence in France to develop, produce and sell electronic medical equipment, electronic machinery and fine chemicals into the European market. *Zhongguo Kexue Bao* (April 28, 1993), p. 1 in JPRS-CST-93-013 (July 27, 1993), p. 3. However, foreign investment in high technology enterprises by Chinese firms is still a small percentage of the growing Chinese total foreign investment.

[24]See, He Jun, "Foreign Funds to Bolster Hi-Tech, "*China Daily* (March 11, 1994), p. 1 in FBIS-CHI-94-051 (May 16, 1994), p. 47.

New Enterprises and New Enterprise Zones

Since its initiation in August, 1988, the Torch Plan has been given a special responsibility to foster new technology enterprises (hereafter, NTEs) and to oversee, and promote the development of special high tech enterprise zones. But activities in these two areas predate Torch, and illustrate another side to China's high technology development story.

As early as 1980, Beijing's talent-rich Haidian district began to see the appearance of new firms growing out of the many research institutes located there.[25] Most were being spun off from the Chinese Academy of Sciences, and still had formal ties with the Academy. Some, however, were started by individuals who broke with "the system" and began pushing the limits of what the reform environment would allow. These typically employed some form of collective ownership, with many also having some sort of relationship with the Haidian district government. The celebrated Stone(*Si-tong*) Corporation was started in this fashion by Wan Runnan. Wan is now in exile as a result of his support for the democracy movement in 1989, but Stone has continued to develop and is now one of China's largest non-state firms.

Under the reform conditions of the 1980's, the number of enterprises continued to grow. Reform policies of two sorts were at work. One encouraged the growth of collective enterprises and technical entrepreneurship, and more generally made the possibilities for technical careers outside of the state sector a reality for Chinese scientists and engineers for the first time since 1949. The

---

[25] The earliest non-state commercial entity reportedly was initiated by Cheng Chunxian of the Academy's Institute of Physics in 1980 with support from the Beijing Association of Science and Technology. This has evolved into a Chinese-American joint venture, the China-Silicon Valley Information System Corporation, Ltd. Chen Zhaoying, et al. *Report on the Development Zones for High and New Technology Industries* (Beijing Science and Technology Publishing House of China, 1992), p. 2 cited in Gǔ Shulin. "Spin-off Enterprises in China: Channeling the Components of R&D Institutions into Innovative Businesses." Unpublished paper, Maastricht, UNU/INTECH (August 1994), p. 7.

other policy involved reducing the guaranteed annual appropriations of established research institutes, thus forcing them to seek new ways of generating revenues and to become more responsive to commercial opportunities. Starting their own firms became one of their responses.

The number of firms in the Zhongguancun area of Haidian district grew rapidly after 1987, and its main thoroughfare, Haidian Road, became known as "electronics street." While some of these firms can be legitimately described as high technology companies (selling products and/or technology, which they themselves developed), many others have been (and still are) better described a technology traders (often offering hard to get foreign hardware) and technical service firms.[26]

In May, 1988, after a thorough investigation by the Party Central Committee, the State Council approved the designation of the area as the Beijing New Technology Development Zone and, in the process, also reshaped the policy environment for NTEs and high tech industrial zones for the country as a whole. While Beijing is legitimately seen as the leader in the new entrepreneurship, start-up companies and special zones were also appearing elsewhere after the mid-1980's. With the formal State Council approval of the Beijing zone, the rush to start high tech zones at different locations around the country accelerated. Many of the new zone designations initially came as a result of local, rather than of central government action and, as a result, there is no one model for the zone.

In her careful analysis of the different zones, and the NTEs within them, Gu Shulin reports that by the end of 1993, there were three types of zones:

> 1. those in cities with high concentrations of R&D institutes and universities, where no special new infrastructure was required(eg., Beijing,,Tianjin, Wuhan, Shenyang, Changchun);

---

[26]During 1989, revenues from trading dropped from 60% of the total for firms in the area to 32%, while technical service revenues increased from 20% to 40%. *XINHUA* (April 14, 1990) in FBIS-CHI-90-074 (April 17, 1990), p. 49.

2. those in existing or specially planned industrial areas where there are R&D strengths, but where the state has invested in infrastructure for large industrial projects(eg., Shanghai's Caohejing); and

3. thoese resembling "research" or "science parks," having newly created infrastructure to attract domestic and foreign investment (eg., Shenzhen).

Gu also notes that by the early 1990's, the NTEs fell roughly into three main types(but with ample blurring of the lines of distinction): (1) those where part of an existing institute is spun off into an independent NTE(the most common form); (2) those where individual scientist and engineers take advantage of new opportunities for career mobility and move to NTEs(the fastest growing form in 1992-3); (3) those where the NTEs remains a part of the existing institutes, existing enterprises, local governments, individuals, and by foreign firms.[27] By the middle of 1994, China's 52 nationally approved zones contained more than 20,000 NTEs with a combined work force of some 700,000. In 1993, the zones earned more than RMB 50 billion, including more than $US 700 million in foreign exchange.[28]

The enthusiasm shown by the technical community for NTEs and high tech zones sicne the late 1980's is closely related to the policy directions of the Torch Program which provided incentives for their establishment and supporting institutions to assist the start ups with their managerial and financial problems. Tax incentives have been especially attractive, with tax holidays enjoyed by the firms during their startup phases, followed by a 15% rate of corporate income tax during the firms' early years. Conventional enterprises in the state sector, by contrast, were paying income taxes at a 55% rate at the time the zones were launched, though this rate was lowered to 33% in early 1994.[29]

[27]See Gu Shulin, "Spin-off Enterprises in China," Gu notes that initially foreign firms were not important initiators - though many of the NTEs did have foreign ties. On the basis of fragmentary data, she speculates that initiatives from foreign firms began to increase in 1992-3, when foreign investment surged and a number of high profile deals were announced.

[28]*XINHUA* English Service(August 25, 1994) in FBIS-CHI-94-166(August 26, 1994), p. 40.

[29]Gu Shulin, "A Review of Reform Policy for the S&T System⋯⋯." p. 28.

In addition to tax policy, other important policies include those which provide criteria for defining the status of NTEs,[30] those providing for incubator services("service centers for scientific and technical entrepreneurs"), and those pertaining to property rights (discussed further below), financing, and foreign participation in the zones.[31] With regard to financing, most NTEs have had to rely on their parent institutes for start up funds - thus making the idea of truly autonomous entrepreneurship more the exception than the rule. The zones have all seen the introduction of innovative banking practices, however, and these have added new options for NTE financial decision making. Bank financing, for instance, along with retained earnings, has been the chief source for the financing of enterprise expansions. With the zone authorities providing for infrastructure, and with the Torch Program(and local science and technology commissions) providing the imprimatur for a NTE's existence, specialized banks have been willing to play more active roles.[32]

By the early 1990's the growth of technological entrepreneurship and high tech zones were "pushing the envelope" of politically acceptable reform practices and, thus, were raising a series of important new policy and management issues for decision makers. These have included questions about financing, about how workdrs in the NTEs should be housed and compensated,

---

[30]The three conditions required to qualify as an NTE are that the firm's technology be "new and high," that the firm have appropriate capital, market potential, and managerial capabilities, and that the chief manager of the firm be a technically trained professional. "New and high technology" is defined in terms of ten categories of technology set by the SSTC. These include: 1. microelectronics and computer technology and products; 2. information technology and products; 3. new materials; 4. new energy or energy conservation technologies; 5. biotechnology and products; 6. space and ocean technologies; 7. lasers; 8. products concerned with the application of nuclear technology; 9. products integrating electronic and mechanical technologies, and 10. "other" new and high technologies. Gu, "A Review of Reform Policy for the S&T System of China," p. 29.

[31]Gu, "A Review……." pp. 29-31.

[32]Gu, "A Review of Reform Policies……." p. 30.

and sensitive and controversial questions about property rights – who should own the NTEs, who should bear the risks of their operations, and who should enjoy the rights to appropriate the profits they might generate.

The nature of these questions point to the close, ongoing relationshipss between strategies for high tech development and the politics of reform, noted at the beginning of this chapter. These relationships have led to joint, cooperative efforts at policy development by both the State Science and Technology Commission and the State Commission for Restructuring the Economy. One such effort, reported in October, 1991, was a nine point policy statement on "deepening reforms in high and new technology industrial development zones and on pushing the development of high and new technology industries."[33] This statement addressed a number of institutional issues about high tech development, and included provisions to enhance enterprise autonomy, expand the range of property rights options, stimulate internationalization, clarify personnel policies, provide new opportunities for financing, provide for alternatives to the work unit in supplying housing and social services, and to encourage local decision making. These issues of institutional reform subsequently were addressed by the State Council in its important "State Medium and Long Term Science and Technology Program" ("SMLTSTP") issued in March, 1992.[34]

In the spring of 1992, in the spirit of the SMLTSTP, the two Commissions identified high tech zones in five cities(Beijing, Shenyang, Wuhan, Chongqing and Zhongshan) as "experimental sites" for intensified reform activity focused on

---

[33]*XINHUA* (October 5, 1991) in FBIS-CHI-91-206, pp. 25 ff.

[34]The text of the SMLTSTP is included in the State Science and Technology Commission's *White Paper on Science and Technology ,#5,* issued in June 1992. An English version of the latter (and SMLTSTP) is available in JPRS-CST-94-005(April 8, 1994). In addition to addressing institutional issues, SMLTSTP also discusses the priorities for key technologies and industrial sectors for the periods, 1991-2000 and 2000-2020.

"... revamping the system of property rights, the pay structure, the system of dispersing scientific and technological personnel, and the means of combining planned management with market regulation so as to promote reform and development of the financial, social security, and socialized supplementary services systems. New operational mechanisms will be introduced in new and high technology enterprises to encourage self-financing, voluntary association, independent operations, accountability for profits and losses, self-development and self-restraint."[35]

With regard to property rights, in particular, the experimental sites sanctioned the introduction of a share holding systems for enterprises.

"Under the premise of ensuring the predominance of shares owned by the state, employees and workers of enterprises will be allowed to own shares. Once approved, publicly floated shares in enterprises may be dealt over the counter or through stock exchanges in Shanghai and Shenzhen."[36]

The increasing movements of scientists and engineers into NTEs and increased foreign interest in the zones in the 1992-1993 period, as noted above, are partially explained by policy innovations contained in the SMLTSTP. Further implications of the NTEs and high tech zones will be discussed below.

Other National Programs

In conjunction with the issuance of the SMLTSTP, the State Council also approved the "Ten Year Plan of Scientific and Technological Development of the PRC Outline of the Eighth Five Year Plan(1991-1995-2000)" prepared by the SSTC. This document contains a section on high technology which generally reaffirms the directions of existing programs(i.e., those discussed above), but provides for some adjustments in national high tech priorities in light of the achievements of the existing programs and changing assessments of international technological trends. The target technologies for the 1990s found in the Ten Year Plan include

[35]*XINHUA* (June 9, 1992) in FBIS-CHI-92-112, pp. 29-30.

[36]*Ching-Chi Tao-pao* (May11, 1992), p. 18 in FBIS-CHI-92-095, p. 29.

biotechnology, microelectronics, photoelectrics, space applications, computers, software, communications, automation, new energy sources, new materials, superconductivity, and laser technology.[37]

Other national programs are also of relevance to China's high technology development. The first is a more focused and better funded commitment to basic research during the 8th plan period via the National Basic Research Priorities Programme.[38] This program allows for investigator initiated projects, but also has "mandatory" and "guidance" plan features which give it a "targeted" or "oriented" basic research quality as well. Some of the targeted priorities are supportive of high technology.[39]

A second program is the expanded support now being given to the establishment of State Engineering Research Centers(SERCs). The promotion of the SERCs, like the promotion of spin-off NTEs, is directed at solving the chronic gap between the relatively abundant technical resources in the state sector and actual production needs. The idea behind the SERCs is to encourage the large number of research institutes which belong to the national industrial ministries to enter into new, targeted, market driven cooperative relationships with the state enterprises. Approximately 39 engineering research centers had been approved by the end of 1993, and a majority have missions dealing with high technology. The SERC initiative is coordinated with the 863 Program and the Key Technologies Program, with projects from the latter being assigned to SERCs(eg., the CIMS research work of the 863 Program is integrated with a new SERC which is dedicated to CIMS).[40]

---

[37]These planning documents are also included in the *White Paper, #5,* and can be found in JPRS-CST-94-005 (April 8, 1994), pp. 122-137. The section on high technology priorities is found on pp. 128-129.

[38]China expects to increase funding for basic research over the course of the 1990's from 7% of national R&D expenditures to 9%.

[39]See, *The Main Programmes* , pp. 18-20.

[40]Li Maoming, "Achievements Seen in Establishing State Engineering Research Centers," *Zhongguo Keji Luntan* (*Forum on Science and Technology in China*), No. 4 (July 1993), pp. 7-9 in JPRS-CST-93-016 (October 6, 1993), pp. 6-8.

The Defense Sector

A large concentration of technical resources exists in China's defense R&D and defense industries. Reportedly, S&T personnel in defense industries have constituted 13% of the work force, in comparison with an average of 3% in civilian industry.[41] China's programs in nuclear weapons and space have spurred development in a whole range of attendant technologies - materials, electronics, new processing techniques, etc. - of potential commercial value.[42] Institutions such as the National Defense Science and Technology University in Changsha, which developed the Galaxy supercomputer, are also active in such fields as artificial intelligence, precision guidance, stealth and counter-stealth technologies, simulator technologies and flexible manufacturing.[43]

Since the early 1980's the defense sector has been given the charge to assist the civilian economy by technology transfers and through the conversion of its plants to civilian production. According to one report, some 3,000 long standing civilian production problems during 1980's were solved with technologies from the defense sector, netting the latter more than 2 billion *yuan* for the know-how supplied; by 1989 the value of production for the civilian economy from defense plants had risen to 66% of total output value, up from 10% in 1979.[44]

While the exploitation of the technical talents of the defense establishment is not without problems,[45] China's leaders believe it holds great potential. Recent moves to accelerate the use of assets from the defense sector include a late 1989 decision to

---

[41]Xiao Qinfu, "The Shortest Route To Two Way Development of S&T and the Economy," *Keji Ribao* (*Science and Technology Daily*, December 25, 1990) in JPRS-CST-90-007 (March 6, 1990), p. 1.

[42]See, for instance, Di Naiyong, "Research and Development of Long March Family of Launch Vehicles,"*Shijie Daodan Yu Hangtian* (*Missiles and Spacecraft*), No. 137 (September 1989) in JPRS-CST-90-007 (March 6, 1990), p. 19.

[43]*Keji Ribao* (*Science and Technology Daily*, February 4, 1989), p. 1.

[44]Xiao Qinfu, "The Shortest Route……."

[45]See, *Ibid*.

declassify some 2,300 defense R&D achievements[46] and, to spur foreign sales of defense sector technology, the issuance of "Provisional Regulations for the Examination and Approval of the Export of Secret Technology," on December 6, 1989.[47]

In addition to being a source of supply for new technologies, the defense sector, of course, is also a major source of demand. Chinese concerns for acquiring sophisticated weaponry to support national security missions have been expanded as a consequence of increased defense budgets in recent years, and as a result of Chinese assessments of the performance of high tech weaponry during the Gulf War. High technology for the military is thus closely related to high tech development efforts more generally.[48] Unlike the Maoist past, however, there is likely to be much greater interaction between high tech in the military and high tech in the civilian sectors, a trend which would be in keeping with the growing recognition internationally that the sources of high tech innovation are more likely to be found in the dynamics of the civilian economy than in focused military R&D.[49]

Major Infrastructure Development

Apart from the various programs to stimulate R&D and cultivate high technology entrepreneurship and new firms, described above, China is also embarking on major infrastructure projects with significant implications for the demand for new technologies. As with defense missions, these infrastructure development

---

[46]China daily (January 24, 1990) in FBIS-CHI-90-018-S (January 26, 1990), p. 42.

[47]The text of the Regulations can be found in Keji Ribao (Science and Technology Daily, December 30, 1990) in JPRS-CST-90-005 (February8, 1990), pp. 1-2.

[48]See the discussion in SMLTSTP. JPRS-CST-94-005, pp. 8-9.

[49]*Ibid.*; Cf., Kosta Tsipis, *New Technologies, Defense Policy, and Arms Control* (New York: Harper & Row, 1989); John A. Alic, et al., *Beyond Spinoff: Military and Commercial Technoloies in a Changing World* (Boston: Harvard Business School Press, 1992).

efforts provide opportunities to go beyond "supply push" approaches to technological development and exercise the "demand pull" side of technology policy.

Perhaps the most significant area of infrastructure expansion for high technology is telecommunications, where the Ministry of Posts and Telecommunications alone is expected to spend some $US 52 billion during the 1990s to more than double the size of its public network. Chinese authorities have recently agreed to allow new entrants to compete with MPT, and have decided to open the operation of the telecommunications sector to foreign participation as well. With China's increasingly complex and sophisticated economy and rising personal incomes, and its very low installed telecommunications capacity, the market for telecommunications equipment is enormous.

Closely related to telecommunications expansion is the growing interest in computer networking. Internet connectivity is improving, plans are being made to link some 1,000 institutions of higher education by the year 2000 via the "China Education and Research Network"("CERNET"), other plans call for new computer networking for credit cards, bank transactions, and customs clearances (the "Three Goldens" project), and talk of a "national information highway" is becoming common among policy elites. In short, the information industry, with its ensemble of technologies, faces a huge demand. How the demand will be satisfied is unknown at this point; what can be said with certainty, however, is that meeting it will have profound effects of China's high technology development.

High Tech Development and the Continuing Challenges of Technology Policy

The discussion above has pointed to a close relationship between R&D and industrial promotion initiatives to stimulate high technology, and ongoing S&T reform and restructuring efforts. In the language of complementary assets with which we began, reform and restructuring are essential if China is to find the institutional flexibility required to locate complementarities and match technological opportunities with market demands. In this connection, the NTEs stand out as an intriguing experience in institutional innovation for a society in transition from socialism. Their existence also poses an ongoing challenge to public policy.

The NTE-State Enterprise Relationship

In less than a decade, the NTEs have emerged as a significant, albeit still small, part of the Chinese economy. Because the number of NTEs has grown so rapidly in various settings around the country, it is difficult to generalize about them. Among the more successful, however, certain features recur. First, most spin-off firms started with the provision of services, rather than the making and selling of products. Second, the service provision mission necessarily meant that technologies had to be adapted to user needs. In the computer industry, for instance, this meant adapting foreign made computer technology to Chinese language needs. Success in this effort then stimulated demand and led to further growth of the computer industry. In the process control industry, as another example, domestically produced equipment from large state enterprises which was not terribly user friendly was made more so. Many NTEs, in short, are using their technical assets to complement established industry with services directed at user needs. According to Gu Shulin,

> "The NTEs are distinguished by their access to the best-educated manpower with the greatest experience in R&D. They serve to support activities in the rest of the economy, helping to upgrade existing production, and to supplement the large-scale manufacturing sectors."[50]

However, the relationship between the NTEs and the large state enterprises is a complex one. Unitl the early 1990's, the latter were often hostile and unsympathetic to the former, and resented the preferential policy treatment the NTEs enjoyed. Gradually, as the roles of the NTEs became clearer, attitudes have become more

---

[50]Gu shulin. "Spin-off Enterprises in China," p. 45.

favorable.

Still, the relationship remains complicated by the distinctly different characteristics of the two sectors. The state enterprises are behemoths, with huge work forces, extensive human and material resources for technological development, extensive fixed assets for production, and an enormous ability to defy reformist change and profitability. The NTEs, on the other hand, have been small, nimble, capital-poor but intelligence-rich entities, who have faced formidable barriers to entry in trying to launch large manufacturing activities in a system which is still biased towards the state sector.

The NTEs, thus, have given China's high tech activities creative and entrepreneurial energy which was not be found in the state enterprises. However, since the latter constitute so much of China's industrial economy, and possess so much of its core technology, it is inconceivable that high technology industrialization can proceed without them. What to do with the state enterprises, and how they should be related to the NTEs, is of course one of the more daunting challenges for technology policy. While the challenge is, in the first instance, a domestic one, how it is approached will increasingly be a function of the broader international environment.

Although the discussion here has focused primarily on domestic programs and issues, China's high technology quest is, of course, no longer a purely domestic matter. China has an intense interest in high technology in the international economy and high technology firms have an intense interest in China. These interests by now take a variety of forms, from non-commercial cooperation in research and educational exchanges, to increasingly sophisticated forms of foreign investment and joint venturing, to trade in high technology goods.[51] The question of how NTE's

---

[51]The value of China's two way trade in high technology products has risen from $US 6.3 billion in 1987 to $US 14.7 billion in 1992. China's exports have risen steadily during this period, increasing from $US 9 billion to close to $US 4 billlion. The value of imports has increased more rapidly, however, with the result that China's high tech trade deficit has increased by more than $US 2

relate to state enterprises is closely related to how China orients itself to foreign technology, to the international high tech economy, and to the foreign business presence in China more generally.

These latter questions are familiar to students of Chinese technology policies. They involve the relative importance to be given to self-reliance and import substitution measures, the extent to which market criteria should inform technology policy, and the ways in which China's strong sense of technological nationalism should be indulged. While the questions are familiar, the circumstances in which they are asked have changed, and continuing to change. China is already in a much more interdependent relationship with the international economy, and in seeking entry into GATT/WTO, hopes to become more so.[52] Around the world, technological change is accelerating, is becoming more expensive, and is increasingly a part of global economic processes from which China does not wish to be excluded.

A number of the themes alluded to above are illustrated in the complex deliberations which comprise China's efforts to devise a national computer industry strategy. On one hand, China has an enormous, but poorly structured, state electronics industry which might be expected to be the backbone of the computer industry. On the other, the most commercially successful players in the industry are the larger NTEs with foreign partners, such as Legend, Stone, and Founder, whose annual revenues now often exceed enterprises in the state sector.[53] Should China's technology policies be directed at the latter, as their leaders are now arguing,

---

billion over this five year period. *China Science & Technology Statistics : Data Book, 1992*, pp. 20-21. Over the past year, China has been gearing up to further promote high technology exports.

[52]These hopes are also mixed with fears, however. Concerns for the negative impacts of China's accession to GATT on high technology have been occurring frequently in press reports over the past few years. See, for instance, Pei Jianfeng. "China to Nurture Its Own Electronics Giants," *China Daily Business Weekly* (April 4, 1991), p. 1 in JPRS-CST-94-007, p. 1.

[53]In 1993, Legend's revenues of $US 345 million were second only to Shanghai Audio and Video ($US 410 million), the nation's largest electronics firm. Pei Jianfeng, "China to Nurture……."

to large technology development and industry restructuring projects in the state sector, or to both?

For Wang Xuan of the Founder Group, whose patented discoveries in the area of electronic printing technology are becoming the standard for color publishing systems for Chinese language newspapers around the world, the answer is simple. China should avoid wasteful technological dead-ends and should instead support those players who have a demonstrated ability to exploit profitable technological niches with innovative technological systems.

In Wang's views, for instance, China should abandon national efforts to develop its own computer chips and home grown operating systems. China is so far behind the world's leaders in CPUs and microprocessors, in this view, that it is unlikely to catch up, even with enormous national expenditures. On the other hand, the domestic and international markets for integrated circuits continues to expand, South Korea has demonstrated how to make a successful entry into this industry, and with the demise COCOM, China would have new opportunities to introduce advanced equipment for its IC industry. Similarly, Wang believes that the prospects for an indigenously developed Chinese character based operating system staving off foreign competition is highly unlikely, given the growing international dominance of DOS, Windows, and Unix. China's efforts should be directed instead to the development of utility software suited to the needs of Chinese users.[54]

Such views are quite in keeping with the formulae for success developed by the NTEs over the past decade. These include the location of niches in large technological systems, and filling them-profitably-with innovative combinations of hardware, software, and service. Advanced foreign technology is not necessarily something to be held at bay in this view; rather it is something to be adapted to Chinese conditions and to the needs of Chinese users.

---

[54]Pei Jianfeng, "Chips are Down in PC Industry," *China Daily Business Weekly* (August 21-22, 1994), p. 8.

The voices of the NTEs can no longer be ignored in technology policy councils. First, the economic importance of the NTEs is increasing; the successful ones have proven their viability and have become important parts of the high tech development. Second, their message is not necessarily completely inconsistent with the interest of the large state enterprises(whose voices have tended to dominate technology policy councils, and whose interests in the past have been closely linked with import substitution policies). Indeed, the NTEs are showing the way out of at least some of the formidable problems the state enterprises face, and as China continues to explore the options for restructuring the electronics industry, both state enterprises and NTEs will figure into the merger and acquisition process which is expected to deliver the kinds of new high tech firms which, following admission to GATT/WTO, would remain internationally competitive.55 In ways that few could have anticipated in the early to mid-1980s when it began, the experience of the NTEs has now become far more central to policy as China tries to use its wealth of human talent wisely in adjusting to global technological realities.

Other Technology Policy Challenges

The institutional challenges of ownership, industrial structure, and enterprise organization, noted above, do not exhaust the problems of technology policy in China. They are, however, closely related to the ways other problems are confronted and attacked. Among these other problems, three warrant brief mention here. First, for all the attention being given to high technology in government policy statements and press accounts, China still seems to be under spending on research and development. At the national level, the ratio of R&D expenditures to GNP remained at approximately 0.7% since the late 1980s, well below the ratios found in both the OECD countries *and* the Asian NIEs. While it is difficult to get good firm level data on the ratio of

---

[55]Pei Jianfeng, "China to Nurture……."

R&D to sales, it is certain that very fe w Chinese enterprises are spending at a level which would define a firm as "high tech" in other countries (at least 5%). In China, the ratio is more likely to be 0.5-1% in enterprises with high tech aspirations.

China's plans for the 1990's include an increase of the R&D/GNP ratio to approximately 1.35%(10% of which will be for basic research) by the year 2000.[56] This increase presumes that R&D spending by the end of the decade will come from three sources: state appropriations, funds from non-state financial sources, and enterprise expenditures, with the relative share of the former decreasing substantially. To achieve this target, Chinese enterprises will have to become more viable financial entities - as successful earners of revenues from sale of product, and as worthy players in domestic and international credit and equity markets. Changes of this sort are inseparable from the institutional issues surrounding the NTEs and the state enterprises noted above.

A second policy problem area has to do with the complex interactions of Chinese enterprises and foreign high tech firms, especially with reference to the powerful demand forces being unleashed by the major infrastructure projects of the 1990s and beyond. The prominence of foreign high tech firms - from the OECD countries as well as from the Asian NIEs - in China's development has increased dramatically since the beginning of the 1990s, and the achievement of China's infrastructure development goals would be inconceivable without foreign capital and technology.

For the short to medium term, at least, and in spite of the ongoing problems of doing business in China - eg., those of regulatory ambiguity, corruption, intellectual property and labor disputes, etc. - China continues to open its open door policy ever wider. At the same time, it remains profoundly ambivalent about doing so because of fears losing control of its own industrial and technological future in the process. Finding the right balance between

---

[56]White Paper, p. 136.

the promotion of national high technology industry and the inevitable sacrifice of national controls which participation in the global economy makes inevitable will not be easy. Clearly a necessary condition for this balance is the existence of domestic firms which are of a scale which would make them both commercially viable and technologically adept, a condition which is again related to the NTE-state enterprise question.

A final problem of technology policy for China as it pursues its high tech aspirations has to do with how the management of information is approached. While high technology is clearly more than information technology, the latter is so fundamental to high technology generally, that failures with policy for information technology can put the entire high tech project at risk.

Students of Chinese history and politics will of course recognize that the channels along which information in Chinese society is supposed to move are far from friction less, or without significant obstacles. Indeed, the protection of bureaucratic, regional, clan and family interests and identities has often provided good grounds in Chinese society for regarding information as privileged, to be marked secret or confidential, and kept from the hands of real or potential rivals. It is by no means clear that there are easy technological "fixes" for this institutional problem of information "cellularization."

Chinese policy makers thus have to ask whether it makes sense to invest in the technologies needed to make an information superhighway a reality if non-technical factors work against the public sharing of socially useful information, as when – as is now the case – databases are kept secret, or when lackadaisical attitudes lead to slipshod approaches to the collection, archiving and dissemination of data, or when telecommunications hardware procurement decisions outrace systems integration strategies. Strong political leadership and far-sighted public policy will be required if solutions to these problems are to be found, but the solutions will also require skillful and aggressive firms who help "make markets" in information and supply the hardware and software needed to make the markets work, needs which also point to roles for NTEs.

Conclusion

China is at a point in its high technology development which is pivotal and especially interesting. Through a series of reforms measures it has induced many important changes in its R&D system(even as other parts remain resistant to reform). It has also launched a variety of national programs to stimulate research of relevance to high technology and to facilitate high tech industrial expansion. Its science and technology are increasingly linked with global scientific and industrial trends. Reform and open door policies have created and identified, and have begun to link, the core technologies and complementary assets from within China and from abroad which are needed to make high technology industrialization in China a reality.

But China is also faced with a series of new challenges to its high tech aspirations. The pace of technological change in the international economy continues to be rapid, and China must find innovative ways to participate in, and learn from, that change. China's entry into GATT, when it occurs, will open the Chinese economy to new levels of foreign competition. Inescapably, China's ability to meet that competition involves finding ways to use the considerable technical assets - human and material - of the state enterprises to serve high value added production.

These various challenges point to the need for technology policies which are "smarter" and more flexible than those seen up to now, and perhaps for new policy mechanisms as well. Over the coming decade, a number of policy areas and policy problems will begin to converge. Policy tools will be required which are grounded in sound understandings of the issues at stake and which are appropriate for managing the convergence.

The tasks ahead have both technical and political dimensions and involve, in particular, the convergence of the needs and interests of the state enterprises with those of the NTEs, and the convergence of domestic R&D and industrial policies with foreign trade and investment policies. The former will require that the progressive understandings of high tech development found in the NTE sector be given a more central place in policy thinking without, in the process, extending a whole new set of subsidies and protective measures to the NTEs. The latter will require an appreciation for the increasingly subtle interactions of trade and industrial policies, and for the delicacy of political intervention decisions to promote the protection of national technical assets in an increasingly international world of high tech commerce.

There are powerful domestic political forces which will work against the achievement of the more sophisticated policy stance described above. It is quite conceivable that these forces will prevail. If so, China's high tech industrialization will look somewhat as it does today – with slowly expanding pockets of technical excellence and small sectors of internationally competitive firms in a large, rather inefficient economy of conventional industry. I refer to this outcome as Scenario 1.

However, China's quest for high technology has also put the economy on a course which might be likened to stepping onto a moving walkway – one having slow, medium, and fast lanes. At this point, China is moving from the slow to the medium lane. On balance, the risks of returning to the slow lane, or trying to get off the walkway altogether, far outweigh those of pushing on into the fast lane. For these reasons, it is likely that we will continue to see the increasingly bold policy innovations and organizational changes needed to address the asset complementarity problems which will shape China's high technology future. This outcome can be referred to as Scenario 2.

As we consider the broader regional and global implications of China's high technology future, it is helpful to distinguish between capabilities and intentions. However, it is also important to remember that capabilities and intentions are related as well, as other chapters in this volume demonstrate. Let us conclude with the thought that one of the issues bridging capabilities and intentions in today's China is the prospect of regionalism leading to some measure national fragmentation. Interestingly, China's high technology development experience is both a force for strong regional economies *and* a critical ingredient for strengthening centrally directed integration.

The China of Scenario 2 clearly has the potential to be a more economically and militarily capable China *vis à vis* the international environment. It is so, in no small part, because it is also a China with a demonstrated capacity to built the institutional infrastructure needed for a highly integrated national market. Without the latter, as suggested above, the technological infrastructure for maintaining an increasingly complex modern national political economy cannot be effectively implemented. Scenario 2 China is one in which the central government has divested itself of the onerous obligations of running a socialist economy and has reclaimed for itself the more limited prerogatives needed for maintaining national unity. Such a China is comfortable with the existence of vibrant regional economies with active foreign participants because it has confidence in the institutional basis for an integrated national high technology economy.

The China of Scenario 1, on the other hand, is a China with an uneasy grasp on central power. It is one which is weighted down with obligations to both provide employment for workers in state enterprises *and* create a high tech future in the face of chronic revenue scarcity. It is a less capable China which, in its weakness, is more dependent on – and beholden to – military and security interests. Though it is impossible to predict the international intentions of either China, one suspects that of the two, Scenario 1 China would be a less reliable economic partner and a more unpredictable neighbor.

PART Ⅳ

Regionalism within China

8

Regional Disparities, Localism and China's Search for a New Regional Development Strategy in the 1990s

Ick Soo Kim
(Korea University)

Introduction

China's regional development strategy ('RDS') is related to the evolution of its open-door policy since 1979, as well as to the development of China's regional industrial organization policy. In the pre-reform era, the rationale of China's RDS was based primarily on defense and integration needs rather than on economic needs and modernization. The "three-front strategy" (*sanxion zhanlue*) of the mid-1960s to early 1970s, according to which heavy and defense-related factories were moved to or built in the inland area of Sichuan, Gizhou, Shaanxi, etc., is a good example.

The RDS in the post-1979 period, however, became tied more closely to the differentiated modernization objective of each region, and efficiency became the prime concern. The partial opening-up and prior development of the coastal region contributed greatly to the revitalization of the rigid bureaucratic economy and to the maximization of the comparative advantages of differing regions. However, administrative decentralization, particularly fiscal decentralization, gave rise to a new form of economic regionalism and exacerbated the income gap between regions. Thus, China in the late 1990s has shifted the focus of its RDS from an imbalanced coastal development strategy to a more balanced RDS supported by the so-called 4-*Yan* Development Strategy (i.e., *yanjiang, yanxian, yanhai, yanbian*) whereby the benefits of opening have been extended from coastal cities to comparatively backward inland or border areas.

This paper shall review the partial opening, fiscal decentralization, incremental price reforms, regional disparities, localism, and overlapping investments, all of which pushed the Chinese government to formulate its new equity-oriented, balanced RDS in replacement of the efficiency-oriented, unbalanced RDS. The paper will also attempt to study how the post-1979 Chinese government compromised these two seemingly contradictory strategies in a decentralized institutional setting.

China's Coastal Development Strategy, Administrative Decentralization of Fiscal Authority and Partial Price Reforms

Partial Opening and the Coastal Development Strategy

China's RDS in the post-1978 period was not implemented in a vacuum. It has evolved along with the progress of China's economic reforms and open-door policy. During the 1979-1988 period, China pursued a partial open-door policy for fear of adverse effects on its socio-political stability, and also because of its initial emphasis on the efficient use of investment resources. It is quite natural that the focus of regional development policy was on the coastal region, which has better initial conditions in factor endowments, industrial structure, technology level, availability of capital, etc. as compared to the inland region. Thus, in July

1979, the first "special economic zone"(SEZ) was established in Shenzhen, and three others appeared in Zhuhai, Shantou, and Xiamen. In April 1984, fourteen coastal cities were opened; in February 1985, three delta zones were established; and in 1988, Hainan Province was designated as the fifth SEZ. Therefore, by the end of 1980s, the coastal development strategy had resulted in a multi-level structure, composed of 5 SEZs, 14 coastal open cities, and various open economic zones. Indeed, up until 1988, China stuck to the partial open-door policy, and its front was restricted primarily to coastal cities, five special economic zones, and economically open areas (*kaifangqu*).

The rationale of the coastal development strategy is that the different provinces or regions may not develop at the same time and at the same speed, given the scarcity of capital and the backwardness of technology and management expertise, and that therefore, development efforts should be concentrated in the coastal region, which meet the conditions for development. The less developed inland region may enjoy trickle-down effects of the partial opening over time. This indicates that the prime concern at the initial stage of open door policy was the effective use of scarce capital and the concomitant maximization of investment returns.

Political endorsement by Deng Xiaoping of the coastal development strategy was an additional boost. In fact, prior opening and the subsequent preferential treatment of Guangdong Province in relation to others is a kind of compensation for Guangdong's help in 1976 when Deng, in the face of political difficulties, found shelter in Guangdong and General Xu resisted the Gang of Four's demand that he hand over Deng. In addition, according to Shirk (1994), partial opening and the small scale implementation of the SEZs was a strategy designed to minimize resistance from the powerful planning, finance, and industrial bureaucracies to full-scale open policies.[1]

---

[1]Shirk, S. L., "Beyond Particularism: The Challenges of the Next Stage of China's Foreign Economic Reforms," Paper presented at the 5th U.S. Korea Academic Symposium on Economic Cooperation and Challenges in the Pacific: Japan, Korea, China, the U.S., and the Economies of East Asia (1994), pp. 12-13.

Decentralization of Fiscal Authority

What went along with the partial opening of the coastal region in the 1979-1988 period came the partial incremental reform of the economic system and the administrative decentralization of the economic management authority.

Various reform measures were taken to eliminate or alleviate the systemic irrationalities embedded in the Chinese economy. However, given the ineffectiveness and socio-political risks associated with one-shot radical reforms, Chinese leaders chose to adopt a "gradual approach" in reforming the systems of planning, price, finance, enterprise management, and ownership structure.

In parallel, the authority of local governments and the incentives of enterprises were expanded in such a way as to facilitate the transformation of the economy into an efficient market-oriented economy with Chinese characteristics. Thus, economic power related to the management of planning, price, credit, budget, investment, and foreign direct investment was devolved from the central government to local governments and relevant authorities.

Of the various reforms and decentralization measures, however, what impinged most on the direction, scope, and focus of China's RDS in the 1980s was the decentralization of the fiscal management authority to provincial level governments, which in turn contracted the revenue sharing with lower level governments. As a matter of fact, the introduction of the "fiscal contracting" system in 1980 and its evolution since then, coupled with other reform measures, led to various undesirable consequences such as localism, uneven growth between regions or provinces, overlapping investments, and assimilated industrial structure, which will be discussed later.

However, before discussing the consequences of fiscal decentralization, it is necessary to review briefly the central-provincial fiscal contracting system which came into being in 1980. Before 1980, the Chinese government basically maintained a centralized budget management system in which each province remitted most of its revenue and was allocated expenditures through a uniform budgetary process. Under this system of "eating from the same big pot"(*chi da guofan*), there was little incentive for local governments make efforts to expand revenue or economize expenditures, which eventually put pressure on the state coffer.

The new system of "eating from separate kitchens" (*fenzao chifan*) aims primarily to expand the national "pie for intergovernmental sharing" by expanding the the fiscal autonomy of local governments and by enhancing local accountability and systemic efficiency in the collection and use of the budget. The intermediary goal of the new system was to arouse local enthusiasm for revenue collection. To this end, the previous principle of a "unified collection of revenues and centralized allocation of expenditure"(*tongshou tongzhi*) was superseded by the "management of budget by different levels of government through vertical contracting"(*haufen shouzhi fenji baogan*). Thus, the central government contracted with provincial govenments the ratio of remission, or fixed amount to be remitted, which once decided, remained fixed for 5 years.[2]

However, regional disparity in the level of development, per capita expenditure requirement, revenue collection capacity, and relative strategic importance has required the central government to implement "four" variants of different revenue sharing schemes in different groups of regions. The three municipalities of Beijing, Shanghai and Tianjin remained under the old scheme of sharing total revenues by the previous year's expenditure-revenue ratio. Shanghai, for example, remitted 74 to 88 percent of its locally collected revenues to the central government, despite a substantial increase in the collection of local revenues during 1985-1987.

Sixteen provinces (primarily coastal and centrally-located provinces) were under the scheme of the fixed percentage deliv-

---

[2]For details of the 1980 revenue sharing system reform, see Cai Yanchu, "Wu nianlai caizheng tizhi he shuizhi caiwu zhidu gaige qingkuang (The Status of fiscal, tax and financial system reforms over the past five years)," *Cai Zheng* (Public Finance), No. 8 (1984), p. 28.

ery scheme, and a major incentive of this revenue sharing scheme was that, provided the central government's requirements are met, provincial governments are, in principle, entitled to local fixed revenues plus a fixed percentage of shared revenues. However, Guangdong Province was under the preferential scheme of "delivering a fixed amount of revenue"(*ding'e shangjiao*); the relatively poor province of Fujian was subject to "receiving a fixed amount of subsidy"(*ding'e buzhu*) scheme; and five autonomous regions (Inner Mongolia, Tibet, Xinjiang, Ningxia and Guangxi) and three poor provinces (Guizhou, Yunnan, and Qinghai), which had heavy minority populations and normally ran deficits, were given "block grants" which grew annually by 10 percent. In 1988, faced with serious criticism and complaints by other provinces, Guangdong shifted to an incremental fixed revenue sharing scheme, according to which the amount of remission must increase by 10% each year, and Shanghai, Shandong (except for Qingdao), and Heilongjiang (except for Harbin) were allowed to move into the more favorable scheme of fixed revenue remission regime.[3]

Despite various changes made since 1980, however, the basic framework of the 1980 fiscal system, which favors Guangdong and other coastal provinces, has been retained; and there have been no drastic changes in the sharing ratios or delivery amounts. The 1980 fiscal system reform and ensuing improvement of the fiscal management system created an atmosphere in which provincial governments with expanded autonomy pursued the expansion of net local revenues. At the same time, the extended implementation of revenue-sharing arrangements to subprovincial levels has caused the stimulative effect to trickle down to the county / city governments.

---

[3]Unlike Shandong and Heilongjiang which are allowed to keep total collected revenue less the amount remitted to the center, Shanghai was still required to share a certain percentage of surplus revenue with the central government even after the remission of fixed amount for the last two years out of the 5 year contract period.

Partial Price Reforms and Price Distortions

A third factor that exerted a great impact on China's RDS in the 1980s is price reforms. The Chinese government, since 1979, has introduced price reforms in agricultural and industrial products. However, the price reform was mainly of a partial, incremental nature, and the coverage was piecemeal and uneven, depending upon the commodity category and the demand-supply situation.

One of the most intriguing aspects of the partial price reform is that it is biased against the interior (central and western) regions, producing mainly raw materials and energy for the industrialized coastal provinces and cities. This is because the pricing, production, and distribution of raw materials and energy resources are subject to comparatively stricter central control than finished consumer goods. As of the end of 1988, approximately 95% of the prices of finished consumer goods produced by coastal provinces were regulated largely by the market.

This implies that the eastern coastal regions, with strong processing industries, were subject to less mandatory targets and more discretion on pricing than interior regions. However, as one can see in Table 1, the inland regions produced approximately 64% of the industrial output related to extractive industries – more specifically, 65% of energy and 45% of raw materials. As a matter of fact, during 1992, 78.1% of coal, 57.4% of crude oil, 74% of natural gas, 56% of iron ore, 73.8% of timber, and 51.8% of electric power were produced by interior regions. By contrast, coastal regions with a traditionally strong base of processing industries produced a substantial proportion of finished consumer goods. Coastal regions were also strong in the production of semi-finished industrial products, which have to be bought by interior products to make finished heavy industry products. In the case of ethylene, 72% of total output originated from the coastal area, whereas the ratio is lower for iron (58.8%) and pig iron (55.4%).

Table 1. The Regional Distribution of Major Industrial Raw Materials

(As of the end of 1991)

	Coal (mil.tons, %)	Crude Oil (mil.tons, %)	Natural Gas (100mil.m3, %)	Iron Ore (mil.m3, %)	Timber (mil.m3, %)	Electric Power (100 mil. kwh, %)	Ethylene (tons, %)	Steel (mil.tons,%)	Pig Iron (mil.Tons, %)
Total	108,740.61	14,099.20	160.73	19,016.24	5,807.33	6,775.47	1,761.050	7,099.97	6,765.27
Coastal[1)]	23,822.34 (21.9)	6,001.17 (42.6)	41.77 (26.0)	12,190.75 (64.1)	1,524.14 (26.2)	3,262.67 (48.2)	1,267,200 (72.0)	4,171.87 (58.8)	3,745.95 (55.4)
Inland	84,918.27 (78.1)	8,098.03 (57.4)	118.96 (74.0)	6,825.49 (56.0)	4,283.19 (73.8)	3,512.8 (51.8)	493,850 (28.0)	2,928.1 (41.2)	3,019.85 (44.6)
Central Area[2)]	63,462.13 (58.4)	6,929.36 (49.1)	38.24 (23.8)	4,482.48 (23.6)	3,317.7 (57.1)	2,319.27 (48.2)	426,590 (24.2)	2,025.01 (28.5)	2,118.82 (31.3)
Western Area[3)]	21,456.14 (19.7)	1,168.67 (8.3)	80.72 (50.2)	2,343.01 (12.3)	965.49 (16.6)	1,193.53 (34.2)	67,260 (3.8)	903.09 (12.7)	901.03 (13.3)

Source: *Zhongguo Gonggye Jingji Tongji Nianjian* (Annual Statistical Report of Chinese Industrial Economy, 1992), pp.197-277.

Note : 1) Figures in ( ) represent respective percentages of the total.

2) Regional classification is as follows:

East coastal region includes the 12 provinces/cities of Beijing, Tianjin, Hebei, Liaoning, Shanghai, Jiangsu, Zhejiang, Shandong, Fujian, Guangdong, Guangxi, and Hainan.

Central region includes the 9 provinces/autonomous regions of Shanxi, Inner Mongolia, Jilin, Heilongjiang, Anhui, Jiangxi, Henan, Hubei, and Hunan.

Western region includes the 9 provinces/autonomous regions of Sichuan, Guizhou, Yunnan, Tibet, Shaanxi, Gansu, Qingjai, Ningxia, and Xinjiang.

Regional Disparities, Localism and Political Discontent

In the above we have discussed China's partial open-door policy characterized as coastal development strategy, fiscal decentralization, and incremental price reforms. As a combined consequence of these, the Chinese economy exhibited various idiosyncracies such as regional disparities, localism, overlapping industrial structure, political discontent.

Asymmetric Effects of Fiscal Management and Price Reforms and the Widening of Regional Disparities

First, the incentive effect of the new system of central-provincial fiscal contracting and the subsequent recontracting with lower level governments was uneven among local governments depending upon the nature of the revenue sharing scheme to which they belong. The incentive effect was most strong in the fixed amount scheme (or Guangdong scheme), which allowed Guangdong to retain all revenues less a fixed amount delivered to the center. The next strongest incentive effect took place in the fixed percentage scheme and its variants, in which provinces were allowed to keep all locally collected revenues less a fixed percentage of shared revenues. The weakest incentive effect was associated with the subsidy scheme under which minority regions and the 3 poor provinces were given a pre-negotiated block grant regardless of the volume of revenues.

Second, the effect of partial price reform was uneven, too. Central and western regions had to provide or sell low-priced energy and raw materials to buy high-priced consumer goods. Such unequal terms of trade resulted in the siphoning-off of scarce investment funds from interior to coastal region, thus hampering the interior region's effort towards rapid industrialization. As a matter of fact, an increasing proportion of investement funds have flowed from inland to coastal regions, particularly to Southeast China. To take Heilongjiang as an exmple, a total of Y 1.3 billion flowed out of the province during the 1st quarter of

1993 alone, in pursuit of quick and high investment returns.[4] The same took place in Shanxi Province, where approximately Y 1 billion of funds flowed out during 1992 to coastal areas in the form of loans and cross investment funds.[5] This outflow of funds made the fund-scarce interior region suffer more from the shortage of investment funds, while enabling the developed coastal provinces to grow faster.

The asymmetric incentive effect of fiscal decentralization, combined with the uneven result of price reform, widened the regional disparities between coastal and inland region, on the one hand, and between rural and urban area, on the other. Moreover, the prior opening of coastal area in the 1979-1988 period and the subsequent influx of foreign investments in the area gave the east region a considerable advantage in the growth race. As a result, regional income gaps and the disparities in growth rates widened.

Table 2 explains the regional disparities between coastal and

Table 2. Changes in Per Capita Income and Absolute and Relative Gaps among Regions (1979 -1992; 1952 Comparable Prices)

	Per Capita Income (Yuan)			Absolute Gap(Yuan)			Relative Differences		
	Eastern	Central	Western	E-W	E-C	C-W	E-W	E-C	C-W
1979	408	216	175	233	192	41	2.33	1.89	1.23
1985	672	346	276	396	326	70	2.43	1.94	1.25
1988	854	420	344	510	434	76	2.48	2.03	1.22
1989	869	426	352	515	441	74	2.46	2.04	1.21
1990	871	426	362	509	445	64	2.41	2.04	1.18
1991	967	443	390	577	524	53	2.48	2.18	1.14
1992	1155	500	431	724	655	69	2.68	2.31	1.16

Source: Computed from *Zhongguo Tongji Nianjian, 1990, 1992, 1993*.
Note: All per capita income figures are at 1952 comparable prices.

[4]Zhang Tai, "Ruhe duidai zhongguo de diqu jingji chabie (How Do We Treat China's Regional Economic Differences)," *Jingji Ribao* (November 26, 1993), p. 7.

[5]*Ibid*.

inland provinces absolute gaps and relative differences among regions for the period of 1979-1992. As of the end of 1988, average per capita income (at 1952 comparable prices) of the east reads Y853, 2.48 times of that of the west(Y420) and 2.03 times of the central region(Y344). Table 3 shows the widening of income gap between rural and urban area. In 1988, urban area's average income was 2.05 times of rural area; and even within rural area the eastern region was richer than the central or the western region.

The point is that the income gap has widened since 1980 mainly because of the combined consequences of coastal development strategy and the asymmetric impacts of fiscal decentralization and price reforms. In both tables, relative income differences between eastern and western regions, or between the rural and urban areas expanded. Thus the coastal region, accounting for only 36% of population and 11.6% of total territory, produced 62 % of GVIO in 1988, up from 60.9% in 1978 (see Table 3). By contrast, interior (central + western) region, accounting for 64% (as of 1991) of total population and 89.4% of total territory,[6] produced only 34.9% of GVIO, down from 39.1% in 1978. Even within the interior region, the west region showed the decelerated growth, as evidenced by the fall of its percentage share of GVIO from 13.2

Table 3. Urban-Rural and East-Central-West Income Gap

	1986	1987	1988	1989	1990	1991	1992	1993
Rural	100	100	100	100	100	100	100	100
East Region	117	122.5	125.7	127.3	124.9	146.1	147.5	
Central	94.2	93.7	89.8	88.0	90.4	87.4	90.8	
West	77.4	77.2	79.4	76.6	76.8	81.0	79.0	
Urban	195.4	198	205.4	209.6	202.1	217.9	232.9	273.3

Source: *China Statistical Yearbook* (1993), p.282; *Renmin Ribao* (1993). 11. 23. 1992 Nian Zhongguo Nongcun Jingji Fazhan Niandu Baogao he Fenxi 1993 Nian Fazhan Qushi (Annual Report of China's Rural Economic Development in 1992 and the Analysis Trend in 1993), (Beijing: Zhongguo Shehuikexue Chubanshe, 1993), p. 73.

[6] *Jingji Ribao* (September 24, 1992), p. 2.

percent in 1978 to 12.7 percent in 1985, and to 12.1% in 1988.

These income differences are ascribed to the differential rates of average annual rate of growth between the eastern (1.39), the central (1.05) and the western region (1.0) during the 1985-1990 period. In particular, South Eastern China recorded faster growth than other coastal provinces. To take Guangdong as an example, its GDP and GVIO grew at average rates of 12% and 18.5% respectively during the 1979-1991 period, which are far higher than the national average of 8.6% 3and 12.2%. Now E.F. Vogel cites it as a strong candidate for the fifth little dragon in East Asia.

Local Protectionism and Inter-Regional Trade Barriers

In the above, we have mentioned that introduction of different brands of "fiscal contracting" at provincial level in 1980, 1985, and 1988 touched off asymmetric incentive effects between provinces. This, however, coupled with administrative decentralization of economic management authority to local governments in planning and fixed investment, resulted in a new form of localism in the 1980s.

First, in order to maximize their net local revenue base as well as their own retained surplus revenue, which can be used to cover new investment or other expenditure at their own discretion, and the expansion of the fiscal independence, local governments competed to promote the massive growth of local investments outside of planning and the budget. Rich provinces expanded extrabudgetary investments; and inland provinces, partly to emulate rich provinces and also to increase their revenue, began to expand investment in industries, processing locally produced raw materials. Under the policy of "own production, own processing and own sales," inland resource-rich provinces such as Gansu, Xinjiang, and Inner Mongolia refused to supply coastal provinces with low-priced raw materials in exchange for high-priced consumer goods and opted for local processing. During 1986, for example, Gansu was adding 16,384 spindles and Xinjiang was building 25 textile factories and some 15,000 spindles.[7]

Table 4. Distribution of China's GVIO among Eastern, Central, Western Regions (1978-1993)

		GVIO (100 Million Yuan)			% Share		
		East	Central	West	East	Central	West
GVIO (Y100)	1978	2,575.3	1,096.1	559.4	60.87	25.91	13.22
	1980	3,069.7	1,301.9	620.0	61.50	26.08	12.42
	1985	4,985.2	2,221.5	1,054.4	60.35	26.89	12.76
	1986	5,446.7	2,410.7	1,121.2	60.66	26.85	12.49
	1987	6,302.9	2,740.0	1,264.3	61.15	26.58	12.27
	1988	7,522.5	3,139.4	1,465.3	62.03	25.89	12.08
	1989	8,045.1	3,340.7	1,559.1	62.15	25.81	12.04
	1990	12,539.8	5,424.5	2,687.9	60.72	26.27	13.04
	1991	18,006.9	6,925.8	3,315.3	63.75	24.52	11.74
	1992	24,363.4	8,627.8	4,074.5	65.73	23.28	11.00
	1993	26,338.8	9,348.8	4,784.3	65.08	23.10	11.82
1986 - 1988		-	-	-	61.28	26.44	12.28
1989 - 1993		-	-	-	63.49	24.60	11.93

Source: 1979-1990 figures are from *Zhongguo Gongye Jingji Tongji Nianjian*, (1991), pp.171-81. 1991 figures are from *Zhongguo Tongji Zaiyao* (1992), p.71. 1992 figures are from *Zhongguo Gongye Jingji Tongji Nianjian* (1993), 1993 Figures are from *Zhongguo Tongji Zaiyao* (1994), p.101.

Note : 1) The coverage of the East, Central and West regions is as follows:
East(12 provinces): Beijing, Tianjin, Hebei, Liaoning, Shanghai, Jiangsu, Zhejiang, Fujian, Shandong, Guangdong, Guangxi, and Hainan.
Central(9 provinces): Shanxi, Inner Mongolia, Jilin, Heilongjiang, Anhui, Jiangxi, Henan, Hubei and Hunan.
West(9 provinces): Sichuan, Guizhou, Yunnan, Shaanxi, Gansu, Qinghai, Xinjiang, and Tibet.

2) GVIO of 1978 is at 1970 constant price; GVIO from 1981 to 1989 are at 1980 constant price; GVIO of 1990 is at 1990 constant price; GVIO from 1991 to 1993 are at nominal price of each year.

[7]Watson, A. et al., "Who won the 'Wool War'?: A Case Study of Rural Product Marketing in China," *The China Quarterly*, No. 118 (June 1989), p. 234.

Second, and most importantly, local governments began to raise trade barriers to restrict imports of high-priced consumer goods, to stem the outflow of undervalued raw materials and energy, and to protect their local infant industries from competition. Resource-producing inland provinces had a strong incentive to prohibit out-of-town procurement, and limit sales of products from coastal provinces. Thus many of inland provinces introduced "local tax" on the imported products. A county in Sichuan not only imposed a penalty on the distribution of imported beer but also collected a 20% anti-dumping tax.[8] In other cases, color TVs imported from Beijing or Shanghai were charged an additional Y 200 when sold locally on top of the imported price.[9]

Another means is to probibit the import through administrative measures. Xinjiang banned the import from other provinces of 48 products, including bicycles, refrigerators, washing machines, and color televisions,[10] and it placed a levy of 30 yuan per ton on exported raw wool.[11] In 1990, a long distance truck in Shandong had to pass through 100 roadblocks to reach Fujian. Export of ten tons of oranges and lemons from Sichuan to Harbin City of Heilongjiang met with Y4,000 taxes *en route* to Harbin.[12]

Some went as far as to establish customs points and organize the militia to block transport which was taking the raw materials out of their jurisdiction. Morover, local blockade escalated over time as provinces or cities levied "taxes" and "fines" and penalized the local traders violating local rules or regulations. Provinces that did not make protective regulations felt exploited and introduced retaliatory measures. Although the State Council in December 1990 issued a circular calling for the immediate dismantling of "illegal duties" and "all unauthorized outposts at

---

[8]See Wang Peixian, "Adrifton the Bitter Sea-Repent! The Shore is at Hand," *Jingji Cankao* (May 29, 1990).

[9]"Zaijan Zhalan (Good-bye, Fences)," *Jingji Cankao* (May 24, 1990).

[10]Simon Long, *China to 2000: Reform's Last Chance?* (London: The EIU, Special Report No. M209, May 1992), p. 108.

[11]*Ibid.*

[12]*Ibid.*

roads, train stations, ports or provincial borders," the policy has yet to see its full success.

At the same time, given the inter-regional trade barriers, resource-poor coastal governments, enterprises, and merchants fought to secure supplies; and resource-producing provinces had to prevent the outflow of above-plan resources from getting into the hands of other provinces. Silk concoon wars (*chuncan dazhan*) that broke out in Sichuan, the Jiangsu-Zhejiang border (1985-86) and western Anhui (in 1988),[13] grain wars along the borders of Guangdong and Hunan and Guangdong and Guizhou, tobacco wars in Yunnan, wool & cashmere wars between inland provinces (Gansu, Qinghai, Xinjiang and Inner Mongolia) and major wool-consuming coastal provinces, and cotton wars between Xinjiang or Henan and other coastal provinces are just several illustrative examples of "economic war-lordism (*zhuhou jingji*)."[14] The regional blockade between provinces or between cites undermined the unity of the "single market" by prohibiting or restricting the free flow of materials, energy and capital among provinces.

Lastly, local governments tend to defy central macroeconomic control over outside-the-plan or extrabudgetary investments. When central control weakens, they resume the projects temporarily put on hold; and when central control is imminent, they accelerate the completion of investment projects, thereby undermining the macro equilibrium.

The combined result is the fragmentation of the Chinese economy and market, as was characterized by A. Donnithorne (1972) as "cellular economy."[15] In addition the localism, eroded the

---

[13]*Ibid.*, p. 15.

[14]For the details of 'wool war,' see Watson, et al., *op. cit.*, pp. 233-38; Findlay C., *Challenges of Economic Reform and Industrial Growth: China's Wool War* (Sydney: Allen & Unwin, 1992), pp. 170-180. Also see Liu Deyou, "Yangmao dazhan ji xu pingxi (The wool war cugently needs to be calmed down)," *Jingji Ribao* (November 15, 1986).

[15]A. Donnithorne, "China's Cellular Economy: Some Economic Trends since the Cultural Revolution," *The China Quarterly* (1972), pp. 605-19; T.P.Lyons, "China's Cellular Economy: A Test of the Fragmentation Hypothesis," *Journal f*

effectiveness of macroeconomic policies. In addition, local protectionism hampered the exit of backward, loss-making enterprises and outdated low-quality products.

Assimilated Industrial Structure and Lack of Specialization

More seriously, however, local protectionism, coupled with the competitive expansion of local investments, led to overlapping investments in the profitable light processing industries. With the objective of maximizing local net revenues, local governments, more often than not, encouraged or even subsidized investments in processing sector such as beer, tobacco, textile & apparel, and consumer appliances. Although these investments are locally essential, they led to the duplication of regional industrial structures at the macro level.

Coastal provinces accelerated their traditional way of developing processing industries; and inland provinces under the minority revenue-sharing scheme, in the face of increasing uncertainties surrounding the receipt of "incremental block grant," and ever-fierce competition for larger local revenue base, felt the strong incentive to emulate the investment behaviour of their rich neighbors to invest. Cotton fabric enterprises sprang up in Xinjiang and Henan provinces; the number of soybean-processing factories increased in Heilongjiang province. As a consequence, high-priced (hence high-taxed) light industries were developed by inland provinces in such a way as to increase their fiscal independence. Distorted relative price structure in favor of processing goods reinforced the emulation motives and competition between provinces.

The subsequently assimilated industrial structure biased towards lucrative processing industries came into being across the nation. In the process, small factories mushroomed across China, with the result of overlapping investments. This is evidenced by the fact that factor endowments and comparative advantages were disregarded. Of the 30 provinces in China, 27

of Comparative Economics, No. 9 (1985), pp. 125-44.

provinces have their own color TV factories, 26 have their own washing machine factories, 23 have their own refrigerator factories, 28 have their own automobile factories as at the end of 1990.[16] In 1988 approximately 144 large or small automobile plants across China produced only 644,700 vehicles, and the largest one has the production capacity of 100,000.[17]

Table 5 shows the similarity trend of the China's industrial structure measured by the standard deviations of the Hoffman coefficients ("Gross Light Industrial Output Value"/"Gross Heavy Industrial Output Value") between 1984 and 1988. The measure of SD(1) (standard deviation of the Hoffman coefficients of total 30 provinces) weakened slightly from 0.416 to 0.413 during the period, but the other measure, SD(2), which excluded the 4 traditional heavy (Liaoning, Heilongjiang, Jilin, and Shanxi) and 4 light provinces (Guangdong, Fujian, Jiangsu, and Zhejiang), fell by 0.019 from 0.33 to 0.31. By region, the western region shows the comparatively greater strengthening of the light industry bias in production, in relation to the eastern or the central region.

However, such similarity of industrial structure goes against the original aims of decentralization to pursue efficient growth based on differing factor endowments and regional comparative advantages. In addition, the redundancy or increase of small-scale investments with quick return not only undermined macro-economic control by intensifying local protectionism and local fights for raw materials, but also hampered the realization of "economies of scale" and specialization. Last but not least, assimilated industrial structure and the production of non-differentiated products in an overlapping and inefficient manner resulted in a substantial weakening of Chinese export competitiveness in the international market.

---

[16]Huang Tianhua, "Zhongguo quyu jingji fazhan yu duiwai kaifang (China's regional economic development and opening to the outside world)," *Jingji Dili* (Economic Geography), 13:3 (1993), p. 6.

[17]*Ibid.*

Table 5. Similarity Trend of China's Industrial Structure Measured by the Hoffman Coefficient s by Province or Region

Year	1984	1988		1992		1984-92
			Change		Changes	Changes
National Average	0.983	0.971	0.012	0.894	0.077	0.089
I. East	1.163	1.115	0.048	1.036	0.079	0.127
Beijing	0.781	0.801	-0.020	0.672	0.129	0.109
Tianjin	1.300	0.075	1.225	0.874	-0.799	0.426
Hebei	0.893	0.944	-0.051	0.810	0.134	0.083
Liaoning	0.543	0.509	0.034	0.425	0.084	0.118
Shanghai	1.271	1.101	0.170	0.873	0.228	0.398
Jiangsu	1.370	1.149	0.221	1.038	0.111	0.332
Zhejiang	1.797	1.759	0.038	1.740	0.019	0.057
Fujian	1.705	1.576	0.129	1.789	-0.213	-0.084
Shandong	1.218	1.068	0.150	0.973	0.095	0.245
Guangdong	1.965	1.903	0.062	1.792	0.111	0.173
Guangxi	1.524	1.217	0.307	1.091	0.126	0.433
Hainan	N.A.	1.666	N.A.	1.886	-0.220	N.A.
II. Inland	0.764	0.775	-0.011	0.669	0.106	0.095
A.Central	0.762	0.767	-0.005	0.648	0.119	0.114
Shanxi	0.390	0.427	-0.037	0.321	0.106	0.069
Inner M.	0.726	0.675	0.051	0.572	0.103	0.154
Jilin	0.643	0.716	-0.073	0.551	0.165	0.092
Heilongjiang	0.514	0.503	0.011	0.438	0.065	0.076
Anhui	1.153	1.123	0.030	0.972	0.151	0.181
Jiangxi	0.909	0.810	0.099	0.776	0.034	0.133
Henan	0.998	0.866	0.132	0.701	0.165	0.297
Hubei	0.924	0.943	-0.019	0.787	0.156	0.137
Hunan	0.825	0.827	-0.002	0.722	0.105	0.103
B.West	0.767	0.792	-0.025	0.716	0.076	0.051
Sichuan	0.912	0.900	0.012	0.783	0.117	0.129
Guizhou	0.605	0.749	-0.144	0.648	0.101	-0.043
Yunnan	0.979	0.989	-0.010	1.020	-0.031	-0.041
Tibet	0.740	0.623	0.117	0.465	0.158	0.275
Shaanxi	0.845	0.730	0.115	0.667	0.063	0.178
Gansu	0.303	0.415	-0.112	0.371	0.044	-0.068
Qinghai	0.658	0.501	0.157	0.406	0.095	0.252
Ningxia	0.414	0.462	-0.048	0.333	0.129	0.081
Xinjiang	0.800	0.910	-0.110	0.854	0.056	-0.054
S.D.(1)	0.416	0.413	-0.003	0.432	0.018	-0.016
S.D.(2)	0.330	0.311	-0.019	0.315	0.004	-0.015

Source: For the computation of 1984 coefficients, see *Zhongguo Tongji Nianjian* (China Statiscal Yearbook, 1985), p.320; for 1988, 1989 Issue, p.269; For 1992, 1993 Issue, p. 416.

Note: Hoffman Coefficient = Gross Value of Light Industrial Output / Gross Value of Heavy Industrial Output
S.D(1) stands for Standard Deviation of the Hoffman Coefficients among the total 30 provinces.
S.D(2) stands for Standard Deviation of the Hoffman Coefficients among the 22 provinces (excluding the 4 traditional light industry provinces of Guangdong, Fujian, Zhejiang, and Jiangsu, and the 4 traditional heavy industry provinces of Liaoning, Shanxi, Heilongjiang, and Jilin).

Underinvestments in Agriculture, Transportation and Basic Industries

The rapid expansion of such local investments has a double-edged effect. Siphoning off funds from locally collected revenue, that could otherwise be used by central government "crowded out" central investments in agriculture, raw materials, transportation, and energy industries. Excessive investment in the processing industries *cum* underinvestment in bottleneck- easing industries, brought about serious consequences in the Chinese economy for the 1980-1988 period. Firstly, underinvestment in agriculture accelerated the faltering farm output growth by weakening the agricultural infrastructure. Secondly, deficient investment in the energy sector aggravated the already acute power shortages, which in turn, combined with material shortages, disrupted the normal production of material and investment goods. Thirdly, unfavorable distribution of investment resources in transportation exacerbated the shortages of raw materials and energy in coastal area.

New Regional Economic Policy in the Post -1989 Period

In the above, we have reviewed various undesirable consequences of partial opening, incremental reforms and fiscal decentralization, which include the widening income gap, disparities in growth rates, local protectionism, overlapping investments, fragmentation of the commodity market, assimilated industrial structure, underinvestment in infrastructure and basic industries, and the loss of central macroeconomic control. Of these, the widening income gaps and the consequent "polarization" of the economy impinged substantially on the political economy of China in the early 1990s by undermining socio-political stability and balanced development of the economy.

The Tiananmen Incident that took place in June 1989 warned the Chinese political leaders of high socio-political costs of partial opening characterized as the coastal development strategy. The sudden collapse of the Soviet Union in December 1991 convinced the Party leaders of the urgent need of rectifying the excessive orientation of regional economic policy towards efficiency. The upsurge of ethnic minority unrests on the western borders of Xinjiang and Tibet accelerated the Chinese government's shift of the principle of the RDS. In September and October in 1987, and March 1988, a sequence of big riots broke out at Lhasa and the capital was placed under matial law from March 1989 to May 1990.

Readjustment of Excessive Efficiency-Orientation in RDS

At beginning in 1989, however, the Chinese government began to seriously worry about socio-political unrest. In an attempt to alleviate the socio-political risks associated with the efficiency-oriented RDS, China in late 1989 began to reemphasize regional equity between provinces or between regions. The preferential treatment allowed to the coastal area was extended to the major inland cities and border regions. The new catch phrase in China's RDS became "let's go to the western interior region" (zhou xikou), notably the Northwest and the Southwest areas.

That, however, did not mean that China gave up the primacy of economic efficiency in implementing regional development policy. Rather, it chose to strike a balance by rectifying the excessive orientation towards efficiency. Such reverse engineering or dialectic development of economic principle is common and recurrent in Chinese economic history, as is supported by oscillations between regional equity and efficiency in the pre-reform regional economic policy. Even in the 1990s, efficiency is still one of prime principles of implementing regional economic policy, but in the process of seeking it, China is taking into account other considerations such as regional balance, socio-political risks, and integrated development of the economy.

Omni-Directional Opening (quan fangwei kaifang) and "3-Yan" Development Strategy: Opening of Inland & Border Cities

Related closely to the shift from efficiency- to equity-oriented RDS is the introduction of full-scale open door policy. The Chinese Communist Party in May 1992 determined the policy direction to be "omni-directional, all-dimensional opening"(quan fangwei duo chengci kaifang),[18] and in October 1992 the 14th National Party Congress formally endorsed the full-scale open-door policy. The main characteristic features of the "omni-directional opening" were materialized in the "3-yan" regional development strategy through Document No. 4, which aims to extend the forefront of the open-door policy from the existing coastal area(yanhai) to minority areas(yanbian) and inland cities/ towns/counties along the Yangtzi River(yanjiang) to outside world.[19]

Thus, the so called "3-yan" development strategy has become the part & parcel of China's regional economic policy in the 1990s. The primary rationale of the "3-yan" development strategy is to revitalize the backward regions through the attraction of foreign capital and technology and also through the expansion of

---

[10]As a matter of fact, the feasibility of 'omni-directional opening' has been under careful study since the Tiananmen Incident of June 1989. In April 1991, the Fourth Plenum of the 7th National Congress decided to include the '3-Yan' RDS in the Ten Year Plan and the 9th Five Year Socio-Economic Plan.

[19]The total length of inland boder with other countries (mainly in *Xinan, Dongbei, Xibei* of China) is 22,000 km. *Jingji Ribao* (September 7, 1992), p. 1.

cross-border trade with neighboring countries.

The evolution of the strategy is as follows:

First, in June 1991, four northeastern cities/towns of Heihe, Shuifenhe (Heilongjiang), Hunchun (Jilin), and Manzhouli (Inner Mongolia) were designated as border open cities; in March 1992 they were given the economic management authority comparable to special economic zones; and in August of the same year Dandong (Liaoning), Yining, Urumqui, Bole, and Tacheng (Xinjiang) were added to the list of border open cities.[20] In June 1992 seven southwestern cities/towns bordering Vietnam, India, and Pakistan, including Nanning, Fengxiang, Dongxing (Gangxi), Kunming, Wanding, Luirui, and Hekou (Yunnan) became open to foreign investment.

Second, speaking of the opening of the Yangzi River Area (yanjiang), the Chinese government disclosed the ambitious Pudong Development Program in September 1990. At the Yangzi Delta Zone Conference in June 1992, 28 cities and 8 districts were declared open cities mainly to attract high-tech and light industries; and in August the same year, 5 cities of Chongqing, Yueyang, Wuhan, Jiujiang and Wuhu were given the authority equal to the 14 open coastal cities. The idea was that the Yangzi Economic Belt could be developed from the western end of Chongqing to the "dragon head" (longtou) city of Shanghai, which would lead the industrial and commercial development of the area.

Third, during the August 1992 to March 1993 period, the front of opening was again extended to the 11 capitals of inland provinces;[21] and they were given the preferential tax treatment

---

[20]Lin Qihui, "Diqu qingxie yu chanye qingxie yinggai jiehe qilai (Regional slant must be combined with industrial slant," *Jingji Daobao* (Hong Kong, December 6, 1993), p. 29. Xinjiang, which has 5,400 km of border with 8 countries, opened 8 inland commercial ports (*tongshang kouan*). Yunnan now has 17 open cities as inland ports, and Guangxi opened 20 odd trading points (*maoyi dian*) to expand trade with Vietnam. See *Jingji Ribao* (September 7, 1992), p. 1.

[21]The 11 open provincial capitals are Shenyang (Liaoning), Harbin (Heilongjiang), Changchun (Jilin), Huhehaote (Inner Mongolia), Xian (Shaanxi), Zhengzhou (Henan), Lanzhou (Gansu), Hefei (Anhui), Nanchang

comparable to that of the 14 open coastal cities.[22]

Finally, dozens of cities/towns along the Trans-China Railway(or TCR) linking Lianyungang to Lanzhou to Urumuqi were also opened to foreign investors (yanxian). Thus the "3-yan" strategy had to be rephrased as the "4-yan" strategy.

As a result, as of 1991 the total number of open cities/towns/counties amounted to 339, with the combined area totalling 545,000 km2, and a combined population of 230 million.[23] By region, the yanbian area (35,000 km2) has a population of 1.3 million, yanjiang area (330,000 km2) has 170 million people, and inland cities (180,000 km2) have 62 million people.

Establishment of Ten Major Economic Regions

At the same time, in order to shift from a region-tilted development strategy to an industry-oriented one, and also to implement the appropriate regional development strategy based on geo-economic idiosyncracies and nonidentical factor endowments, the State Planning Commission (hereafter "SPC") in 1992 publicized 10 major economic zones, replacing the existing 'three zone' concept of dividing China into the east, central and west. The SPC then organized many conferences to materialize the new concept of having 10 major economic regions, inlcuding West-South (Xinan), West-North (Xibei), South China (Huanan), Bohai-Rim (Huan Bohai), and Yangtze River Area (Changjiang). The focus of discussion centered upon the identification of priority sectors in each region.

The upshot of the discussion, albeit temporary, is depicted in Table 6. Each of the 10 economic zones is expected to foster priority industries that have comparative advantages. To take the Yangzi River Delta Zone as an example, it is envisaged that primarily high – and new – tech industries, along with real estate, finance, and insurance industries, will be developed. Overall, the idea of the 10 major zones is that technology – and information –

(Jiangxi), Chengdu (Sichuan) and Yinchuan (Ningxia).

[22]Huang, *op. cit.,* pp. 7-8.

[23]*Ibid.*

Table 6. Major Economic Zones in China and Industries of Comparative Advantage

Economic Zones	Provinces* included in Each Zone	Priority Industries
1) Northeast	Liaoning, Jilin, Heilongjiang, East of Inner Mongolia	Heavy Industry(esp. Steel Machinery, Petrochemical Ind.), Agriculture, Forestry, Animal Husbandry, Food Processing
2) Bohai-Rim	Beijing, Tianjin, Hebei, Shandong	High-Tech Ind., Export-oriented Light Ind., Marine Products
3) Yangzi Delta	Shanghai, Jiangsu, Zhejiang	High-Tech Ind. (esp. Electronics, Semi-Conductor), Finance, Real Estate, Telecomm., Information
4) South China	Guangdong, Fujian, Guangxi, Hainan	Export-oriented Light Ind., Finance & Insurance, Real Estate
5) Yellow River Mid-Stream	Shanxi, Henan, Shaanxi Midwest of Inner Mongolia	Energy Development, Heavy Ind., Space & Aeronautics, Timber Processing
6) Yangzi Midstream	Anhui, Jiangxi, Hubei, Hunan	River Transportation, Light Ind., Food Processing
7) Yellow River Upstream	Gansu, Qinghai, Ningxia	Hydraulic Power, Energy, Foodstuff, Raw Materials
8) Yangzi Upstream	Sichuan, Guizhou, Yunnan	Agriculture, Forestry, Heavy Ind.
9) Xinjiang	Xinjiang-Ugur A.R.*	Energy-Efficient Heavy Ind., Agriculture, Forestry
10) Tibet	Tibet A.R.*	Petroleum & Petro-Chemical Ind., Animal Husbandry, Agriculture

Source: *Jingji Ribao* (September 2, 1989); Renmin Ribao (Overseas ed.) (October 7, 1992).

Note: *Provinces represent provincial level governments, i.e., provinces, autonomous regions, and municipalities. A.R. stands for Autonomous Region intensive industries, export-oriented light industries, and service sectors are attracted to and agglomerated in the coastal area, whereas the interior region specializes in energy, raw materials and heavy industries.

This indicates that the main theoretical underpinnings supporting the differentiated development of the coastal-interior region, or east-center-west, remain unchanged, but only the regional classification has been diversified so as to reflect differing regional comparative advantages and to promote industrial & commercial exchanges between different regions.

Horizontal Inter-Regional Economic Cooperation

Related to the set up of the "10 major economic zones" is the Chinese government's attempt to facilitate inter-regional economic cooperation between coastal and interior provinces and between northern coastal provinces and eastern coastal provinces, under unified national planning and policy guidance. Vice-Premier Zhou Jiahua stressed at the Economic Planning Meeting for the Northwestern Region in August 1992 the strategic importance of the multi-sector (duo menlei), multi-tiered (duo chengce), multi-formed (duo yangshi) inter-regional horizontal economic cooperation.

The rationale is that, to avoid excessive income gaps between regions, trade between regions and factor mobility across regions should be promoted. Thus the focus of new RDS should be on the promotion of inter-regional cooperation and horizontal economic alliances (hengxiang jingji lianhe) between the resource-rich interior regions and resource-processing coastal areas. With respect to the principle of inter-regional economic cooperation, "mutual benefit and risk sharing on an equal footing"(huhui pingdeng) was stressed and the establishment of organizations of economic cooperation between coastal provinces and relatively underdeveloped inland provinces was encouraged. The catch phrase was "let the western region come forward to establish links with the east"(xichu donglian), "expand the opening and develop the market" (kuoda kaifang, fazhan shichang), and "seek cooperation and common prosperity" (lianhe xiezuo, gongtong fanrong).[24]

The main area of horizontal inter-regional economic cooperation was trade between regions, but the area has become diversified to include cross-investment between regions or between provinces on the joint development and use of energy and mineral resources, coordinated planning and construction of trans-provincial infrastructure and telecommunication facilities, exchanges or pooling of technology, knowhow, raw materials, capital goods, etc. To take transport infrastructure as an example, construction of trans-provincial highways and high-speed railway, requiring huge capital and a long gestation period, cannot be undertaken by a single province or a single city, but various bottlenecks related to it should be resolved through coordination and consultation between provinces or cities.

Fostering of Township & Village Enterprises in the Interior Region

Comparatively larger share of township and village enterprises (TVEs) in the East-Central region (Huazhong), notably Jiangsu and Zhejiang, and Southern China (Huanan) has been the primary source of faster economic growth in the East region. As a matter of fact, 80% of the peasants' net income in the coastal developed areas comes from TVEs, which has been the fastest growing sector of the economy. As of 1992, there were 20 million TVEs in China, which accounted for 31% of GNP.[25] The merit of the TVEs is that they operate primarily outside the state plan, and hence are more responsive to market demand than state-owned enterprises. TVEs also contribute a great deal to the expansion of the employment of rural surplus labor, which is estimated to be 150 to 200 million across the whole nation. Therefore, by encouraging the set-up of TVEs in the interior region (central and western region), China may accelerate the development of the economically backward region.

---

[24]*Jingji Ribao* (August 30, 1992), p. 1.

[25]*China Daily* (December 14, 1993), p. 1.

Table 7. Contribution of TVEs to Production and Empoyment by Region

(As of 1991)

	Coastal	Interior Region		
	East	Total	Central	West
(a) Rural Labor Force (million)	153.41	266.67	196.43	70.24
% of National Total	36.5	63.5	46.8	16.7
(b) Labor Force in TVEs (million)	45.68	46.96	39.01	7.95
% of National Total	49.3	50.7	42.1	8.6
% of (a)	29.8	17.6	19.9	11.3
(c) Rural Output Value in the Region (Y 100 million)	9,264	7,355	5,844	1,511
% of National Total	55.7	44.3	35.2	9.1
(d) Output by TVEs (Y 100 million)	6,221	3,359	2,938	421
% of National Total	63.9	35.1	30.7	4.4
% of (c)	67.0	45.7	50.3	27.9
(e) Output by Industrial TVEs (Y 100 million)	5,082.5	2,024	1,788	236
% of National Total	71.6	28.5	25.2	3.3

Sources: Based on the statistics provided by the Ministry of Agriculture. See *Jingji Ribao* (September 24, 1992), p. 2.

Notes: Regional classification of East, Central and West in this Table differs from the conventional wisdom of 12: 9: 9 used in Chinese studies. East region thus includes 10 provinces and municipalities (Beijing, Tianjin, Shanghai, Jiangsu, Shandong, Zhejiang, Guangdong, Fujian, Liaoning and Hebei), and central region covers 10 provinces (Heilongjiang, Jilin, Shanxi, Shaanxi, Henan, Sichuan, Hubei, Hunan, Anhui and Jiangxi), with the west region covering 10 provinces (Inner Mongolia, Ningxia, Gansu, Qinghai, Xinjiang, Yunnan, Guizhou, Guangxi, Tibet and Hainan).

However, the role of TVEs in the interior region in general and in the western region in particular has been minimal. As one can see in Table 7, as of 1991, TVEs in the western region employed only 11.3% of the rural labor force in the region as compared to 29.8% in the east region and 19.9% in the central region. Even in the share of total rural output value in each region, the west showed the lowest (27.9%) as compared to 67.0% in the east and 50.3% in the central region. The regional disparity widens if one narrows down the scope of TVEs to those in the industrial sector.

The western region accounted for a meager 3.3% of total national output value produced by industrial TVEs. Indeed, in Jiangsu Province, well known for the Sunan Model of TVEs, TVEs produced 51.3% of the provincial GVIO, contributed 24.8% of locally collected revenue, and exported 36.8% of the provincial export in 1990.[26]

Underdevelopment of TVEs in the west is also supported by the fact that 9 provinces in the Northwest and Southwestern regions accounted for only 9.24% of the national total output value, whereas the 4 coastal provinces of Jiangsu, Shandong, Zhejiang, and Guangdong took the lion's share of 43.1%. In particular, the total number of TVEs in Yunnan and Xinjiang were only 0.71% and 0.28% of the national total, respectively.

Formation of Cross-Jurisdictional Enterprise Groups

In order to mitigate the aggravating regionalism and the concomitant fragmentation of the Chinese economy, Chinese economists came up with the idea of forming horizontal mergers of enterprises across regions. In 1989, the Chinese plan of fostering 100 big enterprise groups was publicized, and in September 1991, 55 large enterprise groups were listed for the first round of experimentation.

The idea was that, by forming enterprise groups encompassing

Table 8. Changes in the Number of Economic Associations and Enterprise Groups (1986-1990)

By Year	1986	1987	1988	1989	1990
Total Number of Economic Associations Enterprise Groups	65,000	32,000			50,000
• Nationally Approved	1,000	2,000	1,630	4,000	
• Locally Approved	6,833				
Number of Ent. Groups in the State Plan	14			15	18

Note: For detailed sources, see Kim, *Chinese Policy of Fostering Enterprise Groups: Current Status and Prospects* (Seoul: KIEP, 1992) p. 37.

[26]*Jingji Ribao* (September 21, 1991), p. 1.

different regions and cities, China might be able to check the ever-worsening localism, and promote the free flow of production factors across jurisdictions. Indeed, an enterprise group is an independent accounting entity which consists of two or three layers of umbrella enterprises in different regions, which have different degrees of business/technical links with one or two core enterprises.[27] Normally, the core enterprise exercises a unified control over member enterprises' important management decisions on personnel, production, investment, procurement, and marketing, with daily management left to member companies.

This, however, does not mean that before 1989 there were no quasi-groups. As one can see in Table 8, there were as many as 1,630 quasi-enterprise groups as of the end of 1988,[28] but the majority of them were mainly "loosely integrated enterprise associations," which do not have core enterprises, or whose core enterprises perform only a perfunctory role. Some are unlawful groups which merely changed their names to enjoy the special benefits granted to enterprise groups.

The 55 experimental enterprise groups, however, differ from the existing enterprise groups in that the enterprises in different regions may integrate together, regardless of whether their control organs and tax payment channels are changed or not. In addition, many enterprise groups, subject to prior approval from the relevant authorities, are allowed to introduce a "stock" system (gufen zhi), conduct cross-investment between member companies, and set up a financing company within the group. Thus, theoretically speaking, member companies in enterprise groups may liberate themselves from the straitjacket of dual controls both by local governments and relevant central departments.[29]

---

[27]According to the Chinese regulation, "an enterprise group is an economic entity to meet the demand for mass production in a socialist planned commodity economy." The relationship between different layers of member enterprises in a group is usually regulated by a group charter or contracts agreed upon.

[28]China in 1987 publicized the rules and regulations on the establishment of enterprise groups.

[29]Four other major objectives of fostering enterprise groups include (1)

Regional distribution of the 55 enterprise groups reflects the government's policy intentions. As one can see in Table 9, the 55 groups have greater percentage shares in inland provinces than in the case of 1,630 enterprise groups as of 1988. Whereas 58.8% of total number (1,630) of enterprise groups as of 1988 were concentrated in the coastal regions, only 37.3% of the 55 groups were in the coastal provinces (see Table 9). This reflects the government's re-emphasis on developing the comparatively backward inland regions, the area along the Yangzi River, and national borders.

---

improving industrial structure through rapid capital accumulation and technological development, (2) stabilizing the macro economy by exercising effective control over enterprises, (3) alleviating the government burden by enhancing the efficiency in production and investment, and (4) enhancing international competitiveness. More specifically, it is envisaged that the horizontal merger or vertical intigration of firms across regions may improve what Leibenstein called "X-efficiency" by promoting the optimal use of inputs to produce a certain quantity of output, and to increase the efficiency in the allocation of resources between different industries and regions by rationalizing the organization and structure of enterprises. "Risk-hedging" or "entry deterrence" theories of market economies are not sufficient to explain the horizontal merger or vertical integration in China, where the risk of bankruptcy is still low, and factor and commodity markets are underdeveloped.

In addition, Chinese authorities also attempted to use enterprise groups as a policy tool to control the macro economy. The idea was that, by controlling a small number of big enterprise groups, rather than controlling a large number of small enterprises, they may save monitoring and information costs. Such a need became more pressing as neither monetary nor fiscal policies worked to cool down the overheated Chinese economy during the readjustment period of late 1988 to the end of 1991.

Last but not least, Chinese policy makers felt the need to upgrade China's competitiveness and advance into the international market. Yet, this could not be achieved without rapid accumulation of capital, technological development, and the reshaping of industrial structure in favor of high-tech industries. To this aim, the reorganization of the enterprise structure in key industries was one of the few experimentable options open to the Chinese policy makers.

Table 9. The 55 Enterprise Groups by Regions

Coastal Provinces: 18		Non-Coastal Provinces: 37	
Liaoning	4(3 in Shnyang)	Beijing	9
Hebei	3	Heilongjiang	4(1 in Harbin)
Shandong	1(All in Jinan)	Jilin	4(3 in Changchun)
Jiangsu	2(1 in Najing)	Inner Mongolia	1
Fujian	-	Sichuan	5(1 in Chengdu, 2 in Chongqing)
Guangdong	1(Gangzhou)		
Hainan	-	Shaanxi	3(All in Xian)
Guangxi	-	Henan	2
Shanghai	6	Hubei	5(3 in Wuhan)
Tianjin	1	Hunan	1
		Guizhou	3

Source: China State Council (1992), *Internal Document for the Fostering of 55 Experimental Enterprise Groups.*

Effectiveness and Sustainability of the New Regional Development Strategy

Assessment of the New Regional Development Strategy

In the previous section 1, we introduced the Chinese government's "RDS" in the early 1990s to alleviate various undesirable consequences of partial reforms *cum* administrative decentralization in the 1980s. The major policy components of the new RDS include: (1) readjustment of excessive efficiency-orientation (2) omni-directional opening of inland & border cities, (3) establishment of ten major economic regions, (4) promotion of horizontal inter-regional economic cooperation, (5) fostering of township & village enterprises in interior region, and (6) formation of cross-jurisdictional enterprise groups.

It may be difficult and premature to assess precisely the effectiveness of all these policy measures of the new RDS, as we have had a very short observation period since 1989. However, we may be able to assess preliminarily the outcome of the new RDS based upon scattered evidence and available statistics.

First of all, it may be possible to examine the effectiveness of the omni-directional open door policy by looking at the regional distribution of foreign direct investment in China and the increasing trend of cross-border trade with neighboring countries.

Secondly, by analyzing the workings of economic cooperation between provinces and the newly formed enterprise groups, we may be able to assess the effectiveness of China's efforts to overcome local protectionism.

Lastly, by analyzing the changes in the Hoffman coefficients between 1988 and 1992, we may be able to assess whether the investment bias towards light processing industries has been mitigated or not.

Effectiveness of Omni-Directional Opening

- Attraction of Foreign Direct Investment into the Interior Region

Let us start with the assessment of the omni-directional opening strategy. One of the chief aims of the strategy is to attract more foreign direct investment (FDI) into the interior region. Therefore the success of the policy should be proven by a rise in the share of the interior region in total FDI attracted into China. Table 10 shows the regional distribution of FDI contracted during the 1979-1992 period. The percentage share of other regions rose from 5.6% of total FDI amount in 1990 to 9.6% in 1992, and the share in the total number of projects increased from 8.1% to 14.9%. However, analysis of the regional distribution of practically utilized FDI shows that the share of interior (central + western) regions in total amount of FDI only inched up from an average of 8.3% in the 1979-1991 period to 9.8% in 1992, and the share of the coastal area was as high as 90.2% in the same year, only down 1.5% from a year earlier. By region, South China (Guangdong, Fujian, Guangxi, and Hainan) still accounts for the largest share of FDI with 35.1%, followed by Central China (Shanghai, Zhejiang, and Jiangsu) with 20.2%, and Bohai-Rim area (Beijing,

Table 10. Percentage Shares of Major Economic Regions in China's FDI Contracted (1979-1992)

Unit: %

	1979-87		1988		1989		1990		1991		1992	
	No.	Amt.	No.	Amt.	No.	Amt.	No.	Amt.	No.	Amt.	No.	Amt.
South China	75.2	58.9	69.4	61.0	65.8	69.4	61.2	64.5	49.8	62.3	33.0	49.2
Yangzi Delta	6.6	12.6	10.5	14.8	11.5	12.2	12.2	12.5	16.2	13.5	25.3	22.3
Bohai-Rim	7.4	13.2	9.1	13.8	10.4	7.7	11.6	8.9	16.8	12.0	19.6	14.2
Northeast	3.7	5.5	5.9	5.1	6.6	7.1	6.9	8.5	7.2	6.3	7.2	4.7
Other Regions	7.1	9.8	5.1	5.3	5.7	3.6	8.1	5.6	10.0	5.9	14.9	9.6

Source: *Zhongguo Duiwai Maoyi Jingji Nianjian* (China Foreign Trade & Economic Yearbook), each year.

Tianjin, Shandong, Liaoning, and Hebei) with 18.8%.[30]

This indicates that, in spite of the China's strategy of omni-directional opening, foreign investors are still cautious about advancing into the inland area fraught with backward transport and telecommunications infrastructure. As a result, the actual growth of FDI bound for the interior region is lower than argued or desired by the Chinese authorities. However, given that most of inland-bound FDI is known to be increasing faster in 1993 and in the first half of 1994, for which a detailed regional breakdown is not available, a few more years have to pass before one can make a full assessment of the success of the Chinese full-scale open door policy.

• Expansion of Cross-Border Trade in the Border Region

In contrast to the somewhat unclear results in the attraction of FDI into the interior region since 1992, it is clear that China's new RDS since 1989 has exerted a significant positive impact on the expansion of cross-border trade. With the implementation of a strategy of opening the country's borders and improving relations with neighboring countries, border trade expanded rapidly. According to the Ministry of Foreign Trade and Economic Cooperation, the total volume of China's border trade in 8 border

[30] *Zhongguo Duiwai Maoyi Jingji Nianjian* (1993/1994).

provinces, despite the incomplete institutional arrangements, expanded from US $650 million in 1989 to US $1.14 billion in 1991, and to US $1.865 billion (including US $787 million of imports and US $1.078 billion of exports) in 1992.[31] In 1993 the border trade volume more than doubled from a year earlier to US $ 4 billion.[32] As of the 1992, China had 184 1st class border customs posts ("kouan") under central government control,[33] 330 2nd class border points under the control of local governments, and 292 markets for trading among border tradesmen.[34]

Heilongjiang alone has 19 1st class customs posts, including 4 temporary ones including Heihe and Shuifenhe along the 3,045km border with Russia, and the total border trade volume reached SFr 2 billion (or US $1.28 billion), up 95% from a year earlier, accounting for two thirds of the total national border trade volume for the same year.[35]

Jilin Province, bordering 233km with Russia and 973km with North Korea, recorded a whopping 120% increase in the volume of border trade during the first 5 months of 1993 as compared to the same period in 1992.[36] Inner Mongolia, with 3,193km of border with Mongolia and 1,010km of border with CIS, has witnessed a big rise in the volume of border trade which grow from SFr 630,000 in 1985 to SFr 30 million in 1991, and to SFr 843.7 million (US $ 600 million) in 1992. The volume of border trade in Xinjiang (mainly with Pakistan) rose 41.9% from a year earlier to US $ 99.58 million in 1991;[37] Yunnan's border trade (mainly with Miyanmar) increased by 30% to Y1.6 billion in 1991;[38] Guangxi

---

[31]Hua Juxian and Jing Wei(1993), "Border Trade in Minority Regions," p. 14.; Yu Lixin (1993), p. 67.

[32]Lin Qihui (1993), p. 29.

[33]The number of 'kouan' has increased to 216 by 1993. *Ibid* .

[34]*Ibid.*

[35]*Renmin Ribao* (July 1, 1993); *Ibid.*

[36]*Renmin Ribao* (Overseas Edition) (September 1, 1993).

[37]Hua Juxian and Wei (1993), pp. 14-15.

[38]*Ibid.*

Autonomous Region's border trade with Vietnam along the 1,020 km border more than tripled from Y200 million (US $37.6 million) in 1991 to Y620 million (US $112.4 million) in 1992.[39]

As a consequence, per capita income of Shuifenhe in Heilongjiang jumped to Y3,200, and that of Manzhouli in Inner Mongolia rose to Y2,400, far outstripping the provincial average. This all indicates that China's omni-directional opening has been successful and the subsequent expansion of border trade has contributed a great deal to the narrowing of income gap between the the interior and the coastal region.

Effectiveness of Efforts to Overcome Local Protectionism.

- Regional Economic Cooperation

As a result of the China's policy to promote inter regional economic cooperation since 1989, three types of regional economic cooperation bodies have appeared in China. The first kind of regional economic cooperation body is "the inter-provincial economic cooperation organization." Its best example is "the Northeast China Economic Cooperation Zone," which aims to facilitate the flow of raw materials and commodities among Jilin, Liaoning, Heilongjiang, and Inner Mongolia (3 mengs and 1 city). The three provinces of Shanxi, Gansu, and Sichuan formed a similar organization and signed 5,500 technological cooperation project to develop 1,200 kinds of new products and generate Y237 million new revenues. In addition, Xinjiang cooperates with coastal provinces in the industries of textile, electronics, chemical, automobile, and nonferrous metals.

The second type is the cooperation between cities among different provinces. In 1992, fourteen cities in the provinces of Hunan, Hubei, Sichuan, Guizhou, and Gangxi formed an "Economic & Technological Cooperation Zone" to promote exchanges in commodity, raw materials, technology, and capital. A regional economic cooperation association of the same purpose has also been established among 18 cities/districts in provinces

[39] *Ibid .; Renmin Ribao* (Overseas Edition) (June 3, 1993).

of Jiangsu, Anhui, and Jiangxi. In addition, Lhasa in Tibet during the 1989-1993 period garnered Y70 million in profits out of the economic & technological cooperation projects with cities in Jiangsu, Zhejiang, and Shandong, whose total value was Y700 million.

The third type is economic cooperation among cities/counties within a province. The so called "Su-Xi-Chang-Tong" inter-city cooperation network among the four cities of Suzhou, Wuxi, Changzhou, and Nantong is the best example of intra-provincial cooperation organization.

Although detailed statistics are not available, it is known that almost every province has a similar organization or network to deal with trade, technology, and finance between cities/counties. These differing types of regional cooperation bodies might have contributed to a certain degree to the lessening of the local protectionism, but it is doubtful whether the force of regional cooperation has overpowered that of regionalism and local protectionism.

• Enterprise Groups to Alleviate Local Protectionism?

In spite of the increases in the number of enterprise groups (2,000 as of the end of 1992) it is not certain whether or not the formation of enterprise groups relieved localism. The reasons are as follows: First, evidence suggests that the formation of enterprise groups did not substantially change the behaviour of local governments, nor mitigate the local blockade, but merely changed the channel of localism. Many local governments, mainly for fear of a reduction in their power and local revenues, still attempt to hinder or retard the formation of trans-jurisdictional enterprise groups, thereby maintaining the fragmented nature of the Chinese market.

Second and more importantly, the formation of the groups themselves could not cure the irrational incentive structure of Chinese fiscal management and industrial organizations. While not eliminating or alleviating the local protectionism, it has engendered various undesirable byproducts, such as diseconomies of scale and scope, and over-concentration of economic power.

This indicates that, without any fundamental reforms of the price and fiscal incentive structure of the Chinese economy, and without the significant improvement of distribution and transport systems, mere reorganization of enterprise structure could not enhance the mobility of production factors and resources across regions or provinces.

- Continued Civil Riots in Minority Areas : Evidence of the Ineffectiveness of the new RDS in Alleviating Political Localism

The new RDS has aimed at alleviating the socio-political chasm between the rich coastal and poor inland areas. However, scattered evidence suggests that socio-political instability is strongly associated with the economic disintegration of the Chinese economy, the rising income gap, and localism. The number of civil riots in minority areas as a reasonable measure of the sufficiency and effectiveness of the new RDS did not decrease since 1989.

In Xinjiang-Uyigur Automous Region, secessionist tendency was getting stronger at the influence of the Kirghistan's Islamic fundamentalism to form the Great Islamic Circle, and a major uprising took place in April 1990 near the Silk Road terminus of Kashgar.[40] In August 1994 30,000 laborers, soldiers, and civilians at Urmuqi, the capital of Xinjiang-Ugur Autonomous Region, and five other cities including Keshen, Yining, Ahkesu, and Kelamayi were known to take part in a protest against the government's unfair economic policy against minority regions, resulting in hundreds of casualities.[41] Many Tibetans, despite Chinese provision of subsidies and investments, feel that they are economically exploited by the Han Chinese, and this feeling, combined with aspirations of political independence, formed a formidable source of socio-political unrest in the region.

---

[40]For details of ethnic unrests in 1987-1988, see *Far Eastern Economic Review* (August 25, 1988), p. 28; and Simon Long (1992), pp. 108-109.

[41]*Zhengming* (October 1994).

Table 11. Regional Distribution of GVIO (As at the end of 1991)

	East	Central	West
Extractive Industries	36	36	28
•Energy	35	41	24
•Raw Materials	55	29	16
Light Processing	67	18	15
Heavy Processing	81	13	6

Source : SPC Investment Research Institute (1992), p. 16.

Table 12. Regional Distribution of of Total Gross Fixed Investment
(As at the end of 1991)

Unit: Million Yuan, % share

	1989	1990	1991	1992
National Total	4,137.7	4,449.3	5,508.8	7,855.0
	(100.0)	(100.0)	(100.0)	(100.0)
Coastal Region	2,380.6	2,525.7	3,142.2	4,690.1
	(57.5)	(56.8)	(57.0)	(59.7)
Interior Region	1,600.1	1,755.5	2,142.1	2,886.1
	(38.7)	(39.5)	(38.9)	(36.7)
Central Western	1,006.1	59 3.9	1,108.2	647.3
	(24.3)	(14.3)	(24.9)	(14.6)
	1,333.6	808.6	1,799.8	1,086.3
	(24.2)	(14.7)	(22.9)	(13.8)
Nonclassified Inv.	157.1	168.1	224.5	279.4
	(3.8)	(3.8)	(4.1)	(3.6)

Source : *Zhongguo Gudingzichan Tongji Ziliao* (1993), p. 28; *Zhonguo Tongji Nianjian* (China Statistical Yearbook, 1993), p. 147.

The preliminary outcome of the analysis is that the new RDS is neither sufficient nor effective in lessening the socio-political grievances of minority people. This is evidenced by sporadic civil riots and strikes that have broken out in minority regions.

•Specialization/Readjustment of Regional Industrial Structure

It is hard to assess the success of the new RDS in readjusting the regional distribution of industrial structure between the east and the inland. However, as shown in Table 11, the Chinese government's effort to remedy the lopsided industrial structure and the dominance of the coastal region has yet to succeed. The coastal region still produces 67% of light processing industrial output value and 81 percent of heavy processing industrial output value. By contrast, the inland region (central + western) accounts for 65% of GVIO in extractive industries. This implies that the regional bias towards the coastal region in the production of processed goods has not been corrected to the satisfaction of central authorities.

The analysis of the Hoffman coefficients, as shown in Table 5, confirms that light industry bias has improved only marginally in coastal provinces in 1992 as compared to 1988. By contrast, heavy industry bias in the interior region deepened as indicated by the fall of the Hoffman coefficients in the central and western regions. And the SD 2 (standard deviations measured by excluding the 4 traditionally heavy industry provinces and the 4 tradtionally light industry provinces in Table 5) of the Hoffman coefficients of 29 provinces changed little, from 0.311 in 1988 to 0.315 in 1992.

When we look at the regional distribution of domestic fixed investment shown in Table 12, we come to a clearer conclusion that the coastal bias in the distribution of fixed investment, after being slightly improved in the 1989-1990 period, strengthened in the 1990-1992 period. In 1992, the eastern region accounted for the lion's share with 59.7% of the national total fixed investment, up from 56.8% in 1990,[42] whereas inland region accounted for 36.7%, down from 39.5% in 1990. If one looks at investment increment, the coastal-interior comparison is even clearer. In 1991 alone, 61.5% of the increment of fixed investment originated from the eastern region. The regional differences in fixed asset investment is also supported by the fact that the rates of growth of

[42]For the detailed regional distribution of gross social fixed investment among provinces during the 1986-1991 period, see *Zhongguo Gudingzichan Touzi Tongji Ziliao* 1990-1991 (1994), pp. 27-28.

fixed investment in eastern, central, and western regions between 1982 and 1991 were 19.7%, 16.2%, 18.2%, respectively.

Conclusion: The Course of China's RDS in the Future

Thus far, we have assessed the effectiveness of the new RDS in various aspects. The preliminary conclusion is that China's RDS since 1989 was relatively effective in expanding cross-border trade, but it was not very effective in attracting FDI into inland regions or in remedying localism, regional protectionism, coastal bias, and the tendency to invest in light processing industries. Part of the ineffectiveness stems from the imperfect design of the new RDS, which intended to mitigate the strong inertia of localism and irrationalities embedded in the decentralizd economic system. However, it is fair to say that the ineffectiveness of the equity-oriented RDS is related to the incompatibility between policy tools and the changed economic environment in the early 1990s.

First, the new RDS did not fully take into account the marketization trend of the Chinese economy since 1984 and the concomitant changes in the means and channels of resource distribution in the decentralized economy. The domain of the non-state sector economy, encompassing township enterprises, privately owned firms, and foreign joint ventures, which are outside the state plan, continues to expand; and the financing sources of investment have diversified into non-budgetary sources of self-raised funds, bank loans, and foreign capital. As of 1992, the share of extrabudgetary revenue now accounts for 49.3% of total fiscal revenue (budgetary + extrabudgetary revenue), and the shares of local government in total budgetary and extrabudgetary revenues are as high as 63.5% and 55.7%, respectively.[43]

Given this situation, the conventional means of centrally allocating the budget, materials, and fixed investment between regions became ineffective in accomplishing the multi-faceted

---

[43]*Ibid,* p. 57.

policy objectives. Diversified economic entities distributed an increasing proportion of their financial resources according to market signals. Thus, the central government had little leverage to readjust the regional inequality through subsidies or through central redistribution of revenues and investment resources. In addition, the Ministry of Finance, or the central bank, with only a limited pool of financial resources and power, was not able to exercise fiscal or monetary policy to correct the deficiencies of the marketizing economy, and as a result, resources could not be distributed efficiently into the essential sectors and regions suffering from relatively low prices.

Second, despite the implementation of the new RDS, there is no evidence that local governments have stopped acting like central governments in the region. Rather, they wield tremendous power in resource distribution as the main beneficiaries of decentralization. Critics say that China's local governments turned into politico- economic dinosaurs that pay little heed to central directives but try to get around central control. Therefore, without genuine economic decentralization, in which firms, not local governments, have the economic management authority, the new RDS is just one more addition to the list of existing proposals to relieve regional disparities which have been under experimentation. Third, reform of the distorted relative price and tax structure, which favors the coastal region producing high-priced light industry goods, is still incomplete and has yet to achieve its goal. In the meantime, the interior region, producing mainly low-priced raw materials and energy, must make sacrifices. Therefore, without the fundamental price and tax reforms, the government's aim of lessening the regional income gap through regional economic cooperation will be hard to fulfill.

Finally, factor markets, including the capital market and labor market, have to be developed further, thereby replacing the administrative restrictions on the mobility of labor and capital across regions. Without modernizing the factor markets, introduction of a new RDS aimed to relieve local blockades in the future, may be doomed to fail because the rent-seeking local governments have little economic incentive to facilitate the flow of capital across provinces or regions. Marketization of the economy should be supported by the development of commodity and factor markets.

9

China and the Development Trajectory of Northeast Asia

Zhou Yuan
(Chinese National Research Center for Science & Technology for Development)

The Ongoing Situation and the Feature of the Economic Cooperation in Northeast Asia:

The potential for the economic cooperation in Northeast Asia

The concept of a North East Asia (NEA) region is relatively new and in the past, few people considered this area as a region. In view of this past negligence, it is not surprising that the boundaries and characteristics of the region have not been well defined. Usually, NEA refers to the area extending from the Korean Peninsula in the south to Mongolia in the west to Far East Russia in the north and to Japan in the east. It includes both Koreas, Mongolia, Inner Mongolia and the three provinces of Northeast China, the entire Far East and Eastern Siberia of Russia and Japan. It covers an area of 17.5million square kilometers and supports a population of 580 million. The Sea of Japan(or East

Sea as it is referred to locally) lies in the centre of this region. As indicated below, the NEA region thus comprises a highly complementary group of countries.

Japan, which has served as the economic powerhouse for much of the explosive growth observed in East Asia over the past two decades, is by far the largest economy and increasingly has been shifting its less profitable industries offshore to the mutual benefit of itself and its neighbours. South Korea, one of the most successful countries among the East Asian Tigers, has become a strong economy as a result of good economic management and hard work which has enabled it to expand GDP per capita at almost 7% per year since 1980. Such growth has been largely the result of exports which have grown at more than 11% annually over the same period. South Korea, like Japan, is very limited in its own natural resources and has a strong interest in participating in the development of resources in neighbouring countries. Also, South Korean firms are finding that since rising wages and input costs are reducing their competitiveness in certain areas, they are looking for new offshore locations to invest their capital, know-how and access to markets.

China's growth since the opening of its economy in 1978 has been remarkable. GDP per person has grown by almost 8% per year since 1980 and exports grew by more than 12% per year. GDP is currently growing at nearly 14% although inflation is growing even more rapidly. China's successes have largely been the result of an export push which included the creation of Special Economic Zones(SEZ) and Open Cities, export incentives, and mandatory export targets for some state enterprises. The Northeastern part of China has not yet participated in this economic growth although it offers vast potential in view of its abundant but relatively low cost labour and its considerable natural resources, including agricultural surpluses and minerals. The potential is further enhanced by the strong cultural ties that bind parts of the Northeast to the Korean Peninsula. Northeast China also offers a vast market for a wide range of manufactured products and access to this market is highly sought after.

North Korea offers a contrast to its neighbours in many ways yet it too has a resource base and location that makes it highly complementary. North Korea finds itself at a much earlier stage on the path to export growth, however, it has made a firm commitment to this goal by creating its own Free Economic and Trade Zone in 1991. In contrast to South Korea, North Korea has relatively good access to natural resources and has relatively abundant and low cost labour. It also has a number of excellent seaports that are strategically located to serve part of the growing trade from the hinterland. The disintegration of the Soviet Union and COMECON has meant that its trading arrangements and sources of supply for its industries have been severely disrupted over the past four years. As a result, economic growth in North Korea is able to provide access to ports, natural resources and low cost labour that are potentially valuable to its neighbours and thus offers the prospect of mutual benefit.

Mongolia is a resource rich country awaiting its opportunity for development. It has abundant supplies of minerals, a relatively efficient livestock sector and low-cost but limited labour. Its disadvantage is that it is landlocked, distant from the sea and forced to transport exports over long distances on congested and indirect railroads. Along with North Korea, it is suffering the effects of the breakup of the Soviet Union and the disruption of trade and aid.

Far Eastern Russia represents an important but remote part of the Russian Federation. It is a resource-rich area with the added advantage of excellent seaports and a well-developed specialised industry structure. The Far East also contains a very well educated and trained breakup of the Former Soviet Union. Its economy has the task of re-orientation to a totally different set of suppliers and markets from those that existed previously. This task will be made easier by virtue of its location as a "gateway" for Russia to the Asia Pacific region. This provides the area with opportunities to develop new trading partners and to find new sources of supplies of its industries and domestic markets. The area also offers as a considerable attraction to tourists as a result both of its historical origins and its largely unspoiled environment.

An Overview of the Regional Economy in Northeast Asia

As illustrated in the research, China, Russia, North Korea and Mongolia are centrally planned economies, although this is changing: Russia has now largely converted to a market system; Mongolia is in the process of moving towards a market system; and China is well on its way to a socialist market economy. Nonetheless, these economies still retain some of the distortions resulting from the previous planning systems. North Korea is at the earliest stage of reform.

The Chinese economy is the dominant economy of the Northeast Asia Region (excluding Japan and South Korea), and represents by far the largest population. The three Northeastern provinces adjacent to the Tumen River area (Heilongjiang, Jilin and Liaoning) have a combined population of 110 million. Economic reform in these three Northeastern provinces has been slower than in the Southern regions of China, which to some extent have been used as a testing ground for reform. Prior to the opening of China's economy, the Northeastern part of China was relatively more prosperous than many other parts of the nation owing to its well developed heavy industries and agriculture. Even now, the Northeastern part is a major contributor to the national economy producing more than half its petroleum, 36% of its timber, 20% of its steel, 17% of its coal and 15% of its grain.

The economy in this region of China is relatively inward looking. Exports, as a percentage of GNP in 1992, were only 8% compared with an average of 18% for the whole of China and over 40% for most of the Asian Tigers. The economy is dominated by heavy industry, resource extraction and agriculture. The area has a large agricultural surplus which grew rapidly in the late eighties in response to price liberalisation and now provides much of the exports of the region. Many of the resources extracted in the region and the heavy industry outputs are sold in other regions of China often at controlled prices well below market prices. To some extent these controlled prices explain the low rate of growth, but the lack of diversification into the export-oriented light industrial sectors responsible for growth in Southern China appears to be the main factor in the relatively poor growth in the region.

The changes in the Primorske region of Russia have been far more radical and rapid than those observed in Northeast China. Until the dissolution of the Soviet Union, the main activities in the region was defence and defence-related industries. Large parts of the territory were totally closed. The southern areas had minimal population and were largely undeveloped. Economic activity was centered around the defence industries in Vladivostok and northern parts of the territory. The regional economy was heavily dependent on transfers from Moscow and the bulk(70-80%) of consumer goods and industrial inputs came from Western regions of Russia at highly subsidized freight rates.

The economy is still in the midst of a radical restructuring process and an attendant massive change in trading patterns. There is a major shift underway as Primorski ceases "trading" with other parts of Russia and starts trading with Asian countries. It is looking for better and cheaper suppliers in the region for goods previously bought from Western Russia. It is expecting to finance these purchases by increased natural resource based exports (fish products, minerals etc.). The major goals for growth are targeted towards the expansion of resource based industries, development of new industry based on the very extensive capabilities of the old industrial-military complex and the provision of transport and related services to Siberia and Western Russia. Given the particular resource endowments of the region including relatively highly skilled but high cost labour, limited agricultural capabilities and minimal development of light industries, the regional economy will not become self sufficient and will need to rely heavily on trade with its neighbours and other regions of Russia.

By contrast, North Korea remains a centrally planned and largely closed economy. In 1991, exports represented only 7% of GDP and this figure appears to have dropped substantially with the collapse of trade and aid to support its economy and has suffered severely with the sharp reduction in this aid.

The industrial development pattern in North Korea has followed the classical model of an inward-looking centrally planned economy. There has been an emphasis on heavy industry at the expense of light industry and particular efforts have been made to achieve high levels of self – sufficiency. Increasingly, the industrial structure of North Korea is diverging from that of China, creating some short-term opportunities for sale of industrial products into China. Most of these products have not, however, been exposed to competition in open markets for many years and their competitiveness is therefore in question.

Mongolia is also undergoing a dramatic transformation. Before the collapse of the Soviet Union it was totally dependent on Soviet aid. All the capital spending and some of the recurrent spending of the Government was funded by Soviet aid. Three quarters of its trade was with the Soviet Union; the balance with other CMEA member countries. Mongolia is re-establishing its economy based on its comparative advantages in agriculture and livestock and its rich mineral resources. The development of external trading routes and if possible, the development of mineral processing facilities in the region, will be critically important to Mongolia since these measures are the only ones that will enable it to minimize its freight disadvantages.

Trade in Northeast Asia

During the 1980s trade among the Northeast Asian countries was repressed. However, at the end of the decade, this decrease started to change and the process accelerated during the early 1990s. Economic reform in the Soviet Union and China not only led to a redirecting of Russian trade, but also affected Mongolia and North Korea which had been running substantial trade deficits with the USSR until the latter was dissolved. Meanwhile, the economic size of Japan and the rapid economic growth in South Korea led to an increasing weight of these two countries in regional trade flows. The trade matrices in Table 1 illustrate the rapidly changing trade patterns in Northeast Asia since the 1980s.

In 1985, the USSR, China and Japan had multilateral trade

Table 1. Northeast Asia Trade Matrices, 1985-91

1985 Trade Matrix (US$ billons)

Importer	*ROK	**DPRK	Japan	PRC	USSR	Mongolia
Exporter						
ROK		0	4.5	0	.0	0
DPRK	0		0.1	0.2	0.5	na
Japan	7.1	0.2		12.5	2.8	-
PRC	0.4	0.2	6.1		1.1	-
USSR	0	0.8	1.3	0.9		1.4
Mongolia	0	na	-	-	0.5	

1990 Trade Matrix (US$ billons)

Importer	ROK	DPRK	Japan	PRC	USSR	Mongolia
Exporter						
ROK		12.6	0.6	0.5	0	0
DPRK	0		0.3	0.1	1.0	na
Japan	17.4	0.2		6.1	2.6	-
PRC	2.5	0.4	9.0		2.2	-
USSR	0.3	1.5	3.1	1.9		1.7
Mongolia	0	na	-	-	0.7	

1991 Trade Matrix (US$ billons)

Importer	ROK	DPRK	Japan	PRC	USSR	Mongolia
Exporter						
ROK		0	12.4	1.1	0.7	
DPRK	0.1		0.3	0.1	0.2	na
Japan	20.1	0.2		8.6	2.1	-
PRC	3.5	0.5	10.3		1.8	-
USSR	0.5	0.2	3.1	1.9		0.3
Mongolia		na	-	-	0.2	

Source: Sooyong Kim, Young Sun Lee & Kap-young Jeong: *The Current Status and Prospects of Intra-Regional Trade in Northeast Asia*, (December 1993), p.13

Notes: na=not available;-=<$50 million

*South Korea **North Korea

among themselves, although the amount was low. South Korea traded exclusively with Japan, and that amounted to less than a fifth of the South Korea's total trade. Mongolia's trade was totally dominated by the USSR. The North Korean trade was heavily oriented towards the USSR though it had some trade with China and Japan. North Korea did not trade at all with South Korea.

By 1990, the zeros have disappeared from the trade matrix, and only intra-Korean trade and Mongolia's non-USSR trade had become more concentrated with the two market economies (Japan and South Korea) accounting for $30 billion out of $65 billion in total trade.

The 1991 trade matrix is also dominated by Japan-South Korea trade flows, but there have been some major year-on-year changes in the trading relationship. The USSR's trade with Mongolia and North Korea collapsed dramatically while its trade with South Korea grew substantially. Meanwhile, North Korea's exports to South Korea increased from $11 million to $95 million, making South Korea the North's third largest market after Japan and the USSR. For all Northeast Asian countries, Japan was now the largest regional export market, and South Korea the fastest growing market in the region.

These developments continued through 1992-3. Indeed some sources place the decline in USSR-North Korea trade in 1992 rather than 1993 (depending on the exchange rates used). Sino-South Korean trade surged to $6.4 billion in 1992 and about $9 billion in 1993, making China South Korea's third largest trading partner and the South Korea, China's sixth biggest. An analysis of the trade matrix for 1992 and the first half of 1993 (Table 4) indicates a continuation of these trends with some growth in the Russian eports to Japan and China.

Let us investigate into the trade in Tumen River area as an epitome of the whole Northeast Asia. Trade in the Tumen River area was extremely limited during the 1970 and 1980s. In particular, Yanbian Prefecture was closed to foreign trade between 1970 and 1982. Although USSR-North Korea trade passed through Primorski Krai, little of the trade involved products from Primorski or from the Northeastern part of North Korea.

Table 2 shows the gradual reopening of Yanbian's foreign trade after 1982. The value remained small through the 1980s and the direction was mainly with the North Korea. In 1991 and 1992,

Table 2. Yanbian Prefecture's External Trade (million

	Total	DPRK	USSR	Total	DPRK	USSR
1970-81	0			0		
1982-5	68	na	na	71	na	na
1986	31	na	na	32		
1987	41	na	na	48		
1988	52	na	na	52		
1989	83	80	3	113	72	41
1990	59	42	17	70	58	12
1991	309	198	111	296	204	91
1992	841	478	363	676	353	323
1993						

Source: *Yanbian Prefecture Statistical Yearbook* (1993), p.513.
Notes: na=not available.

however, trade began to grow more rapidly with both riparian partners. A substantial part of this trade is transit trade from outside the immediate Tumen River area.

Current trade between Jilin and the two neighbouring countries is dominated by a few products(Table 3). Imports of cars and trucks accounted for over half of Jilin's trade with Russia in 1992 and 1993. In 1992 fertilisers were China's next most important import from Russia through Yanbialn, but their significance declined in 1993 due to supply problems. In 1993 steel trade was more valuable.

Trade between China and North Korea across the Tumen River also has a high degree of commodity concentration. Chinese exports to North Korea are dominated by coal from Heilongjiang, over a million tons in 1993, valued at almost $50 million. Maize, cotton yarn, cooking oil, canned meat, sugar, soap and wheat are also important. North Korea's exports to China through the Tumen River area are dominated by steel and iron ore, together amounting to over 800,000tons valued at more than $150 million in 1993. North Korea also exported(or re-exported) 27,826 vehicles, valued at $49 million, and seafood, fertiliser and alumina.

Russian-North Korean trade has been in severe decline during the 1990s, and its commodity composition is poorly documented. According to the report from August 1993 UNIDO mission,

Table 3. Commodity Composition of Yanbian Foreign Trade

Total foreign trade in $US:
1992-$378m.;
1993 $468m., of which exports $230 million and imports were $238 million

Hunchun

1. Changlingzi (RF) – opened December 1991
   1992 54,788t. worth $42,194,066
   1993 76,326t. worth $56,111,915
2. Shatouzi – opened 1972 (1972-86 for people only)
   1992 49,678t. worth $79,065,390 & 46,000 people
   1993 46,463t. worth $49,173,149

Changlingzi (RF)

	1992			1993		
	Tones	$'000	No.	Tonnes	$'000	No.
Imports						
Steel	227	97		31,993	7.144	
Car	970	2,407	(617)	525	1,143	(465)
Trucks	7,961	20,525	(747)	11,437	27,627	(1,631)
Fertilizer	21,340	3,147		8,390	991	
Timber	108	2		1,573	83	
Seafood	5,247	2,651		596	242	
Exports						
Sugar	1,759	820		4,496	1,647	
Corn	8,685	1,264		400	55	

Shatouzi (North Korea)

	1992			1993		
	Tones	$'000	No.	Tonnes	$'000	No.
Imports						
Steel	313	78		14,717	3,822	
Car	7,870	14,593	(3,676)	9,196	17,346	(4,857)
Trucks	20,789	58,238	(2,113)	10,106	22,560	(1,143)
Fertilizer				61	na	
Timber	1,342	53		2,383	119	
Seafood	6,953	2,323		2,755	1,215	
Exports						
Sugar	1,866	710		200	70	
Corn	7,963	828		3,720	404	

Figures in parentheses=number of vehicles

Table 4. Northeast Asia Trade Matrices, 1992-3

1992 Trade Matrix (US$ billons)

Importer	ROK	DPRK	Japan	PRC	USSR	Mongolia
Exporter						
ROK		na	11.6	2.7	na	na
DPRK	na		0.3	0.2*	na	na
Japan	17.8	0.2		12.0	1.2	na
PRC	3.7*	0.5	11.7		2.7	na
USSR	na	na	2.3	3.5		na
Mongolia	na	na	na	na	na	

First Half of 1993 Trade Matrix (US$ billons)

Importer	ROK	DPRK	Japan	PRC	USSR	Mongolia
Exporter						
ROK		na	4.9	1.8	na	na
DPRK	na		0.1	0.1*	na	na
Japan	9.2	0.1		7.9	0.8	na
PRC	1.2*	0.3	5.9		1.5	na
USSR	na	na	1.3	2.4		na
Mongolia	na	na	na	na	na	

Source: International Monetary Fund, *Direction of Trade* (*Statistics* September and December 1993).

Notes: exporting country data, apart from*=importing country data;
na=not available in the source.

Tumangan rail station handles about 6-7 million tons of traffic a year. North Korea imports crude oil(although Russian supplies ceased in July 1993, and recently most of North Korean oil has come from China, Libya and Iran), steel(by rail to Chongjin West Port), logs(by rail to Ungsang port, for transport to the North Korean sawmills), coal, transport equipment and machinery. Sonbong wharf facilities also handle 300,000tons p.a. of Russia oil/petroleum products in transit to Singapore and Hong Kong. Russia imports fruits, vegetables and food products. Dalso(a Russian joint stock company) imports alumina from Australia and India into Rajin, where it is transferred to rail transport for Bratsk.

The official statistics ignore the rapidly growing border trade by entrepreneurs. Because of its nature such trade is hard to document, and existing extimates are estimates based on the number of cross-border North Korea. Assuming trade per crossing at 1000 Yuan, this would add 250 million Yun(over $40 million at the official exchange rate) to Sino-North Korean trade through Yanbian. It is primarily in consumer goods, with clothes, TVs, household articles and some food products being taken out of China and seafood and other foodstuffs out of North Korea.

Despite recent growth in trade, the three economies that constitute the region are still fairly closed. The 1991 export/GNP ratio of Jilin Province was 9%, or half of the average for China. For North Korea, the ratio was 7%, which is low for a country of 20 million people. The ratio for Primorski Krai was 8% which is considered very low for a region whose name means "near the sea."

Investment and Technology Transfer in Northeast Asia

In view of the presently rapid changes (which is in line with the strong increase countrywide), the figures presented below regarding to investment only convey a snapshot information.

•Starting with merely three joint venture approvals in Yanbian in 1985, the accumulated number grew from 39 in 1990 to 61 in 1991 and 212 in 1992 to reach a total of 355 and 371 ventures as of June and early August 1993, respectively (Table 5). The total contracted investment amount rose almost thirteen times since 1985 reaching US$406 million. The August 1993 foreign investment component amounting to almost US$200 million was almost fifteen times the 1985 figure, representing 48 per cent of the total investment amount.

•In terms of numbers, more than three quarters of the joint ventures were concluded with investors from only three countries: South Korea which accounts for 161 project or 43 percent of the total, Hong Kong with almost a quarter; and Japan with another ten percent. The absence of language barriers, cultural affinities within the Yanbian population and low wage levels

Table 5. Foreign direct investment in Yanbian Prefecture

By number and investment volume, 1990-93 (accumulated)

Year	No. of joint venture approvals	Total investment in million Us$	Foreign investment component million US$	% share of total invt.
1990	39	32.2	13.2	41.0
June 1993	355	391.0	185.0	47.3
August 1993	371	406.0	193.6	47.7

By countries of origin, as of August 1993

Country	No. of joint venture approval	% share of total	Country	No. of joint venture approval	% share of total
Republick of Korea	161	43.4	Singapore	4	1.1
Hong Kong	87	23.5	Macau	2	0.5
Japan	37	10.0	Thailand	2	0.5
Korea, DPR	20	5.4	Australia	1	0.3
USA	19	5.1	Germany	1	0.3
Taiwan	16	4.3	Indonesia	1	0.3
Russian Federation	11	3.0	Malaysia	1	0.3
Canada	7	1.9	Philippines	1	0.3
			TOTAL	371	100

By sectors

Sector	No. of joint venture approvals[a]		Foreign investment component[b]	
	abs.	% share	abs.(million US$)	% share
Agriculture, forestry andhusbandry	7	2.0	4.07	2.1
Industry	274	77.2	148.70	76.8
Service sector	38	10.8	20.33	10.5
Real estate	14	3.9	7.36	3.8
Commerce	1	0.3	2.46	1.3
Other	21	6.0	10.71	5.5
TOTAL	355	100	193.63	100

a: As of June 1993.

b: As of August 1993.

Source: Yanbian Prefecture Government.

clearly contributed to the high degree of attractiveness which South Korean investors found. Investors form the neighbouring TRADP partners, North Korea and the Russian Federation, which account for 5 and 3 percent, respectively. A notable number of contracts has also been approved with partners from the USA and Taiwan, while other Asian or European countries are only about to enter the scene.

• The breakdown of joint venture approvals by sectors reveals a clear focus on industry which absorbs more than three quarters of the total, both in terms of numbers and of the foreign investment component, followed by the service with some 11 per cent.

The eleven largest foreign direct investments approved for establishment in Yanbian Prefecture together make up for roughly 10 per cent of the total Yanbian figures, both in terms of the contracted total investment and the foreign investment component, thus reflecting a rather balaced size structure. Among these companies, seven of which are concluded with partners from South Korea, the foreign share in the respective total investment varies from 17 per cent (Russian partner) to 100 per cent (Japanese partner) and averages at around 44 per cent (Table 6).

A look at the geographical distribution of foreign investments shows the emergence of Yanji and Hunchun as prime locations:

> As of June 1993, roughly half of all joint ventures approved in Yanbian Prefecture were to be located in Yanji alone, accounting for 42 and 45 per cent of the contracted total investment and total foreign component, respectively. Again, with a share of nearly 80 per cent investments are mainly targeted at industry.

A number of foreign direct investment project are at various stages of preparation. Inter alia, negotiations were reportedly nearing completion in August 1993 with a South Korean partner on the construction and operation of a US$110 million animal husbandry farm project foreseen to raise 240,000 cattle with 60,000 slaughterings and 13,000 tons of beef production per year.

Table 6. Largest foreign direct investments in Yanbian Prefecture[a]

No.	Name	Foreign partner	Pruduct	Total investment (US$ million)	Foreign investment component (US$ million)	Contract period (years)
1	Xian Xing New Building Material Co.	Republic of Korea	Wall paper/PPC pipe/PUC pipe	7.95	4.75	20
2	Yanji Er He Pottery Co.	Republic of Korea	Pottery bricks	5.47	1.90	10
3	Yanbian Jintial Wood Products Co.	Hong Kong	Wood processing products	3.92	1.33	10
4	Sheng Long Flax Spinning Co.	Japan	Flax spinning products	3.92	1.33	20
5	Helong Mineral Water Co.	Hong Kong	Mineral water	3.55	1.24	10
6	Longjing Long Qin Edible Oil Co.	Republic of Korea	Edible oil	3.46	1.46	20
7	Yanmo Welding Material Co.	Russia	Welding materials	3.09	0.51	10
8	Yanbian Korean Ginseng Food Co.	Republic of Korea	Ginseng tea/condensed ginseng liquid	2.57	0.54	20
9	Wang Qing Evergreen Towel Co.	Republic of Korea	Towels	2.52	0.88	12
10	Yanji Ahegn Sheng Co.	Republic of Korea	Laser disks/disinfectant	2.42	1.45	30
11	Yanji Zhen Wei Plastic Packaging Co.	Republic of Korea	Plastic packaging products products	2.10	1.06	20

a: As fo August 1993.
Source: Yanbian Prefecture Government.

Potential for an enlarged cooperation with South Korean investors is also seen in the already commenced production of building materials. For instance, the production of in-house bricks, indoor plastic windows and high-standard cement in several ventures is being negotiated and/or desired. Negotiations are also ongoing with KIA of South Korea concerning investment into the manufacture of automobiles; a prefeasibility study is said to envisage an annual output of 100,000 cars.

•Hunchun so for has attracted some 20 per cent of foreign direct investments in Yanbian Prefecture. Of the 70 joint ventures approved, 55 with partners from eight countries had been registered by August 1993 with a total registered capital of US$88.9 million of which the foreign component was US$32.4 million. Half of the registered ventures are in industry.

As of August 1993, a series of seven joint venture projects, primarily in food processing and various light manufacture, were under negotiation for establishment in the Hunchun Border Economic Cooperation Zone with a foreign investment component of a total US$108 million. Some further 13 ventures were being advertised for investment as priority projects, representing a Y780 million total investment amount (see Table 7).

The increasing attraction of Hunchun as a promising trade and investment location is also reflected

•in high double-digit growth rates recorded for gross industrial output in 1992(24 per cent) and 1993(31 per cent; preliminary);

•in the recent establishment of 369 representative offices of enterprises largely from Jilin Province(ca. 150) and other Chinese provinces(ca. 200), but also of foreign companies(19), such as from Hong Kong, the US, Macao, the Russia Federation and North Korea.

•in an expanding stream of foreign visitors seeking information about investment opportunities and facilities in the zone; more than 9,000 domestic and foreign delegations comprising some 47,000 persons were reported to have visited Hunchun for this purpose until July 1993;

•in the rapidly changing face of the Hunchun downtown area where a whole series of tall(up to 20 storeys) office and commercial buildings presently under contruction with capital from external sources will distinct-

Table 7. Pipeline and priority projects for joint ventures within the Hunchun Border Economic Cooperation Zone

Pipeline projects under negotiation

Product	Capacity p.a.	Origin of Partner partner	Total Investment (US $ million)	Foreign Investment Component (US $ million)
Plastic canvas	1,200 million tons	Taiwan	1.7	0.65
Computer tags	2 million dozens	Hong Kong	1.45	0.435
Carpets	384,000m^2	Hong Kong	1.2	0.42
Vegetable and fruit processing	100,000 kilogrammes	Hong Kong	0.52	0.364
Instant Noodles	1.5 million bowls	Taiwan	1.3	0.52
Heat and Power Plant, Phase I	2X21,000 kilowatts	USA	RMB 300 mn	42.1
Leather products and computers	Hong Kong	Hong Kong	RMB 8 mn	0.56

Priority projects (advertised for investment)

Product	(Planned) capacity	77 Total investment (million Yuan)	Product	(Planned) capacity	77 Total investment (million Yuan)
Gas factory	60,000 m^3/day	52	Aluminium alloy pipes	2,000 tons/year	45
Waste water treatment	50,000 m^3/day	200	Light pottery grains	188,000 m^2/year	60
Plastic energy-saving film	3,000,000 m^2/year	28.5	Leather processing	100,000 pieces	6.26
30,000 Telephones	3,900 exchange lines	86.39	High-quality furniture	650,000 units/year	24.4
Fiber plank	30,000 m^3/year	130	Vitamin C	1,000 tons/year	47
Hunchun River Bridge	480X30 metres	52	Carbon Paper	1,000 tons/year	31.20
Hunchun River Flood-protecting Dyke	Lenght: 32.9 km	16.4			

Source: Hunchun City Government

ly change the city's shape within the near future.

With around 20 joint ventures each having been approved for establishment within the boundaries of the areas of Tumen and Longjin foreign investors' interest in these locations so far has been less pronounced than elsewhere. Important joint ventures in longjin relate to the production of ginseng, leather shoes, woollen sweaters, and of energy conservation tubes. Another five ventures including one in timber processing were reported to be under negotiation. Joint venture contracts at finalization stage in Tumen include the badly needed contruction of two four-star hotels, one of which with a Hong Kong investor.

While joint venture approvals clearly need to be distinguished from their actual establishment and the start of business operations, no clarity was to be obtained on the latter. It should, however, be a safe statement to assume the implementation of a rather limited though not insignificant numbers up to the present. The commencement of construction activities and/or production appeared imminent in a larger number of cases, particularly in Hunchun. The few joint venture establishments were all looking back on a rather short period of existence, such as a garment nanufacturing venture (set up in March 1992) and a plastics manufacturing company (since April 1993) in Tumen City, as well as a knitting factory in Hunchun (since July 1993).

As to foreign investments in the Rajin-Sonbong Free Economic and Trade Area no industrial joint venture agreements were reported as having been concluded by March of 1994. Negotiations with a number of potential investors from several countries were, however, referred to as ongoing.

With the opening of the region to the outside world foreign investment inflows into Primorskiy Territory have witnessed a sharp increase in recent years. Within a three year period, the number of equity joint ventures had grown from 24 to 364 by June 1993 with foreign paid-up capital, respectively, foreign investments display a high degree of geographical concentration. Consequently, the structural pattern of investments (countries of origin, sectors of activity) shows little difference between

Primorskiy in total and Nakhodka FEZ (Table 8 and 9). The listing of foreign investments is headed by China, Japan, the USA, Hong Kong and South Korea which together account for 80-90 per cent of the total in terms of both project numbers and foreign in-paid capital. In turn, investors from Europe so far assume only a marginal role. With regard to project numbers, China emerged as the single most important country of origin (54 and 44 per cent share in Primorskiy and Nakhodka FEZ, respectively), while Japan takes a clear lead as to the foreign investment amount (32 and 53 per cent, respectively).

The areas of investment extend over a wider range of activities, as is revealed in a sectoral breakdown available for Nakhodka

Table 8. Foreign direct investment in ventures over time

Number of equity joint ventures over time

Year	No. of joint ventures
1990	24
1991	127
1992	247
1/6/1993[a]	364
memorandum item:	
foreign paid-up capital total	US $208.4 million

Number of equity joint ventures by countries of origin, as per 1 June 1993

Country of origin	Number	Foreign paind-up capital (US $'000)
China	197	27,221.6
Japan	41	65,979.8
USA	33	48,729.3
Hong Kong	30	4,583.4
South Korea	15	7,524.0
Germany	11	467.0
Singapore	9	300.0
Taiwan	5	180.0
North Korea	3	10.5
TOTAL	344	154,995.6

a: Break down does not add up to total in source.

Source: Primorskiy Territory Government.

Table 9. Foreign Investment in Nahodka Fre Economic zone as per July 1993

By type of investment

Type	Number
Joint ventures	113
Wholly foreign-owned enterprises	45
Subsidiaries and affiliates of foreign ventures located outside FEZ Nakhodka	94
Representative offices	
TOTAL	271

By country of origin

Country of origin	Number	Percentage	Foreign paind-up capital (US $)	Percentage
China	119	43.9	15,624.1	12.5
Japan	38	14.0	66,086.8	52.9
USA	23	8.5	25,819.9	20.7
Hong Kong	23	8.5	2,101.3	1.7
South Korea	12	4.4	5,268.0	4.5
Taiwan	6	2.2	100.0	0.0
Singapore	4	1.5	300.0	0.2
Germany	3	1.1	167.1	0.1
Canada	3	1.1	502.0	0.4
North Korea	3	1.1	10.5	0.01
Switzerland	3	1.1	37.2	0.03
Norway	2	0.7	4,395.0	3.5
New Zealand	2	0.7	100.0	0.1
Great Britain	3	1.1		
Finland	3	1.1		
Hungary	2	0.7		
Kazakhstan	2	0.7		
Latvia	2	0.7		
Panama	2	0.7		
Spain	2	0.7		
Sweden	2	0.7	4,032.6	
Vietnam	2	0.7		
Argentina	1	0.4		
Austria	1	0.4		
Cayman Islands	1	0.4		
Estonia	1	0.4		
Israel	1	0.4		
Italy	1	0.4		
Luxemberg	1	0.4		
Netherlands	1	0.4		
Serbia	1	0.4		
TOTAL	271	100	124,904.5	100

Table 10. Amount(A) and volume(V) of Business for Technology Transfer Contracts from Japan to China (unit: 10 thousand US$)

1979		1985		1987		1990		1991	
A	V	A	V	A	V	A	V	A	V
42	147766	217	63818	138	70612	43	9183	63	26928

Source: *Chinese Science and Technology Statistic Yearbook* (1992).

FEZ. About a quarter of all investments are related to manufacturing activities (consumer goods, technological equipment). Other major activities are reported for commerce (some 24 per cent), agriculture including forestry/wood processing (17 per cent), as well as for transport and construction (table 10).

Only a small number of foreign investments are under operation in Khazan District so far, for instance, two of the three shareholders of the East Base Fleet of Russia for Catching and Processing of Seafood Joint Stock Co. in Zarubino are Russian-foreign joint venture undertakings with partners from South Korea (Pacifico) and Vietnam (Dalsiprico), respectively. Shops and restaurants with Chinese participation from Yanji were reported to be under construction in Zarubino. In general, however, foreign involvement to date appears to be largely limited to the extension of infrastructure (road, rail, port facilities), particularly by available Chinese labour.

Regarding to the technology transfer in Northeast Asia, a few information is shown in Table 10.

The Characteristics of Regional Economic Cooperation in Northeast Asia

• Based on natural economic connections, the Northeast Asia countries have the characteristics of an inward trade structure.

The economic cooperation between Northeast Asia countries is different to that between countries of European Community or North American Free Trade Area in that the countries are not bounded together by any agreement or policy but a kind of self generated economic relationship based on natural economic con-

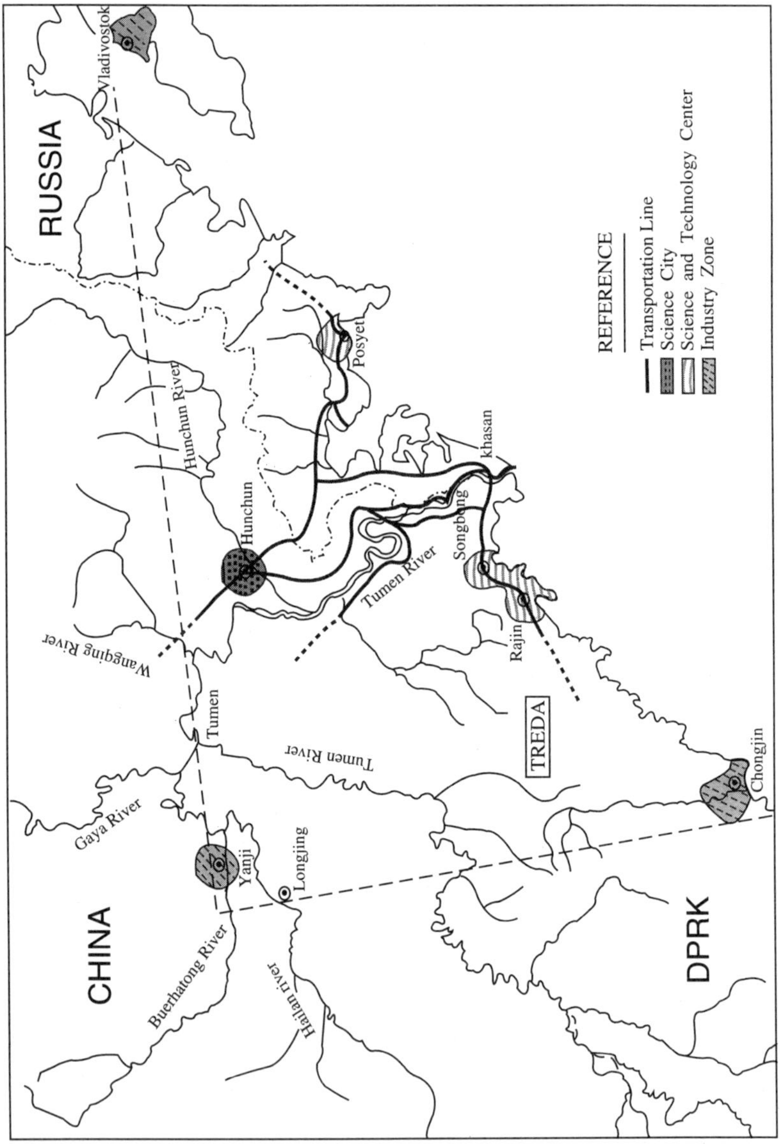
RUSSIA
CHINA
DPRK
Vladivostok
Posyet
Hunchun River
Hunchun
khasan
Songbong
Rajin
Tumen River
Wangqing River
Tumen
Tumen River
TREDA
Chongjin
Gaya River
Yanji
Longjing
Buerhatong River
Hailan river
REFERENCE
Transportation Line
Science City
Science and Technology Center
Industry Zone

nection, which is prominently reflected in the dependence of inner area trade by Northeast Asian countries. Among Northeast Asian countries, The degrees of dependence on inner area trade of China, Japan and South Korea are relatively high, all of which exceed 20% with Japan's over 40%. On the part of China, although Northeast China's dependence on inner area trade within Northeast Asia on the whole is only 23.9%, from the perspective of Northeast China, this degree of trade dependence is higher than the national average level. Take export only, the amount of export to Northeast Asian countries by the three provinces in Northeast China is 44.0% as their total amount of export and such proportion of the whole country is 23%, which shows that Northeast China's dependence degree is two times that of the whole country. What is more, the amount of export of Northeast China does not include the export to South Korea, and the ratio could be even higher considering the fact that the amount of import and export of the three Northeast provinces with South Korea has been increasing enormously.

• Vertical division of work is the mainstay while horizontal work division exists, thus forming the multiaxis trade structure.

In the international system of division of work amount Northeast Asian countries at present, especially amount China, Japan and South Korea, vertical division of work on the whole prevails. Such vertical division of work is glaringly reflected in Sino-Japanese and Sino-South Korean trade. In Sino-Japanese trade, although the percentage of industrial manufactured products, among China's export to Japan in recent years, is increasing rapidly, primary products, among Northeast China's export to Japan, still takes a quite big percentage. Take Liaoning, the relatively most advanced province only, the primary products export occupies 57.2% of the province's total export in 1991, which is higher than the national average of 20.4%. In Sino-South Korean trade, China's exports mainly consists of primary products such as cotton, raw silk, corn, coal and crude oil, while the bulk of Korea's exports are industrial manufactured products like plastic products, clothing, electronic products and machinery equipments. This indicates that Sino-South Korean trade is still based on a vertical division of work model. From the post war development of international trade, it can be seen that such vertical division of work has led to the deterioration of the trading conditions of developing countries, and hindered the development of multilateral economic cooperation. In the case of Sino-Japanese and Sino-Korean economic cooperation particularly, such vertical division of work has been proved to be an obstacle for the international flow of capital and technology transactions, and has brought along a lot of difficulties for Sino-Japanese and Sino-Korean economic cooperation, which is an outstading issue in the regional economic cooperation of Northeast Asia that calls for prompt resolution.

While the above mentioned vertical division of work is in a predominant position, the horizontal division of work is also developing very rapidly. Such development of horizontal division of work is not only reflected in the industrial manufactured products trade between Japan and Korea, but in the rapid development of Sino-Russian border trade. In recent years, with the development of Sino-Russian border trade, the commodity structure has experienced a remarkable change. From the commodity structure, it can be seen that horizontal division of work is the basis of Sino-Russian trade.

The development of horizontal division of work has changed to some degree the old international work division pattern in Northeast Asia area with the vertical division of work as the mainstay. With the increase of industrial manufactured products in China's export to Japan and South Korea, a new international work division system is bound to emerge where the two kinds of division of work cross exist in both developed and developing countries. The formation of the new international work division system will change the regional economic layout in which all countries greatly rely on Japan at the centre, and form a multiaxis trade structure and provide an important precondition for promoting the regional trade development in Northeast Asia.

• Formation of a multilayer economic co-operation with China,

Japan and Korea at the core

The regional economic cooperation system has two major characteristics: The first is concentration on economic cooperation among China, Japan and South Korea. This is because China, Japan and South Korea have an extremely important role in the regional economic cooperation of Northeast Asia as a whole. In the regional trade of the area in 1990, the total amount of Sino-Japanese, Sino-South Korean and Japanese-South Korean trade makes up 78.76% of the total amount of inter-trade. What is worth special mention of is that Sino-South Korean trade surpassed Sino-(former) USSR trade in 1990 although it was still in its early stage.

The second characteristic is its multi-layeredness. There are in the region both economically developed countries and newly industrialised countries as well as developing countries such as China, Monogolia and North Korea. In the three layers, Japan mainly provides capital, high technologies and high-tech products, and South Korea mainly offers middle level technologies and its products and China mainly provides labour intensive products and primary products.

The multi-layered regional international division of work has two meanings. The first is constant realization of industrial promotion with the economic development of countries involved. The concrete content of it is, Northeast China could gradually be transformed into an export base for labour intensive industrial products from the present base providing primary products, and North Korea could be transformed from mainly exporting labour intensive industrial products into an export base offering capital intensive and technology intensive industrial products; at the same time, in the process of industrial restructuring, the countries involved could transfer their industries no longer having their comparative advantages to countries having the comparative advantages so as to realise the optimised distribution of regional industries. The second meaning is, the conducting of economic cooperation between countries of similar developing levels is conducive to the realisation of horizontal mutual flow of commodities and various production elements and to the common development and prosperity, which would surely create a subjective foundation for conducting multilateral economic cooperation in Northeast Asia area, and as a result, enhance the development of regional trade in the area.

Chinese Development Strategy for Northeast Asia

Chinese Development Strategy for Northeast of China

• Basic Strategy

(1) Combine "Openness to the North, Cooperation with the South" and "Import from the West, export to the East," and accelerate the outward orientation of the regional economy. The Northeast region should, giving full play to its own geographical advantages, open to the North and enhance its economic co-operation with Russia, Mongolia and other Fareast Asian countries. It should fully involve itself in the economic co-operation in the area surrounding the Bohai Sea, reach the world through the Pacific Ocean, and speed up the development of the region's western part. It should take an active role in international cooperation and economic integration of the Northeast Asia area, and attempt to form several internationalised "hot spot" for economic progress.

(2) Widen and deepen reform. The emphasis should be placed on the two aspects of transforming the management system of large and medium sized enterprises and energetically fostering a market system. According to the present situation of the structures of the enterprises in the Northeast area, a group of key large enterprises should be chosen as experimental spots to carry out all round reform and implement group management. Effort should be devoted to developing both domestic and international markets, organising production in line with market demand and forming various markets according to actual conditions.

(3) Give full play to technological forces and develop the region with science and technology. The Northeast region has a leading position among the country's major areas in terms of sci-

entific and technological personnel, research organisations and institutions of higher learning. We should truly value their ideas, management systems and scientific and technological policies, and make advantage of and give full play to their talents.

(4) Speed up the reformation and optimise of industrial structure. We should conscientiously promote the development of energy, water resources and communication and transportation, and place the construction of weak links and "bottlenecks" at a significant strategic position and give top priority to their development. We should increase the capital input through various channels and in various forms including state investment, local fund raising and foreign investment. We should actively support the development of several key industries and high-tech industries. The tertiary industry should be vigorously developed. We should push forward and give complete incentive to the development of township enterprises. We should consolidate the fundamental position of agriculture, and take the road of high production, quality and efficiency.

(5) Consolidate cooperation and strive for common development. The three provinces in Northeast and the Eastern part of Inner Mongolia Autonomous Region as a whole have both strong and weak points in terms of natural resources, economic foundations, talented human resources and geographical conditions. The old pattern characterised by administrative separation and regional segregation should be broken up, and a new pattern should be set up to promote regional co-operation and mutual supplementation. We should form a modernised mass production system with the characteristics of group management supported by key bases so as to organise large scope and wide spanning united regional market, and to set large scale enterprise groups of key and pillar industries, and make the most of overall regional advantages. We should establish a multichannel fund raising system, and jointly build up some major projects of energy, water conservancy and communication that cover different areas. We should unite scientific and technological forces to organise high-tech research and development programmes.

•Conception of Regional Economic Layout

Regional layout for economic development in the next ten years can be a "three strips and one zone" pattern determined by their different functions. We can then consolidate classified direction and implement key construction and key breakthrough.

(1) Coastal Economic Strip Centred at Dalian

The Coastal Economic Strip stretches from Dandong in the east to Shanghaiguan Pass in the west, which includes six cities of Dalian, Dandong, Yingou, Panjin, Jingzhou, and Jinxi and 12 counties/cities under their jurisdiction. It represents an area of the Northeast region that is relatively advanced in its economy and culture. The GNP per capita and Gross Industrial Product per capita in the area are 51% and 72% higher than the average ones of the whole region respectively. It has considerable economic strength as well as relatively dense city group and port group with Dalian harbour as the centre and Dandong, Yingkou and Jinzhou as the two wings. The strip is the southern front for the vast Northeast inland to reach the world and serves as its "window" and "door" for its opening up. It can play the role of a "setter" in attracting, digesting and absorbing foreign advanced technologies and passing them on the inner part. Speeding up the opening up the development of the Coastal Economic Strip is of great significance to promoting the region's overall economic development and prospering the Bohai- rim area.

(2) Border Economic Development and Opening Strip

All the provinces (region) in Northeast China border neighbouring countries and have long inland borders. Distributed in the strip are 36 cities and counties of Liaoning, Jilin, Heilongjiang and the east part of Inner Mongolia, the population of which is 8 million, taking up 7.1% of the total population of the region. The Northeastern region is the weakest economically. All the cities and counties along the border should adapt themselves to new international environment, speed up economic cooperation with bordering countries, widen the opening to the outside world, gear up the development and construction of the strip, and make it a new "window place" for the region's opening up and a new economic increasing spot. This is of great importance to changing the conditions of poverty and backwardness and developing an outward-oriented economy in the whole region.

The Border Economic Strip is vast in territory and has abundant resources of land, forestry, hydraulic power, coal, non- ferrous metals and tourism. It boasts some large and medium sized industrial and mining cities like Dandong, Hunjiang, Jixi etc. and relatively convenient communications backed up by large and medium sized cities in the hinterland and has broad prospects for its development. Since the reform and opening up of our country, Manzhouli, Heihe, Suifenhe and Huichun have been approved by the state as border open cities, followed one after another by a group of small land ports at the country level, which has provided an opportunity for the outward oriented construction of the Border Economic Development and Opening Strip.

(3) Economic Strip with Harbin-Dalian Railroad as the Axis

The strip starts from Dalian in the south and ends up at Harbin in the north. It is mainly consisted of the areas along Harbin-Dalian railroad and road, and has a population of 50 million, which makes up 45% of the whole region. The GNP of the region in 1991 reached RMB 130 billion, making up 54% of the region's total GNP; Gross Industrial Product in that year was RMB 240 billion, which occupies two third of that of the whole region. the GNP and GIP per capita in the strip are 22% and 49% higher than that of the whole region respectively. The area is the most densely concentrated with large and medium sized cities and large and medium sized key enterprises. Having solid industrial foundations, strong economic strength, rich talent resources and well developed communication, it is the heartland and essence of the Northeast region. The nation-wide influential industries of Northeast like iron and steel, oil and chemistry, automobile manufacturing, heavy-duty machinery and equipment and machine tools are all located in the strip. Speeding up the renovation and development of this area is the key to reinvigorating the old industrial base and prosperity the Northeast economy as a whole.

(4) Western Resources Development Zone

The Western Resources Development Zone includes

leagues/cities of eastern Inner Mongolia, Chaoyang city of Liaoning Province, Baicheng Prefecture of Jilin Province and Daxinganling area of Heilongjiang Province, and is a less advanced area that is to be developed. The population of the zone is 1.7 million, 14.8% of the region's total. Its GNP, GIP, and GAP in 1991 are RMB 22.5 billion, RMB 20.3 billion, and RMB 13.2 billion respectively, which take up 9.5%, 5.2% and 15.9% of that of the region respectively. The GNP per capita and GIP per capita are respectively RMB 1,360 and RMB 1,229, which are 64% and 38.4% of the region's averages. Excluding few cities with better industrial foundations, most area are very weak in their economic foundations with the east four leagues/cities as the worst, where there is vast land but a small population with agriculture and husbandry still as the mainstay and modern industry in its starting period. However, the area is abundant in its natural resources such as forestry, grassland, coal and non- ferrous metal and therefore has great potential. Through development, it can be built into an important base of the Northeast for energy, forestry, husbandry and non-ferrous metal mining and refining and provide a new channel for opening up. Speeding up the development of this area is very important in removing its own poverty, enhancing and supporting the development of the region's east and middle parts, and prospering the national economy of Inner Mongolia Autonomous Region.

Chinese Development Strategy for Tumen River Area

•Basic Attitudes

(1) It is the view of the Chinese government that the economic development of Tumen River area is a step of strategic importance to China's overall economic progress, and provides an opportunity for development.

(2) On the one hand, China takes an active part in the multilateral cooperation in Northeast Asia area and in the pushing forward of research, organisation and promotion sponsored by UNDP; on the other hand, we base ourselves on domestic and inner province development and opening up to create an

favourable environment for international cooperation.

(3) In 1992, the city of Hunchun was approved by the State Council as one of the first group of border open cities and was granted many preferential policies, which has provided a favourable policy climate for the city's development. China hopes to enhance international economic cooperation in Tumen River area with Huichun as the focal point.

•Strategic Priorities

"Planning Program for the Comprehensive Development of the Lower Stretch of Tumen River area and Hunchun City" was worked out in 1992 under the organisation of Jilin Provincial authorities. It was examined by the Planning Commission under the authorisation of the State Council of China. Following are some assumptions about it:

(1) We should follow the principle of overall planning and step by step implementation and energetically enhance the infrastructure construction including energy, transportation, communication and urban construction.

(2) In terms of the choice of industries, we should give prominence to local advantages, devote effort to some promoting industries or programmes, and make decisions surrounding outward oriented economy. During the starting period, some labour intensive programmes can be conducted and gradually, attention should be paid to the combination of labour intensive and technology intensive industries. Before 2000, we should direct most of our effort to light export processing, food processing and textiles industries. After 2000, we should put the emphasis on trade and gradually development of high-tech industries.

(3) Outward oriented agriculture and tourism should be vigorously developed.

(4) We should speed up border economic cooperation and border trade.

(5) Attention should be paid to talent cultivation. According to the 10 years experience of China's opening up, soft environment is extremely important in attracting foreign investment. Although China has abundant human resources, but the level of quality

needs to improve. At the same time, qualified personnel are in great demand, to which we should also pay our attention.

Prospect for the Future Development of Northeast Asia: the Impact on the Regional Development to Technology Transfer and Layout of "Science Cities"

To forecast the future development of Northeast Asia is very difficult and complicated. In order to find an easier way to do so, let us narrow the topic and just focus on the impact of Tumen River Area development to technology transfer.

Exploitation of methodology

As technology is an important component in production factors, its transfer is inevitable affected by the new features of regionalization of world economy. With regard to the layout of the science cities, it is the result of technology transfer, i.e. technology flow of different levels and kinds stationing in suitable surroundings, and hence, becoming science cities. The reason is that it is an era of globalization of science and technology. For a particular region, the stronger the technology flow, the greater the imnpact would have on technology transfer, and the greater possibility there is for establishing the science cities.

In the past, the impact of regional development to technology transfer was basically in the economic paradigm. When we study these kinds of impact, only the factors on economic development level and the technology itself need to be considered. But it would be more complicated for the impact of regional development to technology transfer after the Cold War. The problem lies in how to determine the impact of regional development on technology transfer under the new situation.

Generally speaking, the impact of regional development on technology transfer under the new situation is far from limited to the economic paradigm itself, since regions that have just gotten over the Cold War would inevitably retain some political influences in their technology development. Besides, due to the importance of trans-national regions in the regional development under new situations, geographical factors can also play a significant role in technology transfer. Among the political influential factors, political stability takes up the primary importance, since political stability in the regions for proposed development would have a direct impact on the quantity and direction of technology transfer. Among the ecocomic influential factors, the degree of market development, comparative advantages, economic potentials and present situation of development (including industrial mix and arrangement of prolductive forces) in the proposed regions will all have an impact on technology transfer. In addition, the geographical influences the state and potential of infrastructure of the proposed regions and the distance from the technology source areas are closely linked to technology transfer. Also related to the technological factors are the orginal technology base of the proposed regions and their difference in technical development level including technical mix compared to the technology source areas. Considering the complexity of the impact of the post Cold War regional development on technology transfer, it can be depicted in an indicatrix system (see Chart I).

In this indicatrix system, the impact of regional development

Chart I. IMPACT OF REGIONAL DEVELOPMENT ON TECHNOLOGY TRANSFE

- POLITICAL (0.31)
  - 1. POLITICAL STABILITY(10)
- ECONOMIC (0.31)
  - 2. LEVEL OF MARKET DEVELOPMENT(2.33)
  - 3. COMPARATIVEADVANTAGES(3.32)
  - 4. DEVELOPMENT POTENTIAL(2.36)
  - 5. PRESENT STATE OF ECONOMIC DEVELOPMENT(1.99)
- TECHNOLOGICAL (0.22)
  - 6. DIFFERENCE IN LEVEL(4.87)
  - 7. ORIGICAL BASE(5.13)
- GEOGRAPHICAL (0.17)
  - 8. DISTANCE(2.27)
  - 9. STATE OF INFRA-STRUCTURE(3.76)
  - 10. POTENTIAL OF INFRA-STRUCTURE(3.97)

on technology transfer is divided into 4 first level indices, namely, political, economical, technological and geographical, which are further divided into several second level indices. 32 specialists on regional development and technology transfer were invited to determine the weight of each indicatrix in the whole system (Chart I) on the basis of stratification analysis. The following steps were taken when we carried out the research in this indicatrix system of the impact of regional development on technology transfer and layout of science cities.

•To establish, according to the target model of regional development, the realm and focus of study, including general concept, location of technology source, destination for technology transfer, and so on.

•Specialists were invited to mark the relevant objects of the various indicatrix in the system. For instance, if to study the impact of technology transfer from Osaka to Dalian on the development of Dalian, specialists were invited to make assessment on the indices of Dalian, except the 6th and 8th items which need to draw study on the comprehensive situation of both cities; if to study the impact of Dalian's development on the technology transfer towards Osaka, specialists were invited to repeat the above assessments on various indicatrix of Osaka. a five-grade marking system is adopted in the assessment. For instance, on the assessment of development level of Dalian's market, the following table is made:

Table 11

level of market development	high	fairly high	ordinary	quit low	low
score	1	0.85	0.7	0.55	0.4

•The impact of regional development on technology transfer can be concluded into 4 categories by induction of the scores given by the specialists: strong impact (7.5 up), fairly strong impact (7.5-6), ordinary impact (6-4.5), less impact (below 4.5).

These 4 categories have their different characters:

(1) Strong Impact – means the regional development in relevant areas are suitable to the environment formed by technology transfer, enjoying political stability; high level of market development, obvious comparative advantage, steady economic growth and huge potentials; indices in other aspects all showing high scores. Technology flows tend to station in such areas.

(2) Fairly Strong Impact – though the impact of relevant areas on technology transfer is not as strong as the "strong impact" areas, yet the fairly high scores show such areas are quite attractive towards technology transfer.

(3) Ordinary Impact – although the overall score of such areas are not very high, the high scores in certain particular items may bring about some large scale transfer of technology.

(4) Less Impact – means the referred areas are hardly attractive to technology transfer and may barely have it stationed there.

• According to the comparison and analysis of calculation results and the existing science cities, scientific and technological centers and industrial zones, regions with the score above 7.5 are considered to be possible locations for large science towns in regional development; those scoring between 7.5 – 6 may become scientific and technological centers, only smaller in scale compared to science towns; regions scoring 6 – 4.5 may become industrial zones of fairly large scale. Therefore, the layout of science cities are listed accordingly.

Table 12

area	Tsukuba	Zhongguanchun	Dalian	Shenzhen	Weihai	Kunming
score	8.8	7.6	7.2	7.3	5.8	5.6

Impact of Development in Tumen River Area on Technology Transfer and the Layout of Science Cities in Northeast Asia

Development of the Tumen river area is a typical example of regional development in the post-cold war period. Locating in the border area of China, Russia and North Korea, the Tumen River region used to be an area of recurrent warfares. Before 1990s, this area was viewed as the military forefront, with hardly any development, let alone technology transfer from the outside world. In recent years, the huge economic, scientific and technological potentials of this region has been gradually recognized. As this region is equipped with all the new features of regionalization of world economy, the indicatrix analysis should be suitable to the study of the impact of development of Tumen River region on the technology transfer and layout of science cities in Northeast Asia.

Regarding the latest progress of the "Tumen River Area Development Program"(UNDP), the present plan, which is acceptable to all the participants (China, North Korea, Russia, South Korea and Mongolia), can be termed into "4 points in 3 lines", i.e. separate economic zones are to be set up in Hunchun of China, Rajin-Sonbong of North Korea, Zarubino of Russia, linked by international corridors with major traffic lines as their mainstay(see Chart II), and establish economic entities for administration. Governments of relevant countries should sign international agreements to guarantee cooperation in the development, and set up inter-governmental committees for coordination and consultation on legislative, environmental and economic issues related to the development. By now, the content of the international agreements is basically defined after several amendments, the construction of railway connection between China and Russia has been completed on the Chinese side and is expected to be completed on the Russian side by the end of this year which is now under accelerated efforts. Work will soon start on the connection of Sino-North Korean railways. The strategic model and actual progress of development in the Tumen River area has constituted the general framework for the impact of the development in this region on the technology transfer. We hold that the Tumen River area, with Hunchun city of China as the center, will become the growth pole of Northeast Asia. In this regard, full advantage would be drawn from human resources, agricultural and industrial resource of China, natural resource of Russia, the harbor of

Table 13

Region	Score	Region	Score
Hunchun	7.6	Vladivostok	5.6
Rajin-Sonbong	6.2	Niigata	7.5
Zarubino	7.1	Osaka	7.5
Yanji	5.9	Changchun	7.2
Chongjin	4.8	Seoul	7.5

North Korea, capital and technology of Japan and South Korea, by sharing the merits of their complementarities. With regard to technology, the technology source of Northeast Asia will mainly come from Japan and South Korea. Hunchun, Rajin-Sonbong area, Zarubino, and to be on larger scale, cities like Changchun, Yanji, Chongjin, and Vladivostok will all become destinations of technology flow. We have invited forty one specialists on Northeast Asian economic studies to give two rounds of marking on the strategic indices of the above areas by using AHP. The result is shown as Table 13.

The result of assessment and comprehensive analysis show:

(1) China and Japan will be under the greatest impact of the development of the Tumen River area on technology transfer in Northeast Asia, symbolized by the emergence of science towns in Hunchun of China and Osaka and Niigata of Japan. Among these centers, science city of Hunchun will mainly be engaged in bio-technology and new material technology, Osaka science city will be developed in the direction of chemical technology on the basis of the present Kansai science city, and Niigata science city will take new technology of machine building as its main industry.

(2) The impact of development of Tumen River area on the lay-out of science cities in Northeast Asia is demonstrated by the prediction that besides a science city in Seoul, scientific and technological centers will appear in Changchun of China, Zarubino of Russia and Rajin-Sonbong of North Korea, big industrial zones will appear in Yanji of china, Vladivostok of Russia and Chongji of North Korea.

Given a comprehensive analysis of the present base of science and technology in various areas, I maintain that once the development of the Tumen River region is put in force, there will be a group of new type science cities in the Northeast Asian region which are led by new material technology and bio-technology, with Hunchun, Osaka, Niigata and Seoul at the core, Changchun, Zarubino and Rajin-Sonbong area as the periphery, and the region composed by Yanji, Vladivostok and Chongjin as the hinterland.

10

Regional Cooperation and Development Strategy of Southwest China

Hieyeon Keum
(Yonsei University)

Introduction

Despite its advantage in raw materials and great potential for economic cooperation with other countries, Southwest China, (i. e., the four provinces of Sichuan, Guizhou, Yunnan, and Guangxi) has not been widely known to the outside world. This is partly because this vast area has not benefitted as much as the coastal provinces from the post-1978 economic reforms and trade opening polices of China. An unbalanced development plan resulted in two kinds of disparities: between individuals and between coastal provinces and interior provinces. To resolve this, beginning in the early 1990's, the Chinese government readjusted its regional development strategy, with more emphasis on balanced development and extension of the direction of development plan, or in Chinese terms, *xiang xibei tuijin* (towards West from East, and towards North from the South).

Comprising twenty-six percent of the total area of China, and 19.5% of the total population, and blessed abundant raw materials, Southwest China, often called *daxinan* (Great Southwest), draws international attention for its potential for development. However, development of Southwest China needs not only more efficient use of resources, but cooperative ventures with other countries. This study analyzes the strategies of economic development of this region and structure of Chinese national economic development on three levels of economic cooperation: international, regional or subregional, and national.

These three levels can be seen as complementary. Regionalization is a part of the ongoing internationalization process, and subregional cooperation can promote development of the region as a whole. Accordingly, cooperation between nation states in the subregion or region is necessary for progress toward an economic development, as it taps the potential of enlarged markets, reaps the benefits of complementary national resource endowments, and eases the movement of goods, capital and labor.

This paper seeks to delineate an appropriate development strategy for Southwest China. While there are already trade and other economic relationships between the region and other areas of China and neighboring countries, the Southwest's strategies for economic development and cooperation with them are likely to draw more attention from domestic and foreign markets. With possibilities for regional development and cooperation based on interdependence and complementarity, the region can offer an efficient means for enhancing East Asian regional economic cooperation.

Reform-cum-Opening Policies of China and Regional Development

Since it launched historic reform-cum-opening policies in 1978, China has experienced the greatest economic development in its history. Many Chinese believe that the stage of *wenbao* ("feeding full" [stomach] and "wearing warm" [clothes] 1.2 billion people) is over and that China has already reached the stage of *xiaokang* ([economic] "convenience"), and is moving towards the final stage, *datong* ("great unity").

In the 1990's China has speeded up the pace of the reform-cum-opening efforts. It has accelerated industrialization and the Four Modernizations Program, in order to achieve a per capita income of $ 1,000 by the year 2000. Because of the fluctuation in the scope and speed of the reforms, or in Chinese terms between "push for" and "retreat from," (*jiasu and tiaozheng*) China had to continually readjust the pace of growth and development. However, China is preparing its economy for further rapid growth, in spite of serious social and economic problems and various unexpected consequences of reforms, especially the growing inefficiency of its industrial structure and the widening disparities between individuals and among regions within the country.

As reform/opening policy continues, the gap between the coastal areas and inland grows. As an integral part of economic reform, major effort has been made since 1984 to promote the growth of lateral , or horizontal, economic relations between geographic regions. Geographic variations are major contributor to perceptions of uneven or unbalanced development.

There have been serious conflicts between coastal and inland areas in the share of resources allocated for economic development and policy implementation related to autonomous administrative power.[1] To gain support from the peasants and to promote a more equitable economic distribution, in the 1950's China set a deliberate policy of avoiding concentration of industrial development in the coastal areas, and industrial plants, resources, and skilled manpower were redistributed to scattered inland provinces. In fact, before 1978, inland regions received a much larger share than coastal provinces of capital investment and fiscal subsidies from the central government.[2]

In 1978, there was a clear shift in China's development strategy.

---

[1]James C. F. Wong. *Contemporary Chinese Politics: An Introduction,* 4th edition (Englewood Cliffs: Prentice-Hall, 1992), p. 153.

Central control over investment and allocation of resources for coastal regions was modified to accommodate the open door policy.[3] Since coastal regions had "good economic foundations" such as availability of factories, skilled labor, and port facilities, they were given higher priority to attractive foreign investors. Moreover, these areas had the experience of capitalist industrialization and commerce to 1949, and many *huashang* (overseas Chinese businessmen) had their roots there.

On the contrary, inland areas began to feel what Shirk termed a "comparative disadvantage."[4] To avoid provincial officials "sabotage of the economic reforms" and mitigate Deng's open door policy, Chinese government embarked on a new strategy of "inter-provincial cooperation," allowing inland and coastal areas to participate in joint ventures and trade with each other.[5] The central government even allowed a coastal enterprises to invest retained profits in inland mines and factories.

Although there are still problems related to uneven development, China nearly completed the groundwork for a market economy involving an experimental mixed economy by the end of 1992. China is now bolstering operation of this mixed economy by reducing the portion of the centrally planned economy, through cut off of government subsidies for money-losing state-owned enterprises (SOEs), granting more autonomy to local government and local enterprises, and reducing the central government's overall control. However, whenever side-effects of these measures have become apparent, Chinese government has tried to regain macro control and reduce the degree of economic decentralization.

Additionally, when Deng Xiaoping travelled to the South in

---

[2]Susan Shirk. "The Politics of Industrial Reform," in Elizabeth J. Perry and Christine Wong, *The Political Economy of Reform in Post-Mao China*, Harvard Contemporary China Series 2 (Cambridge: Harvard University Press, 1985), p. 210.

[3]Wang, *op, cit.*, p. 153.

[4]Shirk, *op, cit.*, p. 211.

[5]*Ibid.*

1992, he noted in his *nanxun jianhua* (Southern Speech) that,

> we must continue our economic reform and open-door policy and speed up economic development ··· anyone who opposes this must be retired.[6]

Later, the 14th Party Congress of the Chinese Communist Party endorsed the principles of Deng's reform policy. According to the CCP Central Committee, all provinces are required to adjust their rates of development. At the same time, it stated that the establishment of a "socialist market economy" offers the best opportunity for the development of Southwest China. The socialist market economy lifts the economic strictures of a highly centralized planned economy, while presenting various opportunities for large state-run enterprises.[7]

The policy of opening to the outside world is supposed to be readjusted and applied not only on the eastern coastline, but along the borders of China, and to be extended to previously neglected interior areas that have experienced difficulties in getting access to the outside world.

Gradually, China is extending direct international links to most parts of the country, making full use of its coastline, its border regions and its rivers. Southwest China is well placed for this. Four provinces, viz., Sichuan, Guizhou, Yunnan, and Guangxi, are target areas for the achievement of China's new balanced regional development and setting up international trade links with countries to the south of China and beyond. The Chinese government has put much emphasis on this region because it can be another window for China to the outside world.

---

[6]"Deng Xiaoping's Important Address," *Chinese Communist Party Document* No. 2 (January 18-February 21, 1992).

[7]Luo Xiduo and Li Junhua, "General Thinking on Northeast China's Development Plan,"in Won Bae Kim, ed., *Regional Development in Northeast China: An International Perspective* (Hawaii: East-West Center, 1994), p. 5.

Developmental Environment of Southwest China

Southwest China has a total area of 1,376,000 square kilometers and a total population of 220.7 million. The region is characterized by a complicated topography, a complex climate, abundant resources but relatively underdeveloped natural resources, compared with other regions of China. This can be seen in the following table.

According to Lian and Tisdell, there are two main reasons why more emphasis should be given to the development of this area: first, it will reduce regional income disparities, thereby enabling a greater sharing of the increasing wealth of China, and will promote social stability, and second it will provide new international trade opportunities.[8]

The per capita income of these provinces is far below the

Table 1. Basic Statistics of Southwest, 1993

	Sichuan	Guizhou	Yunnan	Guangxi
Population (mil.)	109.98	33.61	33.32	43.80
Territory (sq. km)	570,000	176,000	394,000	236,000
GRP (bil yuan)	149.24	33.17	51.0	3.33
GNP Growth Rate (%)	12.9	9.2	10.9	18.3
Annual per capita Income (Yuan)	1,357	987	1,331	1,307
Annual Household Income (yuan)				
Rural Areas	634.31	506.13	617.98	731.69
Urban Areas	1,791.72	1,637.46	1,848.23	1,886.01
Numbers of Foreign Enterprises	2,313	376	249	1,915
Industrial Structure (%)				
Primary Industry	69.8	78	77.8	73.4
Secondary Industry	14.5	10.1	9.6	10.6
Tertiary Industry	15.7	11.9	12.6	16.0

Source: *China Year Book 1993* (1994); Mitsubishi Research Institute, *China Handbook* (1994).

[8]Younong Lian and Clem Tisdell, "Developing China's Southwest: China's Strategy, Regional and Industrial Policy," *China Report*, 29:3 (1993), p. 135.

national average, the economic reform and opening policy has made them much better off than the pre-reform period. In 1992, the national economy grew 13.0%, but the four Southwest provinces only marked averaged 12.82%. At the same time, per capita GNP of Southwest China was about 1,245.5 yuan, only 60.7% of that of the national average. In 1993, the economic positions for Yunnan, Sichuan, Guangxi, and Guizhou in terms of GNP per capita were respectively 1,331 yuan, 1,357 yuan, 1,307 yuan, and 987 yuan, making them twenty-fourth to twenty-eighth among China's 27 provinces and three municipalities. Further, the income gap between the coastal areas and the interior areas has actually increased. In 1993, while the average income of Shanghai residents was 7,925 yuan and of Beijing residents 6,434 yuan, it was only 987 yuan in Guizhou, the lowest level in China.

In order for China to establish an appropriate development strategy, it is necessary to review carefully the actual conditions of this region and its provinces. Generally, this area is characterized by several economic bottlenecks, or developmental constraints. First is the huge population, especially in rural areas. This creates serious difficulties in turning the rural labor force into industrial or agricultural activities.

The economy of this region progressed very rapidly in recent decades, but as a whole, it still lags behind the national economy. In 1993, for example, the Southwest's share of population was 19.5% of the national total, but its shares of GNP and GDP were only 12.1% and 10.2%, respectively. Annual energy consumption of Southwest in 1991 was 829.8 billion tons, which is 11.6% of total national consumption. Annual electricity consumption the same year was 60.92 billion kwh, only 11.58% of the national total. In 1992, the Gross Agricultural and Social Product Output (GASO) of Southwest China was 270 billion yuan, or seventy-nine percent of the national figure. Agricultural and industrial production of the region in 1992 was 471.1 billion yuan, and average provincial production was 117.9 billion yuan, also lower than the national average and only 76.7% of the national level.

Second, there is also large regional disparity within the region.

For example, most of the industrial production is concentrated in limited areas, such as the cities of Chongqing, Mianyang, Chengdu, Leshan, Zigong, Luzhou, and Yibin; Kunming and the surrounding area of Yunnan Lake; as well as Zhunyi, Guiyang, Anshun, Guilin, Liuzhou, and Nanning. These areas also generally have a higher population density than elsewhere in the region.

A third problem is that several key industrial sectors lack close links with other sectors. During the pre-reform period, Southwest China established several industries which played an important role in the national economy, e. g., metallurgical products. However, these industries more or less developed in isolation and as result, the modern notion "industrial clusters" have not been fully realized.

Compared with other areas, Southwest China has favorable conditions for development. As Deng noted when he emphasized the importance of this region in 1992, Southwest China is gradually drawing attention from the central government and is gradually gaining priority in the government's balanced development plan. This is due to the region's favorable conditions: rich natural resources, an adequate technological and economic base, and a favorable geographical location for foreign trade.

Southwest China is rich in natural resources. Southwest China has abundant climatic resources and has a warm winter and cool summer. There is a saying in Guizhou that "the weather is different every ten hours."[9] Since the area has suitable soil and water resources for both intensive crop farming and animal husbandry, in Chinese it is often referred to as the "plant kingdom," or the "animal kingdom." This region also contains the second largest forest in China, and so has been called China's "green house."[10]

---

[9]Zhu Hongfei, "An Exploratory Discussion on the Ways of and Policies for Attracting investments and importing Technologies to Transform Traditional Industries in the Southwest Region," Paper Presented at the International Conference on "Economic Development and Opening Up to the Outside World of China's Southwest Regions" (February 10-12, 1993, Kunming, Yunnan Province), p. 2.

[10]Lian and Tisdell, *op. cit.*, p. 137.

Because the region is rich in both mineral and energy resources, Chinese called it "treasure storage." It has the largest deposits of vanadium, titanium and tin in the world, as well as and the largest deposits of iron, lead, zinc, aluminum, copper, manganese, mercury, phosphorous, antimony and nickel in China. Major energy sources include hydro – electric power, and large coal and gas deposits. Because of plentiful rainfall, the total amount of water reserves in the region amount to 804.8 million cubic meters, accounting for 29.5% of the national total. The amount of hydropower reserves in the region is estimated to be much as 676.1 million kw., or 42.9% of the total for China. Despite abundant water resources, the direct utilization ratio is only 4.6%. This is due to problems such as unbalanced distribution of water resources, low water conservation capabilities, and inadequate water drainage equipment.[11]

The Southwest region is also rich in natural scenery and tourist attractions. Due to the great variety of landform, geology, topography and climate, and its unique rivers and mountains, coupled with many ancient historical sites, there is much potential for tourism. Famous places include the karst land caves, springs and waterfalls in Guilin, Shilin Stone Forest, Ermei Mountain in Sichuan. Such tourism resources can stimulate opening of this region and play an important role in the international cultural, economic, and human exchanges.

Additionally, the region boasts thirty-four ethnic minorities, or 61.8% of China's fifty-five minorities. Partly related to this, the number of counties that are in absolute poverty is 25% of national total. A great variety of local festivals and fascinating local social customs of ethnic minorities now attract the foreign tourists.

Non-agricultural industries in the region also attract the foreign technology and capital. Leading industries include gas and chemicals, aerospace, mechanical equipment, electronics, nuclear power, and food processing. In 1991, the value of annual industrial production was over 249.6 billion yuan and the following year there were over 1,511,500 industrial enterprises in the region.

[11]Zhu Hongfei, *op, cit.*, p. 2.

Some 454 enterprises are classified as the large- scale national enterprises. Motorcycles, cars, sugar and cigarettes produced in this region have a high reputation both in domestic and international markets.

Southwest China has a high concentration of intellectual resources, and a high level of technological expertise. This region has over 133 universities and 757 research institutes, and a total of 1.5 million people are engaged in professional and technical profession. However, these human resources are not evenly distributed. In 1992, the Southwest region had a total about 2,300,000 technical personnel, or 22% of the national total. There are 110 technical professionals per 10,000 people, while the national average is just 98. But the distribution of this human resources is highly concentrated. The cities of Chengdu, Chongqing, Kunming and Guiyang had around 230,000 college graduates which is 40% of the total college graduates in the region. In rural areas, however, there is a severe shortage of educated people, and college graduates account for 1.5 to 2 persons for every 10,000 in the rural population. The rural illiteracy rate is about 28% of the labor force in Sichuan, but up to 40 to 55% in the other three provinces. Furthermore, there is also mismatch of the technical staff and the economic structure. Ninth percent of the total manpower are working in technical and specially-skilled positions, while only 7% of them are agricultural technical staff, even though the agricultural sector still plays a vital role at this stage of development.

Finally, this area has favorable geographical location and so is well positioned for foreign trade. Southwest China faces the ASEAN region. Currently, most of its export goods shipped via Hong Kong or Macau, but as this area develops its infrastructure and communication systems, direct trade will increase. This area has started building a transportation system more suited for foreign trade. This includes the Nanning-Hanoi railway, the Dian-Yue highway, the Dian-Mian railway and two sea ports, Beihai and Fangcheng. There are also various riverports, highways and airline connections. The Nan-Kun railway from Nanning to Kunming, currently being built, will also greatly improve the transformation system.

Requirements for Development and Cooperation of Southwest China

The irrationality of the region's industrial structure manifests itself in various ways. First, basic facilities are inadequate, and this restricts economic development. Most of the railroad network is bound for the east, and there are no high- power locomotives. Few rail lines run across the borders. Highway systems are similar, with low technical standards and quality. Also, few roads connect remote areas to major cities. The most serious problem is that many of the inter-provincial highways have "broken ends," i.e., many navigation lines are obstructed by sluice-gates and dams. Civil aviation, too, is insufficient to transport cargos and passengers.

Secondly, the region's industries are not rationally structured and are at a low level of development.

Third, non-state-owned economic elements accounted for only 23.3% to 36.6% of national totals, which was far below the national average of 45.5%. In fixed assets investments, non-state-owned elements made up 28.2% to 32.4% also lower than the national average of 34%. The difference is even greater when the Southwest is compared with Guangdong, Jiangsu, Zhejiang, and Shandong provinces. Rural enterprises in the Southwestern provinces are small in scale and weak in technological know-how. The slow development of non-state-owned elements is one

Table 2. Economic Structure of Southwest China, 1993 (%)

	Guangxi	Sichuan	Guizhou	Yunnan	National
Agriculture	52	43	46	46	32
Industry	32	36	37	41	50
Construction	4	7	6	4	6
Transportation	3	3	3	2	5
Commerce	9	11	8	7	7

of the major factors that causes the nation's relative underdevelopment.

Fourth, the region has only partially opened up to the outside the world. Foreign capital put to actual use in 1991 in Guangxi, Sichuan, Guizhou and Yunnan amounted to $86 million, $154 million, $1.6 billion, and $21 million respectively, or 0.75%, 1.34%, 0.14%, and 0.18% respectively of total foreign capital employed in China. In 1993, the ratios of foreign trade of Sichuan, Guizhou, Yunnan were 7.26%, 4.94%, and 7.4% respectively, far below the national average of 38.53%. The low degree of openness of the Southwest has directly affected the region's ability to use its resources and markets to develop its economy, and causes it to lose many favorable opportunities, while broadening the gap between the region and the rest of the country.

Additionally, Southwest China has suffered from problems common to underdeveloped countries and regions including an over- abundance of manpower and a shortage of subsidies and foreign capital. The region also suffers from problems peculiar to it, the most important being the poor fit of modern industries in the region. One would expect strong industries in the Southwest to be energy and natural resources and related industries. But, since these industries require concentrated capital, the contraction cycle is long, labor-absorbing capacity is low, and there are no quick benefits. In the absence of foreign investments, it will be difficult for the Southwestern region to develop on its own. On the other hand, if priority is given to agriculture and processing industries, difficulties include lack of demand for the products in the local markets, inability to compete in exports, and backwardness of basic facilities. For example, the elasticity for demand of the residents in Guangxi, Sichuan, Guizhou, and Yunnan was 0.25, 0.26, -0.78, and 0.41 respectively, lower than the national average in each case. The lack of brisk demand directly affected the development of production. For the sake of the region's future development, it is necessary for governments to map out a clear course of development so that the Southwest's economy can be improved and backwardness put to an end.

Formulation of an appropriate development strategy can be

based on a thorough understanding of Southwest China's comparative advantages and developmental constraints. The region's natural resources, materials and technology, industries and products provide the four provinces with obvious joint comparative advantages. Development of the region requires adjusting provincial structures toward regional integration through provincial specialization in accordance with three levels of development strategies.

International Level

Natural economic territories have been forming throughout the Asia-Pacific region. Scalapino defines the natural economic territories as

> regional entities that cross political boundaries, often encompassing only portions of states, but with their raison d'etre resting upon the combination of natural resources, manpower, technology, and capital that can be pooled to maximum advantage.[12]

Thus, Southwest China is a notable example of a national economic sphere, involving market-driven, trans-boundary economic interactions with neighboring countries. International economic cooperation encompasses the Southwestern provinces and Southeast Asian countries. Regional and subregional development can complement each other, while cultural similarities can de facto economic integration.[13]

Southwest China has a geographic advantage as it pursues opening to the outside world. The main railway lines on the primary axis from west to east in the region connect to Special Economic Zones (SEZs) and Hong Kong. The central government

---

[12]Robert A. Scalapino,"The Politics of Development and Regional Cooperation in Northeast Asia," in *Regional Economic Cooperation in Northeast Asia*, W. B. Kim, et al., eds., Proceedings of Vladivostok Conference (August 25-27, 1992), p. 22.

[13]Si Joong Kim, "The Progress of Economic Cooperation in the Yellow Sea Rim," Paper presented at the International Symposium(April 21-25, 1995, Seoul), p. 2.

is planning to build a north-south axis to connect with its neighboring Southeast countries to facilitate economic cooperation.

Several factors have encouraged greater economic linkages and cooperation between South and Southeast Asia, the growing integration of markets, increasing political stability, economic restructuring in Japan and Asian Newly Industrializing Countries (NICs), and shifting comparative advantages of Malaysia, Thailand, and the Philippines, and growing political relationships between China and its neighboring countries. China should take advantage of this change by speeding up the reform- cum-opening, give priority to the development of an export- oriented industrialization (EOI), and more effectively use foreign capital and technology. China should also optimize economic and trade cooperation with developed countries, developing countries, and the ASEAN countries, along with upgrading the Southwestern economy.

Under economic policies advanced by the Central Committee, all provinces and municipalities have begun a competing to take measures to attract foreign investment and introduce advanced technologies. Attracting foreign capital and technology depends on several factors. First, the region should extend the degree of openness with neighboring countries and strengthen economic and trade relations with them. Southwest China is near ten nations in Southeast Asia. Southeast Asia has an economy of $302.42 billion and consists of a huge market of $158.95 billion.

The ASEAN countries are similar to Southwest China in terms of industrial structure. However, while the Southwestern Chinese industrial structure is mainly geared to satisfying the needs of domestic markets, and is therefore self-contained, the ASEAN is export-oriented, and thus more closely linked to international division of labor.

The ASEAN countries mainly have light industries, especially materials assembly and spare parts. In Southwest China, the main industries are heavy and chemical industries. Electronic and machinery products have obvious advantages; light industry mainly depends on local raw materials and the food industry is quite competitive in export markets. Although there are both competition and supplementary relationships between them, at present, cooperation outweighs the competition.

This region should pay more attention to trade routes linking Southwest China with the ASEAN countries. Ships from ports along the North Bay of Guangxi can directly sail to Southeast Asian nations. Opening of Southwest border areas can lead to gradually widening of cooperation in economy, technology and trade. Meanwhile, regional coordination should be conducted so as to form a more comprehensive trade and economic system. Though countries such as Vietnam, Laos, Myanmar, and Kampuchea have a lower levels of industrialization and consumption, they constitute a good import market. At the same time, because the industrial level of the Southwest is comparatively higher, in border trade, it should mainly export processed products and primary raw materials to this neighbors.

Areas for opening along Southwest rivers should include the Xijiang River Basin, the upper reaches of the Yangtze River and the Lanchang River Basin. Opening of these three river basins should take into account the special geographic and industrial characteristics of each basin. They should also become part of the trade and economic channels through with Guangdong, Hong Kong, Macau and Taiwan.

Areas neighboring China, a few sub-areas of cooperation are now in the process of being established. Recent rapid economic growth in East Asia can help promote the development of the "growth triangles," i.e., Hong Kong-Southern China-Taipei, Singapore-Johor-Riaut, Northern Malaysia-Southern Thailand-North Sumatra, and North Thailand-Indochina-Myanmar.[14] These growth triangles can also assist growth in neighboring areas.

---

[14]Wang Huijong, "Representative Presentations: People's Republic of China," in *Subregional Economic Cooperation: Initial Possibilities for Cambodia, Lao PDR, Myanmar, Thailand, Viet Nam and Yunnan Province of the People's Republic of China* (Asian Development Bank, February 1993), p. 98.

National Level

After forty years of development and reconstruction, the Southwest Chinese industrial sector has become the leading sector. For the time being, the Southwest China needs to develop three types of industries: energy and minerals industry, processing and manufacturing, and light/consumer industries. Also important is the formation of a regional market linked to the national market. Transportation and telecommunications are an important prerequisite for this development.

To begin with, better coordination of economic and policies for the Southwest region are necessary. Promises of the region should open up to each other to increase economic cooperation and interdependent regional development. Not only should commodity markets be opened but also capital markets and those for technology, and labor.

Next, the Southwest provinces should be integrated in a way that emphasizes the respective resources and products of each area, so as to establish export production bases with regional characteristics. Then, each province should act as a window for the others. By exchanging market information and cooperating in use of transportation and port facilities, the regional economy will be strengthened and expanded radially. Structural adjustment will also help development of processing industries and rural enterprises.

At present, the industrial structure of Southwest is still in the transition from a rural to industrial economy, and none of its emerging industries yet play a leading role. Only a few industries, such as engineering and electronics have a solid material and technological basis. Since 1949, China has invested over 20 billion yuan in these two industries in Southwest China. However, adequate regional development programs were not set forth because of the dual structure of industry in Southwest China, i.e., the backward traditional agriculture coexisting with advanced modern industry. Manual labor and animal power are still the basic form of agricultural labor, and some areas still practice slash-and-burn cultivation. Precision and advanced technologies such as micro-electronics and biochemical engineering coexist with traditional technology.

The best way to speed up the Southwest's development and reduce the gap between traditional and modern sectors is to develop those industries in which the region enjoys a comparative advantage, but such development should not be confined to the mining of raw materials, as in the past. It should instead exploit the division of labor in China. Industrial activity in the East will become difficult without full development of energy resources and raw materials from Southwest China. As with the rest of China, proper utilization, based on a long-term plan, which emphasizes economic efficiency, is also necessary. From 1986 to 1989, for example, about 35% of Chinese productive capacity was underutilized because of scarce energy resources.[15]

Additionally, the private sector should be encouraged and rural surplus labor needs to be channelled into non-agricultural trades, so that rural enterprises and local enterprises(*xinagzhen qiye*) can be more fully developed. Also, the "third line" defense firms should be turned from military to civilian needs, to exploit their abilities and create a multiplier effect on the overall regional economy.

Regional Level

The development of Southwest China cannot be separated from that of the other regions of the country, especially Southeast China. In order to coordinate different regions, Southwest China should accept industrial transfers from Southeast China, i.e., partial adoption of China's "Stepwise Development Strategy." Southeast China has become the richest region in China, and is over due ripe for structural adjustment. Resource processing and labor intensive industries are being replaced by capital – and technology – intensive industries. About one-third of enterprises in Southeast China are no longer appropriate to the region and need to be transferred elsewhere. Furthermore, the main econom-

[15]Lian and Tisdell, *op. cit.*, p. 143.

ic development districts in Guangdong and Fujian have been unwilling to accept investment in small-scale and low technology projects, but such projects would be welcome in Southwest China.

It is also necessary to improve relations among the four provinces in Southwest China and encourage better cooperation between them. Joint coordinative bodies ought to be set up to foster cooperation among the provinces in resources, industrial development, technology acquisition, market expansion, border trade, trade with other countries and tourism.

In the next ten to twenty years, the GNP of Southwest China will increase by an average of 8 to 10 percent. Through joint exploitation of regional resources, the Southwest will become one of China's most important industrial basis buoyed by development of hydroelectric power, coal and nonferrous metal resources. It will focus on energy-consuming heavy and chemical industries, but with proportionate development in machinery, textile and food industries. Geographical advantage should greatly boost foreign trade, through transportation and communications facilities will be stretched to the limit. Accordingly, the transportation network needs to be developed to provide better links to Southeast Asia and the world beyond. Ongoing projects must serve the needs of leading industries to develop and facilitate foreign trade. The developmental plan for transportation and communications in Southwest China should put more emphasis on multi-directional and multi-purpose development, i.e., construction of roads and railroads in all directions, improvement southward passageway connecting of sea-routes connecting the region with Southeast Asia and other countries and better landroads to Myanmar, Thailand and India. The emphasis should be placed on the construction of highways and rail links from to coastal areas, the establishment or the enlargement of border ports and sea ports, and the modernization of civil aviation and inland water transportation systems.

To enhance provincial competitiveness, the government should adopt a regional developmental strategy. Two elements are critical: (1) strategic planning should be emphasized over mandatory allocation of resources, and (2) the planning system should be changed from a vertical hierarchy to a horizontal structure allowing more autonomy for each province.

Conclusion

Southwest China should be encouraged by the central government policy to foster international cooperation and regional development. This region, with its abundant natural endowments and potential for economic development, has been and will continue to attract domestic and foreign attention.

Much efforts have been made to improve the investment environment and transform the industrial structure in this area. However, relatively less attention has been given to the "software" aspects of building a common commitment to development and opening policies, concepts of the rule of law, the need for economic efficiency, and the idea of providing good service. Instead most analyses stress the "hardware" of construction, transportation, energy and other infrastructure. Until recently, the Southwest emphasizes only economic self-sufficiency without much attention to intra-regional cooperation. There was little understanding of the concepts of interdependence and complementarity.

There remain several developmental constraints. First, the regional economy still depends on traditional agricultural and extraction. As a result, the region suffers from serious structural problems that cause a slow growth and lagging efficiency. Second, the Southwest Chinese infrastructure, especially hydroelectric power, transportation, and communication, is unable to satisfy the demands of heavy and chemical industries, and cause the major bottle-necks of economic development in the region.

Third, domestic capital shortages are compounded by weak attraction of foreign capital. Modern technology has not been brought into full play. For a long time, this area has stressed production over technology development and labor training. As a result, the rate of technological progress in the region has been lower than China's average.

The chief problem of development in Southwest China is a structural one. Thus, for the region's future economic development, governments and enterprises should exploit their advantages and remedy shortcomings by gradually rationalizing industrial structure and slowly integrating with the national and international economies. The basic principle can be summarized in the phrase, "integral structural transformation of the entire region." It has three main points.

To begin with, a successful strategy should transform the economy from its insular orientation to one that is truly to the outside world. It should also help develop a market economy out of the ruins of the old Mao-era command economy. Southwest China will then enter the international stage through economic cooperation and development of competitive industries, Southwest China may then become an international player.

Next, the strategy should promote technologies that can help the region from resource exploition to resource processing. It should also coordinate technology acquisition with economic development. Finally, the new strategy should carry out a gradient shift of industries toward integration and optimization of resources region-wide, to promote the swift development of new regional growth poles. Southwest China should reorganize old industries and launch new ones in order to attain the optimal industrial distribution for the entire region. All this should be carried out in stages and at different levels. Enterprises from both inside and outside the region are the best means to advance the development of new growth poles.

Although progress has been made in developing a case of the market economy in China, a number of issues still remain unsolved, viz., a thoroughgoing capital market does not yet exist, there is still unbalanced economic development between coastal and inland areas due to more intensive development on the latter, and various structural problems persist. Current Chinese reforms are often characterized as "reform within the system," not "reform of the system," and changes in the basic system of property ownership have barely started.[16] All these factors have been hindered full adoption of a market economy and have resulted in unbalanced growth and development throughout the country. Until these obstacles to China's progress are removed, Southwestern China, like the rest of the country, will develop only at a snail's pace.

[16]Clem Tisdell, *Economic Development in the Context of China* (London: Macmillan, 1993), pp. 23-35.

PART V

The Challenge of China in the Pacific Rim

11

The Future Path of China's Defence Industry

Ding Jingping
(Chinese Academy of Social Sciences)

Introduction

The defence industry in China comprises of such industries as nuclear, aviation, electronics, ordinance and shipping. They were former Ministry of No.2, 3, 4, 5, and 6 Machinery Industry respectively before 1984 and directly belong to the National Defence Scientific and Industrial Commission (NDSIC). Although they produced some civilian products, they were mainly controlled by NDSIC until 1984. After 1984, these ministries have shifted to civilian sectors and were controlled by the State Council. The subject to be covered here relate mainly to these industries.

The Third Plenum of the 11th National Conference of the Communist Party of China(CCP) that was held at the end of 1978, forecasted that the peaceful strength will constrain the world war in the next twenty years or even in longer period. Thus, China should turn its direction from political struggle to economic development for reaching the goal of "four modernization." According to the new goal, the defence industries also should change their strategy from preparing against war to economic development.

At that time, the general situation in the world was that few countries were occupied with the arms-race. Many countries worried about the regional war in various places in the world. However, China started to shift its military production to civilian production without concerning itself with the prospect of war. Since 1979, China has been doing this work for fifteen years. From 1979 to 1993, the gross value of civilian production created by defence industries increased to an average of 20 percent per year. Now the ratio of civilian production to total production in value term has reached to 76 percent in 1993 from 8 percent in 1979. However, there were not many people paying attention to this big change until the end of the Cold War. Now the conversion from military production to civilian production in China has attracted many outsiders and has become one of the hottest issues in the world.

The major Third Line Industries are an important part of Chinese military industries. It is necessary to explore the situation of the Chinese third line industries as we discuss the changes of military production. This paper will discuss the present status of civilian production in military industries; the history of combination of military production and civilian production; experience of conversion from military use to civilian use; the formation of the third line industry; conversion of the third line industries after reform and openness; the future of the Chinese military industry and; implications for the Pacific Rim.

Present Status of Civilian Production in Military Industries

Since implementing the principle of "Converting military production to civilian production" starting from the early 1980s, military enterprises have made great achievements in civilian production. According to incomplete statistics of 1993, China's military industries have about 600 civilian production lines and can produce nearly 15,000 civilian products. Over the past fourteen years, military firms have provided a great deal of equipment for other civilian industries such as energy, transportation, raw material, machinery, textile and light industries. In the meantime, large quantities of commercial products have been produced and filled the gap between market demand and supply. So far, the largest Chinese color TV company and the motorcycle company are of military firms. Military firms provide more than 60 percent of the total Chinese-made motorcycles, 30 percent of total color TV sets, 11 percent of total automobiles, 26.1 percent of railroad goods wagon and 24.4 percent of the coal mining equipment in China.

The nuclear industry has produced 1,200 types of product. It also made great contributions in building the Qinshan Nuclear Power Station in Zejiang province and the Dayawan Nuclear Power Station in Guangdong province which are the first two Nuclear Power Stations in China. The aviation industry has designed 3 new models and made more than 200 passenger airplanes. Besides that, there are 5,000 types of civilian products could be produced in this sector.

The electronic industry has formed large capacity for civilian production. For instance, among the 12 million color TV sets produced in China in 1992, 30 percent of them were produced by military firms. Within total exported color TV sets, 20 percent of them were provided by military firms. The ordnance industry has formed a civilian production structure mainly consisting of machine-tools, optic, electric and chemical fields, including many high technology products such as digit control machine-tools, industrial control systems and robots. The shipping industry has almost completed its conversion. About 40 percent of ships are exported. The space industry is utilizing its satellite and rocket technologies to serve telecommunication, nature resource exploration, meteorology and commercial launch for foreign satellites, etc.

The History of Combination of Military Production and Civilian Production

The conversion from military production to civilian production in China actually started very early. China felt the weakness of former Soviet Union's model which completely separated military production from civilian production. In the early 1950s, the Central Committee of the CCP had raised the concept of combination of military production and civilian production. In the Senior Meeting of State Affairs held in 1956, Mao Zedong had pointed that the dual use of production must be paid great attention to. Chinese industries must have two capacities: practicing civilian production within military production, and practicing military production within civilian production. In this way, China can convert its civilian production into military production in the case of the war.

In April of the same year, Mao Zedong re-emphasized that idea. According to his idea, defence industries started to develop civilian products and convert military production to civilian production in 1957. By the end of 1960, the Chinese defence industries had produced thousands of new products for civilian and market demand. However, negative assessments of this conversion became a majority idea since the world political situation was unfavorable towards China by the end of 1960's (e.g. the relations between China and former Soviet Union was severed, while the political situation in the Taiwan Straits was getting worse). After that, military industries stopped producing civilian products and returned to unique military production until 1978.

According to the new principle raised by the third plenum of the 11th National Congress of the CCP held in late 1978, China started to reduce its armament and the number of soldiers from four to three million. Meanwhile, China started to emphasize combination military production and civilian production again because the military budget was also largely reduced and there was not enough orders for military firms from the government. Deng Xiaoping, the former Chairman of Military Commission of the Central Committee of the CCP, pointed out that the structure of the Chinese military industry adopted from the former Soviet Union must be liberated. The defence industry must combine military and civilian production and supporting military in civilian production. The general principle that he raised was to take at least 50 percent of labor to civilian production. Once automation production increases, two thirds of the total labor should be shifted to civilian production.

In January 1982, Deng Xiaoping summarized the principles for defence industry: "Combining military with civilian production, combining normal situation with war situation, giving priority to the military production, and supporting military with civilian production." In November 1984, again, Deng Xiaoping spoke that "Defence industry has better equipment and strong technological strength. It must be utilized and joined with national construction for producing civilian products. There will be a great deal of advantages without any disadvantages." According to these ideas and principles, the Chinese defence industries started to produce civilian products and joined mass production. Since 1979, the process of conversion can be divided into three stages:

Stage of Spontaneous Production

Because China had started strategic transition from political struggle to economic construction, orders for defence industries were largely reduced since 1979. It gave way to military enterprises stopping their military production, especially the third line military enterprises. To find a way out of these difficulties and for its survival, these enterprises had to convert their production to civilian production from military production. At that time, their primary goal was to make profit and there was no strategy or plan for future development. They only produced what they could make. Although some products were successful, many products were not since most of these firms had no experience in civilian production. This sort of civilian production still was blind although it benefited the enterprises. Most of them still thought that producing civilian products was just a temporary method and still hoped for military orders in the long run. On the other hand, many of them only focused on some short-term commercial products such as bicycles, sewing machines and electric fans and so forth and did not think how to make use of their real advantages. Most products were of low quality and high cost, and lacked competitiveness. Consequently, many products were quickly produced, and quickly closed down. Until 1983, defence industry as a whole was still in a difficult position.

Stage of Initiative Development

The difficulties of converting military industries into civilian production were brought the attention of top leaders. Deng Xiaoping again pointed out that all ministries of the defence industry must develop civilian products with all their strength besides fulfilling their military tasks. In August 1983, a conference on "Combination of Military and Civilian Production, and Developing Civilian Production" held by State Planning Commission (SPC), State Economic Commission (SEC) and National Defence Scientific and Industrial Commission (NDSIC) discussed how to develop civilian production in the future. After the conference, the State Council held a special meeting for converting military production, the first time in Chinese history. As the final report of the meeting pointed out, conversion of military enterprises to civilian production, from unique military production and transfer military technology to civilian use from military use, will be a long term strategy and will serve the national economy, not just for "finding meal to eat". Therefore, military industries must have a strategic and fundamental conversion and combine dual productions in the future.

Based on this strategic plan, each military industry made its own plan for a combination of military production and civilian production. For instance, the former Ministry of Nuclear Industry (MONI) raised a principle of "multi-business but centered nuclear business"; former Ministry of Aviation Industry (MOAI) raised a principle of "combining military production with civilian production, taking civilian production as a main task, basing on aviation production and multi-business"; the former Ministry of

Ordnance Industry (MOOI) started to force on vehicles and petroleum exploration machines; and the former Ministry of Shipping Industry (MOSI) started to explore foreign markets and export ships.

In the meantime, technology transfer from military use to civilian use has started. A survey on technology transfer had been taken by a group united by SPC, SEC, SSTC, NDSIC and the Leading Group for Science and Technology, State Council. Since 1985, a series of trading conventions were held in several cities such as Hangzhou, Beijing and Shenzhen. Thousands of military technologies have been transferred to civilian sectors through these conventions.

Stage of Deepening Development

In July 1986, management structure of military production was adjusted by the State Council and the MCOCC for promoting development of the combination of military and civilian production. Some ministries that used to belong to the MCOCC were transferred to the State Council, including MONI, MOAI, MOSI, MOOI and Ministry of Space Industry (MOSI). The purpose of this shift was so that the State Council could make a united plan for all civilian production, including these military industries, and to promote the combination of military and civilian production.

In April 1989, a liaison group was created by SPC, SEC and NDSIC for the conversion of military production to civilian production. In October 1989, three commissions held a conference on the changing experiences of the combination of military and civilian production in the last ten years. Meanwhile, for supporting the conversion from military production to civilian production, other civilian industrial ministries invited military industries to join in their projects, and helped them to enter the market competition. From 1985 to 1990, the "Seventh Five-year Plan" period, China supported 296 military conversion projects with about four billion yuan bank loan. There were 450 civilian production lines set up and about 50 percent of military enterprises had a leading civilian product. From 1990 to 1995, the "Eighth Five-year Plan" period, more than 400 projects related to military conversion have been supported with a 6.5 billion yuan loan. After these projects finish, not only will all military enterprises have its own civilian product and 80 to 90 percent of them have at least 1 to 2 major civilian products, but the military production force will also become an important strength in the Chinese economy.

Technology transfer from the military sector to the civilian sector was largely extended since the middle of the 1980s. During the "Seventh Five-year Plan" period, nearly 2,000 R&D project related to military technology were transferred to civilian use. Military industries had transferred about 3,000 technologies to civilian use and another 30,000 contracts were signed. Some of key equipments which had to be imported from abroad have now been produced by the military firms.

For utilizing their own advantages and avoiding competition with civilian firms at low technological level, many military firms enhance their R&D and turn to develop high technologies to improve high value-added products. For example; using nuclear technology for new farm seeds; using satellite technology for territory investigation, telecommunication, broadcasting and environmental inspection and so forth; using precise processing technology for making precise equipments and parts. Developing and utilizing high technologies made military firms become the leaders in many civilian industrial sectors.

In terms of organizational structure, many military firms merged with local firms and formed many big business groups. Within 55 large business groups that were approved by the central government, seven of them are formed by military firms, including Jialin Group, Xi'an Airplane Industrial Group, South Dynamic Machinery Group, Shanghai Aviation Industrial Group, Guizhou Aviation Industrial Group, Guizhou Aero-space Industrial Group and Hubei Aero-space Industrial Group. For acquiring information and promoting foreign trade, many firms open offices in the coastal area. So far, about 200 joint ventures have been created between military firms and foreign firms. A chain with "internal areas – coastal areas – overseas" has been formed in many enterprises located in internal areas.

Chinese Experience for the Conversion from Military Use to Civilian Use

China's conversion from military use to civilian use is actually following the principle: "Combining military with civilian production, combining normal situation with war situation, giving priority to the military production, and supporting military with civilian production." This principle summarizes both the law of war and the law of economic construction for military industries. Setting up military industries in necessitated by, but not always serve for the war because peace period is always longer than war period. On the other hand, military industries are also dominated by the market law, namely, dominated by prices of products, average profit margin and relations between demand and supply.

"Combining military with civilian production" means that using part of capacity to produce civilian products, or transferring military technology to civilian use in peaceful period, including technology, labor, building and equipments. However, it does not mean that all the military production capacity should be transferred. Otherwise, it will not be a combination of two productions and military capacity would disappear. "Combining normal situation with war situation" means that both ensuring supply capacity for the war and storing military productive capacity in the peaceful period should be concerned when a military project is created. It should be suitable for dual use. "Giving priority to the military production" means that a priority should be given when the nation needs since the national security should always be ensured. "Supporting military with civilian production" means that the military firms use part of the profit earned by civilian business for supporting military production capacity. It is reasonable because the original equipments, buildings and land are for military use, not for civilian use. Since these elements are transferred to civilian use, part of its profit should be returned back to military use as compensation.

In summary, these four principles are reflected in the relations between the "combination of military and civilian production," "conversion from military production to civilian production" and "ensuring military need." These three concepts are related with each other and cannot be separated. "Conversion from military production to civilian production" does not mean that China should convert all the military production into civilian production, but just part of it. Otherwise, there would be no guarantee for military need in case a war starts. In this sense, "conversion" must actually be a "combination." Within "combination of military production and civilian production," one thing that should be emphasized is to ensure military need. In detail, it means to maintain capacity for military production, R&D and testing. Otherwise, it will also be in danger if these basic needs cannot be ensured.

These principles have been implementing in the readjustment of industrial structure and organizational structure in military industries in 1980s. In terms of readjustment on industrial structure, the military industrial structure should be divided into two parts: standing production capacity and mobilizing production capacity. The first one is for arming military during peaceful period, and the last one is for the need of war time. These two types of capacities are all required in such previous military industries as nuclear, aviation, electronics, ship-building, ordnance and space.

In terms of readjustment of the organizational structure, it mainly means to open military industries from a close and single organizational structure. Most of them now have shifted from government departments to industrial corporations with multi-industrial sectors and multi-products. Financially, they have to be responsible for their own profit or lose. The new organizational structure and style is more applicable to market environment and have stronger competition strength in the market. Some of them now even are formed stockholding companies and acting in international market.

The Formation of the Third Line Industry

The construction of the third line was raised by a report of the Headquarter of General Staff in 1964. The report revealed that the distribution of Chinese industries was not good for defence. The existing industries were too concentrated in big cities. In 14 big cities where the population was over a million, there was a concentration of about 60 percent of Chinese machinery industry and 52 percent of Chinese defence industries. Most of the big cities were located in coastal areas and lacked efficient anti-aircraft system. Main railroad stations, bridges and seaports were close to big cities and lacked defence countermeasure. Due to these problems, the Headquarter of General Staff sent a report to the Central Committee of the CCP and suggested that some countermeasures be drafted.

This report was attracted by Mao Zedong, the former chairman of the CCP. He emphasized that China should make preparations for war and should build defence industries in the internal areas. According to his decision, China started a large scale construction for three lines areas.[1] The process of entire construction could be divided into two periods: the Third Five-Year Plan period (1965-1970) and the Fourth Five-Year Plan period (1970-1975). During the first period, the main task was to build railroads in Southwest areas, including railroads between Sichuan and Guizhou, Chengdu and Kunmin, Guiyang and Kunmin, Xiangfan and Chongqing, Hunan and Guizhou; to build five bases for iron and steel industry, including Panzhihua, Jiuquan, Wuhan, Baotou and Taiyuan; and to build some other basic industries such as coal mining, power station, nature gas field, machinery and chemical industries. During this period, investment in internal areas had reached by 61.12 billion yuan, or 66.8 percent of the total state

[1]The first line, second line and third line is divided by Chinese geography. Coastal areas are the first line. Middle areas are the second line and internal areas are the third line. the third line is divided into two parts: one part is including such provinces as Yunnan, Guizhou and Sichuan and part of Hunan and Hubei; another part is including provinces of Shaanxi, Gansu and Ningxia and Qinghai and part of Henan and Shanxi.

investment for fixed assets. Within this investment, eleven province which belong to the third line area took 48.24 billion yuan, or 52.7 percent of investment for fixed assets.

During the second period, the main task of the third line turned to the so-called "Three West" areas, namely West of Henan province, West of Hubei province and West of Hunan province. Meanwhile, the construction in Southwest continued. During this period, total investment in fixed assets in internal areas was 89.87 billion yuan, or 53.5 percent of the total state investment. Within it, the investment for third line areas was 69.10 billion yuan and 41.1 percent of the total state investment in the fixed assets.

There were mainly two methods of the third line construction: One was to build new firms in third line areas and the other was to move the firms from the coastal areas to the internal areas. According to the statistics in 1971, since 1964, 380 firms had been moved to the internal areas, including 145,000 workers, staffs and 38,000 pieces of equipment.

The positive result was, first, a group of important projects have been constructed such as Panzhihua Iron & Steel Works in Sichuan province, Jiuquan Iron & Steel Works in Gansu province, Chengdu Seamless Tubing Mill, Guizhou Aluminum Factory, China No. 2 Automobile Works, Sichuan Heavy Truck works, Sichuan Deyang No. 2 Heavy Machine Building Factory, Guizhou Liupanshui Coal Mining, Gansu Liujiaxia Hydro-power Station and so forth.

Secondly, some new industrial bases have been formed. For instance, a machinery building base in Southwest area including Sichuan, Guizhou and Yunnan province; the manufacturing base centered by machine tools and bearing in Shaanxi province; the machinery industrial bases formed by military industries in the provinces of Hubei, Hunan and Henan. A large iron and steel base in Panzhihua, Sichuan province; a coal and power base in the west of Guizhou province; the high technological center in Chengdu and Xi'an city and so forth.

Thirdly, some areas have formed a complete industrial system with higher degree machinery equipment. The capacity of industry in the third line areas occupied a bigger share in the whole country, especially Sichuan province. The investment in Sichuan province reached 39.3 billion yuan, 33.5 percent of the total investment in the third line areas, 16 percent of the total investment for the fixed assets from 1966 to 1975 in China. During this period, about 250 heavy industrial projects moved to Sichuan from the coastal areas. By the end of 1975, the fixed assets of Sichuan province had reached 18.23 billion yuan and became the second largest province in China in terms of the value of fixed assets, just behind Liaoning province, exceeded Shanghai and Heilongjiang province. Other internal provinces such as Hubei, Henan and Shaanxi also set up a strong industrial base after the third line construction.

Because the third line construction began during the period of the "Cultural Revolution" and was on over-estimation of the dangers of war, the scale and speed of the construction was clearly affected by these elements. The scale of the construction was too large and was built too hastily. Finally, there were a great deal of problems in the third line projects. Most of them had such problems as incomplete construction, could not be formed a complete capacity of production; firms were located in bad sites which were too far in distance; unclear production direction; and finally, backward management practices due to the difficult living and working environment. As a result, the capacity of the third line project could not in fully operational. In 1975, total fixed assets in the third line areas was 35 percent of total national fixed assets, but its industrial output was only 25 percent of the gross industrial output in value term. The fixed assets for per employee in Southwest areas was number one in China, but its industrial output and productivity accounted by per ten thousand yuan fixed assets was the last. It is clear that the efficiency of third line industries was very disappointing.

Conversion of the Third Line Industries after Reform and Openness

Since 1979, the beginning of reform and openness, the third line industries faced severe challenges. The major problem was that China had turned its attention from military industries to civilian industries. The budget for defence was largely reduced. The third line industries were also heavily impacted. In the meantime, military orders are largely reduced. Many of the third line enterprises have even no money to complete its construction and dead on middle way. Openness in the coastal areas, especially in the economic zones attracted huge amounts of capital investment and many talented people from internal areas. Faced with these challenges, China took some countermeasures:

- Relocation of some of the third line enterprises. Some projects have not been completed yet with wrong location and wrong products were closed. Part of them with good productions were moved to small or middle-sized cities near them. Some of them were merged to other firms with better locations or other conditions. However, these were the minority of total third line firms.
- Investment of capital for promoting conversion from military production to civilian production through technology transformation. This is a major method for third line firms.
- Promotion of inter-province business and overseas business. Many third line enterprises opened a "window" in coastal areas, specifically in economic zones, and formed a chain that received orders and information in coastal areas, manufacturied in internal bases, and sold products in both domestic and international markets.

For instance, just in the "Seventh Five-year Plan" (1985- 1990), Central government had invested 2.5 billion yuan capital and readjusted 121 projects. Plus 1.2 billion investment for fixed assets construction and 3.0 billion investment for technology transformation which collected by the firms themselves, total investment had exceeded 6.2 billion yuan. After readjustment, the gross value of civilian products reached over 80 percent of that total products from just 10 percent in these projects. By the end of 1990, there were about 200 civilian products that formed large scale production capacity such as automobile, motorcycle, camera, TV set and various machinery equipments and so on.

Readjusted third line enterprises are now playing more and more of an important role in internal areas, especially in the backward areas such provinces as Sichuan, Guizhou Shaanxi and Yunnan. For instance, an electronic industrial zone has been formed based on the third line enterprises in the Northeast of Xi'an city. In Guiyang city, a machinery, electronic and instruments production zone has created based on "Zhenhua Electronic Industrial Co." and automobile parts and components production zone also formed based on eight aircraft manufacturing companies. Other cities such as Zhunyi city in Guizhou province, Chengdu city in Sichuan province and Xiaogan city in Hubei province also has formed newly industrial zones based on the third line firms.

Future of the Chinese Military Industry

Although the conversion from military to civilian production has been in process for more than 10 years, there are still some problems. In general, these problems could be summarized in the following categories:

- The capacity of military production and R&D are still too large though they have been largely reduced. So far, military order can only meet one third of the production capacity. The idling of equipments and labor not only severely affects efficiency of the enterprises, but also increases the government subsidy.
- Duplicating at low technical level production is existing among the military firms. Many products are not high technology but are produced by many military firms.
- In terms of organizational structure, most of the firms are separated with small scale production. Large industrial groups with highly specialized and large economic scale production are still rare. It also severely affects efficiency.

What is the future of the Chinese military industries? What is the strategy for the further development of the Chinese military industries? At least four aspects can be described as follows:

•Speeding up R&D for high-tech and new military equipments. Along with the collapse of former Soviet Union and the end of cold war, all developed countries are readjusting their military strategies. In the future, these countries will continuously reduce its military strength, but enhance their defence R&D. China is not an exception. According to this military strategy, China will speed up its R&D for high-tech and new military equipments. Some key projects should be ensured. China will be looking for opportunities of international cooperations for its military R&D too since its popular method in the world at present.

•Further promoting combination between military production and civilian production. Readjustment of defence industries is a common task for many countries in the world. Although China has done much for this work since the early 1980s, there is still a long way to go. China will continue to readjust its defence industries. The basic idea is to further reduce the capacity of military production, to concentrate strength for some key projects, to raise the capacity for military R&D and to promote the combination between military production and civilian production. In detail, China will try to solve the problem of over supply of military production and weakness of military R&D. More flexible production lines will be built to use for dual production. Dual technologies also will be the main task for defence industries.

•Promoting reform of defence industries to suit the need of a new market economy. Since China has been implementing market economy and has reformed many mechanisms such as monetary system, taxation system, foreign exchange system, price system and trade system, military enterprises also have to be changed from a central planned system to a market economic system. Otherwise, they cannot survive in the new environment. Therefore, modern corporation system and stockholding system also would be started in the military industries. Unlike before, military products should also be paid according to market price. Furthermore, separating military production line and civilian production line would be the necessary method to be taken so that they can suit different needs between the market and the government plans.

•Combining third line industries with their production structure readjustment. Since the original distribution of military was too difficult to operate, many of them have to move to new places which are closer to cities. This started from the "Seventh Five-year Plan" (1985-1990). During this period, 118 firms moved with the exception of one. All the firms that moved produce civilian products and have been posting profit. During the "Eighth Five-year Plan" period (1990-1995), China will move another 110 firms to restructure their production. After these projects finish, the entire military industries will have a more reasonable industrial structure and location. They will be the normal enterprises to join the market competition.

In summery, conversion from military production to civilian production is a long term strategy for the Chinese military industries. China will certainly keep going in this path to form a dual use strength for both military and civilian production. However, in any sense, the production strength for military use will not be important in quantity, but in quality. In other words, improving R&D strength for high-tech and new style weapons and military equipments will be the central task for China in the future.

Implications for the Pacific Rim

China has been largely reducing its military strength since early 1980s, including the reduction of one million soldiers and a large portion of the defence production capacity. It clearly shows that China has realized that there would be no serious threats for China and nor another world war in the foreseeable future. Therefore, China reduced its military strength with its own initiative starting from early 1980s, though the cold war at that time had not yet ended and many countries were still maintaining their strong military strength. Since that time, China's actions decreased the worries of the neighboring countries and also created a peaceful environment for China's economic construction. The achievements that China has made through economic reform and openness are tightly linked with the reduction of its military strength. Thus, China and the rest of the world, especially the other members in the Pacific Rim have benefitted from China's positive actions.

China's conversion from military production to civilian production has been supported by many countries, including the United States. A good example is the creation of the "Sino-US Commission for Conversion from Military Production to Civilian Production." This organization provides assistance to China to shift its military production to civilian production to the benefits of both sides. To China, it can receive some technology and capital support from the United States to speed up its conversion. To the United States, it can reduce its concerns on China's military strength since it is shifting to civilian production.

The economic achievements that Chinese defence industries have made towards the Pacific Rim are clear. In terms of foreign trade, the defence industries have become a main force in producing export civilian products. China's space industry has launched 7 satellites for 6 countries since 1985. By the end of this century, China will launch another 25 to 30 foreign satellites.

China's nuclear power technology has been exported to Pakistan and Iran and will build two nuclear power stations for them respectively. China's shipping industry exported as much as 2.7 million tons abroad from 1981 to 1991 and earned about $2.58 billion in hard currency. The aviation industry also has exported many civilian products to the world, including aircraft, parts and components and other civilian products. So far, this industry has earned $3.5 billion since 1979. The total value of exports has been increasing by 50 percent per annum since. The ordnance industry in China is one of the largest industries active in foreign trade. It produces various civilian products. The export value, by the end of 1993, had reached to $800 million, 100 percent more than that of the last year. The products have been sold to more than 100 countries in the world. Finally, civilian products in the electronic industry to total products in value term has reached to 97 percent in 1992. In 1993, it had exported $8 billion to the world and accounted for about 7 percent of Chinese total exports.

The joint ventures between foreign firms and Chinese defence firms have also made significant progress in recent years. For instance, by the end of 1993, in the Beijing area alone, joint ventures with military firms have reached to 20 with a total of $20.75 million in contracted value. So far, about 200 joint ventures have been created between military firms and foreign firms. The military industries are playing more and more important role in foreign cooperations in China.

In terms of technology transfer, Chinese defence industries

have not only transferred many military technologies to domestic civilian firms, but also foreign firms. For instance, in the "'93 Hongkong International Exhibition on Peaceful Use of Military Industrial Technology" held in July 1993, China sold US$2.5 billion worth of technologies to other countries just within one week.

The two hot topics in the development of China's defence industries are: defence budget and arms purchasing. In regards to the first topic, it is not necessary to say many words here since many papers have discussed it. A clear example is that China's defence budget in 1992 amonted only US $6.13 billion, a level even lower than India, only US $6.13 billion, and defence budget per capita ranked fainly low as shown in Table 1, only US $6 per person per year. Table 1 shows that China's defense budget was one of the lowest both in terms of per capita amount and gross amount. Both of them are at lowest rank (total defence budget compared to big countries). Actually, this minimum budget is not even sufficient to pay for the military's salary since inflation in China is quite high. Inflation reached an average of 20 percent per annumn in 1993 and 26 percent in 1994. Anyone who is rational would not conclude that China is expanding its military strength.

Regarding arms purchasing, amongest many rumors there is one truth. China has bought some Su-27 air-fighters from Russia. The purpose of this purchase is to protect islands in the South China Sea because the existing Chinese air-fighters cannot reach that area. It is understandable given that every country is interested in protecting its territory. On the other hand, since China concentrates most of its strength in developing its economy, the strength of its defence is severely injured. China has no new weapons and equipment to equip the military for more than 10 years. It is unimaginable for a big country to be without weapons.

Actually, there are different attitudes of China's military purchases among the neighbors surrounding China. The United States, South Korea and Japan do not really care what China does because they know the real purpose of China's military purchas-

Table 1. Defence Budget in Major Countries, 1991-1992

	1991			1992		
Countries	I	II	III	I	II	III
US	290.9	5.3	1,155	270.9	4.8	1,076
Canada	11.52	2.0	426	10.35	1.7	383
France	34.48	2.9	606	34.91	2.9	614
Germany	32.3	2.2	405	31.03	1.9	389
UK	43.21	4.4	762	41.2	4.0	727
Italy	19.72	1.8	344	21.2	1.9	370
Japan	32.68	1.1	262	34.3	1.0	275
Russia	-	-	-	38.53	5.2	259
Span	8.26	1.7	205	7.41	1.4	184
Switzerland	3.8	1.7	584	3.65	1.6	561
Australia	7.06	2.4	414	7.27	2.5	426
South Africa	3.85	3.8	146	3.32	3.1	126
Egypt	2.23	5.7	39	2.47	8.3	43
Argentina	1.41	2.1	42	1.75	2.5	52
Brazil	2.3	0.9	15	2.12	0.8	14
Israel	5.79	11.3	1,138	6.76	11.6	1,328
India	7.41	2.6	8	6.75	2.7	8
Pakistan	2.98	7.5	25	3.29	7.7	28
Philippines	0.99	2.2	15	1.03	2.3	16
China	6.13	1.9	5	6.73	1.9	6

I. Budget (Billion US$).
II. Parentage to GDP (percent).
III. Budget for per person (US$).

Source: *People's Daily*, March 31, 1994.
The original source was from the report of London Institute of International *Strategy*: "Comparison on Military Strength, 1992-1993," etc.

es. These countries know that Russia has made an agreement with China while it is selling Su-27 to China. China should put these aircrafts in South China, not in the North. They also know what the situation of the Chinese military is and how weak the Chinese military is presently. Of course, the media in these countries stir up attention to these issues in order to attract readership. However, the real military people would never thought of it as a big issue.

The most sensitive countries towards these issues are the countries that have tenitorial disputes with China, for example, over islands in the South China Sea. It is understandable why they are more sensitive than others. First, unlike the United States and Japan, these countries do not have the capability to produce advanced weapons. They also have to buy weapons from other countries. Arms purchasing should not be a sensitive issue for these countries. If there are no political reasons and territorial disputes, they should not have any problems with China renewing their weapons. Because they worry about China's military threat, they prefer to make some big noise in order to attract international attention and support. Secondly, compared to US-Japan relations, US relations with these countries is less important after the end of Cold War. In other words, these countries are not the key interest presence of the United States compare to Japan. Finally, originally the weapon system in these countries are similar to that of China. They are all quite outdated. If China produces more advanced weapons, they are afraid there will be an inbalance. For these reasons, these countries are more sensitive to China's arms purchasing.

In fact, as the Chinese government announced, China would like to solve the territorial disputes in the South China Sea with other countries peacefully. The idea is, first, to develop these islands together, and then, to discuss the dispute later on. However, there should be another preparation if the idea is not accepted. Taiwan is another case which is different from other members in this region. It has no reason to purchase new weapons since mainland's purchases is for the purpose of South China Sea purpose and the fighters are put in South China. However, Taiwan uses this opportunity to buy new fighters in order to maintain strong military strength to try to become an independent country in the future. Mainland China will never allow them to do so given the adverse effect of such move to the realization of national unification.

Conclusion

Conversion from military production to civilian production is China's long term strategy. The end of the Cold War has further encouraged China to implement this strategy in the future. Since the competition among the countries in the world now is mainly in such fields as technology and economy, R&D capabilities and economic strength will be more important than military strength. This trend will definitely affect the development of China's defence industries. It will make China pay more attention to the development of technology and economy rather than just maintain a large scale production capacities for regular war materials. For the existing military production force, the main task is still to continuously shift their capacities to the civilian production. Under the guide of this strategy, China will continuously readjust its existing military production, including producing civilian products with their own advantages in technology, equipment and skilled labor; closing down or expending or relocating some firms and so forth. Since the original military capacity is too large to finish the conversion in a short period, this process will probably take another decade.

In terms of long term strategy, third line industrial construction can not be simply considered a failed case in the history of Chinese military industrial development for the following reasons. First, these industries were located in the areas with the richest natural resources in China. These natural resources could be utilized by these firms after they were located there. Secondly, these firms play a very important role in narrowing economic gap between coastal areas and internal areas which is one of the most important issues facing China. It can be an important element for maintaining stability for China of which value can not be measured in economic terms. Finally, these firms are still important in maintaining the capacity for military production. In case of war in the future, they would provide military supply immediately.

In short, as a result of China's military reduction over the last fifteen years, China's military strength is relatively limited compared to its population and its land size. A large country without sufficient military strength will of course make its neighboring countries feel more relaxed. China has also benefitted by its conversion from military production to civilian production as mentioned above. However, , there have been some negative affect on China. The most serious problem for China is that the distance among "four modernization" has been expanding larger and larger. In other words, defence modernization is lagging behind the modernization of agriculture, industry and science and technology areas which is not a normal and balanced development. In practice, it also could cause danger to China because any country could provoke China in the future. Therefore, to maintain military strength to a certain extent with advanced technology and equipment, it will be necessary for China to protect its national security, such as its territorial sovereignty.

12

China and the Changing Division of Labor in the Emerging World Economy

William Fischer
(The University of North Carolina)

The Challenge to the East Asian Growth Experience

It is now commonplace to speak of the East Asian Miracle, as if there were a well-defined formula for economic growth among those nations that have recently been labeled *Newly Industrializing Economies*.[1] Typically, this term is applied to the late-twentieth century development experiences of Hong Kong, Singapore, South Korea, and Taiwan. In each of these cases, the "model" seems to include a combination of factors such as: high societal savings rates, high societal investments in education and infrastructure, high government participation in economic decisions [with the exception of Hong Kong], high export orientation, and a relatively high historical reliance on foreign sources of capi-

[1]Recent examples include: James Fallows, *looking at the Sun* (New York: Pantheon Books, 1994), and James C. Abegglen, *Sea Change* (New York: The Free Press, 1994).

tal and technology, as well as a number of other, less quantifiable, social factors. Yet, while all of this makes sense in a fashion, it appears that the real *miracle* of East Asia was the ability of a group of nations, bereft of raw materials and large domestic markets, to move from the periphery of the world economy to a major position on stage-center.

Despite the magnitude of the NIEs' accomplishments, there has recently been concern expressed over the promise of their achievements. Paul Krugman, in a provocative article in the American journal *Foreign Affairs*,[2] has raised an econometric challenge to the entire issue of the sustainability of the East Asian experience, by arguing that:

> Popular enthusiasm about Asia's boom deserves to have some cold water thrown on it. Rapid Asian growth is less of a model for the West than many writers claim, and the future prospects for that growth are more limited than almost anyone now imagines.[3]

Krugman's point is that the Asian growth experience has been one of mobilizing more resources, rather than getting more out of the existing resources. It has been extensive growth, rather than intensive growth, and, as a result, it is limited by the availability of inputs. Once inputs become scarce, as they will in any economic context, the growth plateaus. This is the real issue: how can *extraordinary* growth rates, built upon savings rates, educational rates, export rates, and the like, which are all already very high, continue to grow, when it is unlikely, if not impossible, for the components that fuel this growth to continue to grow? Left unsaid, in the Krugman article, is that, without some sort of breakthrough to a new model of work organization, such as was seen in the U.S. in the early twentieth century, through the funding of industrial R&D and the application of Frederick Taylor's *scientific management*, it is unreasonable to expect the East Asian

[2]Paul Krugman, "The Myth of Asia's Miracle," *Foreign Affairs* (November/December 1994), pp. 62-78.

[3]Krugman, *ibid.*, p. 64.

NIEs to sustain their present growth rates. In a sense, their industrial firms need to *reinvent*[4] their competitive postures and/or their industries, or else ultimately suffer much lower growth – perhaps even fall back onto the periphery. In a very real sense, then, the key to sustained economic growth, and the role to be played in the international division of labor, rests on the ability of the newly and nearly newly industrializing economies to redefine, reconfigure, or reinvent, their productive assets in such a way that they break out of the old models that limit their growth to resource-limited extrapolations of past growth experiences, and create new models that are no longer resource-limited.

The Emergence of New Manufacturing Practices

At a time when the world commercial arena is expanding well beyond the traditional boundaries that marked most of the twentieth century, the primary wealth-creating business activity – Manufacturing – is also undergoing a revolution that is as wide and as deep as any that it has ever seen. This oldest of managerial functions is experiencing an almost complete redefinition of its role, responsibilities, and practice. To speak of a mere *paradigm shift*, as is now commonly fashionable, is to undervalue the profundity of the change taking place. In geophysical terms, Manufacturing is undergoing conceptual shifts that are nothing short of having *plate-tectonic* proportions. Among the consequences of this upheaval is the possible rearrangement of operating relationships within a multitude of international manufacturing regimes, which could have profound implications for the rate and location of economic development in the newly emerging economies of the world, including China. The purpose of this paper is to consider the nature and magnitude of the changes which could conceivably take place within the Manufacturing function; to suggest their implications for the productive assets of a developing economy; and to speculate about what this means

[4]Gray Hamel and C.K. Prahalad, *Competing for the Future* (Cambridge, MA: Harvard Business School Press, 1994).

for China's role, specifically, in the world economy.

The Old Manufacturing Paradigm and China's Present Situation

The Traditional (Now-Dominant) Manufacturing Paradigm

For more than two-hundred years, at least since the publication, in 1776, of Adam Smith's *The Wealth of Nations*, the pursuit or rejection of economies of scale has been the central strategic theme that has dominated Manufacturing thought. According to Alfred D. Chandler, Jr.:

> "Economies of scale may be defined initially as those that result when the increased size of a single operating unit producing or distributing a single product reduces the unit cost of production or distribution."[5]

What this meant, in its most simplistic form, was that firms that were able to build larger volume facilities would seemingly be able to exploit the economies associated with the low-cost position on their relevant long-run average cost curves. Such an achievement would allow them to occupy market-leadership positions by virtue of their ability to combine product availability (due to their larger production capacities) with lower prices. Such a belief persisted for entire careers, and had a indelible effect on the way that people thought about manufacturing investment and operations:

> "The major innovations made in the processes of production during the last quarter of the nineteenth century created many new industries and transformed many old industries. These processes differed from earlier ones in their potential for exploiting the unprecedented cost advantages of the economies of scale……."
>
> "In the older, labor-intensive industries, increases in the output of a manufacturing establishment came primarily by adding more machines and

---

[5]Alfred D. Chandler, Jr., *Scale and Scope: The Dynamics of Industrial Capitalism* (Cambridge, MA: The Belknap Press of Harvard University Press, 1990), p. 17.

more workers to operate them. In newer industries, expanded output came by a drastic change in capital-labor ratios. It came by improving and rearranging inputs; by using new or greatly improved machinery, furnaces, stills, and other equipment; by reorienting the processes of production within the plant; by placing the several intermediary processes employed in making a final product within a single works; and by increasing the application of energy (particularly that generated by fossil fuel)."[6]

* * *

"The essential first step in exploiting the new technologies of production – the step that led to the creation of the modern industrial enterprise – was therefore, the investment in production facilities large enough to exploit the full potential of the economies of scale···inherent in the new or improved technologies. The critical entrepreneurial act was not the invention – or even the initial commercialization – of a newly or greatly improved product or process. Instead it was the construction of a plant of the optimal size required to exploit fully the economies of scale······."[7]

Economies-of-scale-based-logic changed the way that we thought about operations and resulted in the institutionalization of a surprisingly wide and pervasive range and variety of business practices, that underlie almost all of our current operational tradition, including: increased spatial concentration of extremely large production sites; adoption of performance measures based on capacity utilization and throughput (e.g., productivity and efficiency); accounting efforts devoted to the allocation of fixed costs; and the adoption of return on investment as the ultimate appraisal measure. In the words of one observer, the mass production system – the *Fordist* model – was "the central dimension of the development of capitalism."[8]

In industries where the overhead associated with manufacturing was quite large, such beliefs regarding economies of scale

---

[6]*Ibid.*, pp. 21-22.

[7]*Ibid.*, p. 26.

[8]Oliver Weinstein, "High Technology and Flexibility," in Philip Cooke, Frank Moulaert, Erik Swyngedouw, Oliver Weinstein, Peter Wells, with Martine Lemattre & Patrice Grevet, *Towards Global Localization* (London: UCL Press).

were easy to test and were immediately supported, despite the conclusions of empirical work in the mid-1950s, by the economist Joe Bain,[9] which showed, in a compelling fashion, that for most industries the actual long-run cost curve was shallower, and the point of inflection occurring at smaller rated plant capacities, than would be the case if the long-run average-cost curve was truly an effective barrier to market entry.

In the nineteen-thirties, the recognition of substantial time-savings associated with the replication and repetition of activities in the labor-intensive operations of airframe assembly led to further empirical support for the advantages of division of labor and operational specialization that Smith had also envisioned in the eighteenth century. Such so-called *learning curve* effects ultimately matured by the nineteen-seventies into the *experience curve* philosophy of Bruce Henderson and the Boston Consulting Group, and further reinforced acceptance of the concept that "bigger was better" among the manufacturing activities of firms aspiring to market leadership. The significant change here, however, was the gradual evolution of scale advantages based upon labor efficiencies (the *learning curve*), changing into scale advantages based on repetition, despite the continued reduction of direct labor as a factor in determining the costs of goods sold (the *experience curve*).

Over time, as the role of economies of scale became more central to operational logic, the dominant paradigm became further entrenched through the addition of an increasingly larger and more robust superstructure of supporting conceptualizations. The development of the *product life cycle*,[10] played a particularly important role in this regard, as it not only allowed the justification of an expensive period of innovation in anticipation of a

---

[9]Joe S. Bain, "Economies of Scale, Concentration, and the Condition of Entry in Twenty Manufacturing Industries," *American Economic Review* (March 1954), pp. 15-39; and *Barriers to New Competition* (Cambridge, MA: Harvard University Press, 1956).

[10]Ray Vernon, "International Investment and International Trade in the Product Cycle," *Quarterly Journal of Economics* (1966), Vol. 80, pp. 190-207.

longer period of market maturity, during which efficient manufacturing processes (exploiting the experience economies inherent in high-volume, highly-repetitive, manufacturing) would more than recoup the initial investment, but it also rationalized the internationalization of product markets. According to a number of observers, the key activity to extending the peak-profit-producing mature phase of the product life cycle was by cascading investment into markets ever less sophisticated. Tilton, in studying the semiconductor industry,[11] suggested a linkage between experience-curve production, the product life-cycle, trade protectionism, and "offshore" movement of manufacturing. This marked a major extension of the dominant paradigm to include spatial considerations, as well as issues of timing.

Thus, by the end of the nineteen-seventies, a well-established framework for thinking about Manufacturing, that essentially addressed all of the important strategic facets of the function, was in place and represented the embellishment and refinement of the dominant framework for thought and explanation that had stood for more than two centuries. The spatial implications of this thought-framework are quite powerful, yet straight-forward. Included among the interrelated outcomes are:

1. The preeminence of large firms and high-volume/low-variety manufacturing among market-leaders in the mature phase of the product life cycle. This was largely based upon the expectation that by maturity, most product-markets were characterized by so little functional differentiation, that price became the primary distinguishing characteristic among competing product offerings. In such cases, particularly when experience-curve dynamics were important, the ability to product price-competitive products was determined by the ability to exploit the economies associated with high-volume, low-variety product output, in capital-intensive operations.

2. An apparent preference for larger than necessary firms, unless they spatially-disadvantaged for some reason. [Here, the argument needs to be made (in other than footnote-form) that the perception of the virtues of bigness were probably significantly more compelling that the actual economics, especially when static economies of scale were involved.]

---

[11]John E. Tilton, *International Diffusion of Technology: The Case of Semiconductor* (Washington D.C.: Brookings Institution, 1971), pp. 38-47.

3. The establishment and maintenance of core-periphery manufacturing-sourcing relationships between the developed and developing world, and the usefulness of developing markets as sources of growth when domestic markets mature. From the industrial revolution on, the role of the developing world was seen, first, as a supplier of raw-materials and then, later, as the last in a series of cascading markets, entered in an effort to prolong the mature phase of a product's life-cycle.

4. A strong concern for the full-utilization of the expensive manufacturing capacity associated with the large capital-intensive facilities of the market leaders. Attention to capacity utilization, and return on investment, appears to have grown out of the large investments that high-volume, mass production required, and the need to justify such investments in financial terms. Operationally, however, such considerations have driven increased inflexibility in manufacturing performance, as large-lot production requires fewer periods at which the plant is running at less than full-capacity.

The Chinese Situation & the Dominant Manufacturing Paradigm

In order to speculate about China's evolving role in the international division of labor within the emerging global market, and, in particular, about the role of integrated markets and manufacturing in China, it is necessary to say something about the Chinese situation, as it relates to the issues found important in the traditional manufacturing paradigm.

There is probably no single characteristic of China that is as important to a discussion of manufacturing and market integration as is the world s largest population. The one billion, two hundred million plus people who live in China make up what could be, potentially, the world s largest market – given, someday, national market integration and sufficient purchasing power. This same population provides China with a more immediate asset in the form of a potential manufacturing platform characterized by relatively low wages.

Almost as important as its huge population, is the recognition that China is still a developing country, and, as such, still suffers considerable infrastructure deficiencies, which frustrate the ability to integrate the national market, and serve to impede manufacturing performance that relies on actors external to the factory. China's developing country status has also resulted in, until recently, an unwillingness to allow complete convertibility in the Chinese currency. Historically scarce foreign exchange reserves, and a need to build-up domestic industry, argued against too much openness to the outside world.

A third key determinant of China s situation relative to the dominant manufacturing paradigm is to be found in the country's tradition of post-1949 socialist economic development. This included the adoption of the Socialist enterprise as, primarily, a source of employment rather than an engine of economic efficiency; central planning as the determinant of economic allocation decisions (and the resulting vertical integration and segmentation, under the ministries, of the economy); and the separation of research and development activities, under the State Science and Technology Commission and the Chinese Academy of Sciences, from manufacturing activities, under the ministries and industrial bureaus.

In addition to China's application of socialist economic management, there were also some unique Chinese characteristics which have affected the nature and location of Chinese industry. Among these factors are the tradition of *Self-reliance*, which grew out of the civil war, but was reinforced by major infrastructural deficiencies, particularly in transportation and communication, as well as bureaucratic zero-sum gaming within a centrally-planned allocation mechanism, which limited the integration of the national economy; the development of the third-line industrial system, to protect against the damage of nuclear attack; and the historical external experiences of the Coastal Rim.

• Character of Chinese Industry

The result of China's special characteristics has been the creation of a strongly-entrenched state sector, endowed with large enterprises in backbone industries. These factories are able to produce large volumes of a wide-range of products at acceptable quality for the domestic market, and, in fact, have supplied the needs of nearly one-quarter of the world's population for more than forty years. There is also, however, effectively no national market in many industries. This is the result of a number of factors, most important of which have been: inadequate infrastructural linkages, a tradition of self-reliance within provinces, and inter-provincial trade blockages. Recently, explosive economic growth associated with export possibilities (largely through contract manufacturing and joint ventures) has taken place along China's coastal rim. This phenomenon has both localized a great deal of manufacturing and created the possibility of unleashing centrifugal forces which could threaten the stability of the national political situation.

Foreign Interests

There are several external issues associated with the old manufacturing paradigm that need to be at least mentioned in order to size-up the present situation in China. First and foremost is the assumption of an international division of labor which existed under the old paradigm. This was mentioned earlier, but deserves further mention here. Much of the logic of nineteenth-century colonialism was based upon the need of the mass producing industrial factories of the West for reliable supply relationships with the suppliers of raw materials, in what was then the undeveloped world. Today, while such logic has lost much of its currency, there is still an attractiveness to locate some manufacturing in low-wage countries in order to minimize the cost of the direct labor component of production. Typically, this takes place in mature, "low-tech," industries.

There is also good reason to believe that there is a significant need among the manufacturing countries of the developed world for maintenance of sufficient stability in the current world trade regime to sustain their present societal investment in manufacturing. According to one analysis,[12] the continued dominance of the mass production paradigm is dependent upon some form of *Multinational Keynesianism* in order to avoid the crisis of under-consumption, due to worldwide excess capacity, that has plagued

[12]Michael J. Piore and Charles F. Sable, *The Second Industrial Divide* (New York: Basic Books).

so many industries over the past decade. Institutions such as the GATT, the World Trade Organization (WTO), and the International Monetary Fund, can be seen, in such light, as vital institutional props, ensuring "...that international demand expands at a rate equal to the expansion of productive capacity."[13] Something, that has not been happening, as can be told by the perceived spread of *adversarial trade* in major western markets.

One final thought, with regard to foreign interests, is that the great attraction of China remains more as a place to sell than anything else. The image of China's potentially great market is undiminished by number of recent problems and continues to be the compelling force that draws foreign manufacturers to the country. There should be very little confusion on this matter. Except for a very few, typically mature and low-tech industries, where labor costs remain a critical competitive advantage, there is little attraction to manufacturing in China, except as a means of getting closer to a position of ultimately selling to the domestic Chinese market.

The Present Situation: How well-suited is China to fit the old paradigm?

If we put all of the foregoing discussion together, it becomes possible to speculate intelligently about how well-suited China is to fit into the prevailing dominant manufacturing paradigm.[14] Essentially, China has several large provincial markets (and a potentially huge national market) to draw mass consumption demand. This is an important prerequisite for establishing a tra-

---

[13]*Ibid.*

[14]These observations are built upon a more basic foundation of opinion that first appeared in two prior articles by the author: "China As A Player in the World Economy," *China Economic Review*, 1:1 (Spring 1989), pp. 9-21; and "China and the Opportunities for Economic Development Through Technology Transfer," in Tamir Agmon and Mary Ann Von Glinow, eds., *Technology Transfer in International Business* (New York, Oxford University Press, 1991), pp. 159-175.

dition of mass production, as the demand can fuel, finance, and support, large-scale / inflexible, and small-scale / flexible manufacturing at the same time. In fact, these large markets, and a continuing imbalance of demand over supply, has led China to have many large manufacturers built in a classical manufacturing [mass production] tradition. Furthermore, China s manufacturing base is spread throughout the country, reflecting the absence of the national market, spoken of earlier, but also resulting in a geographically-dispersed manufacturing sector.

It should go without much elaboration to note that Chinese wage levels are a source of significant competitive advantage in those industries where labor is a significant component of cost-of-goods-sold. Although this sector is growing progressively smaller, and although the markets so served are among the more capricious markets to produce for, this is, nonetheless, an advantage that China currently possesses, and one that continues to result in many attractive foreign commercial ties. Internally, China still has a relatively protected domestic market, as a result of government barriers to imports and currency convertibility impediments, as well as intra-provincial trade rivalries. As a result, and because of the effects of scarcity as well as a long-standing record of Socialist abuses of the market-place (hence, little value is placed upon: quality, service, delivery performance, product design, etc.), it is unclear how well-prepared Chinese industry is to address serious foreign commercial competition, should it develop within the domestic market. Clearly, one of the great fears of Chinese government officials, throughout the multiple hierarchies that make-up the Chinese government, must be a fear of widespread enterprise failures, if and when competition with foreign firms is allowed in the domestic market.

In a sense, then, it is possible to conclude that China has grown and continues to grow (albeit imperfectly) within the tradition of the dominant manufacturing paradigm; in other words, exhibiting most of the characteristics cited earlier in the paper. In addition, however, the special characteristics of China, make it less likely that spontaneous change will occur within Chinese industry, if the dominant paradigm is imperiled, in any way. Thus,

China appears to be yet another candidate for inclusion among the resource-limited, albeit high-growth, economies, of East Asia. As it is, the near bankruptcy of much of the state-sector in manufacturing, and the lower productivity evidenced within that sector, despite market reforms,[15] suggests that reliance on these quintessential expressions of the dominant manufacturing paradigm will not serve to bring the Chinese economy into a prominent position off of the world economic periphery in the future.

The Emergence of a New Paradigm and the Demise of the Traditional Dominant Manufacturing Paradigm

After such a long period of intellectual ascendancy, it should not have been surprising when contradictions and tensions began to arise in the ability of the dominant paradigm to adequately explain and anticipate what was going on within Manufacturing practice. A number of factors, including such issues and events as:

- an expanding global arena
- Neo-Kondratieffian technology changes
- the appearance of adversarial trade
- the appearance of new market and resource pools
- the emergence of mega-merchandisers
- the shortening of the product life-cycle and the increased early importance of process innovation
- the emergence of the knowledge-based information economy, and
- an increased acceptance of new organizational formats[16]

have now emerged which render the previous dominant paradigm increasingly less useful in interpreting patterns of

[15]Gary H. Jefferson, Thomas G. Rawski, and Yuxin Zheng, "Productivity Change in Chinese Industry: A Comment," *China Economic Review*, 5:2 (1994), pp. 235-241.

[16]William A. Fischer, "Emerging Patterns of Manufacturing in the Midst of Globalization and Regionalization," in *The Evolving Structure and Characteristics of the Global Technology Market* (Seoul: Korea Institute for Industrial Economics and Trade, 1993).

Manufacturing strategy and practice, and which argue for consideration of alternative ways of expressing Manufacturing behavior.

External (geopolitical) Events

Along with the changes that have taken place in Manufacturing, which threaten to overturn the existing dominant paradigm, a number of external (*geopolitical*) events have also occurred which have a strong degree of association with the paradigm shift, and for China, in particular. Perhaps none of these changes is as important as the loss of resiliency in U.S. & European economies. For a considerable period of time, following the second world war, the economies of North America and Western Europe welcomed imports from abroad, particularly from developing countries, as a way of augmenting their own domestic production to meet seeming insatiable demand. Those days are now past. Western populations are increasingly older, and, consequently, less able to adjust to the employment displacement which has accompanied the imports. New trade barriers have been erected, and in some cases major commitments have been made for capital-intensive manufacturing processes, that can produce at a lower price than even low-wage, labor-intensive approaches.

The inability of the industrialized nations of the world to harmonize their trade disagreements threatens to result in a breakdown of the successors to the GATT, the principle piece in the institutional architecture of Multinational Keynesianism. In addition, the emergence of possible regional blocs in Europe and North America (EU & NAFTA), suggest that significant distortions within the international trade regimes may, in fact, be possible.

On top of all of this, has been the unexpected demise of the so-called *Soviet Bloc*, and the resulting emergence of a large number of transition economies, from middle-Europe, into world markets. This entry has had a somewhat destablizing role on both the developed world (where new markets are available to be served, and new manufacturing sites are arising to challenge the ones at home), as well as the developing world (which faces additional competition for foreign investment). In almost all cases, in fact, the manufacturing situation in these transition economies has been similar to, if not in some cases even better, than that of China.

Implications

The result of all of this is that the world is changing at a far faster rate than manufacturing in all but the most developed countries can keep up with. The movement to:

- perfect quality
- high-service content[17]
- responsive delivery performance
- maintenance of relative price parities between low- volume/ high-variety, and high-volume/low-variety producers
- the ascendancy of knowledge-based work

all defy the traditional dominant manufacturing paradigm and all represent a major dislocation in the evolution of manufacturing capabilities, especially in the developing world.

Changes to be Considered

We seem to be facing a situation where the operating environment, as well as our technological ability to address it, appear to be fast outstripping our institutions and our experience. One observer has characterized it as: "markets…triumphing over government policies."[18] It seems clear that the old dominant paradigm is not only weakened, but now misleading, as well. New approaches and new models must be sought for in order to cope with the new realities of the operating environment. Most of

---

[17]Sandra Vandermerve, *From Tin-Soldiers to Russian Dolls* (London: Routledge, 1993).

[18]Philip Cooke, "Global Localization in Computing and Communications: Conclusions," in Cooke, et al., *Towards Global Localization, op. cit.*

these alternative approaches deal with ways of increasing systemic flexibility, and most of them call for some restructuring of manufacturing relations, either within or outside of the firm. Somewhere, perhaps within this set of alternatives, might lie the potential for an economy, such as China, to break out of the resource-limited growth it has enjoyed to date. Certainly, the failure to develop such a breakthrough approach to the manufacturing function will almost certainly condemn such an economy to a plateauing of growth as the resource limitations are reached.

It seems likely that any new approach to succeeding in the emerging global economy, which is characterized by new technologies, new markets, and new customer expectations, will require a degree of operational *responsiveness* that has heretofore only been approached by a few exceptional firms. To support the development of such industrial capabilities, economies will be expected to develop orientations which advance such competitive characteristics as: information abundance; market efficiencies for resource movement; a degree of casualness regarding national boundaries; and a fair amount of tolerance for local political autonomy.[19] This, in turn, will reopen a series of related arguments that deal with the way in which firms, and regions are addressing tensions between stability and change, flexibility and focus. The existing proposals for accommodating such differences, while still quite immature, suggest significant ways of incorporating spatial issues within the logic of Manufacturing strategy. The major theme in most of these alternatives is the positive forging of the tension inherent in the contradictions between stability and dynamics. As Boynton, Victor and Pine[20] have put it: the industrial revolution was based on a one-way evolution of the firm's manufacturing culture from invention to mass produc-

---

[19]This list is adapted from Tony Killick, "Relevance, Meaning and Determinants of Flexibility," in Tony Killick, ed., *The Flexible Economy* (London: Routledge, 1995).

[20]A.C. Boynton, B. Victor, B.J. Pine II, "New Competitive Strategies: Challenges to Organizations and Information Technology," *IBM Systems Journal*, 32:1 (1993), pp. 40-64.

tion. In the future, organizations will be designed to deliver *dynamic stability*, the combination of the best of mass customization and continuous improvement.

There are several ways of achieving the best of mass customization and continuous improvement which range from increased internal investments in new, flexible, manufacturing processes (ranging from just-in-time types of process redesign, to the use of multiple focused-factories), to the creation of "geographically defined productive systems, characterized by a large number of firms that are involved at various stages, in various ways, in the production of a homogeneous product."[21] One author has addressed this range of options by focusing on the degree of integration that is required: "Each element in the [value] chain may be performed entirely within a single business firm (complete integration) or may be performed by separate, specialist business firms (complete disintegration), or in-between.[22] If we overlay, on top of this continuum of integration-disintegration, the role of the external (foreign) firm, as the originator of the process change, we can create a matrix that is quite interesting in terms of its prospects for success, spatial location implications, and political volatility. Such a matrix is reproduced below:

[21]F. Pyke, G. Becattini, and W. Sengenberger, eds., *Industrial Districts and Inter-Firm Cooperation in Italy* (Geneva: ILO, 1990), p. 2.

[22]Peter Dicken, "The Geography of Enterprise," in Marc de Smidt and Eghert Wever, eds., *The Corporate Firm in a Changing World Economy* (London: Routledge, 1994).

Origin for Change	Degree of Networking: Complete Integration (within the firm)	Degree of Networking: Complete Disintegration (along the business system)
domestic Inspired	Difficult to change existing culture Expensive	Relies on traditional linkages(+/−) More likely to be geographically compact
Foreign Inspired	Probably results in a greenfield site Increases pressure on domestic enterprises Probably will be located on the Rim	Difficult to gain knowledge More likely to be multi-provincial

Type of Change vs. Originator of Change

A casual interpretation of this table shows the attractiveness of foreign-inspired integration as a partial solution to China's manufacturing deficiencies. Without the rearrangement/reconfiguration of China's manufacturing assets, there is little chance that a new, more responsive, paradigm can ever be achieved. A greater foreign role in regional economic systems, in China, is not without its domestic political liabilities, however.

As an alternative, the experience of industrial districts in the so-called *Third Italy*[23] suggests that *flexible specialization,* as the "complete disintegration" approaches would resemble, is not only doable, but also a quite potent means of competing in the world market: "The challenge is [continual] restructuring without hierarchy: the capacity to engage in Schumpetarian competition without the creation of a managerial hierarchy." The experience of similar industrial districts in Japan, suggests in some societies more organized networks, centered around a large firm, might be more appropriate.[24] Other work, of a admittedly speculative

[23]Michael H. Best, *The New Competition* (Cambridge, MA: Harvard University Press, 1990).

nature, but still quite interesting, suggests that such networked systems work best in societies where there are some balances between "the rules which govern individuals in their personal interactions," and the extent to which an individual has group affiliations that overlap significantly to produce a clear boundary between insiders and outsiders."[25]

Either approach appears to require that the prerequisite commitments to information abundance; market efficiencies for resource movement; a degree of casualness regarding national boundaries; and a fair amount of tolerance for local political autonomy; will all be forthcoming. This is not necessarily a given within the Chinese situation. In the absence of such changes, radical redesign/reconfiguration of Chinese industry is doubtful, and escape from resource-limited growth unlikely. As a result, it would appear that China's recent high growth rates will not be forever sustainable, and it's movement away from the periphery not guaranteed.

---

[24]Yoshiyuki Okamoto, "The Viability of Industrial Districts by Flexible Specialisation: A Comparison of Italy and Japan," *Journal of International Economic Studies* (Hosei University), No. 7 (1993), pp. 89-105.

[25]Shaun Hargreaves-Heap, "Culture and Competitiveness," in Kirsty S. Hughes, *European Competitiveness* (Cambridge: Cambridge University Press, 1993).

13

Sino-American Relations: The Impact on Chinese Policy and Behavior

Donald W. Klein
(Tufts University)

Most analysts a few years ago would have named the Soviet-American relationship as the most important in the world. The end of the Cold War has led some to argue that most state-to-state relationships have been superseded by such issues as global economic interdependence, environmental problems, wrenching ethnic and religious conflicts, or terrorism.[1] Yet, with an ever-increasing focus on the Asia-Pacific region, including China's stunning economic growth, the case can be made that the U.S.-China relationship is among the most crucial in today's world,

[1]See Zbigniew K. Brzezinski, *Out of Control: Global Turmoil on the Eve of the Twenty-First Century* (New York: Scribner's, 1993); Daniel Patrick Moynihan, *Pandaemonium: Ethnicity in International Politics* (New York: Oxford University Press, 1993); William Pfaff, *The Wrath of Nations: Civilization and the Furies of Nationalism* (New York: Simon & Schuster, 1993).

and will continue to be so into the 21st Century. The broad contours of Sino-American relations are generally familiar: total hostility during the 1950s and 1960s, a detente of sorts during the 1970s and 1980s, and a testy relationship in the wake of the Beijing Massacre of 1989. If Truman, Acheson, Eisenhower, John Foster Dulles, and John F. Kennedy are long gone, it's well to recall that Deng Xiaoping and many of the powerful "Party Elders" are still on the scene, and they remember the "bad old days." Accordingly, a brief review of the pre-Tiananmen periods is useful to an understanding of current and future U.S.-China relations.

1949-1971

The birth of "New China" in October 1949 took place at the peak of the Cold War. The 1948 Czech coup, Tito's defection in the same year, the Berlin Airlift, and the Soviet Union's mid-1949 development of atomic weaponry were landmarks in that era. Shortly before Mao Zedong proclaimed the establishment of the People's Republic of China's (PRC), he bluntly announced that China was "leaning to one side – the side of socialism."

The American reaction was a classic exercise in using all forms of power to stifle Mao's realm, especially after China entered the Korean War in late 1950. In *economic* terms, Washington slapped a total embargo on U.S.-China commercial links, and pressured its allies to shun all such relations, or at least hold them to a minimum. The U.S. embargo was virtually total through the 1960s. American allies conducted some China trade, but it was generally marginal and did little to aid Chinese economic development. More important, U.S. allies did comply with the COCOM sanctions that prevented the sale of "strategic" goods to China.

U.S. power during those years was such that Washington had little trouble in excluding China from the "keystone international economic organizations" (KIEO), to use the Jacobson-Oksenberg

---

[2]Harold K. Jacobson and Michel Oksenberg, *China's Participation in the IMF, the World Bank, and GATT* (Ann Arbor, MI: University of Michigan Press, 1990).

term,[2] thus denying China the benefits of the World Bank, the International Monetary Fund (IMF), and GATT.

Unsurprisingly, China turned to Moscow for help. Despite the Soviets' own economic weaknesses, they supplied China during the 1950s with substantial economic aid and technology transfers. Yet this aid was dwarfed by U.S. economic aid to West Europe (the Marshall Plan) and Japan. By the mid-1950s, three-quarters of China's foreign trade was with the Soviet Union and the East Europe satellites. In global terms, of course, this was marginal in contrast to trade within the West. On balance, the U.S. was largely successful in this exercise of economic power.

In *political-normative* terms, the U.S. used its ample muscle to deny China its place in the sun. Washington continued to recognize Taiwan, and pressured its allies to do the same. Most American allies went along with this policy. Equally important was Washington's success in denying Beijing a seat in the U.N. (especially crucial since this included permanent membership on the U. N. Security Council). This ostracism also effectively denied China's participation in non-governmental organizations, such as international scientific organizations. In a word, Chinese participation in the "intellectual world" was essentially confined to the Soviet bloc.

Washington's economic and political efforts were paralleled by *military-strategic* policies to "contain" Beijing. Apart from the direct hostilities in the Korean War, the U.S. "encircled" China by a curtain of defense pacts with Japan, the Philippines, South Korea, and Taiwan, plus the formation in 1954-55 of the Southeast Asia Treaty Organization (SEATO) and enormous aid to South Vietnam. The Vietnam War, of course, pitted the U.S. against what Washington perceived as a "proxy" for China-North Vietnam. And thus, as in the Korean War, U.S. forces bombed Chinese allies close to China's borders.

If U.S. military efforts are characterized as having prevented Beijing from spilling over its borders into other parts of Asia, the policy can be described as successful. Yet this "success" must be measured against the familiar costs inflicted on the U.S. by the Vietnam War.

1971-1979

The dramatic turnaround in U.S.-China relations has been exhaustively described by Henry Kissinger and others.[3] In brief, an increasingly aggressive Soviet Union, having proclaimed the Brezhnev Doctrine in 1968, found itself in short-term but potentially dangerous border conflicts with China in the spring and summer of 1969. Simultaneously, Richard Nixon announced the Guam (or Nixon) Doctrine in mid-1969, as part of his endeavor to end the Vietnam War. To Mao's mind, this meant that the Soviet Union (in an offensive posture) was more dangerous than the U.S. (in a defensive posture). The Nixon-Kissinger team thought along parallel lines, and thus a Chinese-American alignment against Moscow made sense to both Beijing and Washington. The combination of Kissinger's 1971 visit to China and Nixon's famous trip in 1972 was among the most crucial diplomatic moves of our era. Over the next few years, Washington diminished or ended virtually all the various forms of power it had used to contain China. On the political front, the U.S. in effect acquiesced in allowing China to replace Taiwan in the U.N. A flood of nations (again with U.S. acquiescence) broke diplomatic relations with Taiwan and established them with Beijing. U.S.-China quasi-diplomatic relations were established in the form of so-called liaison offices in each capital. The euphemisms fooled no-one; Beijing and Washington now had de facto diplomatic relations.

The U.S. and its allies began to move into what all hoped would be the potentially enormous market. China's economy in the early 1970s was still small by most measurements, and its total trade was trifling. A modest U.S.-China trade began with the Kissinger-Nixon visits, as demonstrated in Table 1.

Other key economic relationships – especially direct foreign investments (DFI), foreign aid, and technology transfer – were

---

[3]Henry Kissinger, The White House Years (Boston: Little, Brown and Co., 1979; for a brief but excellent summary, see Michel Oksenberg, "A Decade of Sino-American Relations," *Foreign Affairs*, 61:1 (Fall 1982), pp. 175-95.

Table 1. U.S.-China Trade (1971-79)

(US million $)

	Chinese *Exports*	Chinese *Imports*	Total *Trade*
1971	$ 5	-	$ 5
1972	35	$ 64	99
1973	68	690	758
1974	123	807	930
1975	171	304	475
1976	222	135	357
1977	223	171	394
1978	356	824	1,180
1979	656	1,724	2,380

Source: IMF, *Direction of Trade Statistics Yearbook* (Washington, D.C.), various issues.

virtually nil during the 1971-79 period. Their absence apparently derived from the fact that Mao was still alive (until September 1976), and he apparently continued to stress China's self-reliance.

The rapid political-economic turnabout was not as quickly matched in the military realm. The U.S., after all, didn't end its direct military involvement in Vietnam until early 1973. China still had a formal military alliance with North Korea, as did the U.S. with South Korea. The U.S. was also still militarily allied with Taipei, and even had armed forces (though small in number) in Taiwan. The crux of the issue, however, was the Washington-Beijing understanding that direct U.S.-China military conflict was now out of the question. Both also agreed, at least implicitly, that the Kremlin was the real enemy.

The government-to-government relations were paralleled by a blossoming of so-called unofficial links (in Beijing's term, "people-to-people" diplomacy). Relatively few non-official Chinese went abroad in the 1971-78 period, but large numbers of Americans – tourists, jounalists, academics, and business leaders – began to visit China.

A loss of momentum in the mid-1970s resulted from domestic problems in both China and the U.S. The rise of the radical "Gang of Four," the failing health and then death of both Premier Zhou Enlai and Mao in 1976, plus the horrendous Tangshan earthquake in mid-1976, immobilized Chinese foreign policy initiatives. Watergate similarly immobilized the Nixon administration.

1979-1989

Sino-American relations were re-vitalized in the late 1970s because both sides were increasingly alarmed by Soviet aggressiveness around the globe. Worried by Hanoi's tilt toward Moscow that culminated in a quasi-defense pact signed in November 1978, Beijing faced a new nightmare: a menacing Soviet bear to the north and a hostile, well-armed Vietnam to the south (soon to be dubbed the "Cuba of Asia").

These circumstances led Deng Xiaoping, who emerged as the "paramount leader" in late 1978, to shore up relations with the U.S. on all fronts. First, Deng sought to implement the Four Modernizations (agriculture, industry, science & technology, and national defense) by abandoning Mao's autarctic policies. "Self-reliance" was replaced by interdependence – and the most eagerly prized relationship was with the U.S. and what might be called the "OECD world."

Second, Deng eagerly sought to formalize diplomatic relations with Washington. Urged on by National Security Advisor Zbigniew Brzezinski, President Carter agreed to this move, and thus formal U.S.-China relations were established on January 1, 1979. It's worth noting that this carried great symbolism for China. After a century and a half of national humiliation and second-class global citizenship, China had, so to speak, arrived. It sat on the Security Council, it was recognized by both superpowers, and it was increasingly recognized as one of the great powers in Asia. To punctuate this new-found prestige, Deng journeyed to the U.S. in early 1979 – thereby becoming the first top Chinese leader to visit the U.S.[4] American officials gave Deng elaborate

[4]Technically, Deng had been in the U.S. in 1974 when he spoke before the U.N., but visits to the U.N. are not regarded as "official" visits to the U.S.

red carpet treatment, which was paralleled by equally elaborate media coverage.

Yet China's ability to project power was still very limited. In foreign trade, for example, Beijing remained a pygmy among giants. Investments abroad were virtually nil, and its foreign aid was marginal. Indeed, China rapidly became a supplicant for the foreign aid, direct foreign investments, and the technology needed for the Four Modernizations that was only available from the industrialized nations. Similarly, China's military power was quite limited – a point quickly demonstrated when it invaded Vietnam (February 1979). It penetrated Vietnamese territory a few miles, but at great cost in both men and materiel, and then withdrew – ostensibly having "taught Vietnam a lesson" as punishment for Hanoi's invasion and occupation of Cambodia.

Despite these weaknesses, China had made a major breakthrough in terms of its links to the U.S. Their importance is perhaps best demonstrated by Beijing's relatively mild objections to the U.S. passage of the Taiwan Relations Act (TRA) in April 1979. This law's implementing article provides that the "···United States will [not "may"] make available to Taiwan such defense articles and defense services in such quantity as may be necessary to enable Taiwan to maintain a sufficient self-defense capability."

China's distaste for the TRA was in part mitigated in mid-1979 when Vice-President Walter Mondale visited Beijing where he affirmed strong U.S. support by stating that "Any nation which seeks to weaken or isolate [China] in world affairs assumes a stance counter to American interests." If this represented a high point in Sino-American relations, a year later the relationship was jeopardized when Ronald Reagan, then campaigning for the presidency, indicated an intent to renew relations with Taiwan. Nothing came of this, but Beijing continued its objections to U.S. sales of weaponry to Taiwan. This in turn led to an August 1982 communique in which the U.S. pledged that the arms sales would "not exceed, either in qualitative or in quantitative terms, the level of those supplied in recent years······." Further, the U.S. promised to "reduce gradually" its arms sales to Taiwan. This agreement has never been fulfilled from China's viewpoint, and continues to be a major irritant in Sino-American relations.[5] Beijing insists that the Taiwan factor is still the chief stumbling block in U.S.-China relations. The intensity of China's charges seems to have diminished in direct proportion to the elaborate and ever-growing economic ties between China and Taiwan.

Despite these problems, Sino-American relations moved into high gear in the decade after formal diplomatic relations. For example, in the first half-year after January 1979, no less than 13 government-to-government agreements were signed. Senior, cabinet-level officials regularly moved back and forth between Beijing and Washington. In brief, high-level governmental relations were becoming institutionalized. This also applied to senior military officials, and while neither side sought a formal alliance, the Soviet invasion of Afghanistan in late 1979 bolstered Sino-American military ties. The Soviets were again on the march – not only in Afghanistan (that shares a border with China), but also in Vietnam where the Soviet Union was granted extensive

Table 2. U.S.-China Trade, 1980-88

(US billion $)

	Chinese *Exports*	Chinese *Imports*	Total *Trade*	Annual % *Incease*
1980	$ 1.2	$ 3.8	$ 5.0	108%
1981	2.1	3.6	5.7	14
1982	2.5	2.9	5.4	-6
1983	2.5	2.2	4.7	-15
1984	3.4	3.0	6.4	36
1985	4.2	3.9	8.1	27
1986	5.2	3.1	8.3	3
1987	6.9	3.5	10.4	25
1988	9.3	5.0	14.3	38

Source: Same as Table 1.

[5]See Harry Harding, *A Fragile Relationship: The United States and China Since 1972* (Washington, D.C.: The Brookings Institution, 1992). See especially p.370, which provides the figures for U.S. arms sales to Taiwan.

military base rights. An increasingly important U.S.-China linkage during the 1980s was especially apparent in the field of foreign trade. Prior to diplomatic relations, trade was measured in *millions*; after recognition, it was measured in *billions* (see Table 2).

1989-date

Just as "Munich" and "Sputnik" are part of the international relations vocabulary, so too is the word "Tiananmen." Yet only a half-decade after this tragic event, one might argue that the initial trauma may have been overrated.[6]

At first blush, Tiananmen seemed to be the undoubted "story of the year." The collapse of the Berlin Wall a half-year later put that idea to rest, and the long-running saga of the Soviet Unions's decline and fall far outweighed China's internal turmoil. Moreover, Iraq's invasion of Kuwait only 14 months after Tiananmen, plus the ensuing Gulf War, sharply diminished Tiananmen's impact. It's also well to recall that the most strident hostility toward China came from the West. The Third World, and especially China's Asian neighbors, tended to play down Tiananmen.

Beijing, unsurprisingly, denounced its critics for interfering in China's internal affairs. Nonetheless, Beijing's leaders took active "damage control" steps to lessen the impact. Assurances were quickly given to the outside world (which mainly meant Japan and the West) that the situation was under control, and that business officials had no reason to fear for their safety. On the larger diplomatic front, China played the "good international citizen" role in that it went along with the measures to punish Iraq. It acted responsibly in the difficult Cambodian situation, sending troops and officials there as part of the 1992-93 U.N. peace-keeping operation that led to the Cambodian elections in 1993. Definitive information is lacking, but it appears that Beijing has

---

[6]It's worth noting that many analysts today refer today to the Tiananmen "incident" rather than the more dramatic "massacre" – the word almost always used in the immediate wake of this affair.

played a low-postured but perhaps crucial role in urging North Korea to abandon its attempts to develop atomic weaponry.

China's rapid economic growth in the post-Tiananmen period has also been important in diminishing the Tiananmen stain. It is commonly observed that economic interdependence has replaced military issues in the post-Cold War era. And because China is so large a part of the now-famous Asian economic growth, the world's attention is increasingly focused on this fact. Indeed, one often reads comparisons of China's economic growth as a counterpoint to the chaos and economic stagnation in Russia and the other CIS states. Such comparisons, of course, invariably redound in China's favor.

In various but not all ways, Tiananmen did damage Sino-American relations. President Bush's desire to keep these relations on an even keel are well known. Yet the sheer drama and ugliness of the globally-televised Tiananmen events forced some U.S. retaliation. Senior-level official visits were put on hold. But even this stricture was ignored when Bush sent National Security Advisor Brent Scowcroft on a secret visit to Beijing only weeks after Tiananmen and a open visit late in the year. Bush wanted to convey his concern regarding human rights issues, but he also hoped to prevent a full-scale crisis that might permanently damage relations.

High-level military exchanges were postponed and military sales to China suspended. The U.S. also used its considerable influence in the international financial circles (such as the World Bank) to postpone further loans to China. Unsurprisingly, at the non-official level, the number of American tourists to China dropped dramatically.

If Tiananmen sharply set back political and military relations, the economic relationship tells another and perhaps more important story. Analysts in mid-1989 might have reasonably predicted a sharp dip in U.S.-China trade, or at least a leveling-off for a few years. The facts tell a much different story. The trade growth may have derived in part from a troubled American economy (budget and trade deficits), or perhaps it was simply the continuing allure of the potentially vast China market ("one billion customers"!), or the idea that if U.S. business interests did not continue their economic activities in China, Japanese or West European business groups would take their place. Whatever the reason, Table 3 reveals not simply a continued growth, but a very impressive one that in the mid-1990s continues apace with no sign of a letup.

U.S.-China trade almost tripled in the 1988-93 period. During these same years, global U.S. foreign trade increased at less than 8% a year, but U.S.-China trade grew three times faster (almost 27%). Moreover, the CIA reports that in the first five months of 1994, U.S. exports to China increased by over 12% compared to the same period in 1993, and imports grew by 20%.[7]

U.S.-China trade can be put in another perspective to demonstrate its importance in terms of global trading patterns. In 1993, considering all bi-lateral trade partners throughout the world, the U.S.-China trade was the 13th largest. Current trends suggest that it should move up several notches in the near future.

Table 3. U.S.-China Trade, 1989-93

(US billion $)

	Chinese *Exports*	Chinese *Imports*	Total *Trade*	Annual *% Incease*	Annual % Increase of All *U.S. Trade*
1988	$ 9.3	$ 5.0	$ 14.3	38%	15%
1989	12.9	5.8	18.7	38	10
1990	16.3	4.8	21.1	13	6
1991	20.3	6.3	26.6	26	2
1992	27.4	7.5	34.9	31	7
1993	31.5	8.8	40.3	15	5

Source: Same as Table 1.

[7]*China's Economy in 1993 and 1994: The Search for a Soft Landing* (Washington, D.C.: CIA, July 22, 1994). This is a CIA report prepared for the Subcommittee on Technology and National Security of the Joint Economic Committee, U.S. Congress.

The Future

China is often touted as the world's next superpower. In part, this projection is based on recent re-estimations of China's economic growth, some of which assert that China's GNP will match or even surpass that of the United States in the early decades of the 21st Century. Such euphoric estimates of China's growth seldom deal with the staggering costs of building (let alone maintaining) aircraft carriers that is one of the best measurements of the ability to project global military power.[8] Moreover, Beijing itself freely acknowledges other economic problems that China must deal with in order to muster the economic power necessary for superpower status.[9]

Those who describe China as a budding superpower seem to suggest that this will ultimately pose a challenge to the U.S. along the lines of the challenge posed by the Soviet Union for nearly half a century. In many ways, this is misleading. For most of its existence, the USSR was essentially a self-contained economic unit. The Soviet Union was never integrated economically into Europe, in striking contrast to China's integration today with its Asian neighbors. Moreover, China's economy is vastly more intermeshed with the U.S. economy than the Soviet economy was linked to the U.S. economy during or after the Cold War.

Whatever may loom in the next century, for now China is a regional power with only the most marginal means of projecting power beyond Asia. For example, in the economic realm, China's total trade surged by an impressive $28 billion in 1993 over 1992,

---

[8]For a useful discussion of the possibility of the Chinese building aircraft carriers, see *Far Eastern Economic Review* (*FEER*, October 20, 1994), pp. 14-15.

[9]Senior PRC officials openly acknowledge the enormous problems. To cite only two of them, note the following mid-1994 paraphrase of comments made by the minister of the State Science and Technology Commission: "···by the 2030s or 2040s, China's grain output will have to increase by 50 percent, just to ensure that [supplies] remain at the present modest level. Electric energy production would need to expand 14-fold to main the current per-capita standard of moderately developed countries," *Beijing Review*, 37:25 (June 20-26, 1994), p. 4.

yet U.S. trade (already five times larger than China's) rose $68 billion in the same period. To use another economic perspective, China exported more goods to the Netherlands in 1993 than it exported to *all* of Latin America, and its imports from Belgium-Luxembourg were greater than its imports from *all* of Africa. In terms of economic aid, China has virtually abandoned serious attempts to use this as an instrument of foreign affairs. Instead, China has been one of the world's leading recipients of economic aid for the past several years.[10]

Some would argue that China can exert substantial diplomatic or normative power beyond Asia. Yet it is clear that communism as an ideology is withering on the vine, and most developing nations are probably more impressed with Asia's "NICs" as a model than with China – if only because the vast majority of Third World countries have far more in common with the NICs (small size, relative lack of resources, etc.) than with China. To the degree that China has a global role, it probably applies mainly in the United Nations. Beijing has rhetorically championed Third World causes in the U.N., but it's hard to think of cases in which this has had much effect.

In brief, Sino-American cooperation or conflict will almost certainly have a strong *regional* focus for the foreseeable future. This is probably advantageous to Washington-Beijing harmony. In Latin America or Africa, for example, China's declaratory policies may sharply disagree with U.S. actions, but it is unlikely that this would do real damage to U.S.-China relations.

Factors that Tend to Enhance U.S.-China Relations

We turn now to those elements that should sustain positive U.S.-China relations, and those that might damage them. Obviously, any one element may carry seeds that are potentially both positive and negative. For example, large-scale trade is generally seen

---

[10]World Bank, *World Development Report 1994* (New York: Oxford University Press, 1994), p. 198.

in positive terms, but the very volume may include huge deficits or myriad other problems that exacerbate relations.

If the Four Modernizations are accepted as a defining trait of China's foreign policy well into the future, then economic issues may be paramount in cementing positive U.S.-China relations.[11] The two economies are now essentially complementary, but as China moves up the technological ladder competitive problems will surely arise. Still, for the next decade or so, a "positive" complementarity should undergird the essential trade patterns.

The sheer size of the U.S. market should continue as a very positive force for good relations. Japan is often described as having surpassed the U.S. as *the* economic power in Asia. Yet this ignores what might be called U.S. "market power." With the single exception of Indonesia (which sells virtually all its oil to Japan), all the significant Asian nations sell more to the U.S. than to Japan. In the decade from 1984 to 1993, for example, Chinese exports to Japan totaled $111 billion, in contrast to $138 billion to the U.S.

The U.S. government is concerned by the trade deficit with China, but powerful U.S. lobbies are eager to maintain strong links to China. On the export side, Boeing and mid-west farm groups have huge sales to China, and American importers of toys, inexpensive textiles, and footwear are equally eager to have solid relations. Clinton's decision to "de-link" the most favored nation (MFN) issue from human rights in 1994 was clearly favored by these U.S. business interests. Noteworthy in this regard is the fact that nearly 800 large American companies wrote to President Clinton to encourage MFN renewal.[12] In other words, the trade issue is not simply the "U.S. vs. China"; in effect,

---

[11]Technically, the Four Modernizations plan ends in the year 2000, but that is obviously a symbolical rather than a terminal date. For an excellent article dealing with Sino-American economic issues (MFN, intellectual property rights, prison labor, and textiles), see Yangmin Wang, "The Politics of U.S.-China Economic Relations: MFN, Constructive Engagement, and the Trade Issue Proper," *Asian Survey*, 33:5 (May 1993), pp. 441-62.

[12]*New York Times* (August 1, 1994).

powerful American interests – *both exporters and importers* – have become intermeshed with Chinese economic interests.

Aside from the enormous U.S. market, China plainly wants to avoid an overdependence on the world's second largest market: Japan. Whatever historic animosities Chinese hold toward the U.S., they pale in contrast to the lingering distrust of Japan.[13] Moreover, as of the mid-1990s, both Japan and the EU have troubled economies, which could mean a rise in protectionism in both Japan and Europe.[14]

U.S. investments in China are another positive sign. American *cumulative* investments totaled roughly $5.5 billion through 1993.[15] Because no less than $2 billion of this amount was invested in 1993 alone, it appears that U.S. investors view Tiananmen as a thing of the past. In a sense, investments are akin to what military strategists call "confidence-building measures," i.e., both sides have an ever-increasing stake in stability. For example, the greater the investments, the less likelihood that China might take hostile measures, such as nationalization. If it took such steps, investments would doubtless wither overnight – and not just U.S investments.

Chinese officials understand American influence in the World Bank and the IMF – a point brought home after Tiananmen when the U.S. used its power to deny loans to China. Beijing, as noted, emerged by the mid-1980s as a top recipient of foreign aid from these organizations. It may gall Chinese leaders, but they obviously understand the need to deal positively with the U.S. if they hope to continue the flow of these funds. Similar considerations apply to China's application to join GATT and the World Trade

---

[13]See the article by prominent Japanese political analyst Minoru Morita, "Old Wounds Will Not Heal Easily, *Tokyo Business Today* (August 1994), pp. 24-27.

[14]The year 1993 presents a mixed picture in this regard. China's exports in 1993 to Japan rose 21%, but exports to the EU in 1993 fell by 4%. CIA, *China's Economy in 1993 and 1994*, pp. 17-18.

[15]Harding, p. 368; Nicholas R. Lardy, *China in the World Economy* (Washington, D.C.: Institute for International Economics, 1994), p.119; CIA, *China's Economy in 1993 and 1994*, p. 11.

Organization, scheduled to replace GATT in January 1995. China applied in 1986, and it appeared that it would get in – only to founder on the Tiananmen crisis. To judge from the inconclusive mid-1994 negotiations conducted in Beijing by a senior U.S. trade official, China's prospects are none too good.[16]

China eagerly seeks technology from the U.S., a factor intimately linked to trade, investments, and foreign aid. This can take myriad forms, including licensing, the purchase of patents, as well as the training of Chinese technicians in U.S. factories (such as Boeing). It also takes the form of training Chinese students and scholars in American universities and labs. Between 1979 and 1990, for example, no less than 102,000 had arrived in the U.S. for such study. It is notable that Chinese continued to arrive in the U.S. in large numbers even after Tiananmen. One authority claims that in 1992 there were 10,000 Chinese teaching and researching in the U.S.[17]

Apart from formal training in American universities, China obviously needs to continue its already major participation in the international scientific community – a community in which the U.S. plays an enormous role. Any nation hoping to stay on the "cutting edge" of the world's scientific community must send its scholars to attend international conferences, present papers at these meetings, and to meet and stay in contact with fellow scientists around the world. In terms of international science, any notions of "self-reliance" are pure delusion. That Beijing clearly understands this point is illustrated by the extraordinary rise in the number of international non-government organizations (INGO) in which it now participates. The figure rose from 71 in 1977 to 677 in 1989.[18]

---

[16]*New York Times* (July 24, 1994). For a useful discussion of the GATT issue, see Margaret M. Pearson, "Foreign Investment and Trade," especially pp. 72-75, in William A. Joseph, ed., *China Briefing, 1994* (Boulder, CO: Westview, 1994).

[17]Richard P. Suttmeier, "The Changing International Context for Sino-American Relations in Science and Technology," *In Depth* (Fall 1993), p. 100, footnote 7, citing *Chronicle of Higher Education* (December 5, 1992), p. 836.

[18]Lowell Dittmer, *China Under Reform* (Boulder, CO: Westview Press, 1994),

If economic considerations provide compelling reasons for positive U.S.-China relations, important political and strategic factors continue to play their part. The PRC repeatedly proclaims the need for a peaceful environment to achieve modernization. Cynics can dismiss this as a tactical maneuver to allow China time to gain strength. Yet common sense suggests that the Chinese can and do benefit from a peaceful Asian arena. Moreover, some recent actions already mentioned provide some evidence that there is a congruence between China's declaratory policies and its actions. Cambodia is a case in point, as is the nuclear problem in Korea. After years of a clear tilt toward Pakistan, China has recently moved toward a more even-handed policy in terms of the troublesome Indian-Pakistani issue. Such actions, of course, tend to improve U.S.-China relations.

Prior to the early 1970s, China consistently opposed any U.S. military presence in Asia. Yet since that time, Beijing's opposition has been at least partially changed to a limited support for American military involvement. Most analysts attribute this to Chinese anxieties about the possibility of Japanese rearmament and, in particular, the possibility of Japanese nuclear armaments.[19] Thus, from China's viewpoint, it makes sense to have American forces in Asia, and as a corollary, Beijing implicitly supports the continuation of the U.S.-Japan Security Treaty that presumably lessens the possibility of Japanese rearmament. If there is merit in this line of reasoning, it is even more pertinent if the North Korean nuclear situation becomes a catalyst for Japan to become a nuclear power.

For most of the post-World War II period, Sino-American relations were largely bi-lateral in nature, with very few occasions (aside from the U.N.) in which the two sides dealt with each other within the structure of multi-national organizations and

---

p. 163, footnote 7. Details are lacking, but presumably many of these were associated with science and technology.

[19]Banning Garrett and Bonnie Glaser, "Multilateral Security in the Asia-Pacific Region and its Impact on Chinese Interests: Views from Beijing," *Contemporary Southeast Asia*, 16:1 (June 1994), pp. 14-34.

conferences. Since the end of the Cold War, however, American and Chinese officials are brought together in new and presumably fruitful ways. For example, since the late 1970s, the Association of Southeast Asian Nations (ASEAN) has held so-called post-ministerial conferences, i.e., meetings with ASEAN's "dialogue partners" after the ASEAN foreign ministers hold their annual meetings. The U.S. has been a dialogue partner since the late 1970s, and since 1991 China has joined these gatherings.

A new and potentially important element was added in July 1993 when, between the ASEAN ministerial conferences and the dialogue meetings, officials from several other nations – China, Russia, Vietnam, Laos, and Papua New Guinea – met in the newly conceived ASEAN Regional Forum. Exactly a year later the group met again. The purpose has been to discuss Asia-wide security issues. Nothing of substance happened, but it represented a "first" in that Chinese and American officials have now dealt with security matters in the larger context of an Asia-Pacific gathering.[20]

Senior Chinese and American officials have also met at the Asia Pacific Economic Cooperation (APEC) meetings. APEC is quite new (holding its first meeting in 1989), and doesn not even have a formal structure or organization. Top American officials have attended all these annual meetings, and China began attending in 1991. It was at the November 1993 Seattle "summit" that President Clinton first met Chinese Communist Party General Secretary Jiang Zemin. The two met again a year later at the next summit in Indonesia.

Factors that Could Damage U.S.-China Relations

If there are manifold factors tending to bolster Sino-American relations, there are others that today damage relations, and still

---

[20]For excellent background articles, see *FEER* (August 5, 1993), p. 10, (July 28, 1994), pp. 22-23 and (August 4, 1994), pp. 14-16. For a perceptive evaluation by journalist Frank Ching, see *FEER* (August 11, 1994), p. 34.

more that may do so in the future. From the U.S. viewpoint, the chronic trade deficit with China is very troubling. The 1990s have seen China emerge as the nation with the second largest trade deficit (following Japan) among U.S. trade partners throughout the world. At first glance, the figures seem shocking. From a mere $300 *million* in 1983, the deficit rose 76 times to $23 *billion* in 1993.

The deficit is partially explained by the fact that, to some degree, China has "inherited" the deficits previously held by Taiwan, Hong Kong, and South Korea. All three sharply cut their large deficits with the U.S. by "exporting" more to China in the sense that Taiwanese, Hong Kong, and South Korean entrepreneurs produce goods (e.g., textiles, footwear) in China, which then sells them to the U.S. The data seem to support this. The Taiwan deficit with the U.S. peaked in 1987 at $19 billion, but fell dramatically to $10 billion in 1993. Hong Kong's deficit also peaked in 1987 at $6.5 billion, and then fell to $100 million in 1993. South Korea's deficit rose to $9.9 billion in 1988 and then dropped to $3 billion in 1993.

To put this in slightly different terms, the U.S. ran a total deficit of $13.7 billion with the combination of China, Taiwan, Hong Kong, and South Korea in 1983. Between that year and 1993, the combined deficit rose almost three times to $38.1 billion. That is a substantial rise, but still far less than the 76-fold increase in the China deficit.

The deficit issue also has a by-product that presents special difficulties for the U.S. Any American punitive action against China to curb the deficit would almost certainly economically damage Hong Kong, Taiwan, and South Korea because these three are now so deeply intermeshed with China's economy.

Whatever the facts, it is clear that the deficit is an irritant that receives much negative attention in the U.S. Congress, the America media, and from some (but not all) U.S. business interests. The U.S. Government has tried, with marginal success, to lessen the deficit by pressuring China to open further its market. (Peter Drucker has summed up the problem with the quip that the Chinese export like capitalists and import like communists.)

The deficit problem is unlikely to be solved in the near future; rather, it will probably get worse.

The deficit is by no means the only problem in U.S.-China economic relations. Added to this are various other American charges: false labeling, exports made by prison labor, lack of enforcement of laws protecting intellectual property rights, the need for greater access to the ever-growing Chinese market, and the lack of transparency and consistency in China's trade and tariff regulations. The magnitude of these issues is illustrated by the false labeling accusation. According to U.S. customs officials, in recent years there has been no less than a $2 billion-a-year influx of falsely labeled garments from China.[21] (Many of these problems, let it be noted, also exist in U.S. trade relations with virtually all of American trading partners throughout Asia.)

At times the negotiations on these issues resemble the dialogue of the deaf. Yet some progress has been made. China has taken a number of steps to eliminate problems, but differences still persist between passing a law or issuing a direction and the actual implication of these measures.[22] On the U.S. side there is the further complication that elements in the U.S. Congress attempt to micro-manage trade as an indirect means of keeping the human rights issue on the agenda. For example, soon after Clinton had approved of MFN treatment for another year, no less than 158 members of the House of Representatives voted to impose heavy tariffs on exports from factories owned by the Chinese military.[23] The bill was defeated (270 to 158), yet it illustrates the continual problems that plague U.S.-China trade.

Human rights is another serious irritant in U.S.-China relations. Once again, the problem isn not simply the "U.S. vs. China." On the American side, in particular, opinion is divided. Everyone pays lip service to human rights. Yet divisions exist within both the executive and legislative branches – some argue for stern measures, others claim that is counterproductive. The

---

[21]*New York Times* (Aug. 4, 1994).

[22]Pearson, *op. cit.*, pp. 76-84, has an excellent discussion of these issues.

[23]*New York Times* (August 10, 1994).

same applies to the U.S. media. With some exceptions, American business argues that a continued commerical engagement with China will in time work to improve its human rights record.

There is also the added complexity that the human rights issues has pushed beyond a U.S.-China bi-lateral issue and has, in effect, become a "U.S. vs. Asia" problem. Whatever their political complexion, virtually all Asian countries agree that the U.S. has pushed this issue too hard and that Western standards of human rights do not necessarily transfer to the Asian scene. Such Asian notables as Singapore's articulate and redoubtable Lee Kuan Yew have begun to talk back in messages that can be summed up with the expression: "Stop lecturing us!" Even such staunch U.S. allies as Japan and South Korea have been reluctant to speak for the American hard-line position. Both are hesitant to damage their ever-growing economic ties with China. The Japanese are acutely aware of their own wretched World War II record, and South Koreans know that they too have some human rights abuses that continue to this day.

China has in fact taken sporadic steps in recent years to placate the U.S. For example, a few political prisoners have been released from time to time. On balance, however, Beijing yielded little ground to Clinton's threat that MFN would not be renewed in 1994 unless China demonstrated marked improvements in its human rights record.

Instead, the U.S. in none-too-subtle a fashion backed down and, as noted, "de-linked" the human rights issue from MFN renewal in 1994. Indeed, Washington has apparently decided that more will be gained if American policy focuses more on constructive engagement and less on human rights per se. The U.S. position is perhaps best captured in an article entitled "A New American Approach to Asia? Maybe···"[24] This article contains extracts from an April 1994 memo sent to U.S. Secretary of State Warren Christopher by Assistant Secretary of State for East Asian and Pacific Affairs Winston Lord. Among other things, Lord noted that the U.S. needs to temper its rhetoric and to "pay

[24]*Tokyo Business Today* (August 1994), pp. 36-9.

greater attention to our style."

Aside from economic and human rights problems, military-strategic issues may prove the most serious in Sino-American relations in the 20th Century's final years. In the post-Cold War era, military budgets and arms sales and purchases have declined in most of the world. East and Southeast Asia are the exceptions. Ironically, there is widespread agreement that China is more strategically secure today than at any time in the past two centuries. Yet from 1988 to 1993, the PRC doubled its military budget (after several years of no increases). Beijing explains this by noting that inflation ate up most of the increases, and that in any case China's defense budgets are far below other nations (including neighboring Japan).

Most of China's defense expenditures have been for its air force and navy. In particular, Beijing has gone full-tilt to create a genuine "blue-water" navy with the apparent goal of having the power to control the South China Sea (a possible but yet unproven rich source of oil). From the Southeast Asian view, China exacerbated the matter in early 1992 by passing a law that asserted unambiguous sovereignty over the South China Sea and also stated explicitly that it would use military force to protect its sovereign rights.

The U.S. has said little about the South China Sea issue, but of course is aware of the nervousness among Southeast Asian nations that hope and expect the U.S. to counter China's seeming aggressiveness in this area.

If Washington has been relatively quiet on the South China Seas, it has been quite the opposite in terms of various other military issues – including Chinese arms sales and nuclear and missile proliferation problems. On the face of it, China has seemingly been cooperative in terms of signing various international treaties related to weapons of mass destruction. These include the convention to prohibit biological weapons (1984) and chemical weapons (1993), as well as the especially important Treaty on the Non-Proliferation of Nuclear Weapons (1992). During former U.S. Secretary of State James Baker's November 1991 trip to China, the PRC pledged to support the Missile Technology Control

Regime's (MTCR) guidelines.

The U.S. naturally approved of these actions, but claims that China has violated both the letter and spirit of nuclear proliferation and the MTCR guidelines. In 1993, for example, Washington charged that Beijing had transferred M-11 missile components to Pakistan. And in recent years there have been reports of sales to governments regarded as "rogue" regimes by Washington: Libya, Iran, Iraq, Syria, and Burma. Adding to Washington's consternation were sales of intermediate-range ballistic missiles to Saudi Arabia, and the 1992 Chinese purchases from Russia of Su-27 fighter-bombers and S-300 ground-to-air anti-aircraft missiles worth $1.2 billion.

Beijing has admitted to some but not all of these American assertions, but complains that Washington has distorted or fabricated various aspects of these deals. The Chinese also point to the undisputed fact that U.S. arms sales are vastly greater than China's, noting further that while China sold $17 billion worth of weapons in the 1985-92 period, its sales dropped markedly in 1992 to $100 million. In any case, in August 1993 the U.S. announced two-year sanctions against various defense-related Chinese ministries and commercial companies.[25]

However, in October 1994, a new agreement was signed that seemed to settle the situation. The U.S. agreed to lift the sanctions, and China in turn pledged not to sell missiles that, while ostensibly not in exact accord with the MTCR, might still be upgraded to come under the specifications of the MTCR.[26]

Several days later, U.S. Defense Secretary William J. Perry arrived in China where he attempted to renew the general level of military cooperation that had existed before the Tiananmen crisis. There were no major breakthroughs on this visit, but each side agreed to be more open in terms of defense budgets and military planning. The overall relationship seemed to have improved

---

[25]See the excellent article by Paul Godwin and John J. Schulz, "Arming the Dragon for the 21st Century: China's Defense Modernization Program," *Arms Control Today*, 23:10 (December 1993), pp. 3-8.

[26]*New York Times* (November 12, 1994).

even more in November 1994 in Indonesia when President Clinton and Chinese leader Jiang Zemin met during the Asia-Pacific Economic Cooperation "summit" meeting. Commerce Secretary Ron Brown, who accompanied Clinton, held high-level talks with Chinese trade officials that he anticipated might turn into multi-billion dollar contracts between China and the U.S.[27]

Conclusion

It takes no clairvoyant to anticipate future problems in the Sino-American relationship. That is a certainty. Yet one need not conjure up doomsday scenarios ("A nuclear-armed China running amok in Asia") to recognize that both sides have compelling reasons to minimize problems. Writing fifteen years ago, Michel Oksenberg observed that "China contributes to the global equilibrium simply by governing its huge mass effectively," and that a "weak or divided China would become a source of international instability, as it was from the 1860s to the 1940s."[28] More recently, he has commented that "Uncertainty is a permanent condition of modern China," and thus the U.S. must be prepared "…to deal with a sprawling, territorially amorphous, culturally confident, socially undisciplined, economically vibrant, and politically messy China."[29]

Whatever the problems, U.S. friends and allies continue to count on a constructive American engagement with China. If there are twin nightmares in Asian foreign offices, they are, first, a direct U.S.-China military confrontation, and, second, a total American withdrawal from Asia. Neither, of course, seems likely today. This leaves the only viable alternative: a constructive Sino-

---

[27]*FEER* (December 1, 1994), pp. 14-15.

[28]Michel Oksenberg, "China Policy for the 1980s," *Foreign Affairs*, 59:2 (Winter 1980-81), p. 312.

[29]Michel Oksenberg, "China and the Japanese-American Alliance," in Gerald L. Curtis, ed., *The United States, Japan, and Asia* (New York: Norton, 1994), pp. 111 and 118.

American engagement.

Apart from strategic issues, American business interests are now witnessing the emergence of that famous yet long-elusive huge "China market." China's imports exceeded $100 billion for the first time in 1993, and by all indications this is likely to grow substantially in the years ahead. In many ways, the Chinese view can be seen as a mirror image of the American view. If the U.S. needs the expanding China market, China has an even greater need for the U.S. market, not to mention investments, technology, and foreign aid.[30]

Overall American power has diminished in recent years, but the U.S. still has crucial ties – political, economic, and strategic – to the OECD nations, as well as to the Asian NICs and the ASEAN countries. Hostile Chinese acts against the U.S. would certainly jeopardize China's ever-increasing economic and political ties to these American friends and allies. Accordingly, Sino-American ties can never be divorced from the overall complexity of both Chinese and American relations throughout Asia.

---

[30]Given the mood of Congress in recent years, direct U.S. foreign aid to China is unlikely in the near future. Because the Republicans took control of both houses of Congress in 1995, foreign aid seems even more unlikely than when the Democrats controlled Congress. Moreover, as noted, the U.S. exercises great influence in the distribution of foreign aid through the World Bank and other international lending agencies.

14

A Headless Dragon: Creating Scenarios for Post-Deng China

David Zweig
(The Fletcher School of Law & Diplomacy, Tufts University)

Introduction: the passing of an era[1]

The emperor is on his deathbed, and the world waits and watches. How will China's leaders deal with the policy and power vacuum that his passing brings? Will they fight or hang tight? Turn left or to the right? Will they innovate, procrastinate, democratize, or disintegrate? Will the army, the bureaucracy, or the part rule the roost? These are all valid but enormously difficult questions to answer.

The problem emerges because of the enormity of Deng's contri-

[1]A special thanks to Alastair Iain Johnston, Harvard University. Some of the structure and many ideas in this paper resulted from a collaborative project we did in summer 1994, where we posited a schema for predicting the outcomes of elite conflict during and immediately after the post-Deng succession crisis. Iain also read the draft and commented. Nevertheless, I alone am responsible for the views expressed in this paper.

bution, the passing of the entire revolutionary generation, and the pace of change underway in China. Deng liberated China form its Maoist doldrums. His economic innovations – domestic reform, marketization, and external opening – created an emerging economic giant and an exporting powerhouse whose impact on the world economy will be enormous, whether it succeeds or fails. After he called on the Chinese people to "let a few people get rich first," hundreds of millions of people have dramatically increased their standard of living. His foreign policy acumen normalized Sino-U.S. relations, pressed Britain to return Hong Kong to Chinese sovereignty, opened a dialogue with the Nationalists in Taiwan, diffused the potential for war with Russia, and helped build a peaceful climate in East Asia that is facilitating unprecedented economic growth.

Yet he leaves behind enormous problems. He chose a successor, but never institutionalized the succession process; had he done so we would not be speculating about leadership scenarios. He flirted with elections, but failed to create any institutions through which middle level officials and China's citizens could meaningfully express their political concerns and pursue their interests. And while suppressing the Tiananmen movement kept China unified and communist, the negative example of "Tiananmen" contributed to the collapse of communism in Eastern Europe and Russia, leaving the demise of world communism as a spectre haunting China's future.

This paper presents a framework for constructing scenarios of the post-Deng era and suggests several scenarios that emerge from that framework. The key elements in this framework are fourfold. First, the post-Deng elite structure – how the elites interact – is the most critical element determining China's future. Second, the power of bureaucratic and institutional interests will affect that elite structure and constrain its policy choices, although which elites participate in the ruling group may also affect the policies that China pursues.[2] These three elements –

[2]In our more complex model, Johnston and I looked at specific leaders, their policy tendencies, their potential for alliance formation with like-minded

elite structure, power capabilities, and policy program – form the core of the Leadership/Policy scenarios by determining who is likely to ally with whom,[3] in the pursuit of what policy program, and with what likelihood of success, given the possible reaction from other elites and society. Third, although the responses to elite policy initiatives by China's middle strata and its "masses" may not affect initial elite policy choices – though anticipated reactions constrain elite choices – they can affect the evolution of the system. And finally international factors, such as China's security environment and the status of the global economy, may also affect China's policy choices, the system's evolution, and introduce externally imposed crises that will test the new leadership. Thus the structure of the political elite, the policy program that the leadership adopts, the institutional power base of each leadership configuration, their ability to weather the social stresses of economic growth and the political demands for greater responsiveness from society and the middle strata, as well as the global strategic and economic environment will determine the type of system that emerges in the post-Deng era.

After presenting this framework, the paper outlines the major trends in the above arenas over the past 10 years. These patterns must be factored into the equation to ensure that any model of the future is grounded in today's trends. For while the Soviet experience has taught us that cataclysmic change is possible, most political and economic systems are highly "path dependent" – partial prisoners of the past in terms of norms, culture, and political and economic institutions (or in china's case, lack of institutions).

The third part of the paper presents three core scenarios: a *linear* projection(not the same as a status quo), a *disintegration* por-

---

leaders, the institutional strengths of such alliances, and the probability that such outcomes could occur.

[3]Though alliances may be based on political expediency, in Chinese politics they have often been deeply affected by elite values, such that like-minded individuals who support a common program are more likely to ally. See Carol Lee Hamrin, "Competing 'Policy Packages' in Post-Mao China," *Asian Survey*, 26:5 (May 1984), pp. 487-518.

trait, and a *liberal* model. I explain how such scenarios could unfold and suggest spinoffs that might develop from each trajectory. In conclusion I challenge each of these scenarios, pointing out their weaknesses, and offering some guidance as to which direction China is most likely to follow.[4] *Does Succession Matter?*

Does succession actually makes a difference to China's future development? Scholars posit three views of succession: two prophesy significant change; one suggests "business as usual." The traditional view in the field of comparative communism sees elite rotation as a *crisis*, whose outcome is relatively unpredictable. Without institutional mechanisms for choosing new leaders, the very transfer of power is highly destablizing, putting these systems at risk whenever new leaders are chosen.[5] Even after the initial crisis is resolved, power arrangements may not hold, as elites vie for control over several years until a dominant leader emerges.[6] This perspective suggest that Deng's succession will initially weaken the state's capacity to respond to internal and external threats. Elites, aware of their vulnerability, will follow a cautious policy line to avoid further destabilizing the system. Only a dominant leader's emergence ends the crisis.

The second view sees succession as an opportunity for *innovation*. The centralization of power within the system and the nature of succession give an emergent leader enormous capacity to determine the system's overall development and the mode of resource allocation – plan, market, or a hybrid model – as well as the norms of political conflict.[7] According to Bunce, political

[4]Since the collapse of the Soviet Union, the degree of change that must be included in any calculation of the "possible" is much greater than would have been necessary before the fall of the Iron Curtain in 1989.

[5]Though it rarely happened, foreign analysts always asserted that it was precisely at these moments that the systems were most likely to collapse.

[6]Hua Guofeng's replacement of Mao in 1976 lasted little more than two years, and few would have predicted after Stalin's death in 1953 that by 1957 Khrushchev would have consolidated power. Thus a "transitional regime," with transitional leaders may emerge in the short term in China.

[7]Hamrin, "Competing 'Policy Packages' in Post-Mao China."

mobilization surrounding the contest for power, competition over ideas among contenders who seek innovative suggestions from below, and lobbying for institutional supporters, give new leaders in communist and capitalist systems a honeymoon when they can introduce new initiatives.[8] In fact, every leadership change in China and the former Soviet Union had enormous policy implications for the system. Thus significant reforms could occur in the early post-Deng era or once a new leader emerges after Deng's death.

The third model, sees institutions not as the passive agents of top political leaders, but as autonomous organisms working assiduously to protect their own interests.[9] Socialist systems are "path dependent." Change depends on the existing distribution of institutional interests, which are reinforced by social values, norms, and laws, making it *extremely unlikely* and difficult to introduce. Expansion of private property will be resisted by politicians, workers, established institutions, and social values favoring a more collectivist ethos, as well as a legal system reinforcing those institutional interests. Given the strength of social institutions and the dispersion of power within China's current political elite, this perspective suggests that only continued partial reform is likely.[10]

Leadership Configurations

The structure of a state's elites – and how those leaders interact – affect a political system's stability by influencing its capacity to

---

[8]Valerie Bunce, *Do New Leaders Make A Difference: Executive Succession and Public Policy Under Capitalism and Socialism* (Princeton University Press, 1981).

[9]James G. March and Johan P. Olsen, "The New Institutionalism: Organizational Factors in Political Life," *American Political Science Review*, 78:3 (September 1984), pp. 734-49.

[10]David Bachman, *The Fourteenth Congress of the Chinese Communist Party* (New York: The Asia Society, 1992). For further elaboration of the view that institutions, not individuals, rule China see, David Bachman, *Bureaucracy, Economy and Leadership in China: The Institutional Origins of the Great Leap Forward* (Cambridge: Cambridge University Press, 1991), Introduction.

innovate, to reach consensus on resource allocations, and to respond to crises.[11] While one leader might impose his will upon the system, and collective leadership could breed stability or stasis, a fragmented group could confront great difficulties making any decisions. If China does not collapse immediately after Deng's death, one of three elite configurations will emerge: (1) a dominant single leader or duumvirate, (2) a collective leadership, or (3) a factionalized leadership group.

Communist systems have often been ruled by powerful individual leaders. Some charismatic leaders, presenting themselves as the embodiment of virtue or history, have sought to transform the political and social system. Others relied on institutional forms of rulership, employing the party or police to keep society and the polity in line. Particularly in early stages of a succession, duumvirates, with one person in a more dominating role, have ruled communist systems.[12] If the past is our guide, one or two leaders could dominate post-Deng China.

A *preeminent leader* must neutralize his chief rivals and coopt all other top leaders. But if bloodletting is necessary, the military and the "elders" might intervene to prevent internecine instability. And while a populist strategy might rally society to his side, a preeminent leader would still need strong institutional support. Would other leaders allow one person to dominate the system? Could they trust him to deal with them with equanimity? Knowledge among the current leaders that they either "hang together" or "hang separately" works against any one leader seeking predominance, as does the apparent lack of charisma among any current leader. Similarly, an effort by any one person

---

[11]Robert D. Putnam, *The Comparative Study of Political Elites* (Englewood Cliffs, NJ: Prentice Hall, 1976).

[12]While one person manages party and personnel issues, a second handles the economy. Fewsmith argues that Chen Yun had much more power than was often attributed to him throughout the 1980s and the economic policies of that period depended on the outcome of political struggles between Chen and Deng. See Joseph Fewsmith, *Dilemmas of Reform in China* (Armonk: M. E. Sharpe, 1993). In the USSR after Khrushchev, Kosygin was seen as the economic czar until Brezhnev centralized all power in his own hands.

to strive for preeminence might invite a collective purge of the culprit.

Since 1989, Deng Xiaoping has been grooming Jiang Zemin as his successor, calling him the "core" of the third generation. At Deng's behest, top military officials, especially Liu Huaqing, the military's representative on the Politburo Standing Committee, have supported Jiang, Unlike Hua Guofeng, who failed to become Mao's successor, Jiang has had six years to build a power base. He may prove capable of exchanging favors and using institutional authority to stay in power, at least through the early post-Deng transition. However, other than Jiang, it would be enormously difficult and probably quite bloody for anyone else to establish preeminence. But if Jiang takes himself too seriously, and tries to become the preeminent leader, disorder could follow.

The division of institutional authority in the system makes an initial *duumvirate* more plausible. While one leader handles party-military affairs, a second could administer the economy. Over time the former leader would be well positioned to assume total control, especially if he can find his own economic czar. Also, should one faction win power, the immediate outcome might be a duumvirate as well.

A *collective* leadership, ruling in a consensual manner, is seen as a likely post-Deng structure.[13] Such a group might purge any aspirant for preeminence, but would incorporate most top leaders and institutions, making it a stable, if not immobile, decision-making group. Even before Deng was incapacitated, Lieberthal and Oksenberg's "fragmented authoritarianism" presented a diffuse, consensual, bargaining mode, rather than a leadership structure based on open conflict.[14] Thorny issues, such as

---

[13]Bachman, *The Fourteenth Congress of the Chinese Communist Party*.

[14]Oksenberg and Lieberthal say that 25 people dominate economic decision making system in China. Kenneth Lieberthal and Michael Oksenberg, *Policy Making in China: Leaders Structures, and Processes* (Princeton: Princeton University Press, 1988). See also Carol Lee Hamrin, "The Party Leadership System," in David Lampton and Kenneth Lieberthal, eds., *Bureaucracy, Politics, and Decision Making in Post-Mao China* (Berkeley: University of California Press, 1992), pp. 95-124.

Tiananmen, inflation, and industrial reform would remain problematic. And while Chinese and communist political culture might suggest that an emperor-like, preeminent leader may be necessary for political legitimacy in a predominantly peasant society, such leader could remain on a tight leash, subject to collective authority, a symbol of Communist Party leadership. And while collective leadership has been rare in communist systems, troikas initially ruled the Soviet Union after the death of both Lenin and Stalin and the purge of Khrushchev.

For critics of the "institutional" approach, this scenario is overly deterministic, putting political economy too far above aspirations for personal political power. With no preeminent leader suppressing or managing the individual hunger for ultimate power – much like a hegemon in the international system – the incentives for individuals to seek power may be too great to contain. Moreover, according to Dittmer, institutional power has little utility during succession crises; so why it constrain personal ambition?[15] Also, Chinese politicians are constantly undercutting each others' institutional base, so while all key institutions may be represented, one or two leaders may accumulate enough of them in their personal power portfolios to emerge dominant.

Moreover, given the deep mistrust among communist leaders – here Lenin's dictum, *kto, ktogo*, ("who" will get "whom?") remains salient – a factionalized succession struggle is a possible outcome. For Pye *factionalism* is culturally inherent to Chinese politics, particularly at times of personal insecurity;[16] at these moments, when each policy concession can shift the political balance, paralysis is unavoidable.[17] Similarly, Dittmer's assertion that personal not positional power dominates during succession struggles again presages for the emergence of factional struggle.

---

[15]See Lowell Dittmer, "Bases of Power in Chinese Politics: The Fall of the Gang of Four," *World Politics*, 31:1 (October 1978), pp. 26-55.

[16]Lucian Pye, *The Spirit of Chinese Politics: A Psychocultural Study of the Authority Crisis in Political Development* (Cambridge: The M.I.T Press, 1968).

[17]Lucian Pye, *The Dynamics of Chinese Politics* (Cambridge: Oelgeschlager, Gunn, and Hain, 1981).

Or factionalism could emerge after the succession, keeping the system unstable.[18] For many analysts, the Mao and Deng eras combined a preeminent leader of differing personal power capabilities with factionalism among the second tier. Particularly after the Great Leap fiasco weakened Mao, and for most of the Deng era, factions formed around policy and personal conflicts.[19] For current leaders, factional alignments may be fluid; many have worked together only since coming to the center in the 1980s, making personal ties weaker. Still, a Tianjin-Young Communist League group and a Shanghai faction could emerge,[20] allowing an apparent collective leadership officiating post-Deng China to split asunder within a few years.

Institutions as Power Capabilities

While institutions may constrain elite action, they are *power capabilities* that can determine the succession and the viability of post-succession elite structures. Were I to focus on specific individual leaders and their role in the succession, rather than on leadership configurations, an individual's institutional power base would be crucial in affecting his chance for power. Also, because informal power affects political struggles in China,[21] per-

---

[18]Dittmer's view that positional power dominates day-to-day politics, and that personal power networks cannot be mobilized during normal politics because of prohibitions against open factionalism, suggests that the politics of "new institutionalism" should dominate the post-succession era, allowing for the reemergence of a collective leadership group. See Dittmer, "Bases of Power in Chinese Politics."

[19]Parris Chang, *Power and Policy in China* (University Park: The Pennsylvania State University Press, 1975); Carol Hamrin, "Competing 'Policy Packages' in Post-Mao China"; and Dorothy J. Solinger, "The Three Lines in the Early 1980s," in Dorothy J. Solinger, ed., *Three Visions of Chinese Socialism* (Boulder: Westview Press, 1984).

[20]The Tianjin-Young Communist League would link Li Ruihuan, Hu Qili, Li Lanqing, and remnants of the Hu Yaobang group at the center, while the Shanghai group would include Jiang Zemin, Zhu Rongji, Wu Banguo, Chang Junyun and Huang Ju.

[21]Dittmer, "Bases of Power in Chinese Politics."

sonal networks and animosities, as well as individual leadership qualities, would go into the calculus. However, the desire to create a more parsimonious predictive framework forces me to treat institutions as important determinants both of emerging leadership configurations and whether or not such leadership arrangements will be able to maintain power in the face of social or political challenges to the state.

In brief, what institutions can affect political outcomes? The People's Liberation Army(PLA) and the Chinese Communist Party's(CCP) Central Military Commission which directs it, is a key institutional actor. Any emerging leadership structure will have to placate PLA interests, including its desire for strong national defense and political and social stability. Yet unless the country sinks into chaos, the PLA should avoid the type of political imbroglio it experienced in 1967 and 1989.[22] Its own generational splits weakens its ability to act independently of top politicians.[23] In most cases, therefore, it will be a political resource, supporting the elite configuration that emerges, rather than an independent actor establishing its own candidate.

A second key institution is the secret police. In Eastern Europe and the former Soviet Union the state's coercive arm remained a key channel for new leaders. In China, Wang Dongxing's control over personal dossiers and the inner palace guard made him a key player in the early post-Mao era. Kang Sheng was also a source of enormous dread during the Maoist era, but he died before the succession. Yet it was Beria's ability to threaten the Politburo that led them to execute him right after Stalin's death.

The party bureaucracy, with its functional influence over the

---

[22]According to Joffe, the PLA has not been inclined to political intervention because "political intervention has brought only harm and hardship to the PLA." Thus if succession is smooth, the PLA is unlikely to play a significant role; but "if a succession struggle erupts, the military may be drawn in despite their desires." See Ellis Joffe, "The PLA and the Succession Question," Richard H. Yang, ed., *China's Military: The PLA in 1992/93* (Boulder, CO: Westview Press, 1993).

[23]Michael D. Swaine, *The Military and Political Succession in China: Leadership, Institutions and Beliefs* (Santa Monica: The Rand Corporation, 1992).

economy, politics, personnel, propaganda, and ideology, make it an important power capability. The ability to transfer his people to the center – what became known as the "circular theory of power" – is the standard explanation for Stalin's emergence. Other key institutions would include the levers of economic power, including the "leadership small groups" which set and monitor policy at the center,[24] the State Council which runs the government, the formal state commissions that manage the economy, the Ministry of Finance, and certain heavy industrial bureaus. However, these economic institutions cannot play any direct role in the immediate succession; but as the channels for resource allocation, they are key institutions for building patronage networks and political loyalty that any leader needs in the medium-term succession. Finally, should the CCP follow more democratic procedures, legislatures such as the National Party Congress or the government's National People's Congress, could become political resources abetting the institutional strength of any individual candidate for power.

One diminishing power capability is the group of party "elders" who played critical roles in purging Hu Yaobang and Zhao Ziyang, and who have an abiding belief in the need for stability and communist power. Long-standing personal networks and the prestige of being members of the founding generation of communist leaders may allow these elders to intervene in the succession and the political system that emerges from it. Though it is unlikely, one of them may vie for the position of dominant leader once Deng dies. More likely, they may support a conservative faction which promises to maintain a priority on order and party control. Or they may prevent any leader from seeking dominance and instead empower a collective leadership group.

Reform Strategies

Some analysts posit the possibility of a post-Deng retrogression in China's reform program,[25] and while the signs of an assertive

---

[24]Hamrin, "The Party Leadership System."

"neo-Conservatism" are evident, China's current leaders know that such a policy would not be sustainable for very long.[26] China's budget deficit screams for resolving China's insolvent state owned enterprises. Therefore, I propose only two policy scenarios, "radical" or "partial" reform.

Partial reform includes: support for "guidance planning" – where local and central governments influence market transactions; slow price reform; a neo-mercantilist, export-led growth strategy based on import-substitution and protection of domestic markets; reassertion of collective and CCP authority in the countryside; subsidies for state owned enterprises with closings of some failed enterprises; and nationalism, more than Marxism-Leninism, as the tool for mobilization. Tight party control would persist, as the unresolved dilemmas inherent in this strategy could trigger social unrest.

The dilemmas of partial reform are three-fold: budget deficits from subsidies, the inability to sustain growth and combat inflation due to the center's lack of fiscal policy instruments, and corruption within the mixed economy. These vestiges of the planned economy, which will persist under partial reform, trigger both stability and instability. Subsidies and growth are popular among the populace, while corruption insures that those with political power support continued reforms. Yet enormous graft creates strong social antipathy. Thus leaders committed to partial reform

---

[25]Comments of Dr. Harry Harding at An Asian Studies Center Symposium, "The Promise and Peril of China After Deng Xiaoping," *The Heritage Lectures*, The Heritage Foundation, February 3, 1994.

[26]For criticisms by neo-conservatives see Larry Sullivan, "Assault on Reforms: Conservative Criticism of Political and Economic Liberalization," *The China Quarterly*, No.114 (June 1988), pp. 198-222; Chao Ching-lun, "A Conversation with Deng Liqun," Hsin Pao (October 26, 1994), p. 21, in *Foreign Broadcast Information Service* (*FBIS*)-*CHI* (October 27, 1994), pp. 31-32; Wang Renzhi, "On Opposing Bourgeois Liberalization" *Qiushi*, No.3 (February 15, 1990), in *FBIS-CHI* (February 23, 1990), pp. 12-23; He Xin, "A Word of Advice to the Politburo," translated by Geremie Barme, *The Australian Journal of Chinese Affairs*, 23 (June 1990), pp. 49-76; and Joseph Fewsmith, "Looking at China Through a Third Eye," *The Journal of Contemporary China*, No. 7 (Fall 1994), pp. 100-104.

cannot liberalize the press, which would declare war on officials and a system that generates corruption. Similarly, rapid growth and its resultant inequities are destabilizing; only strong central authority keeps losers under reform in line.

Radical economic reform means a dominant role for the market, widespread privatization, an end to subsidies to state-owned enterprises, significant plant closings, and large-scale layoffs. Industrial output could plummet for 1-2 years, even as rapid price reform decreases consumer buying power. Bureaucratic intervention at all levels of the economic system would end, as would the welfare net. Global interdependence would shrink tariff barriers and place high priority on peaceful solutions to foreign confrontations in order to advance the economic reform agenda. Social mobilization would increase in the face of economic dislocations, even as the party's role in the economy weakened.

Does Society Matter?

I differentiate between a "middle strata" and the masses of Chinese society.[27] The first category includes regional and local political leaders from the province to the township, leaders of various economic and political organizations such as directors of large industrial groups(*jituan*), companies, factories, and development zones at the national, provincial, and municipal level, and directors of labor unions or other party transmission belts such as official student unions or women's federations. The masses includes members of society who are well organized in their work units, such as factory workers, intellectuals, soldiers, as well unorganized groups, such as peasants, itinerant workers, and students..

A major point ignored by most analysts is that the middle strata have enormous vested interests keeping the system from

[27]Xie uses this concept of an active middle strata that can affect policy outcomes to argue that Chinese totalitarianism is "semi-hierarchical." See Weizhi Xie, "The Semihierarchical Totalitarian Nature of *Chinese Politics*, 25:3 (April 1993), pp. 313-330.

extremes. They will support any political coalition that keeps order and growth and many support China's opening to the international system. Drawing their power from their positions within the Communist party, they are unlikely to jettison that political authority except in extreme cases: systemic breakdown, mass defections,[28] a widespread national consensus that the CCP has lost the "mandate of heaven," or if the central leadership's policies prove highly dysfunctional to local interests. Usually they simply adjust national policies to their own interests. However, over time they may press for a new formalized distribution of political authority between the center and the regions, which might include an institutionalized mechanism for local and regional interests to influence central policy making.

Mass society's response will depend upon how central elites and the middle strata deal with many issues. For urban intellectuals, particularly in Beijing, the evaluation of the 1989 Tiananmen mass movement remains an unresolved issue. But for most people, inflation, corruption, inequality, and expropriations of private and public resources by local officials are the sine qua non of successful rulership. But rapid growth breeds regional and interpersonal inequality and massive social dislocations. Inflation decreases the real incomes of those on salaries and fixed incomes. By expropriating peasant resources and imposing arbitrary taxes, local officials increase the capital they control but breed widespread peasant resentment and weaken the CCP's authority. Finally, corruption adds a moral dimension to these inequities that deligitimizes the regime. Numerous stories now emerge of officials privatizing state-owned enterprises; such theft antagonizes a population struggling to make ends meet. The Tiananmen events of 1989 may be seen in this light, as corruption, with its

---

[28]Nee and Lian argue that market expansion pressures cadres to set aside their moral leadership roles and adopt an "opportunistic" response to emerging business opportunities under the transitional economy. If many officials, who support the party's moral leadership but also see enormous chances for personal wealth, defect, the system will collapse. Victor Nee and Peng Lian, "Sleeping with the Enemy: A Dynamic Model of Declining Political Commitment in State Socialism," *Theory and Society*, 23 (1994), pp. 253-296.

immorality, and inflation, helped university students rally the masses.[29]

Still, the CCP's ability to prevent political or civil authorities outside its control from emerging should prevent mass society from taking unified actions to affect either the secession or the post-succession system. Unions, regional-based rebellions or secessionist movements, or organized student political action which have undermined many developing states, face enormous coercive constraints. Strikes, unorganized but widespread peasant tax rebellions and student protests over corruption might influence the succession crisis – if one or two leaders play to the masses. A faltering economy or sudden recession during the transition could trigger massive protests. But ruling elites and the middle strata fear society and will do their utmost to stop it from becoming an active and direct political agent.

International Factors

Can international factors affect the evolution of post-Deng China? Short of major wars, invasions, significant military treats, global economic collapses, or significant actions by key bilateral trading partners, external influences play secondary, rather than primary, roles in the evolution of political systems.[30] Yet a relatively complex relationship exists among external pressures, types of domestic regimes, and the foreign policy proclivities and actions of a state. While a hostile international environment

---

[29]Inflation in 1989-89 had increased significantly, and estimates at that time were that because of the large number of current and former government workers who were on fixed salaries or pensions, at least 20 (and perhaps 30) percent of Beijingers had seen their real incomes drop during that period. See Kathleen Hartford, "Economic Crisis, Social Change, Cultural Disintegration, and Political Stagnation," in Suzanne Ogden, Kathleen Hartford, Lawrence Sullivan, and David Zweig, eds., *China's Search for Democracy: The Student and Mass Movement of 1989* (Armonk: M. E. Sharpe, 1992), pp. 3-25.

[30]Gourevitch argued that external threats affect the type of regime that emerges within a state. Peter Gourevitch, "The Second Image Reversed: The international sources of domestic politics," International Organization, 32:4 (Autumn 1978), pp. 881-911.

might strengthen domestic pressures for a collective conservative (i.e., a partial reform) program, or bureaucratic interests that favor an assertive foreign policy,[31] the same external pressures might constrain such a leadership from a belligerent foreign policy. Star Wars undermined conservatives in the Soviet Union, allowing Gorbachev to insist that radical reform was the only strategy to avoid collapse. Similarly, a more benign environment might permit the emergence of a liberal regime willing to launch radical reforms.[32] Only then can the military be undermined and economic development determine the domestic and foreign policy agenda.

Prescriptive arguments offer two options. Increased interdependence and global norms, enforced by membership in international organizations and regimes, might constrain an otherwise assertive post-Deng foreign policy. Yet more reactive forces in the United States believe that only direct confrontation on trade, human rights, and military issues will limit China's external behavior and trigger the emergence of a liberal domestic regime. But strategies must reflect the conditions of a regime undergoing succession, when normal responses to external stimuli do not necessarily occur.

Recent Trends in China's Political and Economic Process

The rules and norms of conduct among elites and members of

[31]Garver sees China's extension into the South China Sea as the result of unrestrained bureaucratic interest in the military, particularly the navy. See John Garver, "China's Push into the South China Sea: The Interaction of Bureaucratic and National Interests," *The China Quarterly*, No.132 (December 1992), pp. 999-1028.

[32]China's most radical reform period, the "second wave of reform," occurred when the United States improved China's COCOM status, expanded educational, military, and scientific exchanges, and began significant foreign direct investment. See Carol Hamrin, *China and the Challenge of the Future* (Westview press, 1990).

society, as well as the economic and political structures of political systems, are the product of long-term institutional developments and are not easy to change.[33] New institutions, not consonant with political norms, have enormous difficulties embedding themselves into a society. This "path dependence" makes existing institutions and current trends the starting point for any social change. What are those key trends in China today?

1. Central authority has declined. Compare Mao's and Deng's power. Leaders of enormous stature, such as Liu Shaoqi, Deng Xiaoping, and Ye Jianying, feared Mao and deferred to "Chairman."[34] While after 1978, Deng's views prevailed, few feared to challenge his policies. Why? Deng's "polite purge" of his opponents in the early 1980s ended the violent "exit pattern" Mao had instituted, bringing civility to political struggle. But the price of "polite politics" is less power for any aspiring preeminent leader, as great pressure exists for continued political civility.[35]

2. The Tiananmen disaster, increasing corruption, a "fever" for getting rich at any cost, and decreased control over the influx of foreign ideas have undermined the CCP's legitimacy. Widespread cynicism dominates life and politics in China. The return of traditional vices such as prostitution, drugs, gambling, corruption, and wife-buying, portend the passing of the "mandate of heaven." Cynicism and the declining legitimacy of the political system may increase greatly with the passing of its last emperor, Deng Xiaoping.[36]

3. But the new leadership group that came to power at the 14th

[33]Douglass C. North, *Institutions, Institutional Change, and Economic Performance* (Cambridge: Cambridge University Press, 1990).

[34]This is the portrayal that emerges from Li Zhisui, *The Private Life of Chairman Mao* (New York: Random House, 1994).

[35]For a similar argument, see Yasheng Huang, "Beijing's Polite Politics," *New York Tiems, OP-ED* (November 14, 1994).

[36]Comments of Dr. Anne thurston at An Asian Studies Center Symposium, "The Promise and Peril of China After Deng Xiaoping," *The Heritage Lectures* (The Heritage Foundation, February 3, 1994).

Party Congress demonstrates a stong "external orientation."[37] That Politburo included both the Foreign Minister and the Minister of Foreign Trade, as well as the leaders of the five key coastal cities and provinces – Shanghai, Tianjin, Guangdong, Shandong and Beijing. If conservatives could not close down the reforms after Tiananmen, few events could empower them to turn back the clock now.[38]

4. Since June 1989, when it rescued the CCP from society, the military's power has increased dramatically. Also, the success of U.S. "smart weapons" in the Gulf War increased the CCP's commitment to military modernization and renewed budgetary allocations. However, Deng's purge of Yang Shangkun and Yang Bailbing in 1993 greatly reduced the military's direct aspirations.

5. An interest in advancing democracy in rural China has emerged in the CCP, so long as it stabilizes, rather than challenges, party authority. Qiao Shi, a member of the Standing Committee of the Politburo and head of China's rubber stamp parliament, the National People's Congress(NPC), is supporting a debate that suggests that the NPC, not the CCP, should be the highest organ of leadership in the country. While this position may reflect his effort to strengthen his power base, institutional pluralism is a first step towards a more open and democratic system.

6. Inflation hovers at 25-30 percent, but because the CCP's legitimacy depends on economic growth, leaders fear that an economic retrenchment, as in 1988-1991, could trigger social unrest. The center needs calibrated mechanisms for controlling growth, investment, and the money supply. Similarly, only clear property rights and "hard budget constraints" can constrain local investment, which also fuels inflation.

7. The center's fiscal power has shrunk dramatically since 1978. The expansion of factories owned by various levels of the gov-

---

[37]Bachman, *The Fourteenth Congress of the Chinese Communist Party*.

[38]Still, after Tianamen the system was directionless; only Deng's spring 1992 trip reinvigorated the reforms. That fact suggests that after Deng dies, reforms might stagnate.

ernment has put enormous economic power into the hands of local officials.[39] Over 80 percent of all capital investment is based on local, not central, investment. China's weak central finances complicates the redistribution of funds among regions and the financing of major development projects. Yet state firms may be responding to market pressures and increasing their efficiency without changing property right.[40] By devolving more power to managers and expanding the market, China may outgrow the plan and its inefficiencies without massive layoffs.[41] Also, the center's new tax policy appears to be having a positive impact on the central government's finances.

8. Despite the success of rural reform in 1978-1984, rural incomes in inland China have stagnated, and efforts by cadres to extort funds for development and their own pocket have let to peasant rebellions and tax riots. Outmigration into coastal cities where urban residents experience a level of personal insecurity not known since the Cultural Revolution could lead urbanites to prefer authoritarian order to chaotic democracy. Enterprise reform confronts a hostile working class that fears redundancy without a welfare net. For Chinese leaders, these real threats combine with their own psychological fear of chaos to reinforce their resistance to major political reform and the emergence of a neo-conservative trend.

9. Although Jiang Zemin's political report to the 14th Party Congress described China's external environment as benign, there is concern in the military and the CCP over Japanese expansionism, central Asian Isamicism, Taiwan independence, and border disputes. Still, agreements exist with every major border state, including India, Russia and Vietnam. Japanese and

---

[39]See Barry Naughton, "Implications of the State Monopoly Over Industry and Its Relaxation," *Modern China*, 18:1 (January 1992), pp. 14-41.

[40]Gary H. Jefferson, Thomas G. Rawski, and Yuxin Zheng, "Growth, Efficiency and Convergence in China's State and Collective Industry," *Economic Development and Cultural Change*, 40:2 (1992), pp. 239-266.

[41]Barry Naughton, *Growing out of the Plan* (Cambridge: Cambridge University Press, 1995).

Taiwanese foreign investment is at a peak, and all states in East Asia are committed to a peaceful international environment in which economies will compete and grow. Yet, while increased foreign investment, trade, and international engagement offer China incentives for cooperation, the end of the Cold War, the insecurity of a rapidly evolving system, and China's aspirations for great power status generates inducements for China to protect itself from all possible external threats through military self-strengthening. China's efforts at military modernization frighten other regional actors, whose own efforts at self-defense in turn convince the Chinese that their military expansion is justified.

The Scenarios

The scenarios are based on four factors: elite structure, policy programs, elite power capabilities, and societal response. Elite structure affects the leadership's ability to innovate, make difficult allocative decisions, and deal with domestic and global crises. The reform program generates economic and societal outcomes that influence the system's evolution. The power capabilities of each leadership structure says a great deal about the state's ability to weather intra-elite conflicts and social unrest, while society's responses either threaten state stability or afford it breathing room to deal with the problems that emerge.

Combining the preeminent and duumvirate scenarios creates a 3×2 table, presented below. Boxes C and E which are very unlikely, can be discussed briefly.

• Collective / Radical(Box C)

Although a collective leadership's enormous power capabilities would allow it to risk radical reforms, such an elite structure will seek the lowest common denominator, in line with collective preferences, rather than pursue a radical reform strategy which only one or two members of the collective leadership may prefer. Because radical reform involves enormous redistributions of power and resources among competing economic, bureaucratic,

Table 1. Leadership/Policy Scenarios

Leadership Structure	Policy Preferences	
	Radical Reform	Partial Reform
Preeminent/ Duumvirate (elitist model)	A. Resolved factional battle leads to *Linear Model* under "Neo-Authoritariansm" –dominant elite(s) forms(s) winning coalition –medium power capabilities, as some institutions are excluded. –social protest suppressed or molified in medium term, partly through attack on corruption. –**LOW** probability	B. Failed coup triggers Disintegration as power capabilities weak and middle strata and other central elites withdraw support; –MODERATELY LOW Probability
	–if single leader needs legitimacy, possible emergence of *Liberalization* scenario. but **MEDIUM LOW** probability	–successful coup based on "Neo-conservatism," leads to Linear scenario where dominant elite(s) pay off institutional powers and institute limited reform. –social unrest controllable –LOW to MODERATE Probability
Collective Leadership (institutional model)	C. Power capabilities very high, could contain social unrest and succeed at radical reform. –**VERY LOW** probability as leadership will seek lowest common denominator, rather than the redistributive policies of a radical reform program.	D. *Linear* MODEL –Most likely scenario in short-term. –**MEDIUM** probability. –strong elite consensus, –strong institutional capabilities. –social unrest strong but controllable. –corruption a major issue.
Factionalized Leadership (conflict model)	E. No elite consensus, all power capabilities mobilized for political struggle, –very hostile society –results in *Rapid Disintegration*, likely to be followed by a military move unless military is also split along factional lines. –**LOW** Probability	F. Problems amass as elites unable to respond to social and economic problems—short-term *Stagnation;*
		–continued problems lead in medium-term to slow *Disintegration* allowing for emergence of system dominated by regional or military interests. –**MODERATELY LOW** probability.

and societal interests, the consensus necessary for a collective leadership makes such redistributions extremely unlikely. Representatives of any losing interest can veto the radical program, and since each leader's strength is based on their ability to protect the interests of its power base, their personal power interests also lead them to exercise that veto.[42] Without internecine conflict, which would undermine collective leadership, or a major social crisis, such a leadership group is very unlikely to institute this economic strategy, making this elite / strategy combination a very low probability.

•Factionalized / Radical (Box E)

A factionalized leadership pursuing radical reform is either impossible or a prescription for political suicide. Should the balance of power among factions be equal, extreme caution would be the watchword, either because each side's survival would depend on not giving their opponent any political ammunition to launch an attack, or because any policy initiative would be attacked and blocked for political reasons. And, if radical reforms were introduced, triggering social unrest, a factionalized leadership could not respond. On the other hand, should one faction become powerful enough to push a radical program, it would need to be dominant, as in a ruling duumvirate (Box A), for the enormous and immediate problems that a radical program would generate would empower an opposing faction who, with social and bureaucratic support, would overthrow it. Thus a factionalized leadership is either likely to adopt a partial reform program or stagnate and fail to put forward any clear policy program at all (Box F).

Employing this framework, I posit four most plausible scenarios: dominant / radicalm dominant / partial, collective / partial, and factionalized / partial. These models generate four scenarios – lin-

---

[42]For example, Li Peng or Zou Jiahua, who favor a more gradual solution to state enterprise insolvency, would have to capitulate to a more radical solution, which places collective interests above their own personal ones.

[43]Three of these scenarios, excluding stagnation, were seen to be most likely

ear, disintegration, stagnation, or liberalization.[43]

The Linear Scenario

The best predictor of next year is this year. If Deng's passing leads to a stable *collective leadership* pursuing partial reform(Box D), China's prognosis for the next 5-7 years involves rapid growth, increased military expenditures, an inflation rate that does not destroy the economy, and social instability that remains under control. China's GNP would double in 7-10 years, the military budget would allow it to challenge forces throughout the region, and China's foreign trade and global competitiveness would increase. Thus this is a "linear," not a "status quo," scenario.

Under this scenario, no individual or duo of leaders seeks preeminence, as current General Secretary Jiang Zemin, remains an equal partner with a handful of top leaders on the inside but becomes a symbolic source of national unity for the outside. With stability maintained, the "elders" remain backstage to die. Popular politics remains closed, with increased coercive efforts to prevent autonomous political organizations. In limited local elections, non-party candidates are accepted but anti-party ones are rejected; dissidents and union leaders are reqularly arrested and given long sentences. Coastal leaders and central officials dominate Beijing politics, limiting redistributive economic decisions. But on issues threatening political and economic stability, central decisions emerge. Nationalism, with sprinklings of support for party leadership and socialism, remains the core regime ideology.

Economic growth persists, averaging 7-8% a year. But continued bureaucratic interference in the economy generates corruption and popular antipathy. Inflation looms at aound 20 percent,

---

according to Ronald Morse, *China In the Near Term* (Office of Net Assessment, Department of Defense, 1995). The author was part of that team but dissents from its finding that *disintegration* is as likely as a *linear* progression. Nevertheless, 4 of 11 members of the team chose *disintegration* as the most likely scenario, and another 4 chose *linear*. Two picked *liberalization* and one picked both *disintegration* and *liberal*.

but despite a major economic slowdown, does not destabilize the system. State-owned enterprises remain subsidized, but market competition increases their efficiency. Thus budget deficit grow at a slower rate. Joint stock compaines expand, as does the power of economic combines, but privatization of state-owned enterprises remains off the agenda. A new balance is struck between local and central revenues, leaving the center with enough funds for key projects, but the gap between inland and coast expands. Nevertheless, economic activity up and down the Yangzi River, from Shanghai, through Wuhan, to Sichuan flourishes, in part due to central investment in the Three Gorges project. Foreign trade grows at 10-12 percent a year, despite some levelling off in foreign investment. Yet due to external pressures, local desires for greater authority, and entry into the GATT, continued liberalization of the foreign trade regime persists. But China bickers with the World Trade Organization and the United States as it frequently tightens its foreign trade regime and maintains a mercantilist development strategy. Access to China's domestic market attracts foreign investors, but dealing with China remains difficult.

Minor social explosions persist without getting out of control. Workers in threatened state-owned enterprises strike, and closings could trigger worker political action in one part of the country. Massive arrests follow, as do U.S. government protests. Similarly, the floating population's migration to the coast generates instability and a major outburst by migrant workers could follow an economic retrenchment that cuts construction in Shanghai's Pudong development zone, where currently one million outsiders labor. Similar efforts to move 2-3 million peasants out of their homes to build the Three Gorges project could trigger a serious rebellion. But economic growth in the cities and the rural coast, and small-scale privatization expand the percent of the populace that enjoys improved lifestyle choices, greater economic freedom, and increased job mobility. Despite its awareness of global trends to democracy, this class supports a collective authoritarian leadership that keeps social unrest within bounds.

The military implications of the linear scenario are significant for even if the military's share of the budget remains stable, an expanding economy significantly increases its budget. Stable party leadership allows the PLA to improve its professionalism and its rapid deployment forces. Despite continued skirmishes over the Spratleys, Vietnam could back down in the face of a growing Chinese military presence in the South China Seas and Vietnam's own desire for rapid economic growth. But China's expanding military, continued nuclear weapons program, including the devlopment of tactical nuclear weapons, and strengthened blue water capability, will challenge all actors in the region.

Two of four scenarios lead to this outcome. Thus even if a pre-eminent leader emerges, he too could pursue partial reform under a tightly authoritarian system (Box B). He might resort to a neo-Conservative ideology, but still press forward with many reforms, as partial reform has strong backing from the middle strata and the party bureaucracy, whose interests in profit-making are maximized under a system that fuses political and economic power.[44] However, the inability to resolve corruption, inflation, and inequality will surely test mass society's patience, especially if economic retrenchments become the main mechanism for controlling unbridled growth and inflation. A major slowdown in the world economy or a new arms race, following a U.S. withdrawal from East Asia, could also undermine China's growth rates, generating large scale unrest. A single leader would be hard pressed to hold on under partial reform, leading to disintegration or liberalization.

Disintegration Scenarios

The routes to disintegration are numerous.[45] Factionalism,

---

[44]See David Zweig, "Fusion or Fission? Reforming China's Political Economy," *Harvard International Review*, 11:2 (Spring 1989), pp. 4-7.

[45]Some might argue that regardless of the leadership structure, the growing strength of the regions and the loss of fiscal and political power at the center make it almost impossible for China to avoid a slow slide towards disintegration. But such a view is too deterministic, ascribing too much influence to economic trends and too little to politics.

based on deep mutual mistrust and a zero-sum view of politics among Chinese elites could undermine the regime, either in the short- or long-term. Failed efforts by one leader to seize power could lead to disintegration, as occurred in 1916 when Yuan Shikai's bid to become emperor failed. A failed effort at radical reform led by a Chinese Gorbachev could undo the system, but given the Soviet experience, other leaders will try to prevent this from occurring.

Factionalism could lead to *disintegration* either rapidly or slowly (Box F). Due to continuing and sharp elite conflicts, the mobilization of all institutional power capabilities for political struggle, and the inability of the army to bring order due to its own internal fragmentation, the system could collapse at the center. Especially if splits in the army mirror fissures among the leadership, civil war could emerge. Or societal forces may erupt, aware that the center is too distracted to respond, leading to chaos. Such massive eruptions would have enormous costs for East Asia, as Chinese would flood out through boats and over land.[46]

Slower disintegration could follow, as in Box F, where a factionalized leadership, racked by economic and social problems, lacks the institutional capacity to deal with many crises. Economic downturns, continuing inflation. Or a central fiscal crisis, could generate stagnation, undermining confidence within the middle strata who expand their authority and undermine the center. Such a process could evolve without a cataclysm. Should the center continue to resist institutionalizing the new division of

---

[46]To stop the west from pushing for rapid progress on human rights, Deng in summer 1993 reportedly warned that if the center collapsed, Indonesia would be swamped by 100 million refugees, and Hong Kong would be destroyed by a wave of fleeing humanity.

[47]Many analysts see disintegration arising from a regionalized economy and weakened central economic power. But why must increased regionalism become disintegration? A new deal could be cut between the center and the regions which leaves the regions with enormous powers but they would still supply the center with funds to fulfill critical tasks such as defense, foreign affairs, and infrastructural development. Institutional economists would augue that the center's primary role under a successful federalist system would be to

power, the regions may threaten to withdraw, forcing the center to accept a loose confederation.[47]

A one-man coup could lead to disintegration (Box B). Recent events have shown that Secretary General Jiang Zemin either believes that his formal positions entitle him to be preeminent leader or he fears that others will move against him, so he is moving first. But after a coup, his lack of charisma and shallow power capabilities will weaken his institutional alliances. Deng has pleaded with military leaders to rally around Jiang, and while tea leaves suggest that Jiang has strengthened his position in the military, doubts about his leadership persist. He would need an economic czar and support of the middle strata to grow the economy, but capital flight and increased domestic capital speculation, rather than long-term investment, would be a more likely response to a one-man coup. Social unrest and international isolation could doom such a mediocre leader and China to distintegration.

Nevertheless, gradual disintegration of the center (Box F) is unlikely to lead to a total collapse of China's state; instead, a nationalistic military regime could emerge based on patriotism and bureaucratic interest. Social chaos is anathema to military leaders, especially those who beileve that an anti-Chinese world awaits opportunities for territorial acquisition. With a collapsing party threatening to destroy the military, as it did in the former USSR, the military could replace the party as the core unifying institution. If foreign investment continues, which is possible if a military regime emerged, continued growth based on a military-bureaucratic alliance, a mercantilist foreign trade policy, and an assertive foreign policy, could rally much of the middle strata. Alternatively, some mix of Maoist egalitarianism and ardent nationalism might allow the military to draw on former Maoists in the party and appeals to equity grievances of the interior and

---

preserve property rights and legislate away its own ability to intrude on local budgets. See Barry R. Weingast, "The Economic Role of Political Institutions: Market-Preserving Federalism and Economic Development," unpublished paper (November 1994).

the countryside. However, egalitarianism undermines growth; anti-colonial rhetoric and expansionist policies would scare foreign investors, especially in East Asia. Thus the former model which mirrors the business/military coalitions that have ruled Thailand, South Korea, Taiwan, and Indonesia, is a more likely response to disintegration than a neo-Maoist revival.

Arguments against disintegration are formidable. Today's leaders know that factionalism will be their undoing – either they hand together or hang separately – increasing the pressures to maintain collective leadership. Should any individual leader threaten that stability, he could be purged. Second, economic disintegration is made more unlikely by the emergence of a more national market. Third, the middle strata needs a relatively strong center under which they can develop their economies; the transaction costs that would be incurred should independent regions have to create foreign policy establishments, customs services, security forces, and new laws, would be prohibitive. Also, the lessons of Yugoslavia and the former Soviet Union are stark, and with secessionist aspirations only among China's minorities (Mongols, Tibetans, and Uighurs) and Taiwan, the core Han regions will hold fissiparous tendencies in check.

Liberal Scenario: On the Road to Democracy

Two paths could lead to democracy. The most likely would be if a preeminent leader, duumvirate, or victorious radical reform faction emerged from the leadership and adopted a radical strategy (Box A).[48] Opponents of radical reform might be relieved of their posts or be forced to step aside because partial reform and its resulting corruption create too much social unrest. In response

---

[48]The literature on democratic transitions shows that a split within the authoritarian leadership group is necessary for the transition to begin. See Guillermo O'Donnell, Philippe C. Schmitter and Laurence Whitehead, eds., *Transitions from Authoritarian Rule: Comparative Perspectives* (Baltimore: The Johns Hopkins University Press, 1986); and O'Donnell and Schmitter, eds., *Transitions from Authoritarian Rule: Tentative Conclusions About Uncertain Democracies* (Baltimore: The Johns Hopkins University Press, 1986).

to massive protests, radical reformers might reemerge. But for liberalism to succeed, radical reforms must gain popular support.[49] Former General Secretary Zhao Ziyang, who in his retirement speech in 1989 argued that political reforms had to go in tandem with economic reforms, might reemerge to coopt popular protest in the early stages of radical reform.[50] Or supporters of a legalistic, institutionalized political system could push for inner party democracy, allowing competing groups to emerge in the leadership.[51] As in Hungary, these groups could evolve into competitive parties. However, this scenario is ten or more years in the making, as no visible advocates of radical reform are in the top leadership.

While some see a liberal system emerging from a disintegrated system, building democracy is a complex process, needing the development of strong institutions. As most of the third world shows, stable democracy does not emerge from chaos; more chaos or authoritarianism are chaos' most likely outcome. Thus the road to democracy must be slow; new institutions must emerge and develop legitimacy. Perhaps greater inner party democracy will be the first step, or a greater role for the NPC. But Chinese people must be convinced that democracy can bring the stability necessary for economic growth, even as China's elites develop normative perspectives that allow for a level of political civility that has never characterized any Chinese regime outside Taiwan.

Finally, could a collective leadership following partial reform

---

[49]Some analysts see the role of policy advisors and middle strata intellectuals as key. See Merle Goldman, *Sowing the Seed of Democracy in China* (Cambridge: Harvard University Press, 1994).

[50]Robert Delfs, "Zhao Ziyang in the Shadows – Prospects for Party Liberals in the succession Struggle after Deng Xiaoping," presented to the 5th PLA Conference (June 1994).

[51]Peng Zhen believed in increasing the power of the National People's Congress as a representative assembly reflecting popular interests. Today, security czar Qiao Shi appears to be pushing the same line. See Shan Kaochao, "A Challenge to the Dictatorship of the Chinese Communist Party," *China Focus*, 2:11 (November 1, 1994), pp. 1-8.

generate institutional and social forces that over the long-term expand political pluralism and become the roots of democracy? A collective leadership would have little incentive to move towards a democratic system. With legitimacy currently based on economic growth, and rapid growth highly destabilizing, conservative leaders strongly resist such a transition. China's middle strata, who form a bureaucratic capitalist class, engages in widespread corruption. Threatened by a free press, they resist rapid liberalization.[52] Moreover, in both South Korea and Taiwan, a strong leader emerged from within the ruling group to push the system onto a more democratic trajectory despite great institutional resistance. For such a scenario to unfold in China, more and more top party officials and middle strata must build secure economic positions within China's evolving business community (as in Thailand), and become secure that they will not be hunted down by a more democratic leadership. Then they may acquiesce to a strong leader who sees democracy as the linchpin for stability and continued economic growth. But at best China remains 5-10 years away from that point, unless a political crisis telescopes historical processes.

Conclusion

How political elites deal with each other after Deng's death is the most important element in China's future. Collective leadership will try to follow a linear path, while factions or a failed coup could doom the system in the short-or medium-term. But if the

[52]In Taiwan, democracy emerged because a strong middle class dominated the economy and sought influence over the political process. But the evolution of China's economy in a more bureaucratic capitalist direction, where party, bureaucracy, and industry work closely together to suppress ture private enterprise, bodes ill for the emergence of a strong, independent middle class that sees political freedoms as increasing its security. Despite the long tradition of state expropriation of private property, an emerging middle class in China might prefer a more corporatist system under which working class interests would be suppressed in favor of continued economic growth.

leadership splits badly, military intervention might hold China together and keep much of its political economy stable. Finally, only the emergence of a preeminent leader or duumvirate, or massive social unrest, is likely to overwhelm the stasis and caution among today's elites and impel China down the road to radical enomic and/or political reform. But with bloodletting less a part of the political game, and with political power widely dispersed, a single ruler will have difficulty emerging and keeping power.

Thus, in the short-term, no one person will *successfully* rule China after Deng. Rulership under Mao or Deng involved personal commitments to a preeminent ruler by a coterie of leaders who sat atop key economic, military, and political institutions. Unity and stability was maintained only when the ultimate leader, who combined administrative control with personal charisma, could rely on all these actors to implement policy decisions within their respective sectors and not use their institutional power bases to challenge his ultimate authority. But that institutional support for Mao and Deng was buttressed by personal loyalties earned over decades of interactions with a group of revolutionary leaders with whom they had conquered China. Fear, too, played a key role during the Maoist era.

No leader in China today can muster the administrative support and personal loyalties needed to hold China's uninstitutionalized political system together. While some people have influence in the military or security arenas, they lack the legitimacy to speak efficaciously on economic issues. Or if they possess strong links within the state bureaucracy, they have little leverage over the army. At a minimum, some combination of leaders, most likely combining "order" and "economy," can hold the system together, and most contemporary leaders of China know it. Still, one person might misperceive his own capacities and strive for ultimate power. But such an effort, especially by someone such as Jiang Zemin, the man holding the official position of chosen successor, is likely to fail and lead to collapse.

But what of the apparent imbalance between partial economic reform and limited political change? Many analysts argue that such a strategy is a prescription for collapse. According to institutional economics, however, instability emerges from a disjuncture between the dominant form of property rights and the distribution of political and normative power within the system. Given China's hybrid pattern of property ownership, with significant government ownership of industry at all levels of the system, there is no inherent incompatibility with a state- dominated polity. Members of the middle strata who manage China's political economy also control local politics; so no internal contradiction exists within this structure. A third force, mass society, which rebles at inequality, corruption, and the abuse of power in a system where there is no political accountability, will have to emerge to trigger rapid change. And it is precisely fears of the emergence of such a political force that works against rapid political change in China.

Moreover, the lack of any significant institutional basis for the emergence of political opposition means that rapid political liberalization could be highly destablizing, triggering disintegration, rather than political reform. And the middle strata, with its vested interests in the system, knows these risks and will not push for such change.

Yet this middle strata may be the long-term source of gradual political reform. As their economic power grows, and if social unrest increases, they will want to offer their counsel about how China should be governed. In the past 15 years, whenever the center relaxed constraints on political debate, regional,provincial, and municipal officials used the people's congress system to express their views. Simiarly, many middle level officials in Beijing were disappointed by the outcome of the Tiananmen events, hoping for the emergence of a more responsive political system. Thus pressures exist for evolutionary change involving the creation of more regularized and institutionalized opportunities for the middle strata to assert their interests speak on behalf of societal concerns as well.

Finally, will party members simply give up the fight, as they did in Eastern and Central Europe, and accept democratic competition? Or will they hang on and in the end bring down the system themselves through corruption, expropriations, and malfeasance? While Nee and Lian argue that "opportunistic" shifts of party members into business undermines the party's "fighting spirit," and will lead to the party's collapse,[53] this trend may be providential for the peaceful evolution of the Chinese system. If party officials place themselves in stable business positions, insuring themselves high status after their political authority erodes, and if they feel secure that any post-Deng democratization will not target them for recrimination, the middle strata and even top elite may see that the true road to stability comes not from political repression but from allowing a gradual evolution to a more pluralistic system.

---

[53]See Nee and Lian, "Sleeping with the Enemy."